The
BRASS
RING

Also by Patricia Best & Ann Shortell
A Matter of Trust

The BRASS RING

Power, Influence and the Brascan Empire

PATRICIA BEST · ANN SHORTELL

Random House
Toronto

From Patricia: To Carlo

From Ann: To Don McCallum,
with thanks for his lessons in living

Published in Canada by Random House of Canada Limited, Toronto.

First Printing, September 1988
Second Printing, October 1988
Third Printing, November 1988

Canadian Cataloguing in Publication Data

Best, Patricia
  The brass ring

ISBN 0-394-22015-3

1. Brascan Limited.   2. International business
enterprises – Canada.   3. International economic
relations.   I. Shortell, Ann.   II. Title.

HD9685.C34B67 1987   338.8'8971   C87-094306-5

Jacket design: Falcom Design & Communications Inc.
Jacket illustration: Pam Fullerton
Photograph: W. Grieheling/Miller Comstock
Authors' photograph: Falcom Design & Communications Inc.
Typesetting: Jay Tee Graphics Ltd.

Printed and bound in Canada by T.H. Best Printing Company Limited

Contents

Acknowledgments

We would like to thank together a number of people who helped us as colleagues and as friends: Theresa Butcher and the Maclean Hunter library staff; Robbie Grant and the Maclean's Magazine library staff; Buffy Barrett; Fran McNeely, who transcribed tapes and became the book's biggest fan; Catharine Dowling, who provided research support; fellow journalists Sherri Aikenhead, Marc Clark, Barry Critchley, Jacquie McNish, Peter Newman and Bruce Wallace and editor David Kilgour for their helpful insight; Nancy Colbert, Frank D'Andrea and Aaron Milrad for contractual expertise.

There are also a few people whose skills have made special contributions to our work. Duncan McDowell, while working on his authorized corporate history of the "old" Brascan, willingly provided useful background material from his store of knowledge. Angela Ferrante taught us both important lessons about writing and editing.

Patricia would like to particularly acknowledge Kevin Doyle, for his generosity and support. As well, she sends thanks to family and to two special friends, Linda Hunter and Anne McCall, and to Peter Mandic, Tessa Wilmott and Peter Foster for their help and lively interest. Finally, thanks to Carlo Liconti for his faith and patience. Ann would like to thank family and dear friends including Peter Cole, Cheryllyn Ireland, Michael McCann, Brenda South, Anne Marie Smart and Bob Parkins, Marianne Tefft and Harold Burke, with a special bouquet for Marci and Bill McQuarrie.

Theresa Tedesco deserves a separate mention for her loyal friendship to both authors, as well as for carrying the burden of additional work at *Maclean's* while Patricia was on leave.

Of course, this book would not be in print without the continuous faith of our publisher, Ed Carson.

We would also like to send out a special thank-you to Peter and Edward Bronfman for their trust and goodwill.

The Merry-Go-Round

When we began this book, we wanted, simply, to examine the nature of power in Canadian corporate society. We believed that the way business is done in Canada is changing during this decade of international trade, deregulation, competition and aging family fortunes.

That all of us live in a new economic world is clear. The average Canadian has seen plant closings, has felt the effects of the recession, has watched the stock market relentlessly break records, crash, then shakily inch back up, and has suffered as real-estate prices and interest rates gyrate. We have seen some banks fail and others stagger under the weight of bad foreign loans, and we have puzzled over what Michael Wilson's tax reform will do to our pocket-books. We have also heard of corporate concentration, and of the few families who control Canada. Keen observers have detected a change in who holds that economic power. Ten years ago, most people would have said that the Eatons or Conrad Black or the Big Five Banks were the most powerful barons of the Canadian economy. Sixty years ago, when Sam Bronfman was a bootlegger, the big monied families were the McConnells, the Anguses, the Websters, the Molsons and the Killams of Montreal. Today, the McConnell and Molson families are among the nation's wealthiest, but they do not count power among their many assets. But Sam Bronfman's nephews, Peter and Edward, the Toronto Bronfmans — so named to distinguish them from their cousins Charles and Edgar, who live in Montreal and New York — are both rich and, through the efforts of their hired managers, powerful.

What became apparent to us in the winter and spring of 1985-86 was that the corporate empire headed by Peter and Edward Bronfman was at the very centre of Canadian business, politics and high society. Every time we looked at an issue — corporate concentration, conflict of interest, the deregulation of the securities industry, the post-recession managerial order — the Edper group, which we along with many others labelled the "Brascan empire," cropped up as the best example.

The collection of 152 corporations under Peter's and Edward's control infiltrates all aspects of Canadian commerce. By 1988, they controlled the largest number of companies under a single group in Canada. Their assets total almost $120 billion; the combined equity in their companies is $30 billion. The Edper empire has a stake — that is, enough of a piece of the action so that their managers call the shots — in pulp and paper, gold mining, oil and gas exploration, forest products, copper mining, film distribution, Astral photo processing, the First Choice pay-TV network, the Sports Network, the Toronto Blue Jays, coal mining, fertilizer, Labatt's beer, Chateau-Gai wine, milk, yoghurt, soups, frozen foods, animal foods, Catelli-Primo Italian food products, Holiday fruit juices, flour and gluten, 10 hotels (including Toronto's Four Seasons), major office buildings (including Montreal's Place Ville Marie), shopping centres (including Toronto's Yorkdale), Central Park Lodge nursing homes, residential developments in Ontario, Florida, California, and Texas, equipment leasing, Royal Trust, London Life Insurance, Royal LePage realty, Wellington property insurance, and a huge, highly sophisticated financial-services business that includes mortgage lending, stock trading, merchant banking, underwriting, money broking, bond trading, and management consulting. As well, they have been the largest single source of revenue for Canadian stock brokers in the 1980s as the Edper group turned to the public to finance their ventures. No other corporate group in Canada has such a reach.

Add to all that the wealth and magic of the Bronfman name. Peter and Edward are personally worth $1.1 billion. Trevor Eyton, chief executive of Brascan Limited, the holding company for the group's consumer products and some of the natural-resource and financial-services companies, is worth $40 million. Jack Cockwell, the group's financial architect and driving force, is worth $50 million.

We decided to turn on its head the normal approach to Canadian business book writing. Instead of choosing a particular theme, a particular company, or a particular event, we would use this group to illustrate all the themes and all the events that have come to symbolize change for our business community.

In the beginning, we had only a dim understanding of the brothers who owned most of the shares in the empire. We understood the essential Trevor Eyton, and we understood Jack Cockwell as a business manipulator, without knowing much about him as a man. Peter and Edward were shadows; many other group executives were faceless, except a few we had come to know while writing our first book, *A Matter of Trust*. We had not yet heard the group's theory that it is more than twenty-five key people (thirty-six at their latest CEO Day) who make the group operate.

But we were sure of one thing: they were regarded as a bad element in Canadian business: bullies. Jack Cockwell was considered an evil genius, and Trevor Eyton plotted behind closed doors with other members of the oligarchy. They were thought of as machiavellian, as motivelessly malignant. We knew all this to be true because many, many people on Bay Street had told us so — but not for attribution, just in case they had occasion to do business with the group. In short, we had a rather black-and-white view of the organization and the people, the kind of view that generally makes good newspaper copy. But the truth, as we discovered during our research, was more complex and even more interesting.

This is not an authorized corporate biography. We made a conscious decision not to tell the group about the project until we had gathered a certain amount of information. We did this for two reasons: fear and loathing. But almost from the moment we proposed the book, the group knew about it. Some grapevines work very efficiently. When Trevor Eyton first heard of the project, he issued a memorandum to all key group executives dictating that they not co-operate in any way with our research.

Some talked to us anyway. And one of the most illuminating discoveries we made was who would and who wouldn't talk among the lions of Canadian commerce. Hal Jackman did, on the evening he was preparing to attend a gala Brascan-sponsored Canadian Opera Company performance of *Rigoletto*. Conrad Black, on the other hand, was more circumspect. The usually loquacious Black, who sits on an Edper-group board, declined, saying he would require the approval of Eyton or of Peter Bronfman. During an exchange of letters with us, Black displayed his legendary lack of regard for the fifth estate, predicting "another slipshod treatment of a serious subject" and allowing only "the off chance that [we] would produce a fair and serious work." Black, who had earlier sold his energy company to an Edper company, thereby providing the best possible illustration of the changing order of Canadian business, then dutifully sent copies of our exchange to Peter Bronfman.

The group holds up its outside directors as symbols of self-policing. These men (and a few women), Trevor and the company managers say, are strong voices on the boards. They bring dissenting views and fresh perspectives to the table. Yet a number of outside directors were not interested in talking to us, even to explain their roles as independent, impartial thinkers. In the spring of 1987, Lorne Lodge, then president of IBM Canada, was a member of the board of Lonvest Corporation, the holding company that oversees London Life and other insurance investments. At first he said he would speak with us, and then telephoned the next day with a different story. The group didn't want him to talk; he was sure we would understand. A few months later, Lodge was appointed to the board of Royal LePage, the real-estate subsidiary of Royal Trust.

But Alan Hockin, dean of the business school at York University in Toronto, was a different kind of outside director. He disregarded Trevor's obvious discomfort with the book because he believed he should speak about the group. Later, Hockin, a director of Trilon Financial Corporation, could laugh about lunching with us at the Elmwood women's club in downtown Toronto in front of Mel Hawkrigg, the president of Trilon, ignoring Hawkrigg's red-faced disapproval.

In fact, it was Hockin's stance that was the first chink in the group's armour. From the experience with Hockin, we discovered there were schisms developing in the group. There were, for example, differing opinions about who should be awarded official responsibility for the group's success. The book became part of the tussle over a rewriting of corporate history. Trevor Eyton would no longer carry the mantle of group figurehead; instead, a group of key executives was brought onto the stage to share the glory. This was what Peter Bronfman wanted. He was tired of being portrayed as a weakling who neither knew nor cared about the companies he owned and who was at the mercy of the mastermind, Jack Cockwell. It is no wonder: the empire would be left open to panic selling if anything did happen to Cockwell. The market saw one person as the group's biggest asset, and the group decided to fight against that perception, designating new partners at its key companies and emphasizing the skills of its other executives.

Despite this attempt to rewrite history, the market is correct. Jack Cockwell is the one crucial element in the empire, the one irreplaceable person. He is, as Peter Bronfman has said on more than one occasion, "the heart of Edper." But Cockwell doesn't like the limelight, and has been fighting against any scrutiny. At one point in the spring of 1987 he suggested that he didn't want a book written because he hadn't finished the job he had set out to do, that he still had to turn around the natural resource companies. In five years, a book might be a good idea. By the fall of 1987, he had a slightly different reason. At a reception after a Labatt's annual meeting, he expressed the conviction that any co-operation on his part would undermine his efforts to massage the empire's history. But most of the time he simply smiled and was silent.

Cockwell also took great pains to ask his friends not to speak to us. We beat him to some of them.

Trevor Eyton had the most to lose from the book. He already was suffering from the media's changed perception about who held power at Edper. In 1986 *Toronto Life* magazine named him the city's most influential person; the following year he was demoted to a position down the list, and it was noted that he held less power in his own group. Meanwhile, Cockwell was attracting more and more media attention — and Eyton did not like it. This book would only worsen his already-eroded position of power. He was furious about not being kept fully informed about the book; as a result of this oversight, and other simultaneous events, the group's long-standing media liaison, Wendy Cecil-Stuart, was stripped of her role. One of the "simultaneous events" was Wendy's new role as Jack Cockwell's common-law wife. The public pairing of Wendy and Jack had caused great discomfort and consternation among the group's top people. Eyton, in particular, was worried about how straight-laced Bay Street would react. Cecil-Stuart was moved out of Brascan and into Edper temporarily to keep up appearances — and to keep the peace. But she persisted in her favourite pastime of society-doyen-in-waiting. When she presented the Brascan award for cultural writing at the National Magazine Awards in May 1987, and Peter Bronfman learned of it for the first time after the event, he was palpably annoyed. By summer she was running her own consulting business out of her home.

At the same time, our initial black-and-white view of the group began to change as we did our research. Our many interviews as well as our study of publicly available information could have formed a respectable effort at detailing a corporate empire. But we wanted to go further, to capture the essence of the unique relationships among Jack Cockwell and Peter Bronfman and Trevor Eyton and the others.

Although not kept fully or officially informed about the book, Trevor Eyton had always had access to a good deal of information about the project. Powerful men inspire powerful loyalties. Eyton believed, and not without some justification, that the book would offer strong criticisms of the group. In a letter to us he outlined the argument for not co-operating. "Obviously we can't object to the publication of articles and books concerning the Edper/Brascan group and its senior management so long as they are accurate, fair and balanced. However, you should know that much of what has been published in newspapers and articles to this time has not met that test, but is less damaging because these publications have only a passing impact and are quickly forgotten. The same cannot be said for your book which may become, for some, a reference and therefore part of Canadian business history."

The issue was control. The Brascan group is arguably the most control-driven collection of companies in Canada. Jack Cockwell, who orchestrates the group's approach to the public, treats public companies as if they were a private fiefdom. The philosophy is: Trust us and let us show you how we can succeed. It is Cockwell's philosophy, but it is also the belief of Peter Bronfman and Eyton. They do not accept that there is valid reason to question and room to criticize. For stockholders, falling into line behind the Brascan bandwagon has, for the most part, been a profitable decision to make. Through Trevor Eyton's easy, anecdotal style, the group for years had controlled access to those at the top of the Edper empire. But the group does not understand that the same approach cannot be taken by the media. They were terrified of losing that iron grip on how the group would go down in history. Their manufactured version of events was being challenged by an independent study that promised to demote Eyton and throw an unwelcome spotlight on Cockwell and the Bronfmans. They feared judgement, especially because the group is, at its core, a family dynasty.

Despite these fears and Eyton's argument for noncooperation, by the spring of 1987 we reached a rapprochement with the group. Peter and Edward Bronfman agreed to answer written questions; Peter Bronfman and Trevor Eyton agreed to approve our requests for access to group executives. At their annual CEO Day, where thirty-six chief executives and execs in training gathered in Toronto, we were on the agenda.

Managers later said they were amazed that we had "cracked" Peter and Edward. Once that door was opened, other executive-chamber doors also swung wide.

Mike Cornelissen, the chief executive at Royal Trustco Limited, had taken umbrage at our portrayal of the people who worked for Brascan and Royal Trustco in *A Matter of Trust*. But he was perhaps the most co-operative of all group executives for this book. He sat down with a two-page list of questions from us and dictated a thirteen-page response that was triple-checked; he also provided an addendum. But what Cornelissen was most determined to display was the human side of the group. After our interview, he screened for us a video prepared for a sympathetic audience of in-house managers to enjoy at a Christmas party, in an effort to let us know that the group has a sense of humour.

Peter Widdrington, a charming bon vivant known for his ribald sense of humour, also co-operated. But he was as far from the Cornelissen mould as is possible. Lounging in his personal sitting room at Labatt's Toronto office, Widdrington interrupted the interview for regular dispatches from his secretary on the score of a Blue Jays baseball game. He had left his owners' box at the stadium only minutes before in order to see us. And when his secretary confessed to not knowing whether it was the top or the bottom of the ninth — "I always get confused with the bottom and the top" — Widdrington advised her: "Don't ever do that." On corporate matters he was somewhat less enthusiastic, and clearly had not looked at the written questions he had asked for from us. Although a director of Brascan Limited and one of two people Peter Bronfman had suggested we talk to, Widdrington was fuzzy on most things in the empire outside Labatt's.

All this co-operation was, in turn, being closely monitored by those at the top. Peter Bronfman decided the book was too important to ignore, and wanted to go on the record with his vision of the group. He invited us into his home for the first interview he had given in many years — an interview he devoutly hoped would be his last.

At the eleventh hour, Trevor Eyton decided to approach us about an interview to ensure his voice also would be heard.

But long before we were admitted to the corridors of Edper power, we had changed our minds somewhat about the group; they are very persuasive people. They are also brilliant, profit-driven, and they do use their incredible power. At the beginning, we thought we already knew much of what there was to know about the Edper-Brascan empire. But that was before more than two years of exhaustive research and extensive interviews with the group's top people.

If nothing else, the extraordinary people in the Edper empire make a fascinating study in human nature. But there is more. The group's influence reaches into our daily lives through the companies it controls, but also through the significant role it has played in Canadian politics and charities. And finally, it has become a pattern for a new way of doing business. Canadian business has had to shift, in little more than a decade, from a parochial, complacent system to the fast, unforgiving world of international power plays. The group is billed as the model for that change. Is this a new breed of corporate animal with a truly innovative approach to doing business? Is it a manipulative force that takes advantage of the system? You decide.

CHAPTER ONE

In The Beginning

*I don't see myself as being in a position of power.
I don't think a lot about power. And I am underwhelmed by people who fashion their lives around
power. I know Edward feels the same way.*
— Peter Bronfman, 1987

It was the Great West Life deal that changed the lives of Peter
and Edward Bronfman. It was a proving ground, a litmus test
of nerve and will. And they failed it. The two brothers, exiled
from the family fortune, cast out from the family business,
had reached for the brass ring. Their fingertips had touched
it, but their grasp fell short of their aim. When the hard knocks
and tough realities of the business world impinged on their
lives for the first time, Peter and Edward lost their nerve.

But it was the last time they were the pushed-around
stomped-on "poor" Bronfmans. Out of the Great West Life
experience emerged a determination to build, albeit slowly and
cautiously, their own empire. They chose the quiet way: no
headline-making takeovers for them. Rather, they would build,
negotiate, form partnerships. Stay non-threatening. It was the
natural thing to do for Peter and Edward.

Edward Maurice, born in 1927, and Peter Frederick, born two years later, grew up in the coddled environment of the very rich. A sister, Mona, was two years older than Edward, but she died in 1950, committing suicide at the age of twenty-seven. Their father, Allan, was a brother to Sam Bronfman, builder of one of the world's great fortunes, the Distillers Corporation — Seagram's liquor empire. Sam had four children, two of them boys, Edgar Miles, born in 1929, and Charles Rosner, born in 1931. Although always second to Sam, Allan was almost as wealthy and had built his family a massive mansion on Belvedere Road, next to Sam's, in Montreal's Westmount neighbourhood. Peter and Edward were pampered, protected, sheltered children. They knew there was an outside world, knew that most people lived differently from the way they lived, but they rarely got a chance to examine that world. Bundled off to American preparatory schools at an early age, and constantly aware of the excruciating tension building between their father and Uncle Sam, the boys acquired more than their share of insecurities and phobias.

By the time the Bronfman boys were in their teens, it was generally believed that the family differences had yielded to a wall of silence between Allan and Sam. Cousins were prohibited from playing with cousins; there was barely any communication between the families. These, however, are not Peter's memories. "Sure there were strains between my dad and my uncle, and they were large, probably. But, I mean, I always remember wondering why they were extremely cordial to each other." Sam's family holdings, consolidated in the CEMP trust, were much more powerful within Seagram's than Edper, Allan's family trust. Many people who know Peter and Edward firmly believe that the seeds for the ambitious growth of the Edper empire were planted as a result of the bitterness that Peter and Edward felt had been created in the split between Allan and Sam. These same people also believe that Peter and Edward were driven to gain the respect of Sam's family. "They certainly have succeeded and deserve it, and deserve credit for it, but that has a lot to do with the motivation in my opinion of what got them to where they are today," said one business associate familiar with the Bronfman family. But Lionel Schipper, a close friend of Peter's and a director of the Edper trust, says, "I think that's a crock, but I can't prove it one way or another." Schipper adds, "I don't think he [Peter] set out to become one of the leading industrialists of Canada." Peter Bronfman maintains that there was never a grand design to build himself an empire: "You don't plan for those things. They sort of happen."

Peter and Edward have consistently denied publicly the theory that the bitter family backdrop motivated them. "It had absolutely zippo to do with what Trevor and Jack were trying to do," Peter says. "I wanted to prove something to myself only. That still holds true today. I mean, what kind of motivation would it be to start out, when you think of it, as a young person and be motivated to be better than a cousin or a relative or an uncle?"

But those who knew the family in Montreal say that for many years relations between Peter and Edward, on the one hand, and Charles and Edgar, on the other, could only be described as antagonistic. In recent years, however, with the older generation gone, the two sides have warmed up enough to talk to each other occasionally, and can be found attending the same functions as well as supporting some of the same — often Jewish — causes.

While Allan, who had functioned as Sam's polished, university-educated front man at Seagram's, was content to play a secondary role, he had hoped his sons would have a more important place in the family business. But in 1952, just after he graduated from Yale, Peter discovered he would not have a role in Seagram's. Sam and Allan's shares in Seagram's were lodged in a private company called SECO Investments. CEMP, Sam's trust fund for his children, owned two-thirds of the shares, and Edper, Allan's trust fund, only a third. CEMP's majority allowed Sam to pass a resolution barring Allan's children from joining Seagram's. Peter Bronfman recalls his mixed emotions upon learning that he would never have a place at Seagram's. He was, he says now, "disappointed to learn suddenly that we weren't 'allowed' to join the company, but

I soon became optimistic that I'd learn more about life operating on my own.''

Barney Finestone, a wealthy Montreal insurance broker who has known the two brothers since the late forties, and continues to be one of Peter's friends, recalls the event differently. ''I got a call at my office; it was a Wednesday morning. Peter said, 'Barney, let's go skiing this afternoon.' I said, 'Come on Peter, I'll ski with you Saturday.' He said, 'Barney I want you to go skiing with me this afternoon.' I'm not insensitive, I said okay. So we got in the car and we went to probably St. Adele and on the way up it all tumbled out, what was in the course of happening. He was absolutely shattered, I mean, being tossed out of Seagram's. He was literally thrown out of the nest and he was told you can't even keep your offices in the building. It was a trauma for he and Edward and I listened to it and I said, 'That's pretty rough stuff. Why do you put up with it?' And he said, 'Because if I don't, my father will get beaten around the head.' I said, 'You mean, you have to capitulate for your father?' He ran over it and yes, it was obvious that Sam had all the cards and they had to get out and do what they were told or their father would bleed for it.''

There was good reason for Peter's anxiety. ''After all, ninety per cent of our assets were tied up in SECO, a private company of which Edward and I owned only one third,'' says Peter. ''We were locked into a company whose principal asset was Seagram's stock and we did not have access to what was really going on in that company — an unhappy position for us to be in due to the difficult relationship which existed at that time between our father, Allan, and my uncle, Sam, whose family controlled SECO.''

During the conversation that Wednesday afternoon, Finestone asked Peter why he was so worried. ''I said, 'Peter, what assets do you have?' So he told me. And I said, 'What are you worried about? The way you live, you've got about five times too much money.' He said, 'What am I going to do with the rest of my life?' '' Peter was twenty-three, Edward was twenty-five. Peter instantly rejected the usual option of the very rich, a life spent clipping coupons. ''I'm not a playboy,

I'm not a jet setter. I can't see just clipping coupons and chasing women and drinking for the rest of my lifetime. It's not me," he said to Finestone. Over the course of the intense conversation, Peter also declared an interest in making the world a better place, but he felt that he lacked the proper training for social work. He knew he wanted to leave his mark in a tangible way. Perhaps an important building or a major charitable foundation, something people could point to and say: That wouldn't be here if it weren't for Peter Bronfman.

Peter and Edward set up their own office in the Peel Centre, which they had created out of the former Mount Royal Hotel, and began dabbling in small-time investments, mainly in real estate. Recalls Peter: "I personally found the experience to be exciting and challenging — in other words, I was plenty nervous." Says Finestone, "It wasn't easy. These were two sheltered youngsters, much younger, for example, than I was at their age. They had been in the nest from the day they were born. And they were tossed out at a fairly advanced age. Most of us have to face the realities of life earlier than that. I don't think they said, we would like to be the biggest or the best or we would like to control this asset or that asset. They were like two decent human beings trying to decide, what are we going to do with the rest of our lives."

In 1960, Uncle Sam struck once again. He suddenly decided that he wanted half of Edper's Seagram's holdings. The shares were selling for twenty-eight dollars each on the market, but Sam offered only twenty-two dollars a share. It was outrageous, but once again Edward and Peter accepted because Sam had hinted that a refusal would mean the removal of Allan from his vice-presidency at Seagram's. The forced sale left Edper with 500,000 shares of Seagram's, compared to CEMP's 2.8 million shares.

With the money from the sale, Peter and Edward began to build a stock portfolio. They also bought into a number of small ventures, usually run by big-thinking, under-funded entrepreneurs. Peter and Edward were putting themselves in the worst possible position: minority stakes in small, private companies. Part of it was their own fault. The two displayed a lively interest in leisure activities, charitable efforts, and family life, but exhibited only a passing interest in business. Even today, with his new-found zeal for corporate life, Peter says that his first priority is his family. "I am more concerned that my children will feel that I have been a good father and a decent person." And, unlike the austere, cold, remote father that he grew up with, Peter strives to be an accessible, concerned dad. "I have always tried to keep my children informed of my interests but have encouraged them to choose their own paths to follow while being *always* available for discussion when they seek it."

To their peril, Peter and Edward left their financial fate to a collection of outside advisors. Barney Finestone describes the early years on their own as "a bit of a rocky sail at first. They weren't all good investments. Some of their early advisors weren't great." A number of the Bronfmans' early real-estate ventures quickly soured. The two became involved in some deals in which they were the victims of the next best thing to a swindle. "They bled to learn their trade," says Finestone, in typically hyperbolic style. "They learned their trade like everybody else and they paid for it." Other investments succeeded, however. In joint ventures with Bob and Jack Cummings, members of a prominent real-estate family in Montreal, Peter and Edward first saw how their capital could be used effectively.

But the two brothers continued to be shackled by problems with the limits of their trust fund. Two trustees of Edper, Lazarus Phillips and Philip Vineberg, were also trustees for CEMP and top advisers to Sam. Phillips, widely described as the most influential Canadian Jew of his time, had been with Sam since the 1920s; he had designed the original family trusts and, until the death of Sam, had mediated between Sam and Allan. Vineberg, Phillips's nephew and a partner in the law firm, took on many additional duties as the latter grew older, becoming in the sixties and seventies the family's pre-eminent lawyer. In fact, Vineberg thought up both the CEMP and Edper monikers. Barney Finestone says that these two men, as trustees for Edward and Peter, "made it very hard for them to get going. They just didn't give them much money. They said, "The purpose of the trust wasn't for you fellows to go into business. The purpose of the trust is to look after your children.' They couldn't spring a hundred million out of that trust and really start to swing. They got a relatively small number of dollars. It wasn't like Charles and Edgar who started off probably with a quarter of a billion dollars to play games with. Peter used to be pretty mad about it.''

In 1962, Peter and Edward hired Austin Beutel, who quickly became the brothers' right-hand man and the senior officer at Edper. At the time, Edper's total assets amounted to about $150 million, of which two-thirds was the stock they held in Seagram's. Beutel had hired Ned Goodman, and the part-time services of Paul Lowenstein, a young accountant who had been the auditor for a number of companies in which the brothers had invested. (Lowenstein's father had been Allan Bronfman's personal doctor.)

In 1966, Ned Goodman stumbled on a small public company called National Hees Enterprises Limited, which had been around since 1887, founded by the grandfather of long-time federal Tory cabinet minister George H. Hees, who had severed his ties with the company in 1954. For much of its existence, the company had been a leading manufacturer and wholesaler of venetian blinds, draperies and window shades. As part of its operations, it also made precision metal casting. Goodman, who was a geologist, thought the company had potential. He brought Edper in as a substantial investor, putting one million dollars into convertible debentures.

But soon after, Beutel and Goodman suddenly announced they were going to leave Edper to set up their own investment counselling firm. The move was a surprise to the others at Edper, including Peter and Edward. Beutel had proved to be a top-notch advisor. But the departure was amicable — so much so that Beutel continued to sit on a number of boards as the brothers' representative. Peter and Edward also gave him a large portfolio to manage at the new firm. The departure of Beutel and Goodman coincided with a growing feeling in Peter that he should change direction and move from passive stock portfolio investments to more active corporate life.

The vacancies at Edper were filled by Neil Baker, the respected chief of research at the Montreal stockbroker firm of Morgan, Ostiguy and Hudon Inc., and by Len Spilfogel, a junior from the same firm, who moved into Goodman's job. Baker hired Lowenstein full-time, and the two became interested in expanding Edper's stake in Hees Enterprises. They knew that Hees was controlled by another company, Great West Saddlery, which was listed on the Toronto Stock Exchange. The chairman and controlling shareholder of both companies was A. T. (Dutch) Holland, a jolly, self-described promoter who has sat on the Ontario Securities Commission since 1982. Holland recalls the way in which he was approached and the deal that resulted: "Paul and Neil had said to me one time, 'If you ever want to do something with the company, let us know.' I was getting tired of working with limited resources, so I phoned Neil. He was in New York. So I phoned his hotel and said, 'You want to make a deal?' " Holland wanted some cash and would take the rest in notes. Neil Baker agreed and said he would call back in fifteen minutes. He did, asking Holland if he could travel from Toronto to Montreal the following day to do the deal. "I'm not going to be there," said Baker, "but I've just told Peter Bronfman what we said and he agreed. See Peter tomorrow and he can firm up the deal." When Holland met with Bronfman the following day to draw up an agreement, he knew him only slightly. Peter told Holland, "I don't know other than these five or six things that Neil has given me. You'll have to dictate it." Holland did, taking a half-hour to construct the complex agreement. Recalls Holland, "That's about the largest amount of paper we had between us."

Holland sold his interest in Great West Saddlery to Edper for fifty cents a share, which, together with the purchase of some treasury shares, bought Edper control of Saddlery and total ownership of Hees for less than $800,000. Saddlery was a bargain; its stock value depressed as a result of a sordid past. Holland had picked up the company cheaply after its two owners, known familiarly as Pete and Doug, had run the company into the ground in the late fifties and been sent to the penitentiary on conspiracy to defraud convictions in 1961. But before that, Saddlery had enjoyed a proud history since Confederation, providing saddles and harnesses to cowboys, Mounties, and the Allied cavalry, later moving into wholesale distribution of hardware, dry goods, and footwear.

Edper's purchase of Saddlery soon stirred up the stock market. Saddlery's shares, which had sold for as little as a dime each in 1967 and had traded at forty-six cents in early March, had bounded to $9.25 in trading the day before the company's annual meeting convened in mid-June to ratify the deal. The reason, according to the *Globe and Mail*'s Report on Business: "In part, at least, it is the Bronfman name — a name that is stock-market magic to some people."

Magic, indeed. Some people may have been a little fuzzy on which Bronfmans they were, but what did it matter. "With the Bronfman backing, it [Saddlery] is unlikely to face any shortage of expansion funds," the *Financial Post* confidently predicted. And expansion plans were already formed. "We are not interested in building an empire, but in making money," said Neil Baker, the newly appointed chairman of Saddlery. Baker was set to move into the glamour industries of the sixties. Trevor Eyton, a young lawyer who had just become a partner at the prestigious Toronto firm Tory, Tory, Deslauriers & Binnington, acted for the Bronfmans on the deal. Lowenstein, who had found Eyton a year or so before on the recommendation of a Toronto broker he knew, Chuck Loewen, had already bought a few shares of the affordable Saddlery. As part of the deal when Edper bought in, Peter and Edward offered some of the people who worked for them a cut of the action, in some cases helping to finance stock purchases by executives. It was the beginning of the Edper creed.

What followed was a series of small acquisitions for Saddlery: a computer service company specializing in the insurance business; then another, similar company in Quebec; and a space research company with a link to McGill University that was doing ballistics research for the Israeli and United States governments. Baker, who had a certain flair for public relations, thought the purchases would attract investors to Saddlery. The stock continued to move higher, topping $14.50 by mid-July. Dubbed "this year's fastest flyer" by Bay Street, the investment had taken on the proportions of a stock promotion. Baker asked the stock exchange for a temporary trading suspension to cool out the stock and to give him time to make an important announcement.

Meanwhile, in Montreal, Sam Bronfman was growing increasingly uncomfortable about the attention the press was paying to Peter and Edward, referring to them as members of the Bronfman family, as if that were description enough. He objected to them *using* the Bronfman name! Sam's trusted advisor, Lazarus Phillips, called Peter, asking him to back off. Peter replied that it was his own name and he didn't see any reason he should stop using it. Soon after, the Edper executives concluded that Saddlery needed a "safety net" beneath it, because much of its assets were speculative and the stock price was still moving upward. Baker, Lowenstein and André Bruneau,* who ran the real-estate division of Edper, suggested to Peter and Edward that the potpourri of real-estate assets owned by the brothers be moved into Saddlery in exchange for stock. The two brothers had hooked up with a number of successful real-estate developers, including Samuel Hashman of Calgary, then the west's most prominent real-estate developer. Peter and Edward had invested in or owned several office buildings in downtown Montreal, Calgary and Edmonton as well as shopping centres in British Columbia. By the end of the summer of 1968, Peter and Edward had agreed to merge their real-estate holdings, valued at $14 million, with Hashman's, worth $9 million, and put them all into Saddlery in exchange for stock. Edper would remain the controlling shareholder. When the new Saddlery was unveiled in September — the stock had ceased trading for two months — it had a net worth of $25 million and an annual cash flow of more than $1.5 million.

That move, which sowed the seeds for the later creation of the Bronfmans' giant Trizec real-estate development company,

* Bruneau has led an eclectic life, writing movie scripts, buying race horses, making a fortune in oil and gas, and divorcing four wives. He lives in Montreal now, having given up residing in the tax havens of Monaco and the Cayman Islands.

gave them the confidence to do many other things. Indeed, the corporate restructuring led to another turning point in the evolution of the Bronfmans' nascent empire. With the financial complexities of the non-arm's-length transfer of assets, Edper needed top-rank auditors. They decided to use Touche Ross & Co., and the man assigned to the account was the manager in the Montreal office, Jack Cockwell. He was a tightly coiled but brilliant twenty-seven-year-old, who had moved to Montreal in 1966 from his home in South Africa. The other fellow on the Edper file, Cockwell's junior, was Tim Price, who came from the "poor" side of the Price family of Abitibi-Price fame.

Dutch Holland, who carried on as Saddlery's president for a short time after Edper bought control, and who continued to hold a large number of Hees shares, recalls his first encounter with Cockwell. "The Bronfman brothers and Sam Hashman had put all their real estate into Saddlery to give it some lift-off. And it meant it all had to be independently valued — quite a big job putting it all together. I remember being most impressed as an old auditor, because people were saying, 'Well, we're going to have to do this' and there was acres of paperwork. And Jack was saying, 'No problem, when do you need this?' And someone said, 'Geez, this is Tuesday. We need it Thursday morning, nine o'clock.' 'Oh, no problem. That's easy,' Jack said."

The restructuring of Saddlery made another splash in the financial press. Once again Sam Bronfman was angry and he let them know it. At that time, Peter and Edward worked out of a suite of offices situated right across the street from Seagram's head office, an architecturally amazing feudal castle affair situated on Peel Street. Although Sam had evicted Peter and Edward from Seagram's sixteen years before, the brothers had continued to have all of Edper's calls go through Seagram's switchboard.

But Sam's irritation at their growing publicity had become so great that he cut off the Edper line. Peter and Edward were disappointed, but even they had come to accept that a total separation was inevitable. Peter, in particular, was anxious to be his own person, to take his side of the Bronfman family to greater heights. Other Edper executives were elated at the news that the final tie had been cut. Perhaps with it the brothers' caution, reluctance, second-guessing, and lack of confidence would also disappear.

In the year that had passed, Saddlery's stock had risen to sixteen dollars from forty cents a share. The company seemed headed for more success. Peter and Edward had set out to extricate themselves from a beholden position in the family liquor company. They were acquiring the self-confidence of independence. But there would be one more lesson to learn about the real world: the Great West Life debacle.

Neil Baker felt it was time to do a big deal, something that would put the Bronfmans on the map and put some beef into Saddlery. He had been looking for takeover prospects and had come across Great West Life Insurance Company of Winnipeg. It was the country's fourth-largest insurance company, an establishment dowager in a blue-chip business with thousands of scattered shareholders and no one controlling owner. Almost two-thirds of the shares were held in the United States, with the remaining third held by Canadians. At $85 a share, the company was trading at far less than the estimated value of its $1.5 billion assets, although it was hard to tell for certain because the company was notoriously reluctant to disclose details of its finances. Finally, Baker was familiar with the company because he was from Winnipeg, where his family owned Winnipeg Supply & Fuel.

The strategists at Edper — Baker and Lowenstein and, to a lesser extent, Spilfogel — began to talk about Great West Life. Then, at one of their usual sessions in Peter's office, the three brought up Great West. Peter reacted favourably. Edper began to quietly buy shares, using funds from Saddlery and a bank line of credit. Baker used several brokers, including

Jimmy Connacher, a former Winnipeger and a close friend who worked in the Montreal office of Wood Gundy.*

Meanwhile, Lowenstein had been sent down to New York to raise more money for Saddlery. He began negotiating with Cogan, Berlind and Wheill, an aggressive, creative firm that was the Drexel, Burnham of its day. At that time, several takeovers of life insurance companies had already taken place in the United States, and Cogan, Berlind and Wheill was also advising a comer named Saul Steinberg, who would go on to personify corporate raiders on Wall Street in the 1980s. The firm was comfortable with ideas presented by Edper. Lowenstein was able to raise $70 million in New York through a private placement of Saddlery notes and shares to a group of institutions. Recalls Lowenstein: "We weren't terribly anxious to raise the money in Canada because this was the late sixties and there was really a very closed club institutionally."

During the closing months of 1968, Edper had continued to discreetly acquire shares in Great West Life. But rumours of an impending takeover were becoming widespread. The price of stock in the life insurance company had climbed to $110; Saddlery was trading in the $20 plus range. Edper executives were growing nervous about the publicity and feared the takeover was taking on the appearance of a shady stock promotion; Trevor Eyton, as Edper's Ontario lawyer, was advising almost full time and suggested that Edper go to the securities commission and ask officials to close down trading in the stock, pending an announcement.

On January 29, 1969, Baker announced plans to bid for all the outstanding shares of Great West Life for $170 a share

---

* In the same year, Baker became a five-per-cent founding investor in a new Montreal brokerage firm, Gordon Eberts Securities Limited. Other founders were Monte Gordon and Gordon Eberts. In 1970, Connacher joined the firm as well. Gordon Eberts Securities moved to Toronto, became Daly Gordon Securities, then Gordon Capital Corp.; now it is one of Canada's largest and certainly the most aggressive firm on Bay Street.

in cash and securities. Baker told a meeting of Saddlery shareholders that the main objective in buying Great West Life was to return control of the company to Canada. When reporters referred to the irony of Saddlery using American money, he replied, "That would make a great headline. You can use it if you want to." But when Baker was asked by his minority shareholders why Saddlery really wanted a life insurance company, and why Great West in particular, he retreated to characteristic secrecy: "I think we'll leave the philosophy for another meeting." Although it was not revealed at the meeting, the takeover offer would mean that Saddlery would have to issue another six million shares, thereby swamping the company's existing capital base of six and a half million outstanding shares.

The immediate reaction from Great West's president, David Kilgour, was vague; he hadn't heard anything official and he could hardly take these upstarts seriously. (Kilgour is the father of federal Liberal party leader John Turner's wife, Geills. He is also related by marriage to Jimmy Connacher.) Still, annoyances seemed to be all around Kilgour as he prepared himself for his company's annual meeting the following week. It should have been, by all rights, yet another tranquil Great West meeting. But dissident shareholders had already planned a proxy fight because they were unhappy with the company's miserly dividends and lack of disclosure.

At the meeting, however, Kilgour moved decisively, proposing that the company double its quarterly dividend, form a holding company to allow it to expand into other financial businesses (thereby offering up the impression of progressive management), and increase the authorized capital to ten million shares from one million. Finally, he wanted to issue a stock dividend of one million shares. For the first time in its long corporate life, Great West Life released profit figures. And what figures they were: $9.76 a share for 1968, up from $7.66 a share in 1967, up from $6.30 a share in 1966. This was clearly a stock worth keeping. Strangely, Saddlery — as a shareholder at the meeting — offered no opposition to Kilgour's proposed anti-takeover measures.

Great West Life's directors were not as silent; they officially stated their opposition to Saddlery's bid, and Kilgour launched a smear campaign. Noting that Saddlery's stock had gone from forty-six cents to twenty-four dollars in just one year, Kilgour suggested his shareholders would have to "form their own opinion as to what the market may be when they eventually get the stock or they try to sell it." Amy Booth, writing from Montreal in the *Financial Post*, declared that it "seems to be all part of the instant money game." Tracing Saddlery's ballooning share issues and heady stock-price run-up, she wondered, "Is this kind of result plausible or, what is more important for shareholders of both companies, sustainable? Only time will tell." She estimated the intrinsic value of Great West Life at $150 a share, and then added, "Just what the intrinsic value of Saddlery is, is more difficult to determine. The Bronfman name behind the company is undoubtedly one of its major assets."

It was also one of its major problems. Among the people at Edper, an uneasy feeling was developing that Sam Bronfman was also against the takeover. The mutual trustees, Lazarus Phillips and Philip Vineberg, told them as much, and Sam had exercised his influence over the Bank of Montreal; the country's financial institutions were falling into line — behind Sam. Recalls Lowenstein, "Negotiating the lines of credit at the time weren't quite as fluid. It [financing] just wasn't quite as forthcoming." And Barney Finestone says, " I know for a fact that Sam got very upset at the way they [Peter and Edward] were behaving — and they very politely told him that they understood his concern but they had been told to get out and paddle their own canoes, and that's what they were going to do."

To outside observers and Great West Life shareholders, the Bronfman forces had been strangely quiet. Baker had promised to reveal Saddlery's precise holdings in Great West Life after its annual meeting, but he had not done so. Moreover, no formal takeover offer had been filed for a month. Now street talk had it that the likelihood of a takeover happening was fading with each passing day. It was rumoured that once co-operative Great West Life shareholders had changed their minds about selling when they had heard Kilgour's proposals or that maybe the Bronfmans were manoeuvring for an easy profit from a rival bidder for Great West Life.

In fact, Peter and Edward held about thirty-five per cent of Great West Life; they were on the brink of seizing control. But Trevor Eyton was concerned that, because it was a mutual life-insurance company, in which the policyholders had votes, Edper would not have voting control. Baker and Lowenstein argued that, as with other takeovers of mutual companies, the policyholders could be won over and that the company was a jewel of an asset worth the risk-taking. Eyton's caution, combined with the invisible presence of Sam Bronfman, pushed Peter to call a Saturday meeting.

Peter was hearing conflicting advice from his people. Some were urging him to stay and fight to the end, while others argued that it was not a good time to go for broke, that Edper was too small to essentially take on the Canadian establishment. "God, he was stressed," recalls Finestone, who was with Peter the night he decided to withdraw from the race. "He was making the decision and he was finding it very hard . . . It was a very traumatic experience for Peter," says Finestone. "He was really rocked that night and it influenced his judgement of Baker. He resented what happened. This was a Baker deal and then it became dirty and motives were being challenged and Peter was being accused of being a corporate raider and so on, and he wasn't." It was Peter's first excursion into a real, tough world. "They didn't have the stomach for that fight," Finestone recalls.

First thing the next morning, Peter called Jacques Courtois, the brothers' principal lawyer. Courtois was a prominent Montreal lawyer who also acted as a close advisor to Paul Desmarais, the brilliant reverse takeover artist who had assembled Power Corporation during the 1960s. Peter offered the block of Great West Life stock to Desmarais. The wily businessman quickly accepted. Later he would make a follow-up bid for enough Great West Life stock to give him fifty-one per cent control and go on to roll the company into a huge financial conglomerate that combined Great West, Imperial Life, Montreal Trust and Investors Group mutual funds. The Bronfmans would walk away with a $25 million profit, thereby making them the corporate greenmailers that the establishment forces had said they were all along.

The Saturday morning meeting was a turning point for the Bronfmans and their advisors. Sam Hashman, who held about twenty per cent of Saddlery as a result of selling his real-estate holdings into it, came in from Calgary. Eyton flew in from Toronto. The Edper team assembled. Peter told them what he had decided to do. As usual, Peter made the decision, Edward supported him. The others were stunned. Baker protested long and loud. Lowenstein recalls, "We were almost there and when he sold our block at cost I was very, very discouraged. I said to myself, these boys will never have the confidence to do anything significant." Lowenstein resigned over the decision to pull out of Great West Life and went on to form a venture-capital company with friends. Baker stayed on and hired Jack Cockwell to take Lowenstein's place as vice-president and treasurer of Edper.*

At the meeting, it was decided that Sam Hashman would become president of Saddlery and direct all operations out of a head office in Calgary under a new name, Great West International Equities. Edper was left with its ownership of Hees and another obscure publicly listed company called Marigot Investments. Neil Baker had picked up Marigot for Edper when its entrepreneurial owner had come looking for money. Marigot consisted of two ski hills and some Caribbean real estate — all of which remains in the Bronfmans' vast collection of real estate today. Marigot was later renamed Mico, a company in which Jack Cockwell gained a large personal stake; he turned it into the Bronfmans' first significant sortie into merchant banking.

The dream at Edper had been to create a conglomerate overnight. Len Spilfogel had witnessed the drama from a vantage point slightly off centre stage, and he stayed on long enough to see the effects the Great West Life experience had on Peter's approach to managing Edper. The intense publicity surrounding the takeover battle profoundly affected Peter and Edward,

---

* Not only did Cockwell replace Lowenstein as treasurer, he also married Lowenstein's secretary, Norma. It was his second marriage.

who were accustomed to living a quiet life. "I think, in retrospect," says Spilfogel, "for a first thing, maybe we jumped too much, too quickly. It was reachable but it was a tall reach. One of the things one must avoid in the investment business is believing your own BS and I think at that time people very much got caught up in what was going on."

But the mood at Edper had irrevocably changed. Peter was mentally worn out by the experience, and he was angry at Neil Baker for having put him through it. Baker had moved too quickly for the cautious Bronfmans. "In hindsight," said Spilfogel, "Neil deserves a lot of credit because he was the guy that got this ball going, and he was the guy that had the understanding and the mental strength to be able to convince Peter and Edward to do this kind of thing. And over the fifteen- or twenty-year period, it has proven to have been the right thing for them." Nevertheless, Baker was asked to leave.

For the next year and a half, the Bronfmans analyzed what they had done and finally came to the conclusion that the bold route mapped out by Baker was, in fact, the way they wanted to go. They could, they decided, live with the pressure and scrutiny. The style of the organization changed. Gone was the idea of having one chief guru, and a more collegial atmosphere developed. A larger circle of people was consulted by the brothers. "There was a real kind of meshing of idea and thought and development of what was happening," says Spilfogel. "Long debates on what they wanted to do."

Austin Beutel had shown the Bronfmans one way to move; Neil Baker had shown them another way. Jack Cockwell was still only a junior player at Edper, and had yet to prove his worth and earn the trust of Peter and Edward. That would come over a number of years. "When you work for Peter and Edward," says Spilfogel, "even though they will bring you up [through the ranks], you have to earn your marks before you really gather their trust. Trust is one of the key words." But Cockwell was a methodical, organized person, and his very way of doing things reassured Peter and Edward, who themselves were starting the slow work of rebuilding their self-confidence.

In the early months of 1971, the Bronfmans cashed in their

Great West Saddlery investment. At the end of the previous year, the country's largest publicly held real-estate company, Trizec Corporation of Montreal, had taken control of the property company owned by the Cummings family.* By March 1971, the Bronfmans and Sam Hashman had sold their seventy-two-per-cent interest in Saddlery to Trizec in return for $12 million cash — a twenty-four-fold return — and nine per cent of Trizec stock. As a condition of the deal with Trizec, they sold off the incompatible computer and space-research companies.

Jack Cockwell was handily managing their stock investment portfolio, constantly dreaming up new ways to make money. The portfolio had never done so well, and Cockwell was eventually able to convince the brothers to sell their remaining Seagram's stock. With the Saddlery retrenchment and the new cash, Peter and Edward focused their energies on a new business, which they had acquired at the beginning of 1972: Canadian Arena Co., owner of the Montreal Canadiens (described as "the winningest team in hockey" the day the Bronfmans bought it), the Nova Scotia Voyageurs farm club, and the Montreal Forum. The Bronfmans bought it from the Molson family through a holding company called Placement Rondele Ltée — Puck Investments. They put Jacques Courtois in charge of running the company, and he became the public face for the Canadiens' new owners. "Their first real move on their own was the purchase of the Montreal Canadiens because they came out of the box into the limelight," says Paul Lowenstein. "They started to understand that it wasn't the end of the world that they had a little bit of public exposure." And besides, Sam Bronfman had died on July 10, 1971.

Peter and Edward were free to use the Bronfman name.

---

* Jacques Courtois and Lazarus Phillips already were directors of Trizec; two Phillips boys, Ivan and Neil, were investors in Cumming and partners in the family law firm, Phillips, Vineberg, Goodman, Phillip & Rothman.

CHAPTER TWO

The Taking of Brascan

*There are a lot of other things to do in this world
besides acquiring companies.*
— Peter Bronfman, 1979

It was known as "the Light," and it was for many years a beacon of the modernity and prosperity that Brazilians embraced early in the twentieth century. It was as much a part of Brazil as the famous string of lights that ringed Rio's harbour. In fact, the Light supplied the electricity that powered those lights, as well as providing the developing country with its open-air electric streetcars, the telephone system, gas, and water. The Light, as Ronald McEachern wrote in the *Financial Post* in 1952, is "quite literally the arterial system of Brazil's business life." It was also a gold mine for its owners, a group of Canadian and European investors who allowed managers from the upright Bay Street law firm — Blake, Lash and Cassels — to run the company's affairs for many decades.

The company was officially called Brazilian Traction, Light and Power Company Limited (in 1969, the name was changed to Brascan). Its headquarters were on King Street in Toronto, but the action was all in Brazil. That sprawling, verdant country, for so long so much an unrealized promise, was a profit waiting to be taken when the rapacious Canadian railroad builder, Sir William MacKenzie, happened along in the late 1890s and bought a tram-line franchise for Sao Paolo. The eager vendors had predicted the decline of the donkey-powered streetcar, but the bewhiskered MacKenzie, who was once described as having an adrenal complex for achievement, was a visionary: he was one of the first to spot the opportunity for electric trams in the developing world. He picked up concessions, often in perpetuity, with guaranteed rates of return and the comfort of a monopoly.

In 1899, Sir William MacKenzie sent Alexander MacKenzie (no relation) to Brazil; the latter was a junior lawyer with Blake, Lash and Cassels who hailed from Kincardine, Ontario. He was to take charge of the tiny power and traction company. Lawyers at Blake, Lash and Cassels played an important role in running MacKenzie's Brazilian holdings, partly because of the legal work, which involved franchises, and because of financing and local politics. Because of the nightmare of foreign-capital regulations and currency-exchange boondoggles, others who worked for MacKenzie were drawn from the accounting firm of Clarkson, Gordon. The younger MacKenzie began building the Light in what became the golden industrial triangle in southeastern Brazil, bounded by the cities of Santos, Sao Paolo, and Rio de Janiero. Fortuitously, he picked up a succession of gas and telephone franchises as incidental rights while building the power system. And along the way, he became an expert on Brazilian law. He also became fluent in Portuguese and adept in Brazil's unpredictable politics. MacKenzie used his Canadian legal and financial expertise; he sold stock and bonds in Canada and Britain to finance the company, and drew his master engineers and equipment from the United States. By 1928, when he retired as president, MacKenzie — by then Sir Alex — left a thriving complex of jungle hydroelectric plants and hundreds of miles of tram lines.

Other people had tried to exploit other developing countries. They fell prey to nationalization or political turmoil, like British Utilities in Argentina. But the Light was different. It made money — potsful — it stayed private, and it sailed through sixty years of Brazilian politics essentially undisturbed. The reasons were the quality of the company's management in Toronto and a corporate ethic that put Brazilians in charge in Brazil. Despite the company's nickname — "the Canadian Octopus," which was used only half affectionately — Brazilians even today say, "Yes, the company made a lot of money, but we are the foremost nation in the developing world industrially and a lot of it is due to the power we got from the Canadian company."

The 1940s were halcyon years for the Light. The company reached a peak in terms of manpower — almost 50,000 people were on the payroll — and the spread of its concessions. Certainly, the Light was everywhere, its tentacles wrapped around every aspect of life in Brazil. A Carioca got up in the morning and heated his water for coffee on gas from the Light; the water was also from the Light. He went to work on a bus or tram owned by the Light. The electricity in his office or factory was, again, from the Light. And the level of service was, by and large, excellent.

In 1945, Brazilian, as the Light was more formally known, was still being run by the people in Toronto who had built the company from the turn of the century to the Second World War. They were men like eighty-year-old Sir Thomas White, who had been Canada's finance minister during the First World War and a senior man at National Trust. But younger, forward-thinking board members and officers like George Troop, who was company treasurer, were worried about the formidable growth projections for Brazil and the company's pressing need for capital. The old guard had always favoured taking a handsome dividend. But Troop and others realized the post-war economy in Brazil was about to go off like a bomb. To cope, the company would have to make huge capital expenditures. In the boardroom at Brazilian's headquarters in Toronto, there was tremendous debate over whether the company could do it, or whether they should sell out right away. The people in favour of staying on and tackling the problems found a young corporate lawyer named Henry Borden and named him new chief executive. Borden had just completed a wartime stint with C.D. Howe in Ottawa. He was handed a huge estimate for enlarging all the power plants and the distribution system; he had to find funding for it.

In 1946, there was very little money around to be borrowed. The major industrialized nations had, as part of the Bretton Woods agreement of 1944, set up the World Bank; the articles of its charter made it clear that both member states and private organizations were free to apply for loans. However, no private companies had applied. Borden saw an opportunity. With some lawyers and treasurer George Troop, he went to Washington. They booked an entire floor of a hotel and began pounding on the door of the World Bank. At first, World Bank officials refused to deal with them because Brazilian was a company, not a sovereign state. Borden pointed out the clause in the Bank's charter setting out provisions for corporations. Finally, the officials agreed to consider the loan request if it had the blessing of the Brazilian government. Borden quickly summoned his chief of Brazilian operations, Antonio Gallotti, to present "the Brazilian side of things." He came, and Brazilian made financial history. It was the first company to negotiate a loan with the World Bank. The money — about $75 million U.S. — was applied to the massive hydroelectric expansion of the 1940s and 1950s. Out of that came the Paraiba-Parai water diversion project, considered a masterpiece of engineering because it created a vast storehouse of water *inside* a mountain, and the Forcacava power plant, which generated 320,000 kilowatts of electricity from water that fell a thousand feet down a twenty-foot tunnel. Said one expert on Brazilian, "It was really the saving grace for the company and in many ways a saving grace for Brazil when the so-called economic miracle happened in the late fifties and sixties. It was a neck-and-neck race with the demand, but basically they kept up with it. It was a tremendous Canadian adventure."

Until he stepped down in the early sixties, Borden ran the company masterfully in tandem with Antonio Gallotti, an Italian-born member of one of Brazil's establishment families. Borden steered the company through the turbulent forties and fifties with leadership and vision, and his initiatives, such as a buy-Brazilian policy, ensured that Brazilian never became an ugly Canadian company. By contrast, the president of the large American utility there, Amcorp, was fond of flying down from the States, having the limo stop at the American Embassy to pick up the ambassador, and then going straight to the foreign ministry. That did not go over well with the proud Brazilians.

In 1952, Brazilian hit an earnings record of $42 million, which it would never achieve again. The 1950s ushered in the era of high tech — switching gear in the telephone companies and hydro substations — and the giant utility began cutting back on its work force even as the phenomenal growth of the country and the company continued unabated. Then, in the early 1960s, the trams were pushed out as the car was embraced passionately by Brazilians. A quick succession of populist governments that promoted economic nationalism made doing business more difficult and uncertain. In 1960, the company was forced to hike employees' wages by thirty-eight per cent, but there was no corresponding increase in its rates. In 1961, the government levied a sharp rise in the withholding tax on profits of foreign-owned companies. In 1962, it threatened to enact a law that seventy-five per cent of proceeds from any nationalization be re-invested in Brazil. The company had always rewarded its investors generously by paying good dividends, but in the early 1960s, it didn't pay dividends a number of times when hyperinflation of two hundred, three hundred, and four hundred per cent sent the *cruziero* through the floor. Meanwhile, consumer demand for electricity had outstripped the capacity of the company. The company's rates of return could not sustain the growth needed, and for two years in a row the company lost money.

But the political worries that had plagued Brazilian under the populist rule of Janio Quadros, and later, Joao Goulart, disappeared almost overnight when, on April 1, 1964, the military took over the government. Given its strategic importance to the industrial life of the country, Brazilian sustained little damage from the coup, save bullet-riddled telephone poles. Under the new government, foreign investors were once again welcome in the country. The company's dividends improved; the regulated rates became acceptable; the company's stock price edged upward. After years of negotiation, in January 1966, the state officially took over Brazilian's telephone utility and, thanks to Antonio Gallotti's superb connections, the company did considerably better than American giant IT&T had done three years earlier. Under the terms of its deal, Brazilian managed to pull $10 million out of Brazil and deposit it safely in Canada, while a balance of $86 million was to be paid over twenty years with twenty-five per cent repatriable to Canada. With the proceeds, Brazilian made its first Canadian investment in April 1967: the company bought a million shares of John Labatt Limited. It was the beginning of a new era.

In 1969, Brazilian changed its name to Brascan Limited, to reflect a growing emphasis on Canadian investments as the remittances from Brazil trickled back to Canada. Also in 1969 the company gained a new president, John Henderson (Jake) Moore. Outgoing, an important player on the little-league, blue-blood London, Ontario social scene, Moore began his mission to give Brascan a high profile in Canada. At the age of thirty-seven, Moore had joined London, Ontario-based John Labatt Limited as treasurer and finance director. His family was not part of the city's most rich and prominent families, and Moore would remain forever a hired hand, no matter how affluent he became. But he had gone to the right schools — Ridley College and Royal Military College — and had started his career as an accountant with Clarkson, Gordon, where he had worked on the Labatt's audit.

By 1956, Moore was running the brewery for the Labatt family, and he had embarked on a strategy to build a truly national concern. At that time, Labatt's held less than thirteen per cent of the Canadian beer market. Nine years later, its market share had shot up to thirty-six per cent. In the process, Moore had acquired a string of local breweries, and in swallowing them up he had been involved in a few corporate scrapes. In 1964, the owners of the giant Milwaukee-based Schlitz Brewing Company acquired 1.7 million Labatt's shares (or thirty-nine per cent) for $39 million, with the blessings of the Labatt family, who sold a large chunk of shares at a handsome premium over the market price. But the company's management and the majority of the board vigorously opposed the sale to the foreigners. Fortuitously for them, the U.S. Department of Justice ruled that the purchase could be in violation of American anti-combines legislation and issued a restraining order to prevent Schlitz from voting the shares until the Supreme Court could decide the case. Moore embarked on a search for a friendly Canadian buyer of the shares, should the court decide against Schlitz. To help in the matter, he hired Tony Griffin, then president of a small merchant banking operation in Toronto called Triarch Corporation. But they faced a near-impossible task, and prospective buyers shied away time and time again. Then, in April 1967, Brascan — at the time headed by Clarkson, Gordon alumnus Grant Glassco — made its first Canadian investment: it purchased one million of the Labatt's shares held by Schlitz for $21 million. A life-insurance company bought three hundred thousand shares, and a newly formed investment company, Jonlab Investments Limited, bought four hundred thousand shares. Jonlab had been formed by Moore (who borrowed $300,000 to take a twelve-per-cent stake) and some of his friends. Meanwhile, the Schlitz sale had split the Labatt family and the company's management into two warring camps with very different objectives. Already, one seventeen-year board veteran had resigned over the sale, taking with him the long-established company solicitor, the company's bankers, and its principal underwriter. By 1968, the last two family directors, one of them Jack Labatt, left the company board. In 1969, the board named Moore chairman of Labatt's. At the same time, he was invited onto the Brascan board.

Moore arrived to see a company in turmoil. Glassco had died a year earlier and Brascan was then in the tight control of one board director, Neil McKinnon, who was chairman of the company's bank, the Commerce. Robert Winters, a former Cabinet minister who had run for the leadership of the national Liberal Party in 1968, losing out narrowly to Pierre Trudeau, was the company's president. He was ineffectually facing a building crisis in Brazil and a takeover threat from the Philadelphia-based utilities giant International Utilities Corporation, which had acquired ten per cent of Brascan's widely scattered shares. By the end of 1969, Moore was moved into the president's slot and Winters became chairman.

A few months later, Moore began consolidating his position. In February 1970, Jonlab Investments sold at $27 US a share the Labatt's shares it had acquired from Schlitz for $21 US. The shares had split in 1967, so it was a handsome profit. With the proceeds, plus a $12-million loan from Moore's good friends at the Commerce, Jonlab bought out International Utilities' block of Brascan shares. That made Moore's Jonlab the largest shareholder in Brascan, and Brascan the largest shareholder in Labatt's. Then Moore launched a diversification plan for Brascan in Brazil and Canada that laid the groundwork for a holding company that, by and large, exists today. Between 1971 and 1978, Moore increased the company's non-Light assets to more than $900 million from $262 million. He bought stakes in Great Lakes Power Corporation (at twenty-six per cent over book value) and London Life Insurance Company (some say in an attempt, with the Jeffrey family, to ward off a takeover threat from Edper). Often, however, his grand plan failed magnificently. In 1970, Moore sank $40 million into Elf Oil and Gas, and soon after he had to write off $10 million of it. In 1972 he spent almost $10 million on an investment in the Sukunka coal fields in British Columbia, and subsequently wrote the whole thing off. Explorations in the Philippines, United States, and Canada failed to result in any commercial production. Meanwhile, Brascan's rate of return in Canada and Brazil steadily plummeted. In 1976, Moore initiated a change in the company bylaws so that foreigners were banned from owning more than forty-nine per cent of the stock, which had the effect of depressing the value of the shares on the open market.

But the corporate manoeuvre that attracted the attention of Brascan's shareholders (and, in 1977, the attention of the Bryce Royal Commission on Corporate Concentration) was Brascan's acquisition of Jonlab. In 1975, Jonlab shareholders — among them Jake Moore; Eddie Goodman, a Labatt's director; Peter Hardy, chairman and president of Jonlab, vice-chairman of Labatt's, and a director of Brascan; John B. Cronyn, a Labatt's director; and three Brascan officers, including Antonio Gallotti — wanted to get out of their debt-laden investment. For several years, Jonlab, Labatt's, and Brascan had bought and sold each other's stock, maintaining the status quo, repelling outsiders. Triarch, a merchant bank owned by Griffin, had earned fat fees participating in some of the deals and, in typically incestuous fashion in 1971, Triarch was bought by Jonlab — at a sixty-nine-per-cent premium. In 1975, Jonlab shareholders scored their biggest deal when Brascan paid $8 a share for Jonlab. The Bryce Royal Commission on Corporate Concentration put the value of Jonlab at $5 a share. But in addition to the price tag of $13 million, Brascan had to assume a $30 million debt when Jonlab's bank, the Commerce, cashed in some preferred shares it held in the company. Brascan's legal officer resigned over the purchase.

Despite the shenanigans, Brascan was by the mid-1970s a major corporate player in Canada. It was one of fifteen Canadian companies singled out for study by the royal commission because of their size and influence. In 1975, the *Financial Post* said that Brascan was the sixth-largest Canadian company in terms of assets, and tenth in terms of profits. In August 1975, *Fortune* magazine ranked Brascan fifty-fourth out of three hundred of the largest industrial companies outside the United States. That year, of Brascan's $2.2 billion US in assets, $292 million US were actually in Canada. The Light still boasted 4 million customers, compared to Ontario Hydro's 2.6 million and Consolidated Edison of New York's 3.1 million. Recalls good friend and fellow Jonlab shareholder Eddie Goodman, "Jake Moore was an important person in this country at that time."

But Jake Moore was not well liked. He was a large man physically, and within the company he played the part he looked

— a bullying capitalist. Moore relished the trappings of office. In 1978, his salary was $250,000 a year; he was the country's third-highest-paid executive. He enjoyed doing business in his Lear jet and often chartered helicopters for mid-week trips from his Toronto office to his London farm. He sat on all the right boards of directors — Canadian Pacific, Bell Canada, Hudson's Bay, Morgan Guaranty Trust of New York, and the Canadian Imperial Bank of Commerce — and he had constructed a disproportionately large head-office staff, numbering 150, which, by the end of his reign, included eight vice-presidents. Other holding companies, such as Conrad Black's Argus Corporation and Paul Desmarais' Power Corporation, employed perhaps fifteen or twenty people. Moore liked to have a lot of staff around; he particularly wanted young MBAs to be available at a moment's notice to do an analysis of anything that struck his fancy. That sort of meddling and second-guessing of their work drove executives at some of the subsidiaries crazy. One wag said that Brascan under Moore had a genius for turning gold into brass.

To make matters worse, the 1970s were tough years for Brascan in Brazil. In the early part of the decade, the country's economy reeled from the effects of the first world oil shock. Brazil's currency devaluation went wild. Meanwhile, Brascan was suffering from a slow strangulation of rates as the government developed its own hydroelectric generating capacity through state-owned companies. Brascan simply did not have access to adequate capital, and it faced the prospect of eventually having little leverage in striking a sell-out deal with the government.

During its last five years, until the great pull-out in 1979, the utility became less and less profitable, the going tougher and tougher. On dark days, expropriation seemed moments away; on good days, a deal seemed possible. The operation continued to be awash in dividends. Some of the money — like the payments for the telephone company — could be repatriated. But much of it had to stay in Brazil because of government regulations. Moore did the logical thing: he began to spend the money in Brazil, diversifying into real estate, financial companies, a brewing concern, tourist sites, cattle ranches, and the InterContinental Hotel in Rio. But the diversification was a shock to the people at Brazilian Light, Power and Traction, who were accustomed to running a utility and were now being asked to operate a diversified holding company. Predictably, many of the investments turned sour.

Still, Moore had the good sense to tread carefully in Brazil. While he continued to make life unpleasant for people such as hotel staff and company middle managers, he was wise enough to take Antonio Gallotti's lead when he dealt with political power-brokers. In Brazil, it has always been a matter of who one knows and how one's family is perceived. The urbane Gallotti had ample qualifications. As well, he had a masterful and deft touch. Gallotti managed to keep the ever-present nationalist element at bay. He was convinced that the Canadian utility could not be perceived to be doing anything more than any large Brazilian company would do; to do otherwise would draw the envy and hostility of Brazilian business. "He was very adroit at getting the right measure of things," said one former Brascan employee familiar with the Brazilian operations.

By 1978, Gallotti was in Brasilia, the capital, almost continually, where he was paving the way to a pull-out. Late that year, Moore and Gallotti arranged to sell the utility to the Brazilian government for $380 million US (about $447 million Canadian). More importantly, they had succeeded in securing from the government a commitment to pay the sum in two instalments, the second payment due the second week in April 1979. They would get all the money out of Brazil quickly and cleanly before the nationalistic backlash, certain to surface after the sale was announced, could gain ground. Critics in Toronto said later that Brascan was forced to take half the book value of its assets. But others realized that, given the realities of the Brazilian regulatory and political system, Brascan was lucky to get the money out of Brazil. Ironically, the very success of Brascan's pull-out, and the amount of executive time and effort spent on it, left the company vulnerable to attack at home.

The slow strangulation in Brazil in the 1970s was well known in Canada. Brascan's stock price had been sliding steadily, and the diversification that Jake Moore had set in motion had attracted criticism. Once the payments for the utility were deposited in a New York bank, the company would be vulnerable to a takeover. In November, Bob Simon, Brascan's director of taxation, wrote a memo to his boss, Bill Miller, vice-president of finance, on what to do with all that cash. Much would be made of the memo later, mainly as proof of the chaotic vacuum in the company's executive suite. Peter V. Gundy, a Brascan vice-president at the time and the executive in charge of examining investment prospects in the United States, says, "Simon's memo was a joke. I threw it out. But a senior lawyer in New York later told me it was one of the most important factors in clouding the judge's perception of Brascan — that is, our motivations as Brascan senior management." Simon wrote, "The collective reaction in Brascan has been an increasingly feverish thrashing about for quick and large investments, so as to shovel out . . . the cash as fast as it comes in, thereby reducing vulnerability."

Jake Moore had teams of analysts combing the financial statements of literally hundreds of companies, looking for a suitable takeover target, one that could soak up the Brazilian money. But there was another option: the liquidation of Brascan. Shareholders could be paid between $22 and $30 a share. Moore had chosen not to call a shareholders' meeting, despite the fact that the company was, with the Brazilian sale, shedding its main line of business and most of its assets. Liquidation was more attractive to outside shareholders than to those on the inside. Simon's memo pointed out that liquidation would mean an end to the jobs of Brascan's senior management after a few years, although, the memo noted, the idea "would be met with favour from our shareholders who do not regard us as an organization with drive and promise, but as a dormant piggy bank; a view not wholly unjustified from where they sit."

Simon proposed another alternative, which he called Project Navel. Brascan's senior officers would incorporate a private company, secure a $650-million line of credit — both Morgan Guaranty Trust in New York and the Bank of Commerce were approached — and bid $25 a share to gain total control of the company. Simon wrote in his memo: "The idea is based upon the proposition that if our vulnerability is real (and I strongly believe it is) then it is visible, and the first takeover artist with enough gumption will waltz away with the whole cake. That being so, those who are most acutely aware of the true values in Brascan are those who are in the best position to be first, and to be successful. It follows (outrageously but logically) that this group is Brascan's management (or very carefully selected members thereof)."

Simon's audacious proposal received little support from top management, and eventually the senior officers decided instead to find a big company to take over. On the short list was giant worldwide retailer F.W. Woolworth of New York. Still shackled by old-fashioned stores and methods, with $6 billion in annual sales, Woolworth had enough cash-generating power to match the Light. The idea of buying Woolworth surfaced in February and was pursued into March. Brascan would bid $35 a share, or $1.3 billion, which would be a huge financial burden. Two outside assessments commissioned by Brascan management were unenthusiastic about the proposed purchase; both pointed out Woolworth's considerable drawbacks. But time was running out. The reports lay largely unread at head office. A day before a board meeting to vote on the Woolworth takeover, the Bank of Commerce came through with $700 million in financing. On April 6, Brascan's directors voted to launch a takeover for Woolworth.

Peter Gundy insists that "nobody was thrashing about for quick and large investments. The pace wasn't dictated by the possibility of a takeover of Brascan." And indeed, Moore found the idea hard to credit. In the unlikely event a threat were to materialize, Moore was certain the friends he counted among the institutional investors holding Brascan stock would help to defend his company. Several Brascan insiders said Moore expected a loyalty that was not there. The business world was changing.

But Bob Simon, the creative memo writer, was prescient enough to warn his bosses in a January 30 memo that "We will be taken over, like the ripe plum that we are. This will be done by an organization which . . . is staffed and serviced in its own right. Such an organization needs Brascan's assets, but not its people."

The takeover of Woolworth brought out the worst of Moore's weaknesses, and in many ways seemed nothing more than a personal indulgence. As the battle grew more and more heated, Moore began spending money extravagantly. He had a jet standing by at the airport to take him to New York; he hired a retired journalist to record the momentous events. He surrounded himself with legions of lawyers and posted Pinkerton's guards at the door.

Things began to go wrong for Jake Moore and the dowager Brascan. It began to be apparent that the takeover was not going to be a great coup, but a disaster. "It was incredibly stressful," recalls Peter Gundy, who ran the "war room," as it was known. "We didn't have an adequate anti-takeover defense." That was the responsibility of Moore and his lawyers from Blake, Cassels. "When Edper came through the back door like they did, it was a sort of breathtaking moment," said one Brascan employee. "People realized, these people are very smart. I had the sense that Trevor Eyton and his team were incredibly cagey, steely minded lawyers just chopping it up, and Moore was being more and more exposed."

In late December, Edper bought fifty thousand shares of Brascan, a foothold following the announcement of the Light's sale. Then in early January, Tim Price — who had followed Cockwell from Touche to Edper ten years before — called Jimmy Connacher at Gordon Capital and told him that Edper was thinking seriously about making a takeover offer for Brascan. The ambitious Connacher had had a small hand in the Great West Life attempt while he was a broker at Wood Gundy in Montreal. Then, in 1970, he had joined Gordon Capital, where friends Neil Baker and Gordon Eberts had set up a fiesty little stocktrading firm. Connacher bought more shares of Brascan for Edper and in mid-February he, a Gordon analyst called

David Dorian, and Price and Cockwell met to discuss the merits of Brascan as an investment. The attraction of an acquisition as large as Brascan was, recalls Eyton, "to make us into more of a player." Connacher also told Cockwell who some of the big Brascan shareholders were. By the end of February, with more buying, Edper held eight hundred thousand shares.

Meanwhile, Eyton had been busy lining up a partner for Edper. He and an old friend, Pat Keenan, an accountant who was the North American representative for a Dutch-domiciled company, Patino NV, talked several times about some sort of association. Patino was an international family-owned company built upon a tin mining fortune in Bolivia; Eyton was corporate counsel for the company and other Patino family interests. It was headed by forty-nine-year-old Jaime Ortiz-Patino who lived — and still does — in a chateau just outside Geneva, Switzerland. Ortiz-Patino had been something of a playboy until he turned thirty, when he went to work for the family company. Then, in 1960, he was forced out by other family members, who proceeded to run the company into the ground. Ortiz-Patino was brought back in by an uncle in 1974, and together they took control and revived the company. Ortiz-Patino, Pat Keenan, and a favourite broker of theirs, Fred McCutcheon, had spotted the possibilities of a cash-rich Brascan back in November, but had decided that, as a foreign-owned company, they couldn't do it.

For Edper, a partnership with Patino offered two advantages: Patino had holdings in Brazil and understood the country; and it had plenty of cash. During February, people from Edper and Patino met formally about forming a partnership to bid for control of Brascan. On February 27, Patino began buying Brascan shares, acquiring 460,000 by the time the two partners met on March 26 to officially create Edper Investments, two-thirds owned by Edper Equities and one-third by Patino. They already held five per cent of Brascan.

At Edper's initiative, at 1:00 in the afternoon on April 5, Jake Moore and his lawyer, Bruce Lockwood, from Blake, Cassels, met secretly with Eyton, Cockwell, Keenan, and Ortiz-Patino in a suite at the Royal York Hotel. Eyton informed Moore that his group was contemplating a bid for fifty per

cent through the Toronto Stock Exchange. He was hoping for
Moore's endorsement. Eyton proffered the usual comforts,
including management security. But Moore seemed doubtful
— it was not the policy of the Brascan board to recommend
to shareholders offers for less than all of the outstanding stock.
"He didn't express any violent opposition, which of course
was the right thing to do because he immediately went to work
full-time to make sure that we weren't successful," recalls
Eyton. Finally Moore said that the board would meet the next
day, a Friday, and he would take the offer to them.

"We were really kind of outsiders at the time," Eyton says.
"I was kind of more accepted, I would say — in Jake Moore's
terms — than the travellers from the east." But by the end
of what became a bitter battle, there was more to it than that.
Says Eyton, "It wasn't just a battle between the new investor
and the establishment. It was also the struggle between law
firms." Indeed, Blake, Cassels and Graydon on the one side,
and Eyton's Tory, Tory, Deslauriers and Binnington on the
other, had only a few weeks before concluded a rancorous fight
over the control of Hudson's Bay Company. Tory, Tory,
representing Ken Thomson's Thomson International Incorporated, had won. Then there was the rivalry of Brascan's auditors, Clarkson Gordon, and Edper's accounting firm, Touche
Ross. "It wasn't a solitary figure here and a solitary figure
there," says Eyton. "They were little battalions marching to
war."

The first troop movement was ordered at the Brascan board
meeting the next day. The directors decided to make a cash
offer for all the outstanding shares of F. W. Woolworth Company of New York — a move that would cost at least $1.1
billion. Edper's overtures were firmly rebuffed. Not knowing
this, Eyton delivered to the board while it met a letter stating
Edper's desire to make a bid for forty-five per cent of the Brascan stock at $27 a share.

There was no word from the Brascan board over the
weekend. Early Monday morning, Eyton prepared a press
release announcing that Edper was "considering" making an
offer for 11.7 million Brascan common shares at $28 each,
up a dollar from Thursday's offer. The offer would be condi-

tional on Brascan not making any material changes to the company, such as a takeover offer of its own or a special dividend distribution. Later that morning, Brascan publicly announced its proposed bid for Woolworth. At noon, Eyton was told that Brascan's management did not consider Edper's offer to be in the best interests of its shareholders.

The people at Edper took a closer look at Brascan's bid for Woolworth. With the help of Duff Scott from Greenshields Incorporated, Jack Cockwell prepared a cash-flow analysis of the proposed Woolworth deal and its effect on Brascan. He concluded that the takeover would reduce the intrinsic value of Brascan shares by more than $10 a share, and would produce a negative combined cash flow. Cockwell put out the word to the press that the purchase of Woolworth, which would force Brascan to borrow more than $800 million, would be disastrous. (It was the start of a brilliant disinformation campaign by the Edper side, often using Andy Sarlos, who held some Brascan shares. Sarlos was frequently quoted in the press making negative pronouncements about Brascan management and its takeover bid for Woolworth. Brascan officials, on the other hand, were restricted by American securities laws from saying anything about the fight.)

Trevor Eyton called Woolworth chairman Edward Gibbons in New York and told him that "on the basis of study we as a shareholder felt that the deal didn't make sense." Gibbons said he wasn't in a position to reply to that comment.* On the same day, Eyton called Woolworth lawyer, Joe Flom, a high-flying takeover-defence specialist. Flom pointed out that if Edper were to successfully take over Brascan, it would have to submit to U.S. Securities and Exchange Commission disclosure rules, or the deal would quickly fall apart. Edper and Woolworth could profit from each other's opposition to the Brascan takeover.

* This conversation was revealed later during court testimony about the takeover. The *Globe and Mail*'s Report on Business pointed out that on April 19, Trevor Eyton had told a *Globe* reporter that he had never called Gibbons. In fact, the contact between Edper and Woolworth was extensive. For example, a memo obtained by a New York court showed that Eyton knew that Woolworth would oppose Brascan's bid a full day before that opposition was announced publicly.

At noon on April 10, Eyton issued a press release saying that Edper was reconsidering its proposed offer. That night, Eyton issued a second release saying the offer would not proceed. Eyton also launched the next phase of the Edper offensive: it began to play the injured Brascan shareholder. The Woolworth bid, Edper maintained, "would convert Brascan from a highly liquid company to a debt-burdened company." The takeover was not in the best interests of Brascan shareholders, several of whom, Edper added, had expressed concerns. He also noted that Brascan management had not consulted shareholders on the sale of the Light or on the bid for Woolworth. The Woolworth bid effectively prevented Brascan shareholders from cashing in on any offers for Brascan, likely at premium prices.

In New York, Woolworth chairman Edward Gibbons filed suit against Brascan, charging that the Bank of Commerce had used confidential information, gained as a result of its role as Woolworth's international banker, in its decision to lend Brascan $700 million to bankroll the unwanted bid.

During the next two weeks, the people at Edper mulled over how to acquire a major stake in Brascan. Edper could make an offer on the Toronto Stock Exchange, conditional on Brascan dropping its Woolworth bid. Edper could buy up Brascan on the American Stock Exchange because, as an unlisted company, Edper could purchase a large block of Brascan stock without issuing a notice of intended takeover. Or Edper could sell its stake for a small profit. Edper people began to talk to other Brascan shareholders about the advisability of the Woolworth bid; they didn't mention their own takeover plans. On April 17, Edper applied to the Ontario Securities Commission for approval of a takeover offer that was conditional on the abandonment or failure of Brascan's Woolworth bid. Three days later, after a brief hearing at which Brascan management and a Brascan shareholder opposed Edper, the commission ruled no. Edper withdrew its offer, warning that it would "pursue other avenues to have the Woolworth acquisition abandoned."

With the Edper bid apparently off, shareholders turned their attention to the fight developing in the United States between

Brascan and Woolworth. In the end, Moore's Brascan would pay out $5 million in legal fees alone. In New York, Woolworth had assigned thirty lawyers to the Brascan repulsion. They brought a series of large and small suits in an array of U.S. state and federal courts. They launched a hard-hitting innuendo campaign on Wall Street — the typical stuff of American takeover battles, but quite a shock for Canadian onlookers. Jake Moore's record as a chief executive was displayed. Opined the *Financial Post*: "True enough, every multinational has its triumphs and failures. Brascan's problem is that there are enough of the latter to make it simple to dispell the impression that this is a corporate knight in shining armour ready to lead Woolworth to the stars."

Meanwhile, Peter Bronfman, in a rare press interview, maintained that failure to win Brascan would be no big deal. "We may go after something else. Anyway we've no need to rush. There are lots of other things to do in this world besides acquiring companies." That seemingly casual, laid-back attitude prompted an enthusiastic Amy Booth of the *Financial Post* to write: "It's this dichotomy which makes Peter Bronfman an enigma to some. North America is more used to the hard-driving, fast-talking, media-sharp entrepreneur with a banker in his back pocket. Openness, casualness is mysterious . . . even underhanded, some think. It's not, of course. Such a devil-may-care attitude is simply not encountered in the business world." Still, Booth concluded, "Somehow, one gets the feeling it's not yet game over between Edper and Brascan."

A few days later, Edper began exploring the possibility of an end run through the American Stock Exchange, along with the alternatives of unconditional or conditional offers in the United States and Britain. On April 24, and again the next day, Jimmy Connacher met with Tim Price, Jack Cockwell, and Fred McCutcheon. (McCutcheon's father had been one of E.P. Taylor's original partners; he owned a chunk of the brokerage firm Loewen, Ondaatje, McCutcheon and with his brother, Jim, he controlled Traders Group, a Toronto financial services holding company.) The men discussed the alternatives and lined up Connacher's help, should they need it, in buying on the American Stock Exchange. He could help them get an American broker, advise on the appropriate commission, and sort out currency hedging problems. They discussed how many Brascan shares Edper needed, and what the prices might be. Cockwell asked Connacher if he would be available for a trip to New York with Price on the twenty-ninth to help. Connacher had become crucial to the operation. But later, in court hearings, Edper people said there was no talk of compensation; Connacher was performing these services simply on an unpaid, friendly basis.

Work had progressed on a number of fronts. Fred McCutcheon flew to London on April 26 to meet with a firm of "jobbers" on the London Stock Exchange whose task it was to buy shares. Jack Cockwell had called in Greenshields Incorporated to discuss with Edper's lawyers the details of a tax-proof paper offer in Canada that would be unconditional. Printers had already been hired to do the circular. Edper had spoken to Brascan's transfer agent, National Trust, about a list of shareholders.

At an evening meeting on Sunday, April 29, at the Tory, Tory boardroom, the people at Edper decided to bid for Brascan. Price had already left for New York that evening, but Connacher attended the meeting before departing. Pat Keenan, McCutcheon, Cockwell, Eyton, and Peter Bronfman convened to decide how to proceed.

Initially, according to testimony at a later court hearing in New York, the meeting was called to take stock of the situation — despite the fact that Price was on his way to New York. But events were pushing things forward rapidly. Keenan, representing Jaime Ortiz-Patino, reported rumours circulating in Europe that a competing bid for Brascan was about to come from Noranda Mining Company. As well, despite pressure from Edper for a Brascan shareholders' meeting, Jake Moore had already announced that the annual meeting, originally scheduled for May 23, would be deferred to June 26. He also said that if the Woolworth bid failed, he would pursue other acquisitions.

At the Sunday meeting, it was decided to bring Edper's stake up to ten per cent, "so we could call an annual meeting [of

Brascan] in our own right," said Cockwell. That level of ownership might force Moore to take them seriously, and would give them more clout at a court hearing scheduled for May 10 in New York. The group then discussed the matter of price, agreeing to pay as high as $25 a share. As the meeting broke up, they decided to buy on the American Stock Exchange (AMEX), subject to one more night's thought and a review of the decision in the morning. They also decided against putting out a press release, unless required to by regulators. Just how much stock they would buy was not discussed, except that McCutcheon was authorized to pick up two hundred thousand shares on the London exchange the next morning at prices in line with the closing price on the AMEX. His instructions were to go gently and to check back if a lot of shares became available. McCutcheon rose very early Monday morning and began placing telephone orders by 4:30 AM. He bid $21 US for a hundred thousand shares of Brascan. By nine o'clock, McCutcheon had bought fifteen thousand shares; he stopped because the AMEX was about to open.

In New York, Tim Price and Jimmy Connacher checked into the Waldorf and Price arranged a breakfast meeting for the next morning with Jay Goldsmith, president of Balfour Securities. Price had been with Edper for ten years and was a vice-president, but he did not have ultimate decision-making authority. His qualifications for this particular job were that he had some experience in the stock market and was friendly with Connacher. In reality, Price had been sent to New York to carry out Jack Cockwell's detailed instructions. On Sunday night, Cockwell had telephoned Price at his hotel to inform him of the tentative-final decision to go ahead with a stock-exchange buy. They would tell him the final decision in the morning, Cockwell said to Price. After hanging up, Price relayed this to Connacher.

Early the next morning, Edper started to move on the AMEX. Cockwell called at 7:30 AM to tell Price to go ahead. Price and Connacher met with Goldsmith at breakfast, and the three settled on a commission of five cents a share. Price said Edper was interested in buying a million shares. After the meeting, Price and Connacher went to the offices of Gordon

Securities on Fifth Avenue. Connacher called his Toronto office to say that Balfour would be buying Brascan stock on the floor of the AMEX on Edper's behalf. Don't discuss this with anyone, he warned.

The exchange opened at nine o'clock. Cockwell called Price and told him to place a buy order for one million shares of Brascan at the best price, and authorized up to $21⅞ US. Sometime between 9:30 and 9:45, Price told Connacher of his mandate, then started buying at $21.25, soon raising the bid to $21.50. A meagre twenty-eight thousand shares turned up at that price.

Around ten o'clock, Price said to Connacher that if three million shares were available, he believed Edper would pay a premium to get them. Connacher, telephoning from a desk only paces away from Price and Goldsmith, contacted large shareholders of Brascan who were also clients of Gordon Securities. Assisted by some of his salesmen, Connacher contacted between thirty and fifty institutional shareholders and about a dozen individuals with large blocks of Brascan stock. Their message: if three or four million shares could be found at $22.75, Edper might buy them.

It was a strange situation: buyer and seller were within ear-shot of each other, and seller was a confidant and adviser to buyer. Later, Brascan would seek an injunction to prevent Edper from voting the shares it had obtained, charging that the buying was nothing more than a back-door tender offer that deprived shareholders of their rights. Brascan also claimed that the trading was pre-arranged, because all the shares had been obtained at essentially the same price, which was a mere $2 over the market price.

In New York District Court, Judge Pierre Leval, after a three-day hearing in mid-May, found that "in contacting shareholders on those days, Connacher and Gordon did not act at the instructions of, or as a representative of, Edper. To the contrary, Connacher and Gordon acted independently as a sellers' broker because it was in their financial interest to do so." The judge went on: "It is true there was a good deal of communication between Connacher and Price, often in the nature of Connacher informing Price of the volume that was shaping up on the sell side." In the name of mutually advantageous transactions, the American way and all that is good, Judge Leval concluded, "Such communication is normal."

Besides, the decision-makers at Edper in Toronto said that, unlike Price, they were unaware of Connacher's activities, although they assumed he would be participating in the opportunity to earn lucrative fees by soliciting sell orders. All they knew was that Connacher had volunteered to furnish friendly, unpaid-for advice.*

Shortly after noon, Duff Scott at Greenshields told Jack Cockwell that Noranda and Brascan were planning a share swap, which would effectively provide a takeover defence for both companies. Cockwell decided to boost the price he was willing to pay to $22.75 or more, and to aim for three million shares. He told that to Price.

Connacher said to Price that he figured about 1.5 million shares might be had for $22.75. At about quarter to three, Price put in an order for 2.5 million shares at that price, then told Connacher. Balfour's floor trader found very little available at less than $22⅜; he bought what there was and bumped up the bid to $22.75, looking for two million shares. Gordon Securities was in the market to sell two million shares, 1.7 million of them on behalf of clients, at $22.75. In an avalanche of selling, Balfour's floor trader was able to pick up 3,104,800 Brascan shares on the AMEX by the close of trading. About 2.1 million of the shares came from Gordon Securities, on its own account or for clients. At one point, the largest single block of shares in AMEX history had crossed the ticker tape, thereby entering the record books.

That evening, after inquiries from the Ontario Securities Commission and the Toronto Stock Exchange, Edper released a statement identifying itself as the purchaser and once again railing at the Woolworth bid.

---

* In court, Cockwell insisted that Connacher's presence in the scheme "had nothing to do with Gordon Securities. My testimony is that Mr. Connacher was there as a friend." Connacher did not testify: the sharp-witted New York lawyers representing Brascan were not able to serve him with a subpoena.

The Edper group had agreed they had more than sufficient shares for their purposes, and decided to stop buying. They told Price. But they did not include the decision in the press release. Trevor Eyton received a telephone call that night from the *Wall Street Journal*'s wire service, Dow Jones. Were they planning to make any more purchases? No, said Eyton. A *Wall Street Journal* article the following morning told interested readers that the buying spree was over, according to Eyton.

But also on Tuesday morning, Fred McCutcheon, oblivious to the decision to stop, which had been taken after he left the Edper office Monday night, once again rose at three o'clock and put in an order on the London exchange for up to 200,000 shares at $22.75 or better. By nine o'clock, when he issued an order to cease buying, he had acquired 132,200 shares. He returned to the Edper offices at about nine-thirty, where he learned of the previous evening's decision.

Edper's strategists convened once more to discuss Moore's reaction to their coup on the AMEX. Brascan appeared unimpressed with Edper's gains, and Moore said publicly that the purchases would not dissuade Brascan from going ahead with the Woolworth bid. Jaime Ortiz-Patino was upset. He believed Edper had taken a tremendous risk without accomplishing anything. He urged more buying. Connacher told Price he had customers interested in selling large blocks at the previous day's price, $22.75. Goldsmith tested the water at $22.25; very little was available. At $22.50, Goldsmith found 110,000 shares by 11:45. Then Connacher called to say there was a lot of Brascan stock available; Gordon had been buying heavily on the Toronto Stock Exchange, in the hopes of selling to Edper.

The Edper people reconsidered their decision to stop, and came to the conclusion that a bigger stake was needed. Given Moore's reaction, Eyton says, they thought a bigger chunk would bring them more "respect." It was a huge risk, and Peter Bronfman was nervous. But the consensus, recalls Eyton, was "in for a dime, in for a dollar." They waded into the AMEX again, scooping up another 2,000,000 shares, 900,000 of them from Gordon, by 12:15. Price ordered 1,000,000 more, then another 250,000. By one o'clock, Goldsmith asked Price if he could halt buying to get an accurate count of what they had.

The buying stopped. Of the 3,250,000 shares acquired that day, 1,550,000 had come from Gordon.

They did not issue a press release advising the public of their change of mind. By five o'clock, Brascan had asked for and received a temporary restraining order barring Edper from making any more purchases, and from using the shares it already owned to exercise its shareholders' rights.

Two weeks later, on May 14, high-priced Wall Street lawyers and their witnesses filed into a United States District Court in New York City to settle the matter. Brascan, represented by law firm Simpson, Thatcher, Bartlett, argued that Edper had deliberately deceived the public and Brascan shareholders when it said on the evening of April 30 that it had stopped buying on the AMEX; it had proceeded the next day to acquire more shares of Brascan. Brascan charged that the statements made by Edper were confusing and misleading and designed to keep the price of Brascan stock down. Edper's lawyer, Raymond Falls, Jr., of Cahill, Gordon and Reindel, countered that Edper was entitled under U.S. securities law to certain exemptions, and that its actions were proper. The misleading statements were "innocent in nature," ruled the judge, who had clearly become a fan of the Edper organization. "Throughout the events which were the subject of the hearing, Edper's managers conducted themselves scrupulously, fairly, and with good faith efforts to observe the requirements of law," he wrote. Many observers considered Judge Leval's ruling controversial, given the appearance of many of Edper's actions.

During the hearing, Brascan lawyers introduced a memo apparently prepared on April 11. It was titled "Timing" and was prepared by a lawyer at Tory, Tory, Deslauriers and Binnington. The opening paragraph contained the words: "Press Release — April 10, 1979 — desired reaction, market down." Brascan contended that those words documented an intention on Edper's part to drive down the price of Brascan shares with its press release. When questioned, Trevor Eyton testified that the memo meant something altogether different. He said the words "desired reaction" were used in several instances in Edper's memoranda, and that they referred to the hope that Brascan's dissatisfied shareholders would press the management to abandon the Woolworth bid. The words "market down," Eyton said, referred to the fact that the market was down for Brascan shares, and did not indicate any causal relationship with the press release. "The item is somewhat confusing," admitted the judge, who throughout the hearing had taken an active role in questioning witnesses. The author of the memo was not called to testify.

Brascan also argued that Edper's managers had planned a surprise buy on the American Stock Exchange all along, despite what they were saying publicly. Judge Leval ruled that, until the evening of April 30, Edper's managers continued to weigh several courses of action, one of which was a swoop on the AMEX. "In these, as in other findings," wrote the judge, "I rely in part on the testimony of Jack Cockwell, who I found to be a thoroughly credible witness and completely honest and forthright in his business dealings." Indeed, the entire case had come down to the crucial issue of whether the Edper people could be believed. Judge Leval decided that Edper's omissions occurred "with knowledge but not with any intention to defraud or deceive." He accepted Edper's evidence entirely. Leval lifted the injunction and freed the Edper forces.

Victory came on May 29. Late in the day, after a two-and-a-half-hour board meeting, Jake Moore conceded defeat. Edper was a powerful minority shareholder, and after the court decision, public opinion was turning against him. "The fatal flaw," says Peter Gundy, "was that Brascan was not ready to defend itself. Jake just didn't believe he'd be exposed. It was a judgement call and it proved to be wrong." At five-thirty, Brascan announced it would drop its bid for Woolworth and that it would settle all litigation with Edper. For Brascan insiders, the bitter irony was that Woolworth officials had sent word earlier, through lawyers, that they were ready to concede if Brascan were not taken over by Edper.

On a Sunday two days before, the opposing battalions had met in the Tory, Tory boardroom. Eddie Goodman, a Labatt director and general company counsel since the 1950s, had approached Edper after advising Moore, "We've lost and we should sue for peace." On the Sunday night, Goodman, Moore, Alec McIntosh from Blake Cassels, Eyton, Cockwell and Peter Bronfman gathered in Tory, Tory's panelled boardroom. As a gesture of accommodation, Eyton had convinced Peter to dress up for the occasion. Instead of the customary turtleneck and desert boots, Peter arrived looking, Eyton recalls, "probably the nicest he had been since his wedding." When Moore arrived it was clear that his advisors had also thought of sartorial accommodation. The formal, status-conscious Moore was dressed in a slightly soiled sweater and corduroy pants.

At first, emotions were running too high for anyone to comment on the extraordinary sight. Finally, Goodman broke the tension and said the best thing was for everyone to start acting like adults and settle the matter. Eyton responded by saying that Edper was happy to do that — all the group wanted was a majority on the board. By the end of the meeting, relations had thawed sufficiently for a few jocular comments about dress habits. For the Bronfmans, the victory was a personal turning point. Long-time friend Barney Finestone concludes that, "Great West was the early, early days. They didn't have the stomach for that fight. Well, they encountered the same thing with Brascan. By then they had the stomach for it."*

The day before Jake Moore left the forty-eighth floor of Commerce Court West for the last time as chief executive, the walls of Brascan's world headquarters were covered in art: Joyce Weiland's lipstick-kissed bed sheet, Brazilian naïve art. The works, all of them from Moore's personal collection, were shipped to London.

The company was about to undergo a wrenching change. In Henry Borden's time, the environment in the old Commerce building on King Street was a reflection of the era. It was a structured company, ever observant of the hierarchy. Employees were addressed formally, with the secretaries at their wooden desks on the first floor, middle management on the second floor and, on the third, the top executives, dwelling

---

* Eyton, whose strongest memory of the entire episode is the fear that he and Cockwell felt, agrees: "We had a little more persistence and courage. And Peter and Edward knew better what they could do and who they were." Recalls Cockwell, "That was the worst period of my life."

in a place to which one was summoned. With Moore's reign
and the company's move to the newly built Commerce Court
tower, the rigid culture relaxed, although Moore's domineering personality curbed that somewhat. One employee described
Moore as commanding the company like Henry VIII.

With the arrival of the people from Edper, there was a clear
sense that the mood of the place, the role of the company was
about to change. Edper redecorated at great expense, swath-
ing the premises in tasteful plum and taupe and corporate art.
The next task was not so simple, but in the end it, too, became
a matter of spending enough money. Edper wanted to win-
now the staff down. The lean, sure-footed Edper team had
no need for the legions of executives that Moore's ego and
the Brazilian utility had sustained. Already, the inherited staff
was becoming more and more idle. Then early one Friday
morning, the old Brascan corporate culture literally went out
the door. It came to be known as Black Friday. One staff member recalls arriving at the office one morning; at 9:30 AM, with
military precision, all of the telephones began ringing, sum-
moning people into their superiors' offices. In the space of
two hours, Edper took the staff from one hundred and fifteen
— to sixty. The night before, all of the senior managers had
been told and had been instructed to tell certain of their people the next morning. The discarded were given generous sever-
ance packages, some the equivalent of a year's salary. In offices
nearby, Edper had arranged for counsellors to help former
employees deal with the shock and find new jobs. "As brutal
as it was to do it all in one morning, it was probably the most
humane way, rather than just let it happen in dribbles over
the next few weeks," said one Brascan employee. Later that
Friday evening, in a bar in the Toronto-Dominion Centre, they
called it "Brass Canned."

Over the course of the summer of 1979, Eyton and Cockwell worked on a business plan for their new prize. They visited
the Brazilian outpost to see first-hand what it was that they
had purchased.

One visit to Rio stands out in Eyton's mind as capturing
the difference between his regime and that of Moore: "On our
first visit, Jack and I checked into the InterContinental Hotel,

which we owned eighty per cent, as ordinary travellers. About half an hour later, I got a panic-stricken call from the general manager. 'Mr. Eyton, you're in the wrong room,' he said. I replied, 'I'm undressed now and about to take a shower.' He said, 'No, you mustn't.' '' The manager was so upset that Eyton agreed to move to more luxurious quarters. Then the manager asked Eyton to persuade Cockwell to move as well. "I said, 'Well, you can try, but you'll have trouble budging Jack. He's happy with his little room.' So I moved, partly to accommodate him. Jack didn't, which again is fairly predictable. The bottom line is that Jake [Moore] had never stayed in the InterContinental Hotel. Brascan then used to have the top suite of the CopaCabana Hotel on a permanent basis, so Jake used to stay there. In those days," Eyton concludes, "people lived more grandly at other people's expense."

By September, Trevor Eyton had assumed the post of president and chief executive officer. Cockwell was given the amorphous title "senior vice-president, planning." That fall, Eyton began to take centre stage as the public face of Brascan and Edper. Years later, Eyton would say he had become involved in Edper's affairs with the acquisition of Hees and Saddlery. "I do not feel that my role shifted markedly during the takeover of Brascan," he said in the fall of 1987. Others in the Edper group, however, take vigorous exception to this version of events, and insist that Eyton's role changed when Edper acquired Brascan. In the fall of 1979, Eyton was profiled by Peter Cook in *Executive* magazine. Eyton took pains to point out to Cook that Jake Moore's reign had come with a heavy price tag: $7 million in general corporate expense — that is, aside from routine expenses — in Toronto and another $7 million in similar expenses in Brazil, a hefty amount when set against a net income of $128 million. Wrote Cook: "With the ostentation has also gone some of the geniality and roguishness of Jake Moore's Brascan." Eyton was pronouncing a new image for Brascan, even as others lamented the passing of an age. "The kind of attention that we have got may have helped us in our objectives. It is useful when you see people, to have a reputation, and for them to know who you are. It also helps that we are, I think, perceived as people who move pretty quickly and have had to be fairly aggressive to do what we have done,'' Eyton told Cook.

By January 1980, the *Financial Post* said that "brilliant corporate lawyer" Trevor Eyton was "drafting a militant strategy that will make Brascan the pre-eminent shareholder of Alf Powis's Noranda." In the back room, the lights in Jack Cockwell's office burned late into the night.

CHAPTER THREE

The Financial Genius

Jack almost always gets his own way, partly because in a technical sense, at least, he is always right.
Tom Kierans, himself described in 1987 as the brightest guy on Bay Street

Children arrived late in life for Jack Lynn Cockwell. By the time he first fathered a child, in early August 1986, he was forty-five years old. His common-law wife, Wendy Cecil-Stuart, was thirty-six when daughter Tessa was born. For both, it was a not-so-minor miracle. Wendy would later say that Tessa was just as important to Jack as to her. Although he had two stepdaughters from his second marriage, Jack had always wanted children of his own. It was his only unachieved goal. Cockwell, a short, solid man with piercing eyes, is a millionaire fifty times over. He is at the pinnacle of his profession, and he has masterminded the growth of a conglomeration of holdings that is a symbol for a new way of doing business in Canada. For years, it was that prize that drove him as he used his clear-cut vision to create an empire. During those years, he didn't have time for much else. A decade or more earlier, friends had asked Jack and his second wife, Norma, why they didn't have children. Norma replied in jest, "Well, that was on Jack's list during our last vacation, but he didn't get that far down the list." The only thing that was not believable about that reply, said the friend, was that Jack would not complete everything on his list.

Yet Jack Cockwell, usually characterized as a rigid man with a set agenda, has shown remarkable flexibility in the way he shaped his own life. When he arrived at the doors of 2055 Peel Street in Montreal in 1968, he was expecting to remain with Edper for a few years. He had already stayed in Canada longer than he originally planned. He had arrived from his native South Africa with a young wife in 1966, at age twenty-five, intending to learn whatever he could as an accountant at the international accountancy firm Touche Ross, then move on to the United States. When he had mastered that country's system of accountancy, he intended to return to South Africa and practise his profession. He wanted to return to the farming community outside of Cape Town where his parents had raised their three boys. "I did not leave to escape the political situation," he says. "I believe South Africans will work out their differences without a blood bath if they are given the time." He and his wife found a walk-up on Sherbrooke Street in Montreal and began to acclimatize themselves to a new country and a new city. For Cockwell, that meant setting about his business.

Cockwell is still seen by some people in the business establishment as the classic immigrant, one who starts with nothing but is determined to end up with it all. Certainly, at times he has been contemptuous of Canada's endemic lack of competition. He was schooled at British-style boys' schools and on his family's farm in Boer country, outside Cape Town; in that environment, stoicism is an art and discipline a craft. Says Cockwell: "South Africa is a country where you are taught very early to think about survival."

Jack Cockwell liked that life; he initially decided to try accounting as a safety play in case he couldn't make a living on the veldt. In December 1958, he began articling, and in January 1960, he met Bryan McJannet, who, he says, "taught me how to make the dullest audits come alive." (McJannet is now a managing partner at Hees.)

But Cockwell had a mentor who would point him in a different direction. Stan Wilson, then president of Mobil Oil Africa, hired the young Cockwell to run his deep-sea tuna-fishing boat "as a sideline," Cockwell recalls. Wilson used to while away the hours telling Cockwell about North America, and urging him to broaden his horizons by spending a few years abroad. Cockwell looked up to Wilson. "I was fortunate to become his surrogate son when his own son left to work in London and later South America," says Cockwell. "He was a very patient teacher, and eager to share his own special values with the younger generation."

At Touche Ross, a raw young Cockwell found a world of clubs and old-school ties; longevity with the firm was used as the yardstick for promotion. That would never be a reasonable measure for Cockwell. But the winds of change were blowing through the stuffy accounting profession, and talent was being recognized in accountants who had only a little bit of seniority. Cockwell was, from the start, the star pupil of George Buckingham, the senior partner at the Montreal office who was in charge of the new recruit. Buckingham kept samples of Cockwell's work for years, much the way a teacher keeps the exceptional work of a bright student. One word Buckingham likes to use for Cockwell is "genius"; another word is "organized." Certainly, a strong yen for organization has always underlain Cockwell's performance. With Jack, Leonard Spilfogel says, "You don't sit back and say, what am I going to do today. That's not Jack Cockwell. He has sat down and he's got nine piles on his desk and he's going to do them all today. And they are all figured out and they are all properly analyzed." For much of his career, he would arrive at the office at four o'clock every Sunday and stay through the evening, organizing his files for the week ahead.

Despite the clubby atmosphere and the antiquated office procedures at Touche Ross, Jack Cockwell felt lucky to have joined the prestigious firm. Some of the men he worked with would become friends, advisors, and even partners in the Edper group. At Touche Ross, these young turks eagerly grabbed hold of a more modern way of looking at business. Royal Trustco president Mike Cornelissen says with pride that they learned from the man Cornelissen describes as Cockwell's mentor, Donald Wells. Only ten years Cockwell's senior, Wells had been made a partner at Touche Ross at a young age. He was part of the new breed storming the Touche Ross gates. Says Cockwell: "Don Wells was a breath of fresh air." He was university-educated, and he had a mentality Jack Cockwell could identify with. Always, with Cockwell, respect begins with a meeting of minds.

Wells still has a vivid recollection of the first time the Cockwell style emerged. "I put Jack on the audit of the Canadian National Railways. It's not a popular audit," he reminisces, "because it's so large." For large audits, the firm had a choice: send in a large squadron to blanket the client company's books for two months or so each year, or set a few people to work steadily for some months. The CNR audit was a never-ending affair. "I thought it was a good place to try him out," says Wells, a genial, intelligent survivor of the accounting profession. But what happened instead was that Jack tried out the old system, found it wanting, and made a few modifications.

"One day I got a call," Wells remembers. "One of the managers said to me, 'You better get over to the CNR because Jack is changing the nature of the audit.' "

What Cockwell was actually doing was changing the way business was done. Traditionally, work would be written out, checked, rechecked, gone over months later. These working notes would form the basis for the actual report. "Jack was suggesting significant changes. He had a full-time secretary. And some of the working papers were starting to get typed. That was highly unusual. But Jack's philosophy is that you only did work once. So he got it typed," Wells says. Cockwell was revealing his prefectionist philosophy, which has endured through his years with the Edper group and has become part of his mythology. "He has a character best described as disciplined." muses Wells. "He is determined, persistent, very systematic."

The CNR incident was the start of a very close working relationship for Cockwell and Wells. "And," Wells adds, "we were friends." Cockwell usually made his friends at work. Tim Price, Tim Casgrain, and David Kerr, all now group executives, were Wells recruits. Another old friend, Anthony (Tony) Power, was recruited from university by Wells and is still at Touche Ross. He is perhaps Cockwell's closest confidant. Mike Cornelissen was a junior to Cockwell at Touche Ross for a short stint. He returned to South Africa, then decided eight years later that he wanted to live in Canada again. He went to see both Wells and Cockwell in Montreal. Wells was working for the Royal Bank of Canada and didn't have a job to offer him. Cockwell told Edper that Cornelissen should be brought on board. This is typical of Cockwell, Wells says. "Jack Cockwell seems to only associate himself with people he knows. He never uses a headhunter. He gets to know someone and then brings them on the team."

This is more than the "slide rule intellect and tax assessor's eyes" Peter Newman once ascribed to Jack Cockwell. From his earliest manhood, Wells says, "The man's competence was obvious. He was extra good at discovering facts, putting them together and arriving at intellectual judgements." Touche Ross's Tony Power has the same approach to auditing company books, says Wells; that is why he and Jack remain so close. "You don't get along with Jack otherwise."

Cockwell is also a man of imagination, and he reveals his imagination in many ways. When the Edper group's real-estate fortunes were the centre of his focus in the mid-seventies, Cockwell devised a new method of depreciating assets. He decided the sensible approach was to match the value of a building to its income flow. The building would depreciate more quickly as it aged; it became a less attractive location, and the potential income stream fell. Cockwell set up individual "sinking funds" to account for the timing of depreciation on each building, and insisted on their use, even though such funds were not accepted practice in the profession. In the next decade, the Canadian Institute of Chartered Accountants adopted the sinking-fund method. "Jack doesn't look things up in the

CICA handbook," notes Wells. "Jack has created some accounting."

After the Brascan takeover, Cockwell shifted his vision to the financing needs of the group as a whole, and set about renegotiating the very basic relationships between stockbroker and client in this country (see Chapter Ten). Perhaps the most vivid illustration of his imagination is his ability to see qualities in the people he meets, and to redirect those people to fit specific roles within the group. Within a year of his arrival at Edper, he brought Tim Price and David Kerr from Touche Ross. Tim Price has been the executor of the Cockwell programs ever since. David Kerr learned company operations, then was groomed to take over operations at Noranda in 1986. "He's not just a numbers guy," Toronto stock-market guru Ira Gluskin says of Cockwell. "He thinks about slotting people, he thinks about it all the time."

Jack is a multi-dimensional thinker, and long-range plans spring from his mind in detailed form. There is always an angle with Cockwell. His designs are as elaborate as computer programs, and he has the programmer's attention to detail. "He has a vision of what he wants to accomplish," says Wells. Because of his vision, Cockwell is accused by his detractors of being machiavellian, a chess player seventeen moves ahead of everyone else. But his ability to see all the ramifications of every plan means that he can perfect his strategy and position his staff. Says Wells, "There is always a purpose to everything Jack does."

Still, loyalty is a sentiment that can interfere with the most set regimen. When he decided to leave Touche Ross and work for Peter and Edward Bronfman at their private investment company, Edper, Jack went through "a certain amount of agony," says Wells. "He had come from South Africa, he was well treated by Touche Ross, and he felt badly about leaving." Touche Ross has profited from his loyalty — even guilt — in the decades since. The majority of the Edper group's companies use Touche Ross as an auditor. One Brascan watcher says that only recently has Cockwell felt that his old commitment has been fulfilled. In 1986, Cockwell declared privately, after handing Touche Ross another account, "That's the last. I've paid my debt."

On the other hand, Touche Ross has lost a lot of talent to Cockwell's team over the years. The group asks for names of Touche Ross's top ten people every few years, and has plucked Manfred Walt, George Myhal, and Bob Harding for Hees, and Laurent Joly and Courtney Pratt for Royal Trust. "The list is endless," says Barney Finestone, an old friend of Cockwell's and Peter Bronfman's from the Montreal days. "I wonder what the top management of Touche Ross has said in retrospect, whether what they got out of it [the relationship] was worth what they lost to it."

The Touche Ross–Edper connection arose from a serendipitous contact with Peter Bronfman. Howard Ross, a senior Touche Ross partner, was fund-raising for a McGill University research project and approached Bronfman and Neil Baker. Cockwell, who by this time worked for Touche Ross, was assigned to the Edper account that eventually arose from this meeting.

When they decided to hire Jack Cockwell, Peter Bronfman and Neil Baker offered him a good deal of money, certainly more than an associate at Touche Ross earned. But another important factor in the offer was the Edper group's appeal to Jack's ego; for all its praise, Touche Ross had not offered the young star a partnership. Neil Baker and Peter Bronfman let Cockwell know they really wanted him. He went to South Africa over the Christmas holidays in 1968. Recalls Cockwell: "I received a telegram from Neil Baker saying, 'We have made up our minds — welcome aboard.' " To Cockwell, this aggressive courting was unusually satisfying. He accepted before he returned to Canada, but on his return received the blessing of Wells and Howard Ross.

Jack Cockwell joined the Edper group as a junior to Neil Baker just before the Great West Life takeover try. When Baker left six months later, the group adopted a team approach to decision-making. "Jack only earned his marks after he worked several years in the office, where Peter and Edward began to have a great deal of faith and trust in him," says

Leonard Spilfogel, who was part of the tightly knit group from 1968 to 1979. "It certainly didn't happen in 1970."

As he had at Touche Ross, Jack inevitably imposed his own way of doing things on the Edper team. Neil Baker had been a concept thinker. Spilfogel says, "He paints his picture and says, 'You can have it. Go do what you want with it.' " In contrast, Cockwell was a program man; he didn't ever hand over his concepts. While he would hand over some of the work, he would monitor each idea until it was perfectly executed. The others in the group had to curb their egos, march to Cockwell's tune, and work Cockwell-style sixteen-hour days. Says Spilfogel: "You either love what he's doing or you're working in the wrong place."

Cockwell's organized, directed approach was just what Peter and Edward Bronfman needed after the scare of Baker's brilliant, half-formed plan to take over Great West Life. In ten years, Cockwell had cemented his place at Edper and had become indispensable to Peter Bronfman to such a degree that, during the Brascan takeover in 1979, Bronfman described Cockwell as "the heart of Edper." From the start, the match of personalities was perfect. Peter Bronfman recalls that when Neil Baker left Edper in 1969, "I asked Jack if he would stay. He looked at me and said, 'Of course I will.' That has always been Jack's attitude."

In the 1970s, Ira Gluskin was a real-estate companies analyst. He visited Cockwell at the Peel Street office. Gluskin remembers, "Jack used to say, 'Our job in life is to make Peter and Edward comfortable.' " (That line, which was vintage Cockwell, was one that Trevor Eyton would later graft onto his public persona as group front man.) Jack liked to serve, and he made a much better executive than outside advisor. At Edper, he could give as much as he wanted, pour his soul into his work. His dream of returning to South Africa began to fade, and the one time he voiced that desire, Peter talked him out of the idea.

Money meant little to Cockwell. Peter Bronfman recalls: "In the early years, I would ask Jack annually to put down on paper what he felt he should be paid for the coming year. He always wrote down a figure that was half of what I felt he was worth. At times I would ask if he wanted to try challenges elsewhere. 'What? And report to eighty-five committees?' was his response. We have our differences from time to time, but we have been supportive of each other for a long time. The basic trust is there, always.''

There were plenty of occasions to test that trust during the 1970s. After Neil Baker left, Edper's real-estate holdings in Great West Saddlery were merged with two other groups' holdings, and management was transferred to Calgary under the mantle of Trizec Corporation.

At the same time, Jack was ready to take the group in a new direction. He wanted to try a type of investment that the great European families had been practising for years, a hands-on, systemized approach to active corporate holdings in a variety of companies. Edper would walk into companies, provide the strategy and the financing and, when necessary, the people. At Touche Ross, he had enjoyed this management-consulting approach to accounting; now he wanted to apply the same lessons to the family holdings. Cockwell introduced the Edper group to merchant banking, and the group never looked back. A decade later, Edper would revolutionize the Canadian financial community through its aggressive merchant banks (see Chapters Five and Ten). But first there was the learning curve, with Mico Enterprises Limited.

Mico was a shortened version of Marigot, a company named after Marigot Bay in St. Lucia by Toronto promoter Ken Patrick. Patrick, who later started Canadian Aviation Electronics (CAE) Industries Limited, was well known as a brilliant entrepreneur but a poor manager. He saw Marigot Bay as a potential gold mine, and spent years talking up the idea of admitting the island as an eleventh province, a southern tourist and business idyll for Canadians. He bought real estate; he also bought a trading company in Antigua called Brydson's, and a nifty item known as the West Indian Stock Exchange. Dutch Holland, who bought a few shares in Marigot from Patrick when the company was started, visited the property at Marigot Bay during a sailing trip with his wife, Frankie. "It was very picturesque." He chuckles in remembrance. "But God Almighty, it was a hundred miles from civilization, a goat track!"

The Edper group lent money to Marigot, which eventually fell behind in its debt payments. So Cockwell announced that he intended to exercise Edper's option to exchange its notes for stock in the company. It would be the first corporate workout, the precursor of some of the most important deals made in Canada in the next two decades. With Marigot, "the boys" learned that the other side could try to bend the rules when pushed against a wall. Patrick issued himself a passel of stock at a fraction of its value. But he backed off when Jack threatened lawsuits, and Edper moved in. Tim Price, who had recently arrived at Edper, became president of the new public company, and Cockwell became secretary-treasurer. Marigot's holdings were so badly run that Edper had to send Tim Casgrain and then David Kerr to Antigua for two years each to sort out the businesses.

At Mico, Cockwell enshrined the corporate philosophy that would become a tenet of life with Edper (see Chapter Six). At the back of the Mico annual reports were little homilies devised by Jack. The 1978 report featured an essay titled "Money and Business." It began, "Corporate management intent on self-perpetuation is one of the ills which has plagued business in recent years." It went on to point out that "poorly operated companies run by executives who have neglected to generate a proper return on the shareholders' equity often provide attractive investment opportunities for others." The essay said these new investors would benefit all shareholders, and that there was a trend towards these investors pushing for more say on corporate boards. This, the essay concluded, was "corporate redemocratization." The Toronto establishment would find out exactly what that all meant in the years to come.

As part of the Mico corporate philosophy, and at Peter and Edward's urging, Cockwell gained his first personal stake in the group's holdings. In 1974, he personally went underwater to borrow $1.2 million from Peter and Edward with backing

from the Bank of Montreal to buy stock in Mico, thereby forming the basis for Cockwell's present holding in Hees. (Price
also borrowed and bought stock.) Cockwell's personal fortune
was now linked to the growth of the empire.

Perhaps that added incentive led Cockwell to take on some
giants he thought were damaging the group's future. Two years
earlier, in 1972, Mico had diversified from some of its holdings in the southern climes and invested in a real-estate company operated by Bruce McLaughlin, a Mississauga, Ontario
entrepreneur. McLaughlin's personal lawyer was Trevor Eyton.
McLaughlin had a genius for buying land in the right parts
of Mississauga, a city booming and set to boom more. He practised high-ratio debt development, and he knew he was always
right. By 1976, Cockwell thought McLaughlin and his business philosophy were very wrong. Recalls Barney Finestone:
"When Cockwell said Bruce is mistaken, he is not going to
succeed, Peter was into bed with him pretty deeply." Instead
of pulling the plug, Edper spent three years trying to ease out
of the situation. They froze their investment and said they
wouldn't take any profits from ventures; they just wanted their
money back. Meanwhile, Cockwell and Tim Price moved in,
spending three or four days a week in the company, and emerging several months later with a classic Cockwell "book" on
S.B. McLaughlin's financial situation. It was a documenta-
tion of what existed, and also a forecast. "I'm sure there was
nobody else who knew, including Bruce McLaughlin himself,
where all that stuff was," says Dutch Holland.*

Mico waited three years before it received the money from
McLaughlin, and almost had to take over the company to
obtain it. As he juggled the investments of the public company he controlled to pay back his private company's debt,
McLaughlin made headlines by claiming Mico was trying a
back-door takeover. Cockwell did a bit of his own media

---

* Cockwell helped Holland out of a financial crisis in 1981, when Holland
feared his bankers would call in his loans. Holland called Cockwell. "I said,
'Jack, I've got a liquidity problem. I could use a few bucks.' He said, 'How
much do you need?' I said, 'I'd like half a million bucks.' And he said,
'That much money — I'd prefer Peter sign the cheque. It would be in
Toronto tomorrow. Will it wait? If not, I'll send it over today.' "

manipulation, leaking information to selected reporters about the state of McLaughlin's desperate manoeuvring. In early 1980, Mico was paid back. Major shareholders, including the Thomson family and large institutions, remained as minority shareholders in the public firm. Three years later, McLaughlin lost his company, and to this day the minority shareholders are suing him for $26 million, which they say he owes the company because of personal deals.

Through the entire Mico affair, Cockwell was learning as he went along. "Jack's experience in doing this — whatever it became — was zero," Leonard Spilfogel recalls. "He had to grapple with who he is and what he is going to do and where is he going." And always, the Great West Life debacle haunted Cockwell and the Edper group. They would never reach beyond their ability to carry through again; in future, everything would be planned by the obsessive, perfectionist Cockwell.

In 1976, the same year that he suggested Peter and Edward should cut their losses and get out of their investment with McLaughlin, Cockwell was busy solving another major problem in the Bronfman real-estate investments. The problem was at the heart of their investment portfolio, at Trizec, their real-estate joint venture in Calgary (see Chapter Five). In 1976, Cockwell's cash-flow analysis showed that Trizec would go into the red in a year and a half if the company wasn't turned in a new direction. Cockwell took a brave stand; he said that Trizec chief James Soden had to go. Soden had rescued the company after its founder, William Zeckendorf, had built Montreal's Place Ville Marie, then bankrupted Trizec with other deals. Soden was a man with a proven track record, unlike Cockwell. Barney Finestone recalls: "It takes a special kind of guy to buck the whole establishment and the whole system and say, 'I don't care what anybody tells me, this situation is turning sour.' And Jack was not the senior man. Soden was the senior man and Jack was Peter's advisor. So it took some guts to say, 'Bang! Mr. Soden,' because Soden would immediately say, 'Bang! Mr. Cockwell.'' You don't tackle a guy who took the Zeckendorf mess and turned it into a successful empire and say, 'You were great for ten years but boy, you're finished now.' ''

The tightly composed Cockwell could take on these challenges because he sincerely believed in his own methods. An entire corporate philosophy has grown from Cockwell's ideas, which were first revealed in those Mico reports, then nurtured at Hees, and are now an inescapable part of the Edper group's way of doing business (see Chapter Six). The investment positions of group managers, the belief in taking risk positions when buying into other companies, the adherence to a demanding work schedule are all part of the Cockwell bible. In 1986, some parliamentarians wanted to know if Cockwell would be asked to leave a company boardroom when a deal between two group companies was to be discussed. Cockwell replied that he would not need to be asked. ''We recognize it is the right thing to do and we get up and leave.'' He is almost self-righteous, and there is an element of the visionary about him. In the early years, Holland recalls, Cockwell would talk about his visions. They would walk the streets of Toronto and Cockwell would point to buildings as he built his castles in the air. All his dreams were of corporate growth.

Cockwell's sensitivity is not usually so openly displayed. And his belief in his own rightness is often a result of a narrow-minded insistence that, because he is technically right, he should prevail. When opposed, he can be very prickly. Any opposition is personal, and any wound cuts deep. He can be mortally offended, observers say, over companies paying high income taxes; it isn't right, and he won't put up with it. One Edper insider says that the secret to arguing with Cockwell is to avoid debating the logic of his argument. Rather, the way to get Cockwell to change his mind on something is to introduce a new element, to say, ''I agree with you, Jack, but here's something you haven't thought of.'' If people don't follow him quickly enough, Cockwell is contemptuous of their abilities. Jim Leech, president of Unicorp Financial Corporation, admires Cockwell, but calls him a tough negotiator. In 1985, Unicorp purchased Edper's Union Gas shares, which Cockwell wanted badly to sell. But he wouldn't move from his asking price. Leech recalls: "He said, 'This is my hurdle, and you've got to get over this hurdle, it's got to be this price.' I'd try a couple of different wrinkles on him and he would figure out what that was worth, and he'd say, 'Yeah, but you haven't hit my hurdle price.' " Leech capitulated, but he's never again negotiated directly with Cockwell.

The steamroller approach doesn't always work; while the other members of the group bow to his judgement and sublimate their own egos to his greater goals, the rest of the world isn't always so accommodating. Cockwell finds it difficult when the other side won't or can't give way. There are legendary stories on Bay Street of Cockwell's predilection for kicking filing cabinets and raging when someone does not agree with his approach or stands in his way. He is well known for swearing like a trooper — his every-day talk is peppered with profanity as long as there are no females around. His concentrated storm is difficult to withstand.

Tom Kierans, president of the Toronto stockbrokerage firm McLeod Young Weir, thinks in theoretical terms about the world in which he operates. On a number of occasions, he and Cockwell have disagreed, not about the technical correctness of Cockwell's plans, but about their effect on Canadian business, their *rightness*. Cockwell does not like having his moral code challenged. Kierans sees his rigidity partly as a newcomer's reaction to a system set up to protect the status quo. "In the course of breaking down the rules, he hasn't always done the right thing," says Kierans. In the early 1980s, Kierans recalls, "Everyone used to tell [Cockwell] that he had to come and deal with me because I'm supposed to be smart, and Cockwell would come and preach at me. And I would say no, not because what he was telling me was wrong technically, but because I didn't want to do it. We used to have these humungous arguments." At times like that, adds Kierans, "He just can't control himself."

To be a truly great tactician, Cockwell had to compensate for his own shortcomings. But because of his sensitivity, he has almost overcompensated. However central he was to the Edper group by the late 1970s, Cockwell wouldn't be pushed into any roles he didn't want. He always preferred to be the invisible hand, more than advisor but less than chief executive. Cockwell does not sit on many boards of directors. He decided that Edper companies would have public ownership, but he also decided he wouldn't deal with that public. He would have the power without the cloak of office. As Cockwell once said about the group's role, "When we talk of power, if anything it is a power to support."

Cockwell chooses and handles his team well. He controls from behind the curtain, the *deus ex machina* who places the characters on the stage. "Jack creates people," says one analyst who has watched him since the Montreal days. The most important creation is Trevor Eyton, who became chief executive of Brascan in 1979, and the face of the Edper empire. This does not mean Eyton does not exert influence, that he does not fulfill an important role in the group. Cockwell would not have him there if he did not do a good job. But as Leonard Spilfogel points out, there are different approaches to exerting power. "Trevor is out front and Jack is behind. I think it's pretty evident who is more powerful." Adds Barney Finestone, "Cockwell does the planning for a lot more than Brascan. All of the bright boys everywhere are his apprentices. He is their mentor." Spilfogel is even more blunt: "All the presidents run their companies, okay. And Jack runs the presidents, even though he's the secretary-treasurer of the company."

Before 1979, Tim Price dealt with the press. But Trevor Eyton is much better at it. He is a good raconteur. In contrast, Cockwell talks in the language of profit and loss. When he described his group's contribution to the changes in the financial-services business to a *Financial Post* reporter, he could have been describing any aspect of his business philosophy: "[It] has been to define rules and principles. They govern us and we are prepared to be measured by them." The same mix of rigidity, pomposity and executive "overspeak" was demonstrated at a House of Commons Finance Committee hearing in mid-1986. Although he was talking of matters that are close to his heart, he couldn't escape the strictures of his business dialect. "We have an investment principle that we expect those with the operating knowledge to provide whatever protections, beyond normal corporate standards, to the investing companies," he said when explaining the group's influence on companies it controls.

And when he was questioned about the group's investment in the Continental Bank, Cockwell criticized the Bank of Canada because it takes a position senior to the other creditors and "chases away other deposits. We have chosen to do it where we think is the right place, and that is at the equity level." At the same hearing, Cockwell lashed out at Cadillac Fairview Corporation chief Bernard Ghert, who was sitting, unable to defend himself, amidst a sea of reporters and parliamentarians. After the hearings, a story floated around that the Edper group was worried that Cockwell had tarnished its public image and that the group would be sure to keep Jack in the back rooms. But within the group, the rumour became a joke; worshipful colleagues teased Jack about living in "the back, back, *back* rooms" and being thrown food like a chained animal while he laboured through the nights.

Trevor Eyton is many things Jack Cockwell is not. Perhaps most importantly, he adds what Peter Bronfman describes as "class" to the group. Eyton, like Cockwell, treats his work as an extension of his life. But he leads a different kind of life. Says Merv Lahn, who deals with both of them at the Labatt board table: "Jack is extremely able, direct, to the point. He doesn't brook a lot of small talk. He's a hundred per cent business." It is common knowledge that Cockwell has little patience with incompetence; no one can bullshit his way through a meeting when Cockwell is sitting at the table. By contrast, Lahn describes Eyton as a "regular fellow" who doesn't mind straying off the topic to enjoy a few laughs. "He's well rounded."

The single most important thing about Jack Cockwell is that he is irreplaceable. He is the *only* executive at Edper essential to the continuing vibrancy of the empire. They need him more than he needs them. The empire, after all, has been moulded by Cockwell's vision. Both Mike Cornelissen of Royal Trust, the man viewed by others as most like Cockwell, and Peter

Bronfman turn to Cockwell when it comes to recalling group history. And Cockwell's view of the future is as clear as his memory of the past. "Jack Cockwell is a long-termer," says Peter Bronfman. "I've never met anyone more long-term." Barney Finestone recalls a conversation he and Cockwell had after Michael Wilson's tax reform. Finestone was twitting Cockwell about the change to financing rules: "I said, 'Mike really put the boots to you now. Your preferred shares are down the drain.' And he laughed, and he said, 'Well, not for ten years.' I said, 'What do you mean, not for ten years?' So he told me what his strategy was. He had anticipated every single thing and had provided for it. So just out of curiosity, I said, 'Okay, have you got a strategy for ten years from now?' He said, 'Yes, I have.' And he told me what that one was. Well, that's what a genius is."

In 1985 and 1986, Cockwell was preoccupied with bailing out Continental Bank, nineteen per cent owned by the group's Carena Bancorp, and restructuring the group's hard-hit resource companies, including Noranda, Westmin Resources, and other oil and gas investments. Continental was sold to Lloyds Bank Canada in mid-1986; the resource companies benefited from a 1987 rise in the price of precious metals. Cockwell's work was trumpeted at Brascan's 1987 board meeting as a new face for Brascan's entire corporate structure was unveiled. Executives had been shifted, companies regrouped; money would be raised through new public companies. Paul Marshall; David Kerr; Alf Powis; the list went on as the key managers were asked to take a bow for the audience. Cockwell smiled and bowed in his turn. Finestone reflects on Cockwell's penchant for planning: "Ten years is forever when you are planning. Nobody is that good." Then he changes his mind. "Nobody plans beyond five years, except maybe a Cockwell."

After years of successful protective colouring, Jack Cockwell is in danger of being lionized — with reason, but without discrimination — by the business community. Barney Finestone describes a recent incident that reflects Cockwell's reputation. A very major businessman had asked for a favour in early autumn 1987. "Did I think I could arrange for him at any price an hour of Jack Cockwell's time. I said, 'What the devil do you want with an hour of Jack Cockwell's time?' He said, 'That guy is a genius and I'm puzzled as to what to do with my little empire. Whatever he charges it will be worth it.' I said, 'I don't think Jack Cockwell is in the business of selling his time. But he is a nice guy. Phone up and tell him I told you to call. If he wants to give you an hour, he will.' "

Time is perhaps the most important commodity for Jack Cockwell. When he works in the evening, he often doesn't go home until one o'clock. "To describe him as a workaholic in the sense that we understand it, that it's negative, is not correct," muses Spilfogel. "That's his life." Of course, there are necessary casualties. Ten years ago, when he was in his mid-thirties, Cockwell looked like a teenager; now he looks his age. The stress shows on his face the way it did on Jimmy Carter after he had served a term in the Oval Office. And he didn't bear all the stress alone. "If you have fourteen hours a day at work, there's not much of a family life," says Spilfogel. "You don't have a family life unless you don't sleep."

Cockwell has tried for years to fit a family into his chosen life-style. Sometimes he succeeded; he would often get up early to take his two young stepdaughters swimming on winter mornings. Just as his business colleagues have become his friends, Jack has also met his wives through his work. His second wife, Norma, was a secretary at Edper in the Montreal days; she was there when Cockwell arrived. Wendy Cecil-Stuart, a wide-eyed blonde with a china-doll demeanour, a country-girl smile, and a talent for disarming ingenuousness, was his colleague for five years before she became his companion. Now, with Wendy, daughter Tessa, and a baby boy, Jack Lorne, born in February 1988, Jack Cockwell does have a family life. He and Wendy purchased a home in Rosedale from Merrill Lynch Canada chief, Michael Sanderson, in 1986. In typical style, Cockwell began to program improvements. Some changes had to wait; a large addition needed the approval of the City of Toronto's committee of adjustment. But Cock-well began to fix up the garden immediately. Cecil-Stuart says he spent hours on the roses, drawing up a master plan for planting and compulsively trying to nurture them to perfection. He is the same with gadgetry; he must understand the workings of any machine he uses. Don Wells says this obsession with perfection is the force that drives him to work; it permeates his attitude to life. "He sees something, and he wants to make it better. That's what drives him. He buys a house and he immediately fixes the basement. He does it personally; it is a form of therapy."

Cockwell's attitude to money certainly hasn't changed. His personal holdings in the Bronfman empire total about $50 million, and are concentrated in the Hees-Carena companies rather than the Brascan holdings. He pays close attention to the way those companies, particularly Hees and the real-estate holdings, are run. Says one old friend, "If you think he doesn't take his own money seriously, I suggest you are profoundly mistaken." In 1979, Peter Bronfman, referring to his spending habits, described Cockwell as "tighter than the bark on a tree." When he takes notes, he covers both sides of a piece of paper. Bronfman also called Cockwell "a sandwich guy." In September 1987, after the Labatt's annual meeting, Jack handed Wendy a cracker and cheese and said, "Here's your lunch." Her rejoinder: "Oh, a typical Jack Cockwell gourmet lunch." Jim Leech of Unicorp has seen Cockwell on the subway travelling to and from work more than once. But Cockwell once gave Don Wells a lift to the airport in his Jaguar. Wells twitted him about owning such a luxurious and ostentatious car. Cockwell the ascetic was embarrassed. "He got mad at me for ribbing him about it," said Wells. "He'll be mad that I told this story."

Cockwell is tight-lipped about money even with his family. He has two brothers — one, Ian, is an accountant and freqently works for Hees in addition to running his own consulting service; the other is an engineer living in Johannesburg. The three recently bought their widowed mother a new house about half an hour's drive east of Cape Town. They wanted her to move from the somewhat isolated family farmhouse because she is getting older and living alone in an increasingly troubled country. The new home is comfortable but not luxurious, and it needed some repairs. Barney Finestone visited her there on a recent trip to South Africa. "The kitchen was kind of shabby, and they were having it remodelled, and she was very worried about the amount of money the boys were spending. Genuinely worried. And I said to her, 'Mrs. Cockwell, do you know how rich Jack is?' She said, 'Jack is rich?' I said, 'Well, beauty is in the eye of the beholder, but I can tell you he can furnish this kitchen a couple of dozen times over, and not notice it very much.' Mrs. Cockwell's voice dropped to a whisper as she asked incredulously, 'He has that much money?' "

Cockwell has travelled a long way since he decided to join the Edper group. "Jack is a different guy from the guy in the Sherbrooke Street walk-up with a South African wife," Donald Wells says. Finestone says that Cockwell still returns his calls, the way he used to, but other old-time acquaintances say he doesn't waste his charm on them anymore. But Cockwell is still extremely shy about exposing himself. When he and Wendy go to a dinner party, Cockwell prefers, when he can, to let no one know what he really does for a living. When asked, he will answer, "I'm an accountant." He has, if possible, less time for tomfoolery than he ever did. That includes his attitudes about some of Wendy's pursuits. In late 1986, an article in the *Globe and Mail* described Jack and Wendy as "joined at the hip," happy to run together. Wendy, a marathon runner, was supposedly the faster of the two: "He can beat her on a flat stretch, but she outdistances him on the hills." The article infuriated Cockwell.

But just as his attitude towards money hasn't altered with the years, neither has his essential approach towards the use of his time. Cockwell doesn't like to let externals interfere with the way he orders his life. He has come to an understanding with Wendy that he will make room for her carefully cultivated and fully booked schedule — but work is still the priority. Cockwell escorts her to the opera, his body encased in black-tie. But his soul is free. He sits at functions with a notebook in his hand; he works through performances. He is proud to tell this to friends when they ask about the "new" Jack Cockwell. One close colleague recalls going for dinner soon after they began living together. After dinner, Jack started to wash the dishes. The friend was nonplussed, and joked that it was nice to see Jack doing the chores normal people do every day. Replied Jack succinctly, "It's part of the deal."

CHAPTER FOUR

The Twenty-Per-Cent Factor

*There tend to be no greys with Peter. You are either
a good guy or a bad guy.*
— Lionel Schipper, a close friend

The dressing room smelled like success. This was the Montreal
Canadiens during the glory days of the 1970s, when Guy
Lafleur and Ken Dryden and Larry Robinson and Bob Gainey
and a gallery of others inhabited the pantheon of Canadian
sports superstars, when coach Scotty Bowman and general
manager Sam Pollock were gurus, their pronouncements delivered to the country during *Hockey Night in Canada* with the
straight-faced awe that only a winning dynasty of Stanley Cups
could command.

But the Habs had two major players who were almost
unknown to regular fans. Outside Montreal, people rarely
talked about the ownership of the team. That family, the
Bronfmans — not the Seagram's ones, but some cousins —
owned the team from the end of 1971 until August 1978. In
those years, the team won four Stanley Cups. The TV cameras
picked out the two brothers in their seats in the reds once or
twice a season, during lulls in the play. But because Peter and
Edward didn't interfere with the team, they weren't really a

part of the equation from the outsider's perspective. "As an owner," Edward Bronfman explained to a writer in 1975, during an interview given while he watched a pre-season scrimmage, "I've got to have faith in the people working for me."

For the players, the ownership of the team was a big part of the winning equation. Ken Dryden was a Canadiens goalie for eight seasons; he captured the essence of the team's success in his book, *The Game*. "There was never a moment that as a player I felt that any decision was being taken except with the goal to win the Stanley Cup," he now recalls. "I never once felt that a compromise was being taken that might add to the bottom line but would make us more vulnerable and put a Stanley Cup in jeopardy." When a team had that kind of support from its owners, there was no excuse for not winning.

Peter Bronfman, the more active brother in their joint business dealings, and his quieter older brother, Edward, were at the heart of the team. Regularly, after games, Peter would visit the players. "That was a new experience for people, that an owner of the team would come into the dressing room afterwards and talk," says Dryden. "There was actually somebody living and breathing who owned the team." He believes that it was the best strategy the owners could have worked out.

In terms of hands-on management, Peter and Edward Bronfman were the antithesis of the Harold Ballard or George Steinbrenner school of second-guessing employees and usurping the role of ultimate decision-maker. Sam Pollock, the team's general manager through four owners, says that the Bronfmans never reversed any of his major policy decisions. "When things weren't going well, they were there trying to lift our spirits. They certainly weren't around to pick up the roses that were being handed out." For the public-relations duties, there was Jacques Courtois, a lawyer whose Montreal connections rival those of Trevor Eyton in Toronto. Says Dryden, "If you're saying to yourself, let's try to put the Canadiens down on paper, and we will develop some kind of business management strategy, you would say that it's textbook. It's perfect right down the line."

Peter Bronfman tried to adopt a carefully paced approach. First he would seek Scotty Bowman's and Sam Pollock's approval, then he would deliberately go to the dressing room on winning nights when the players might be in the mood for a chat. His motivation was as Dryden had divined. "In a very quiet way you show some interest," Peter Bronfman says. "Over five or six or seven years, I guess they would have felt the owners had some interest in them as human beings." Peter is quick to say that he was acting to satisfy his own feelings of what is right and proper, not because he figured the players would think it a thrill to shake a Bronfman's hand. "I'm sure they didn't give a damn."

But Peter cared; he thinks sometimes he cared too much. A sports team can be an adult's Disneyland of sight and sound and colour, heroic battles and camaraderie. Before he bought the club, Peter read sports books and tried to buy a Montreal football club, the Alouettes. He jumped at the chance to buy the Canadiens when the team went on the block. A natural fan of achievement, he liked all the players, but there is only one player Peter held in awe. His face still takes on a pensive, admiring look when he talks about the Big Bird, Larry Robinson. "He was so tall — although Ken Dryden, Bobby [Gainey] and these guys are not small — but Larry was bigger than them and he was bigger than life. I just thought he carried that team. If they don't retire his sweater, I'll eat mine. He was just such a star." He worried over each penalty call, and the referees drove him crazy. In fact, he still gets riled just thinking about it: "It's the only professional sport I know of where the penalties are called in part because of the score," he said recently, his anger mounting.

Peter's emotional involvement with the team became too much for him. He fretted so much about the Habs that he would often develop a splitting headache by the end of the game — "because the good guys have been hurt," he would say. Finally, after seven years, Peter had his fill of Disneyland. "I had seen ten thousand hockey games. I wasn't getting as much of a kick out of it as you're supposed to." He asked Edward if it would be all right to sell the team. Edward was initially reluctant. He liked the game and enjoyed being involved with the players. But, as usual, the milder older brother eventually agreed.

Years later, Peter has plenty of excuses to back up his decision to sell. The group was shifting operations out of Quebec. There were wars with the competing league, the World Hockey Association, for players, and salaries were skyrocketing. "It was becoming obvious that big-league teams should be owned by corporations with something to sell." But as he explains, he sounds like a fan weaning himself of an unhealthy obsession as well as a pragmatic businessman making a smart decision.* The day it was announced that the Bronfman brothers had sold the Canadiens, it was Edward who bravely held the press conference. Peter had escaped south to the sun.

That incident with the Canadiens was only a minor trial in the close and trusting relationship between the two brothers. They have survived six decades of emotional turbulence, public family fortunes, and corporate character-building. The two have remained partners in all senses, and invested their inherited fortune together. The brothers have been so close for so long that people sometimes mix up their names when speaking about them. They never mix up their personalities, though. The late Philip Vineberg, their family lawyer and an early mentor to both sides of the Bronfman clan, said shortly before his death in December 1987 that he could not remember a single dispute between the two brothers. The relationship works, he said, because the two have different ways: "Two Peters and two Edwards, perhaps, would clash with each other. But their personalities are complementary and they make an excellent team. And one and one makes more than two."

One of the secrets of their successful partnership is that Edward has happily and willingly been a passive player. Many people who understand Edward's role are not so certain about Peter's. Which is the real Peter Bronfman: the emotional

*The team was sold at the top of its form, netting a $10-million profit on what had been a $20-million holding. The arena remained the property of the Edper group's Carena Bancorp; a ten-year lease with Molson's is up this year.

aficionado or the smart business executive? Which voice is heard at boardroom tables and in private meetings with company managers and personal advisors? Is Peter, the brother with the presence in the group, a force? Does he use his power? Or does he play the role that he played for the Habs, the non-role? Financier and power-broker H.N.R. (Hal) Jackman, who calls Peter "an intelligent guy," no small accolade from Jackman, says that some people think Peter and Edward are out to lunch and have no power in the group. But Jackman poses a different series of possible roles for Peter: "Does he know, does he know and care, or is he really the mastermind?"

Says one long-time Bronfman watcher who knows Peter and Edward: "There is a ten- to twenty-per-cent possibility that Peter is quite a force now, that he encourages Cockwell to go forward every day, that he wants to own the world." The real test, people say, would be to sit in a room and watch Peter question Trevor Eyton and Jack Cockwell and the boys during their weekly catch-up meetings. Peter answers that the people suggesting such a test have obviously never sat in the room. "I don't think those weekly meetings say anything about my role."

Peter Bronfman is a slight, balding man with a smile that steals the spotlight and measuring eyes that peer over his glasses. He darts from subject to subject with a practised agility and a private road map; he seems scattered, but he is not. People are won immediately by the gentle smile, which shows he is warm and sympathetic and, well, soft. Peter understands people. Later, they might notice the shrewd glances that are cast in their direction. This also means that Peter understands. His ingenuousness is balanced by his constant urge to analyze. Peter Bronfman is a man of sharply defined and contradictory characteristics. "The first impression is that maybe Peter is naïve," says Dryden. "Then with each subsequent time, [one thinks] well, I'm not sure anymore at all. And over time I think the balance starts to shift the other way." Indeed, Peter has a hard inner streak of self-righteousness. He loves to learn about people and takes joy from their successes, but he can be judgemental, critical, and opinionated. He likes to think he has an uncanny ability to slot people into convenient categories of good and bad, although he admits that at times he sizes up people too quickly. And he can be swayed by small things that make an individual seem somehow lacking. A man of minor obsessions, Peter seizes on causes, groups, or events. Once focused on someone or something, he is not easily distracted. He pushes, prods, and suggests until his tenacity wins him a point or two.

Peter loves to joke, to pun, to schmooze. He has favourite lines — for example, "I *resemble* that" — which he never tires of repeating. At Brascan annual meetings, he will conduct his chairman's duties with a dash of Groucho Marx. He enjoys using acronyms such as BCNU ("be seeing you") at the end of letters. And he is consistently self-deprecating; putting himself down is a staple of his patter. But the self-absorbed Peter doesn't always cotton on to others' jokes; then he worries them until he understands. He also likes to think of himself as a blunt man. He doesn't believe in holding back his opinions; he doesn't suffer fools; he doesn't blanch at four-letter words.

His friends and supporters point out the casual way Peter dresses. He is the quintessential millionaire, according to family friend Barney Finestone: oblivious to the conventions that dictate a three-piece suit for business wear. Peter stopped regularly wearing a tie decades ago, and jokes that ties affect blood flow and stifle thought. Most at home in an open-necked shirt or turtleneck, casual pants, any old shoes, and a windbreaker or black leather jacket for outdoors, he likes to look the way he says he likes people to act: candid, casual, open. Dryden, like most people, assumes Peter's dress is a statement. Peter is saying: "That's the way I am. I have the right to be the way I am."

His candour can lead to the belief that Peter stands apart from those involved in the day-to-day fray of the business world, like the gods on Mount Olympus, possessed of human qualities but unaffected by the normal stresses of depending on a weekly pay cheque. Peter professes amazement at the toadying and dissembling that go on in corporate life. At a high-level reception hosted by Merrill Lynch International in Toronto, he asked about a Merrill Lynch broker who had been a boyhood friend. The sycophantic Merrill Lynch bigwig courting Peter tried to fake knowing the fellow. But Peter responded that no, the bigwig probably wouldn't know the broker. And then he made it clear that when he thinks of Merrill Lynch, he thinks of his lowly friend. Still, despite his contempt for artifice, Peter says: "It's easy for me to criticize. I say why don't these guys say something? Maybe if I was vice-president of the company, or treasurer, and I was dependent on that organization for my livelihood and had a wife and three children, maybe I wouldn't be mouthing off, either."

But while he always proclaims that he likes forthright people, Peter's own skin is paper-thin. He was very worried about how Ken Dryden might describe him. Advisor Lionel Schipper says: "Peter is just as happy when [people] don't say anything, but if somebody is going to say something, he really does care what they say." Peter still has a trace of the unconscious arrogance bred in him long ago in the hot-house environment of the Bronfman family.

Perhaps his sensitivity fuels Peter's desire to escape definition. He spent a reported twenty-five years in analysis, and he seems to understand many of his own motivations and characteristics. But he throws up walls behind his surface candour. When his wealth and his life-style don't isolate him enough, he can use his humour to erect another barrier. "I think of myself as a kind of a nice, humble, easy-going person, fairly likeable," he says in a self-mocking tone that leaves the listener wondering. Peter has always been the keener businessman of the two brothers. When he is asked why he went off into his own business, he answers, "It's better than the alternative!" It is almost an automatic reaction to reach for a little humour to shield himself. Yet his candour and hypersensitivity can be detected in crucial actions taken by the businesses he oversees from his seat in the stands.

Behind the barriers is a man who studied at Yale. ("What did I take? The easiest courses I could find!") A man who has written poetry, who studied piano and collaborated on an album of original material while a college student. ("Everybody likes songs and poetry, the usual stuff.") A man who says, "I always pride myself on being very introspective." Yet Peter feels guilty because he hasn't travelled the world in search of the great novel. Once, when he was ill in bed, he hoped that it would magically come to him. "When I was on my back a couple of years ago, with a herniated disc, and I was lying there waiting for the great Canadian novel to happen . . . I mean, it didn't happen." He feels that he lacks something because he hasn't achieved in the arts. Business alone isn't enough.

Peter's secretary, Sue McGovern, sits just outside the brothers' offices. She is a friendly, relaxed woman with laughter lurking just behind her official voice, a Maritimer who moved with Edper from Montreal. Sue usually places Peter's calls, and she often knows why he is calling. Inside Peter's office, the furnishings are deliberately homey. An antique Quebec maple desk is augmented by a small, round Quebec-style table, which Peter proudly proclaims is a fake.

Tossed in one nook is a rather large plastic Mickey Mouse. It is not placed with any real thought, but it emits a distinct message on behalf of the office's other occupant. Peter received the icon from a promotion campaign at a company of which he owns a chunk. Another business figure might have asked his secretary to get rid of it, or taken it home for his grandchild. But Peter keeps it in the office. Like much of Peter's style, Mickey says that Peter doesn't take all this too seriously.

Aside from the office paraphernalia, the room is defined by family. Peter has two bulletin boards crammed with family photos, some faded from exposure to decades of sunlight. Others, such as a photo of his granddaughter, are recent. He likes to take them down and tell stories about the people in them; he likes to layer them in a pentimento of his own life. Peter has a second telephone line in his office, used only for his family. He will place just about anyone on hold when it rings. When close friend Rosie Abella, the Toronto family court judge who married Peter and Lynda, called him on the family phone recently, Peter was shocked, although he was sure that Rosie was right and that he had given her the number.

Within shouting distance of Peter, should they ever choose to shout, is brother Edward. He is right next door in a neater office with a similar view of the Toronto skyline and a more conventional desk. There is, however, the incongruous note of a life-sized fabric Folies Bergères-style dancing lady lounging casually in an armchair.

Edward, at sixty the elder brother by two years, is a gentle soul who prefers his own world of charity work, family, and travel to the Bay Street circle. Edward is devoutly committed to his jogging and skiing — he likes to ski in the deep Rockies snow reached only by helicopter — and to his three sons. Paul, aged thirty, works at Montreal movie-production and distribution house Astral Bellevue Pathé, in which the group has an investment; David, twenty-seven, worked at Merrill Lynch Canada for a year; and Brian, twenty-three, is in his first year of law at McGill University in Montreal.

Edward only recently completed the move from Montreal to Toronto. His home town meant more to him than it did to Peter. "If Montreal had maintained its rate of growth of the fifties and sixties, I am sure we wouldn't have made the move," he says wistfully. And he still spends one or two days a week there, as well as time at his country place in nearby Vermont. Until early in 1988, he maintained an office at the Edper group's tiny Place Ville Marie outpost, which is staffed by Sam Pollock; Leonard Spilfogel, a former Edper employee who leases space to run an investment portfolio with some Bronfman money behind him; and Sheila Zittrer, who looks after the brothers' charitable foundations. Edward's Montreal office is, like Peter's in Toronto, filled with family photographs: son Paul and his wife, Judy; son David's college graduation; Edward and girlfriend Janice; his parents, Allan and Lucy. There is also an old photo of Edward jogging with Sheila Zittrer's husband, Jack, who was once Edward's accountant. But while Peter tacks his photos to a bulletin board as a collage of his feelings, Edward has his neatly framed and ranged around the office, so that everywhere he looks he can see family.

Toronto has some bad memories for Edward. He was divorced from his wife of twenty-two years, Beverly Chertkow, in 1978. And he still suffers from any reminder of the 1983 loss of his live-in girlfriend, Delores Sherkin. In a sad, senseless accident, she fell backwards out of a window at their newly leased three-storey Toronto townhouse in the middle of the night. Edward had to testify at the inquest. He has taken a long time to recover from her death, and those close to him say that any time he sees a public mention of it, the tragedy is revived. But beyond that bizarre event, the very private Edward says that, while he is still bothered by being considered public property, "I have become somewhat philosophical about it and have accepted it as part of the game." In the spring of 1987, he was venturesome enough to attend a singles cocktail party at a refined Toronto women's club, wearing a name tag that read simply, "Edward." But the atmosphere didn't attract him and Edward left early.

Shy and soft-spoken, Edward has long suffered from an image problem. Many people misinterpret his motives and slight his abilities. One Toronto business acquaintance who has known Edward for some years remarked after working with him closely on a Jewish charity matter: "I always thought Edward was a no-brainer, but he is not that dumb." Part of Edward's problem has always been that he simply is not that interested in business. And, like Peter, he says that he easily detects and is not interested in people who kowtow to him because he is a Bronfman. Edward is candid about the choices he has made. "Over the years," he says, "I have been able to recognize those people I feel are important in my life and to whom I can give of myself."

But in his own circumscribed sphere, he can comfortably display the warmth and humour that is expected of a son of Allan Bronfman. In fact, Peter teases his brother that he gets more like their father every day. Dutch Holland, who has known Edward since the old days on Peel Street when Holland sold the brothers the interest in Great West Saddlery, calls him "one of nature's gentlemen."

"You should see Edward in a community setting in which he is comfortable," says Montrealer Sheila Zittrer. By "community" Zittrer means Jewish community. "He is just marvellous. He has a way about him, the most appealing, convincing manner. He speaks in a very soft, informal way, but he has a lot of impact." She realizes this is different from his behaviour in other settings. "With Edward, you have to see him in different environments. He seems to shrink from the business environment. We're all like that — it depends on our comfort level."

Peter and Edward both balk at the suggestion that there is bad blood between them and their cousins, Mr. Sam's children, Charles, Edgar, Phyllis Lambert, and the late Minda de Gunzburg. "Zippo, zero," says Peter. "I'm convinced that Edgar and Charles don't think about it for a second. I know I don't, and I know what goes on in my brother's mind — we're very close — it's never ever come up once. (I could even take a lie detector on that one," Peter says. "Maybe not on everything you're going to ask me, but on that one!)" That there were strains in the family when they were growing up, they will admit; but they call the idea that being shut out of Seagram's would be the motivation behind their decision to succeed in business a fiction played up by the press. Says Edward: "Personally, I think it is a bunch of nonsense."

But they were indelibly influenced by their dynastic background. For Peter and Edward, going into business was the responsible thing to do. Peter says that he felt it was the best way to learn about people; it was a solid, serious choice. He did not want to become a dilettante. That they were denied the right to work at Seagram's — aside from one summer job Peter had at the Ville LaSalle company plant — made the decision to go it alone a more painful one, but a natural choice nonetheless.

To prepare his eldest son for the business world, Allan Bronfman asked Philip Vineberg to take Edward, then in his late twenties, on a business trip. The lawyer was closing a corporate buy-out of the assets of United Distillers for the family in British Columbia, and it was Edward's introduction to corporate manoeuvring. One of the assets the family was buying was a resort north of Vancouver. When Vineberg and Bronfman arrived, the manager met them fully prepared to give them VIP treatment, including massages by a Swedish masseur, quite a big deal back then. Vineberg was adamant that there would be no massage for him, and the manager was crestfallen. When they reached their rooms, Vineberg said, Edward had a talk with him. The manager was very upset, Edward told Vineberg. Couldn't Vineberg see his way clear to having the massage? Edward's main worry, said Vineberg with a smile, was whether people's feelings would be hurt. Today, Edward sees that caring attitude as a link between him and the less fortunate. "People have discovered and are shocked that I do not live in an ivory tower."

Peter is, naturally, happy about Edper's phenomenal business success, but he flatly refuses to ascribe any reason to it. "You plan to succeed," he says, "but you don't plan for success." He compares it to other times in life, when decisions are made that last for years. "It's like a coincidence, when you meet someone at the right time, and marry, and hopefully live happily ever after. But so many things are chance in this world."

Peter's relationships with his three wives may have been at the back of his mind when he made the statement. In 1953, he married Diane Feldman, a Montreal native. Their life together was traditional Westmount on the surface: community work, travel, a cottage. They had three children, Linda, now thirty-two, Bruce, twenty-nine, and Brenda, twenty-seven. One old friend says that Peter used to be irritated by Diane's demanding approach and strong will; there were fundamental differences of opinion. In 1973, they separated. Soon after, Diane moved to Israel, and for a time Linda lived with her. Diane has been involved in philanthropic work there, and worked for a program that provided meals, alert systems, and other supports for geriatric patients.

Peter's second marriage was to Berlitz teacher Theodora (Dora) Reitsma. It lasted six years and ended in the early eighties, shortly after Peter and Edward transferred their business affairs from Montreal to Toronto. A few friends say some of the strain revolved around children. With Lynda Hamilton, whom he married in 1985, life is more serene. Yet Peter has pictures of all three wives in his office, and he speaks of his ex-wives with the wistful fondness of memories safely viewed from afar.

Peter's concentration on Edper affairs has ebbed and flowed through the years, and depends partly on the state of his personal life. With Lynda, he is the happiest he has ever been, friends assert. Eighteen years his junior, Lynda is a slight, delicate blonde woman with an independent streak; she prefers to hold a steady job as a human resources consultant. A native of British Columbia, she was brought up in a large family of modest means — a wealthy grandfather lost his life's savings in the 1929 crash — and she has few pretensions. Peter enjoys travelling with Lynda, especially when they visit spots that she has never seen before. Unlike the hard-driving Jack Cockwell, who directs the group's success, Peter cannot work around the clock or a hundred hours a week. "Peter needs to rest his mind and body," says his advisor and friend Lionel Schipper.

Home these days is a three-storey house in mid-town Toronto, a nicely renovated Edwardian home indistinguishable from any other on the street. Peter had already done "the big house thing," as he calls it, with Diane. He and Lynda prefer quiet comfort, and they pamper their cats, Mozart and Muffy. The house's main surprise is the artwork. Peter enjoys collecting, and the walls contain some of his Group of Seven collection, pieces by artists such as David Milne, and folk artists from the north-east American states. The Group of Seven entries include some obscure works by Lawren Harris, A.Y. Jackson, Emily Carr, and Tom Thomson; Peter managed to buy some of these from Bess Harris's estate. In Lynda's upstairs study hangs a Chagall; it is not downstairs because "that would be heavy." With art, as with life, Peter can be bothered by little things: he sold one painting because of a small white cloud that he felt marred the horizon. Later he met the couple who bought it at an exhibition where it was on loan. He pointed out the bothersome cloud, then went home and worried that he had interfered with their enjoyment of the painting.

Yet with this art gallery on his walls, Peter finds it easier to be proud of and amazed by his new Jacuzzi bathtub. Vineberg said that neither Peter nor Edward is by nature acquisitive. "They are not terribly interested in money for money's sake. They have a very modest individual standard of living, compared to their wealth. It is inconceivable to me that they would buy a yacht or a jet or go in for heavy consumer expenditure." Peter picks up only his share of bills at restaurants; he lives like a comfortable businessman rather than one of the wealthiest men in North America. And it is a good thing that Peter's tastes are simple. When asked whether Peter had a personal jet for the extensive travelling he does, Lionel Schipper replied: "I don't think [Jack] Cockwell would let him."

Peter's natural enjoyment of people is curbed somewhat by his constant wariness. He prefers dinner at his home or a small gathering at a restaurant to a large party any day of the week. He must feel confident that the people he is with are there because they like him, says Schipper, and not "because he's a Bronfman, and now because he is Peter Bronfman." His ambition is to be an ordinary person, and often he succeeds. One former Brascan employee recalls a staff Christmas dinner shortly after Brascan was taken over by Edper in 1979. The employee and his wife found themselves, after drawing lots, at Peter Bronfman's table. They were surprised and delighted when Peter, with obvious relish, discussed at length Maple Leaf player Dave Keon, who hails from Noranda, Quebec, the home town of the employee's wife.

The wariness Peter feels about protecting his own life is increased a thousandfold when his children are involved. He stresses security when discussing them. He has reason to fear. The daughter of his old Calgary friend Sam Hashman, once a partner in Trizec, was kidnapped; so was Edgar Bronfman,

Junior, the son of Peter's cousin Edgar. As well, in 1970, Peter's family home was damaged by a bomb planted in a nearby building. At the time, standing with Diane outside their Montreal home, clad only in nightclothes and a light raincoat, Peter talked with a reporter about fears for safety as he stared at the ruins of his family playroom and bathroom. "I read a lot at night in the bathroom. If I'd decided to read when I came in last night you wouldn't be talking to me today."

Sheila Zittrer, who works in Edper's Montreal office, says that Peter is like Edward; he will cancel anything to be with his children. And his naturally sensitive outlook is heightened by their desire to stay in the background. Since the children's mother moved to Israel, Zittrer adds, much of the responsibility for taking care of the children rested with Peter. "Peter particularly has been the Rock of Gibraltar to his kids, supportive no matter what has happened to them, or what they've been through."

Linda, the eldest, is now married to a rabbi and divides her time between Toronto and New York. One friend suggests that it is her influence that has strengthened Peter's impatience with some of the organized Jewish fund-raising milieu. He supports a new grass-roots organization in Israel called the New Israel Fund, and for a while helped sustain *Moment*, an American Jewish commentary magazine.

In mid-1987, Brenda, the youngest child, gave birth to Peter's first grandchild, a girl name Marissa. Brenda is a tall, delicate, and willowy brunette. Bruce, Peter's only son, was married in 1987 and is with Trizec's leasing operations in Toronto. He has black, curly hair and presents a serious demeanour behind glasses at group annual meetings. Bruce has recently become more involved in group strategy, and now attends meetings every two weeks at Hees. He has worked hard over the years to straighten out his life after a rocky period during his mid-twenties when he had received two convictions for impaired driving — the second time because of Valium. Following that, he successfully completed treatment at an addiction centre in Minnesota and enrolled in Alcoholics Anonymous. "There have been bad times for Peter. Every-

thing passes, and his kids are working out very, very nicely,"
says Zittrer. "It is hard to bring up children with a name to
bear."

Both Peter and Edward are very conscious of their heritage;
they have had to live with it themselves. Allan Bronfman always
placed his children first, according to lawyer Philip Vineberg.
But he didn't make a lot of time for his sons. "The boys were
not as close to their father as is always the case, because he
was so very busy and so much out of town," said Vineberg.
He remembered Allan speaking at the Forum during World
War Two, at a rally to support Soviet military forces. "Mac-
Kenzie King, if you please, was one of the speakers, and so was
Allan, in front of fifteen thousand people. He was the most
outstanding orator." In contrast, Edward is always rushing
back from trips to be with his family for special dinners or
birthdays. For his sixtieth birthday in 1987, Edward returned
from a cycling holiday in Italy to a party thrown by son David
at David's Toronto apartment. Of the fifty guests, many were
old Montreal friends who flew in, including one-time Canadiens player Frank Mahovolich and his wife and Edward's
friend Sam Pollock.

But like their father, Edward and Peter are preparing for
their children's role in the dynasty. Before the Brascan
takeover, they had agreed that Peter would eventually have
voting control of Edper, and his children would succeed as
Edper's prime movers. That left Edward, particularly, re-
thinking his children's role in the empire. Last year, his eldest
son, Paul, turned thirty — the age at which the children begin
to receive capital from the trust under arrangements designed
by Vineberg long ago for Allan's children and grandchildren.
In the past couple of years, Edward recognized that it was time
to restructure his own family's trust.

In readying his sons for their inheritance, Edward has
adopted a very different approach from his father, who seemed
to assume that his children would be involved in business and
would work together. In early 1986, after some soul-searching
and talks with his brother and with his sons, Edward called
Herb Solway, managing partner at law firm Goodman and
Goodman, and asked if Solway would do some restructuring

of his trust agreements with Peter. Solway, who had met Edward many years earlier during a trip to Israel laid on for big fundraisers for the Hebrew University, agreed. Solway thought at first that it was a one-time piece of work. But he soon discovered it was only the first in a series of major shifts in thought and action that would be needed to prepare the boys for their inheritance. Solway brought in another advisor, Arnie Cader, a former Goodman and Goodman partner who left in 1979 to join Izzy Sharp at the Four Seasons Hotels. In 1986, Cader began a real-estate investment company, and he had experience in sorting out family trusts. Says Solway, "It was apparent to both Edward and Peter that you couldn't keep everybody together. There are six kids, three on each side, and you couldn't say to these kids, 'Just be nice and we'll take care of you.' "

Edward and his three sons meet once or twice each month in Solway's Goodman and Goodman offices to evaluate every aspect of the trust and to set in place plans for the next three to five years. "My number-one priority today," says Edward, "is the direction my family will be taking and our future structure and objectives." With the children deciding, in part, what to do with their money, questions arise about the eventual future of their investment in Edper itself. Right now, Edper is secure. But the plans, no matter what they mean for the empire, have already altered the relationship between Edward and Peter.

One of the first things that changed was Edward's involvement in the business. Until recently, he took a low-key interest; he performed board duties and he was the chairman of Hees. Now, while he still goes to board meetings and some committee meetings, he does not attend the weekly meetings with Jack Cockwell and Trevor Eyton that so occupy the attentions of outsiders. Herb Solway, Arnie Cader, and Edward's three sons replaced Cockwell and Eyton as trustees of Edward's family trust in the autumn of 1986. Cockwell had been in favour of such a move for some time, and the family agreed it was the right way to go. "Edward and his children were anxious to have some people who would look at the world from their eyes only, rather than Peter's and Edward's," says Cader.

Before his involvement with family trusts, Cader had only met Edward once, years ago, skiing in the Bugaboos. But he feels intensely involved with the family now; when discussing Edward and his sons, Cader has to catch himself from talking about "our" family. The sons deliberately are not following the style that has been so successful for Peter and Edward. "It will be healthy to give the children the opportunity to do things on their own," says Solway, "so that when they are at the stage in life that Edward and Peter are today, their late fifties, they won't have to start to think about whether they want to work together or separately."

Edward, for once the initiator and the decision-maker, appears comfortable with the new order and with his unusual degree of independence from Peter. "From here on, to some extent, we'll be heading in different directions," he says. He plans to do more community work. As Sheila Zittrer explains: "I think Edward still has a need for public affirmation." She named some of the community projects and big-name groups Edward is interested in. "He hasn't rid himself as completely as Peter of the cloak of public expectation," she concludes. But Edward's son David is taking the community work into a new sphere. David, the middle son, has been most active in seeking a future that is aligned with the group's aims and the family's aims, but is not part of the group. He has visited a number of people, including Toronto alderman JoAnne Campbell, wife of Gordon Cressy; Chaviva Hosek, Ontario's housing minister; Peter Widdrington, Sheila Zittrer; and others. "He's been seeing a lot of people and trying to find out which things he is interested in, which is to his credit, I think," says uncle Peter. David will be running the Edward Bronfman family's new foundation, which will for the first time make donations separate from Peter's family.

Brian, the youngest son, is absorbed in his law studies. While he is interested in the changes, they will not have much impact on him in the next few years. But Paul, the eldest, has immediate plans. After almost a decade of working for Astral Bellevue Pathé, a company in which Edper has an interest but which is controlled by Montreal's Greenberg family, Paul is committed to life as a businessman. He is starting his own investment portfolio. "Paul is very sure of his direction," says Herb Solway. "He is an entrepreneur. Paul has every intention of being independent of the Edper group."

The changes were inevitable. But Peter is sensitive about the shifting roles, especially about the idea that Edward's moves are motivated by any particular agreement between the two brothers. "I am choosing to play a certain role and he is choosing to play a role. If he were that uncomfortable, he would do something else." Peter believes their relationship and attitude to the group and each other are based on their personalities, not on some piece of paper. "The bottom line is, nobody is forcing us."

Still, the brothers were close for a long time. "There has to be an adjustment, and that's just starting," says advisor Arnie Cader. "It may take several years and maybe forever." Herb Solway described the brothers' relationship for the past thirty years by twining his hands into a tight clasp. Then he slightly loosened his grip, so the hands were still clasped, but not as tightly. "Instead of being like this, they will be like this." But while they are no longer inextricably bound together in making every decision, the two brothers haven't really changed their attitude towards each other. "I am sure that for the rest of our lives, in some way, we will always be partners and continue to work together and enjoy our lives as brothers," Edward muses.

Peter always finds it hard to let people go. Irv Grundman was once a partner with the Bronfmans in a bowling alley. He joined the Canadiens at Peter's request. Grundman says Peter likes to keep up to date. "I called Peter and said, 'I'm going to be in Toronto. Can I drop by?' He said, 'Fine, sure, what time?' We sat and talked and talked, and when I was leaving, he said, 'Okay, I'll see you out.' So he walked me to the elevator, and then he got into the elevator with me, and he came downstairs and we talked in the lobby. And we went outside the building — now we're on the sidewalk. I said, 'Well, Peter, I think it is time to say goodbye.' "

When he isn't with his acquaintances, Peter is constantly thinking about this one or that one. He is a famous letter-writer. He is one of the few people who takes the time to clip articles that remind him of someone, and then to send them off, sometimes with a typed note, sometimes with a scrawl on notepaper or on the clipping itself. Ken Dryden treasures the letter he received after *The Game* was published. "It must have been five or six pages long, and this is all typed, and it was like a very elaborate book review, but done in a very personal way." Dryden is careful to note that this is not just politics on Peter's part. "Peter is not blindly kind. It's not a matter of writing a rave on a piece of paper. He will personalize what is there. He will mention something that kind of knocked him out, and then draw on a personal experience that he has had that might relate to it, and he will always have questions about it."

His careful attention to people is part of his enjoyment of their successes. Peter is constantly amazed by people; he describes their achievements, their intelligence, their savvy, even their good looks. And he always listens for a response. Recently, Peter has become enamoured of a number of strong, successful women in Toronto, including Rosie Abella; feminist Ontario Minister of Housing Chaviva Hosek; and writer and do-gooder extraordinaire June Callwood. Sheila Zittrer, who has seen his interests reflected in his charitable donations, such as an interest in a rape-crisis centre, believes that his wife, Lynda, has broadened Peter's awareness of the achievements of women and his perspective on their role in society. "Perhaps he was brought up to believe that women were sort of subservient to men," Zittrer suggests, as she tries to explain why Peter is impressed by dynamic women. These days, Peter has expanded his non-fiction reading habit beyond international politics, sports, and general social issues to include books on women's issues.

When Peter talks about his involvement with June Callwood in a home for unwed mothers called Jessie's, he displays what is almost a hero-worship of those whom he judges to be achievers. Callwood, he says, mentioned "all these big names" for the advisory council for Jessie's, people he had only read about. She was having trouble getting a co-chair, however, because of the fear of disruption by right-to-life groups, and approached Peter about the post. He couldn't understand why she wanted him to co-chair the council with all these big names around. "Finally, she said, well, you're important, too, you know. It was kind of cute." This man, who is "underwhelmed" by the idea of his own power, is overwhelmed by other people's profiles. When this is pointed out to him, he insists he is not being falsely modest. "I may be naïve, but I'm not lying to you."

Sheila Zittrer believes Peter's innate ability to choose the right people is evident in both his personal and his business life. "He has an uncanny ability to select people and place them in special roles around him." But he worries that he uses people in his relationships. Certainly when Peter moved to Toronto, he consciously sought out a few personal advisors to counterbalance his professional advice from Jack Cockwell and the Edper group executives. What the personal advisors have in common with each other and with Peter is a lively sense of humour, intelligence, and a broad streak of independence. One contact led to another; through Brascan's ownership of Labatt's, Peter met Labatt's chief Peter Widdrington, and board director Eddie Goodman. With McLeod Young Weir president Tom Kierans, Goodman was Ontario Conservative leader Bill Davis's most loyal and crucial political advisor. He is at the centre of the Jewish business community in Toronto, where he plays much the same role that Philip Vineberg played in Montreal. Indeed, the two law firms, Phillips and Vineberg and Goodman and Goodman, recently set up a joint international operation.

Peter was happy with his new friendships with Goodman and Widdrington, but he wanted a more formalized advisory set-up as well, and asked the pair for suggestions. Widdrington introduced Peter to Lionel Schipper, a long-time Goodman and Goodman partner who "retired" at forty-nine to pursue an active yet well-paced business life, scheduled handily between tennis games. The choice was inspired; Goodman says "Widdrington gets to chalk up for that one."

Goodman refuses to act his age; Schipper doesn't look his. He could be fifteen years younger that his fifty-five years, a fact Peter never lets him forget. Julian Porter, who has worked with Schipper on political campaigns, says Schipper would make the ideal advisor. "Schipper would be a good ally. You could trust him, he has good judgement, and he also has a great advantage: he is an idealist." For example, Porter says, Schipper doesn't really care about the profit projections when he sits as a board member of the *Toronto Sun*. And he is a fierce partisan. "If people crossed him he never moved," recalls Porter of one campaign experience. "If he went into a war he was on one side. He believed open treachery was quite duplicitous."

Schipper remembers his first encounter with Peter Bronfman, in late 1981 in Widdrington's office. Peter showed up in an open-necked shirt and a scarlet crew-neck sweater. "I remember thinking, who is this guy? Where's Peter Bronfman?" Some months later, Bronfman called Schipper and said he would like to meet again. They arranged to have dinner. Recalls Schipper: "I didn't know quite how to handle something as impressive as this on my own, so I invited my wife and Sue and Eddie Goodman, who are about our closest friends, to join us." The "arranged" friendship worked, perhaps because of Schipper's basic attitude: "I don't need to make a living off Peter Bronfman."

Peter also asks Eddie Goodman for advice. "I guess I'm too old to have any hidden agenda," says Goodman. And the small circle of friends now meets every few months for dinner. But it is Schipper to whom Peter takes his thoughts and queries. "He seeks in his personal relationships people who he thinks are honest and who will tell him what they think," says Schipper of their conversations. "He might talk to me about the profiles of the companies, and his concern for anonymity and privacy, and might want to know what I think of this article or that interview. He might expect me to say, 'Gosh, it is terrible and you guys have got to go underground.' And I might say to him, 'Peter, if you want to be one of the most important businessmen in this country, you had better be prepared for some publicity.' "

Schipper says that after five or six years, he knows more about Peter than Schipper's own life-long friends know about him. "What he will give you of himself, in terms of knowledge, is not usual for men." Still, it is clear that while the relationship is close, it is Peter who is seeking advice, rather than the other way around. At one point, when Peter is asked how much he knows about Schipper's affairs, there is an awkward pause. "I know a couple of things about Lionel but — I guess I wouldn't know as much about him as he does about me," admits Peter. "My loss."

The two certainly have developed a joking camaraderie. Five years ago, Peter wanted to join Toronto's York Racquets Club, a Jewish antidote to the establishment's Badminton and Racquet Club. Schipper belonged and had taken Peter there many times. Peter made an application; a year went by and he still had not been accepted. He mentioned it to Schipper: "I thought you were an important person. How come I'm not in?" Schipper consulted with Kenny, the club's pro, an Australian with a special devotion to beer, and learned that Peter's name simply had not made it to the top of the lengthy waiting list. "For a truckload of Labatt's Blue [the pro's favourite brew] I'll see that he gets moved to the top," the pro told Schipper. Peter has yet to join the club. "Now, when Peter questions me about York," says Schipper, "I simply ask whether the Blue has arrived at Kenny's home yet. Peter is pretty sensitive about it, because he's mad as hell that he's not a member at York."

Peter doesn't let the friendship override his carefully set rules for donating money. Several years ago, Schipper's mother died of Alzheimer's disease; Schipper became deeply involved in the Alzheimer's Society and asked Peter for a small donation to a fund-raising drive. But Peter was deliberately tough minded. He asked for all available information on the society, and Schipper spent hours briefing him before he succeeded in getting a donation. "Peter doesn't like anybody to take him for granted," says Schipper.*

---

*That scrutiny of donations applies to almost everybody. Peter admires former president Jimmy Carter, but, while he says he feels guilty about it, he did not donate $1 million to Carter's post-presidential project, a peace-centre library at Emory University in Atlanta, even after a meeting with Carter. On occasion, however, both brothers have written cheques for emergency causes without any documentation.

These days, with Herb Solway and Arnie Cader on the scene, the small circle of Peter's Toronto advisors has overlapped a Goodman and Goodman fraternity. Both Solway and Goodman are at Goodman and Goodman; Schipper and Cader were partners there, so they all know each other well. In fact, Edward, in choosing Solway as his advisor, chose Lionel Schipper's best friend. "If you look at Widdrington and Goodman and Lionel as Peter's advisors, and look at Arnie and me as Edward's advisors, you'd say the whole thing is very incestuous," says Solway. "But that's not the way it works." Instead, he says, the relationships don't interfere with the advice. They just make it easier to work together, because the people all like and trust each other.

This situation should suit Peter and Edward well. Always, for both friends and advisors, knowing the Bronfmans has that one, hard-earned requisite: trust. Leonard Spilfogel, a former employee who watched Jack Cockwell's relationship with the brothers from the time Cockwell arrived at Peel Street, says Cockwell had to prove himself trustworthy, just like everyone else. "You have to earn your marks before you really gather their trust. I think trust is one of the key words. They have to feel they trust you."

Spilfogel is an example of the loyal backing that Peter and Edward offer friends. He worked for them for about nine years, then opened his own business as an investment advisor. A few years later, he decided he would rather play with a portfolio of stocks than counsel people on investments. He returned to offices in Edper's Montreal wing as a tenant, and Peter and Edward became his only clients, matching his own investment base dollar for dollar.

Jack Cockwell, who long ago passed the trust litmus test, has become almost an alter ego for Peter. Explaining that his memory is faulty, Peter defers to Cockwell on all detailed historical matters. Peter thinks of the group's advisors in terms of when Cockwell started, not when others arrived or left, and he works out when people worked for him by starting with the fact that Jack Cockwell arrived in Canada at the time of Expo '67, when he began working on the Edper account at

Touche Ross. From the start, Peter appreciated Jack Cockwell's long-term investment perspective. They saw eye to eye, Peter remembers, then adds, "He's a lot smarter than I am, of course." When Peter was thinking about the importance of different events to the group's development, he sorted out his thoughts with Cockwell. They didn't quite agree — Cockwell sees the rescue of Trizec as a turning point equal to the Brascan takeover; Peter says that Brascan was the one key event — but still, Peter listened. Why else ask people for their opinions, he says. Lionel Schipper describes it as a natural give and take. "Jack plays a very big role in the way Peter thinks, and vice versa."

In contrast, Peter and Trevor Eyton, Brascan chief executive and the group's self-described senior spokesman, do not have minds that work along the same grooves. That is why Cockwell and Bronfman brought Eyton in; but it also makes for an interesting relationship between Peter, the self-effacing but strong-minded shareholder, and Eyton, the conciliating but quite egotistical executive. Peter wants to ensure that Eyton receives his due, and rushes to point out that he "sets the tone" for the group. There is, for example, the matter of the Christmas parties and annual dinners. If he were in charge, Peter might not handle them as lavishly as Eyton does; Peter might only have the staff gather. But he accepts Eyton's judgement. As Peter explains, "Trevor paints with a broad brush, and I don't know that he's wrong. Everybody still has a good time." For his part, Eyton seems to be one of very few people who calls Peter "Pete," even at annual meetings. And the two have their own camaraderie. Bronfman has a penchant for poking at little digressions, and Eyton has a bawdy sense of humour. Bronfman can't abide people peeking at the notes he is constantly scribbling, be it sideways, upside down, or over his shoulder. On occasion, at meetings such as Brascan's annual meeting, where they sit side by side, Eyton can't resist. He'll find Peter writing a message just for him: "Fuck off." It is by now a little private joke between the two.

In talking about the group these days, Peter likes to mention the young guys, like Manfred Walt at Hees, and the older executives who have played a key but back-room role, like Bob Dunford at Brascan. He also looks at people not just in terms of their performance, but in terms of heart. As an executive — overall, including heart, Peter emphasizes — he would choose Brascan Brazil's president, Jacky Delmar, as ranking with Cockwell as the two top people in the group." But he is afraid to single out this one or that one, fearing that others will be hurt. "You have to be careful when there are a lot of people involved. You don't want to hurt anybody."

At the companies Peter is most closely involved with — Trizec and Labatt's, to name two — he is valued for his people sense. He likes to see the operations, the grass roots. Widdrington says that when Peter visits Vancouver, he might ask if he can drop in on one of the plants. "When he is on tour, he occasionally finds somebody that he relates to very well. And then they have lunch together from time to time, or they talk together, and in a couple of cases he sees them socially. He's very much at ease, and he puts them at ease." Is it unusual for an owner to make friends with employees at the company? Peter tries to deflect the question with a witty rejoinder: "No, I don't like to speak to anybody under senior vice-president." Relenting, he tries to define his constant interest in people. "I think the number nine guy may be just as important as the number one or two guy. He may not be, but he may be."

People have trouble thinking of Peter as an empire-builder because of his personality. To Sheila Zittrer, there is a large gap between the public man she reads about and the Peter Bronfman she knows. "I have this constant dilemma of trying to remember who he is sometimes. I can't sometimes isolate this powerful individual that I read about, and this very sweet man . . . Peter is the guy who calls and is more excited about the jar of strawberry jam that I brought him from the country than if I bought him the most elaborate gift." Zittrer says Peter is not faking his casual attitude to his position: "I don't think he realizes the extent of the power he holds."

Barney Finestone disagrees with Peter's perception of how the group's power lines work. "He's a very humble man. He says, 'Well, you know I'm a slow man, these are geniuses that are doing all of that [analysis].' But I always laugh and say, 'Peter, but who has the final yes or no?' He says, 'Well, obviously, me.' I say, 'Do you ever say no?' He says, 'Not very often.' I say, 'Do you say no?' He says, 'Yes, sometimes I say no.' "I say, 'Fine, then you take all the credit.' "

That Peter would never do. But recently, despite his protests about his contribution, he hasn't been too happy about some of the depictions of his "non-role." Some critics have taken the same deprecating stance he sometimes adopts. When the *Wall Street Journal* ran a profile of Edper and portrayed Peter and Edward as passive, know-nothing owners, Peter was incensed. But he had only agreed to answer written questions for the story; he had given Edper's media wrangler of the day, Wendy Cecil-Stuart, his answers verbally, and she had fashioned the written replies. The replies had reflected his desire to take a background role. But when the story appeared, he was offended by its tone. Such a reaction is only natural when a person is made to look ineffectual, Edward says. "I am sure that Peter no more enjoys being depicted as a rubber-stamper than I do."

The best explanation may come from Peter Widdrington, who sees Peter Bronfman from the perspective of company executive and friend. Says Widdrington, "At the Brascan level, there are three key people: Trevor Eyton, Jack Cockwell, and Peter Bronfman." Cockwell has the intellect, Widdrington continues, and Eyton has the contacts. Bronfman adds an unconventional dimension, a human side. When he hears that, Peter, in characteristic fashion, tries to knock it down, to deflect it with a joke, to veer away from definition. "That's probably exaggerated. Everybody is human — some a little less than others."

"The next time I come into this world maybe I'll own a baseball team," Peter muses. "It is a bit like *déjà vu* because I see the guys in the Labatt's box and you have a sense of kinship with the players and with the coaches and the scouts." Although Brascan controls Labatt's and Labatt's controls the Toronto Blue Jays, Peter doesn't feel a real connection. He remains the disinterested observer. Says Peter Widdrington: "I'm not sure whether Peter knows the game is played with bats yet."

But he is far from the disinterested observer about the lives of some of the Canadiens players. He still keeps in contact with Bob Gainey and Ken Dryden, still worries about what Larry Robinson will do when he finally retires. Once someone has captured Peter's imagination, he or she is not easily relinquished. Dryden, the hockey player turned philosopher, sees a familiar aura surrounding the Edper-Brascan-Hees empire. An unobstrusive man, hovering, prodding, asking pointed questions, passing out gentle reminders, signing the cheques, letting the managers do their jobs, testing them time and time again to ensure they are trustworthy. "I don't know how much of it is conscious, but at a certain point, rightly or wrongly, you do start to ask these questions. There is a pattern here and the pattern is compelling enough that it does force you to ask whether this is all quite accidental — or whether there is something else."

As for the weekly meetings, Peter says they could be held to discuss the annual Christmas party or group financings. They are catch-up sessions, since people don't usually get a chance when "everybody is running." He might ask to be filled in on something; he might ask some questions. "It could be something quite important, or it could be something very minor." He believes he provides some perspective, like a person watching a game of chess who can spy the move that should be made. Peter says he assumes that all companies probably get together once a week. Then he backtracks; maybe he doesn't have enough knowledge to make that assumption. "I haven't had that much corporate experience," says the active controlling shareholder of Edper. "I don't pretend to have had it." And his role in this vast empire? "I'm not a vice-president, I'm not a treasurer. I'm a chairman of the board of some companies. It means I'm pouring coffee and adding Twin."

CHAPTER FIVE

Spheres of Influence

*If Jack ran away to Brazil, I wouldn't sell my Trizec
shares; maybe I'd sell my Hees shares, but I probably wouldn't sell my Brascan shares.*
— Ira Gluskin, a Toronto
investment advisor

The tread of the Bronfmans on their way to the heights of
greater corporate glory became more certain with every step.
During the 1970s, the team of people working for the brothers
began to coalesce, and Jack Cockwell, using his back-stage
brilliance, began to fashion a strategy for success using tax
laws, stock-market financings, a bone-cutting management
style, and well-orchestrated expansion. Cockwell was a numbers man, part of a post-war generation that knew financial
strength would decide who would dominate the world. He knew
that refinancing a company so it could withstand the pressures
of inflation was more valuable than building that company.

Jack Cockwell has always recognized the value of a product,
and he knows how business operates. But he approached business from a new vantage point. He saw that the old operational lines could be knocked down to accomplish goals more
quickly. He is from a new group that will never love the product

the way the old mercantile class did; they will never savour the joy of copper-mining or brewing beer. But he knows how the structure of a company can be reorganized to make the company more efficient without giving anything away in the process. And in the end, the company respects him for it.

The Bronfmans provided Cockwell with money, the best raw material. In return, Cockwell provided a multidimensional framework for exploiting that resource. Cockwell's plans would take at least a decade to develop. The framework is complicated, with holding companies for Peter's and Edward's personal investments, with as many as eight layers of control, and with ownership positions that flow into, out of, and at times around companies.* The aim is maximum control at minimum cost. Cockwell does not believe in the inefficient use of power. He likes to have his money making money — at all levels, at any sum. And, through his holdings, particularly in his pet company, Hees International, Cockwell has amassed at least $50 million in stock holdings. Peter and Edward Bronfman have gained in kind. Between 1976, when they purchased Trizec Corporation, and 1988, their equity stake grew from a few hundred million dollars to $30 billion. The Bronfmans entrusted Jack Cockwell with their family legacy, and he created a corporate empire larger than that of their cousins Charles and Edgar, and one that rivalled Sam's.

Cockwell built his empire around three spheres: natural resources, financial services, and consumer products. He began with real estate, with Edper's Carena Bancorp. Then Edper purchased Brascan and Noranda Mining in the same year; Noranda has acquired oil and gas companies since then. Brascan was bought for the cash it generated, but with Brascan, Edper also acquired John Labatt Limited, one of the country's largest consumer-products companies, and also the second-largest advertiser in Canada. (The federal government is the first.) The acquisition of Brascan in 1979, with its cash treasure of $500 million and its holdings in Labatt's and London Life opened the door to a new area of expansion: Jack Cockwell thought it was natural to take the group into the

---

* See Appendix for the full range of the group's holdings and structure.

world of financial services. The 1982 silent march into Royal Trustco Limited brought the group into the realm of investment management and stockbrokering. Royal Trust provided a starting point for the group's progress to the dynamic, expanding world of international financial services.

For the most part, Cockwell's strategy to build a business empire has been wildly successful. But there have been mistakes. For a time, the worst, the one ill-wishers thought could topple Cockwell's so-called empire of cards, was the group's investment in Noranda, which lost money from the time Edper bought it. Even Cockwell had his doubting times. In March 1987, at the Royal Trust annual meeting, Cockwell worried that it would be another five years before Noranda began to pay off. It wasn't that he had given up on the commodities businesses; indeed, they occupied much of his time after he had the financial institutions running the way he wanted them to. Rather, he wasn't sure whether his restructuring of the oil and gas, forestry, and metals companies would be viewed as wallpapering over old problems rather than as a true assault on a troubled business. But the world commodity markets were smiling on Cockwell. The price of copper executed a spectacular climb during 1987; the price of oil also rose. Demand for paper products, after a five-year slump, began to increase. Because of tension in the Middle East and in South Africa, the price of gold soared. At Brascan's annual meeting in May, 1987, Noranda was the featured company of the day. Cockwell announced a new corporate face, and, for the first time, there was no awkward, painful shareholder probing about the group's resource investments. The last stage of Cockwell's strategy was securely launched.

Jack Cockwell thinks a dozen moves ahead, and he always assumes success. But his predictions are not as comforting to doubting shareholders and financial analysts as his track record, which is not so much a happy series of achievements as a careful adherence to a blueprint laid out long ago. When Edper acquired Trizec Corporation in 1976, the Bronfmans gave Jack Cockwell free reign. He set the financial people in place and he set the agenda. Troubled Trizec would soon become proof of Cockwell's genius.

Trizec Corporation Limited was founded in 1960 by three companies — Eagle Star Insurance, England's largest insurance company; Second Covenant Garden, Eagle Star's real-estate subsidiary; and a New York commercial real-estate firm, Webb and Knapp — in a desperate attempt to complete the three-million-square-foot Place Ville Marie office complex in Montreal. Under the supervision of Webb and Knapp (Canada) Limited, a subsidiary of the New York company, Place Ville Marie was the first major building project proposed for Montreal in more than fifty years. Webb and Knapp was a giant U.S. commercial developer headed by the colourful and daring William Zeckendorff, which built Century City in Los Angeles. Zeckendorff, an Illinois-born innovator, liked to open his projects on Friday the thirteenth.

Soaring construction costs and high inflation had led the company into debt. In 1958, Webb and Knapp owed $31.8 billion, including U.S. $2.48 billion to the Bank of Nova Scotia. One of Webb and Knapp's creditors, Marine Midland Trust Company of New York, forced the company into bankruptcy because of U.S. $4.3 million in outstanding payments. So Zeckendorff formed a new real-estate business with his son William. Then, in 1960, Zeckendorff teamed up with a large British company. Eagle Star and its real-estate arms, Second Covenant Garden and English Property, bought $16.3 million worth of debentures towards the funding of Place Ville Marie. The new team was called Trizec.

Trizec grew rapidly during the 1960s through the acquisition and construction of properties. But the company's early history was marked by financial disorder and bitter personality clashes between the risk-taking American, Zeckendorff, and the cautious British. By 1965, Webb and Knapp declared bankruptcy — again — and their major Canadian properties were taken over by Trizec. Zeckendorff was out; Eagle Star was in control. By 1971, Trizec had assets of $241 million, and had moved into the lucrative U.S. market. At the same time, Trizec purchased Cummings Properties Limited, a Montreal family-controlled real-estate company whose assets totalled $115 million. Also in 1971, Trizec bought Edper-controlled Great West International Equities Limited, a real-estate investment firm set up in 1969 with assets totalling $77 million. By the end of 1971, Trizec had assets of $500 million. In 1972, Trizec became the largest publicly owned real-estate holding company in North America.

As part of the 1971 Great West sale, the Bronfmans acquired ten per cent of Trizec and two seats on the company's board of directors. But Peter Bronfman and Calgary developer Samuel Hashman, his partner in Great West, were isolated from Trizec's management, particularly James Soden. The situation was best described as a constant executive war. By 1975, Trizec's financial fortunes were worsening; the company was due to pay $66 million in debt in 1976. In December 1975, it sold properties worth $150 million to residential property developer Bramalea Limited, another firm backed at one time by Eagle Star Insurance. The deal was the largest exchange of real-estate assets in Canada at the time, and involved sixteen properties, including a majority interest in two Hyatt Regency hotels, one in Toronto — now the Four Seasons Hotel — and one in Vancouver. As well, Bramalea acquired a fifty-per-cent interest in nine of Trizec's shopping malls in Western Canada and in the IBM building in Edmonton. But Trizec's expenses were so high that if it continued to spend it soon would not be able to meet its payroll.

By the spring of 1976, Jack Cockwell and the Bronfmans, minority shareholders in Trizec, could no longer tolerate a company whose management decisions seemed to be illogical. English Property acknowledged the company's weakness and asked the Bronfmans to refinance Trizec. The complicated transaction was achieved by selling the Bronfmans a 50.1% controlling interest in Trizec in exchange for $52 million in cash and a 49.9% interest in Carena Properties Limited, a holding company created by the Bronfmans to oversee the Trizec holdings. For $52 million, the Bronfmans gained control of a company with about $900 million in assets.

Edper's first step was to make a study of the troubled Trizec. To manage the study, Jack Cockwell, who had structured the deal, brought in Mike Cornelissen.

Cornelissen had met Jack Cockwell in 1967, when he was transferred by Touche Ross to Montreal from South Africa.

He emigrated to Canada in 1976 and started to work for Hees and Mico Enterprises, the Bronfmans' personally held merchant bank. Cornelissen helped Cockwell with financial innovations. He has an analytical mind, fuelled by pungent pipe tobacco and intent on the details. At Trizec, says Cornelissen, "I went in full time, and Jack Cockwell made himself available for huge chunks of time."

The transformation was a step-by-step process up what one analyst called "the ladder of financing." Ken Clarke, a group executive who was then at Touche Ross and part of the refinancing team, described it as working on a company by starting at the bottom right-hand corner of a balance sheet, with shareholders' equity. This is the classic Edper formula. A stronger backing is supplied whenever the group walks into a company. The next step is the banks, who have to give up something to make a new company viable. Group backing means the banks are more willing to provide new loans. At times, Brascan or another Edper holding company has acted as lender, issuing shares and using the money to provide financing.

At Trizec, Cornelissen and Cockwell first put together what they called a blue book, which evaluated the company and the managers' plans for dealing with its problems. Cockwell and Cornelissen wanted to build a secure financial base for the company, and cement it with layers of financing. The first layer was a preferred-share issue. The group issued retractable floating-interest-rate preferred shares — one of the first issues of its kind — and, to create a link to institutional investors, sold them to large institutions. Then they issued debt-income debentures, and after that, more senior-ranking debentures, including bonds in the Eurobond market.

Finally, Cockwell arranged for Trizec revolving-term loans with thirty-five banks — "so as not to create undue reliance on the whims of any one particular financial institution," recalled Cornelissen. While all this was happening, management was buying common stock, to demonstrate their belief in the company, while they cut expenses throughout the operation. Said Cornelissen: "The financial restructuring [at] Trizec was to set new standards, certainly for the real-estate industry, but also for other group companies. The Trizec experience was also a major and successful test of group business values.''

Once they had restructured Trizec, Cockwell and Cornelissen flew to Toronto to sell their job to the bankers. Cornelissen recalls his first meeting with Bill Poole, the Toronto-Dominion banker in charge of real-estate lending for decades: ''I walked into his office to explain the situation. He looked at me with very cold blue eyes and listened to my chat. After five minutes he said, 'Just a minute young man, do you really know what you're doing?' It really threw me. I blushed and said, 'Well, I think, I really think we do know what we're doing.' And I took him through the blue book. At the end of it, he came and put his arm around me and said, 'You know, I really think you got it right.' ''

Other bankers, operating in the freewheeling spirit of the day, only had to see the book's cover. For example, Charles (Chuck) Young, at one time president of Citibank Canada, reacted this way: ''Mike, I don't even want to read it. That book looks so beautiful, I just want to lend you some more money.'' But that wasn't the way the group liked to do business. Cornelissen always disapproved of the idea that ''business was done much more over lunches and martinis and the old boy network.'' He added: ''Which I don't think is business-like when you're dealing with hundreds of millions of dollars. You can't deal with shareholders' money like that. It has to be written down. And you have to be very clear and crisp about what you're going to do and what you have done.'' At the time, he says, ''We didn't realize that we were doing anything different, we just wanted to do it right.''

Harold Milavsky was hand picked by the Bronfman brothers to head Trizec after they gained control in 1976. Milavsky, an accountant, was a Saskatoon boy who had made good in the real-estate business, with the Mannix Group and Paul Desmarais' Power Corp., and since 1969 with the Bronfmans and partner Sam Hashman. When he was named president, Milavsky was loathe to leave Calgary, where he had lived all his life. So, the Bronfman brothers went to him. His job was to pick the properties. Cornelissen had an able lieutenant named Kevin Benson who would implement the financial plan.

Years later, Cornelissen would compare Trizec's books to those of a financial institution — what mattered was the spread, the difference between the cost of financing and the return from development. Real-estate expert Frank Mayer says the numbers boys simply look at their budgets and figure out how to reach their targeted returns. "What they do is make investments that don't have a negative drag and push this return down."

Whoever deserves the credit, Trizec worked. The Eurodollar debt issues sold in the late seventies. The banks co-operated. The stock price rose. By 1979, Cockwell's financial strategy at Trizec was in place. But the Bronfmans weren't the only ones who knew it. Paul, Albert, and Ralph Reichmann, the ultra-orthodox Jews who had ratcheted a tile company into the largest family financial empire in the country, knew it, too. They realized that the time had come in the real-estate business when acquisitions made more sense than wholesale building programs. Trizec was their first run at a major stake in a public company.

When the Bronfmans made their deal with English Properties, the two groups signed a stand-still agreement. Neither would sell their stake before July 1, 1979 without giving the other first option to purchase the shares. But by January, analysts were speculating that English Properties, which had financial troubles at home, was looking to sell. The Reichmanns cannily approached the British development firm and, by the expiry of the agreement, they were well prepared to immediately make a public offer in Britain for the shares of English Properties. The Edper team had been caught flat footed. Cornelissen, Milavsky and Eyton flew to London to take a look at English Properties' books and quickly prepare a counter offer. They set up their headqarters at the Churchill Hotel.

Recalls Cornelissen: "Late one night, as we were returning to our hotel, we bumped into Paul Reichmann literally in a revolving door of the hotel — he was leaving and we were entering. In typical style, Trevor Eyton suggested to him that they sit down and talk things over. They did this then and there, in a corner of the hotel lobby." As a result of this, the two parties agreed to work out their difference over the ownership of Trizec. They had the same aims and it proved to be the first in a happy history of the mingling of mutual interests.

The Reichmanns proved to be invaluable partners at Trizec. The Reichmanns' foremost expertise is in the real-estate business, and this was soon to work to Trizec's advantage once it had two very strong, supportive shareholders. In 1980, Paul Reichmann introduced Milavsky to Ernest (Ernie) Hahn, who had a U.S. development company with twenty-eight shopping centres, eight under construction and twenty more blueprinted. Sixty per cent of the properties were in the booming state of California. Hahn wanted to sell control of his company. Reichmann wasn't interested, but he thought it would be a good deal for Trizec. And when the $250 million deal was done, Trizec paid for it by inviting shareholders to buy additional common stock, in proportion to their holdings. Both the Reichmanns and the Bronfmans bought. And Paul Reichmann's instinct about Hahn was right; for U.S. $270 million, Trizec gained a company with almost $1 billion in assets.

Mayer says the Reichmanns' effect on Trizec has been "profound." "They, probably more than anybody else that I know, blend real estate and financial sophistication." It has been Milavsky's job to balance the two groups' philosophies. And, as Mayer points out, "If you stop and think about it, if you were running a real-estate company and you had Paul Reichmann on your board, wouldn't you go and check before you do anything?" And the Reichmanns put Trizec's interests first when there was a conflict, according to Benson. For instance, when both were qualified to tender for the Canadian Broadcasting Company's new Toronto headquarters in 1987, Olympia & York withdrew after the Reichmanns discovered that Trizec was planning a bid.

The partnership with the Reichmanns had another effect as well. "They view the world from a different perspective," says Cockwell, by taking a much longer view of things than most business people do. "They have always made time for us when we have needed advice. Albert Reichmann taught me in 1979 how he had learned not to let business problems cause personal aggravation. Whenever times get tough, I think of Albert

Reichmann and silently thank him for the advice he gave me in the London airport when we were adversaries.''

For their part, the Reichmanns valued the Edper group's business expertise so much that they invited Brascan to come in and be the active partners in the ownership of Royal Trust, which led to the creation of the Trilon financial services conglomerate.

Trizec fell into Cockwell's hands because it was in financial difficulties, good assets aside. And Trizec was the number-one real-estate company during the eighties because of its superior financial structure.

For other real-estate companies who followed a more risky philosophy during the late 1970s and piled up debt, this basic lesson would be learned in the early 1980s' recession. As a result, the Bronfmans' property portfolio was bulging by the latter part of the decade. Through Carena — Trizec's parent company — it bought control of Toronto-based land and housing company Costain Limited, renamed Coscan to distinguish it from its British parent. Carena also slowly took on more and more of a dominant role at Alberta's Carma Limited, a decades-old land company that started as a co-op for local builders and expanded its holdings in the boom days to include at various points a trust company, oil and gas investments, and a casino in Nevada.* Both these investments contradicted the group's basic philosophy not to get involved in major land-banking, but the assets were so cheap they just couldn't resist. Carena truly became the group's real-estate sphere by practising Hees-style workout plans.

But the big news was the 1985-86 takeover of control of Toronto's Bramalea Ltd. Like Trizec, it was an office-retail developer, although it had begun as the firm that redeveloped Brampton Billy Davis' home turf. Indeed, after the takeover, in 1987, Davis assumed the chairman's position. Davis would need all his political prowess to keep the balance of power between Bramalea's two chief executive officers, Kenny Field and Benjy Swirsky. Both had been in the business at Bramalea for more than a decade, with founder Dick Shiff. Ironically,

---

* It finally sold the casino in late 1987.

it was the purchase of assets from debt-ridden Trizec in the mid-seventies that had put Bramalea on the income-property map. But, by the early eighties, Dick Shiff wanted to retire and he needed someone to buy his chunk of shares. In 1981 Bramalea was approached by Cadillac Fairview Corp. chief Jack Daniels about a merger, but Daniels was on his way out and didn't have the management support to pull it off. The deal with Trizec was of a very different nature.

One of the big differences was that during the eighties Bramalea latched onto Coseka Resources, an investment that proved to be a big problem. It was following common wisdom of the day: diversify. And what better than an oil and gas company, the highest flyers in the country. But this, like so much common wisdom, proved false when the recession hit and Ottawa's National Energy Program followed like the right fist after the left jab. When Bramalea made the deal with Trizec, it had to deal with this problem on its books. It had to essentially write off its Coseka investment, and that would mean a huge loss that could place in jeopardy some of its commitments to preferred shareholders' and debenture holders'. But with true Cockwellian finesse, a solution was dreamed up that solved that little problem and, by the way, restructured both Trizec and Bramalea.

First, Bramalea sold a package of shopping centres to Trizec. It recorded the profit on its books — meaning it could record the sales price whereas before it could only use the value of the malls at the time they were built. This helped it to camouflage nicely the Coseka writeoff.

Next, Trizec sold those centres, plus its own mall portfolio, back to Bramalea. They created a new company, Trilea, a subsidiary of both, with Trizec owning two-thirds and Bramalea one-third. There was talk of a new office subsidiary, as well. Eventually, these new companies could raise more money for new development by selling more shares to the public rather than borrowing from the banks. A familiar scenario, only now Trizec would end up being another holding company, another layer between Jack Cockwell and the possibility of failure.

About a month after the deal was arranged, Cockwell invited Field and Swirsky to have lunch with Eyton and himself at the posh Toronto Club. He congratulated the Bramalea boys on their successful company and said that Trizec's pre-eminence in the industry would bode well for the firm. "My mouth fell open," Field later recalls. After explaining to Cockwell that he considered Bramalea to be a more successful company than Trizec, Field went on to dissect the advantages — mostly cash — that Trizec had over the years, compared to Bramalea. "I said, 'Jack, If you measure the return on what we have compared to what return on Trizec has, we think we've done the best of anybody.' "

Cockwell challenged Field to detail the "fantastic story" on a sheet of paper comparing the financial performance of both companies. "Trizec has always been one of Jack's favorite companies," Field recalls.*

In fact, Jack Cockwell maintains, whatever Peter Bronfman and Trevor Eyton might say, that Trizec was just as important to the group as a watershed as the 1979 taking of Brascan. Certainly, Jack is still "actively involved" with Trizec, according to those close to the company. One explains with a sage nod that Trizec is in the segment of the empire — the Hees-Carena spheres — where Jack has a very personal investment stake. "Look where the bulk of his money is invested."

Sooner or later, life teaches you a lesson by giving you what you want. For the Edper boys, that lesson was Noranda. Managing their way out of Noranda was as tough a test of the patience and skill of Jack Cockwell and Trevor Eyton as they would encounter. Says Barney Finestone, a long-time friend of the Bronfman brothers, "They didn't want to fight Alf Powis for Noranda. That's not their style. And they came back a year later and Powis welcomed them with open arms. They gritted their teeth and went through some bad years without a murmur."

---

* In mid-1988, Field sold his 7% share of Bramalea to the Edper group.

When Cockwell and Eyton began their two-step on Noranda in October 1979, it looked like another brilliant move. Prices for copper, gold, and zinc — Noranda's products — had risen steadily in the late seventies. Inflation was a fact of life: spending lots on expansion today was smart because the price tag, and the loan that went with it, would look minuscule by tomorrow. Adam Zimmerman was president of Noranda then. He recalls the late seventies and early eighties as "unduly euphoric and optimistic." Investment, in plants, equipment, and other resource companies — flooded out of Noranda's executive suite. A new mine in Arizona and another in British Columbia; a renovated pulp mill in New Brunswick. "We seemed to be riding a high. And our judgement was ratified by Brascan, who wanted to own us," recalls Zimmerman.

Noranda, a huge, widely held resource company with a powerful entrenched management, had already caught the eye of Conrad Black. That had made Alf Powis, Noranda's chairman and chief executive, uncomfortable, and he had discouraged any ambitions of Black's for control. Now he faced a threat from the even more powerful Brascan.

On September 28, 1979, Jack Cockwell learned from an investment broker that Conrad Black was willing to sell his stake in Noranda. The price for his 7.9 million shares was steep — $21.50 a share, compared to a trading price of $21. There was a rumor that two other groups were interested in Black's shares. Cockwell and Eyton were able to convince the Bronfmans that Noranda had strong management and good positions in mining and smelting, forestry, and oil and gas, and on Monday, October 1, Eyton and Black shook on a deal. Four days later Eyton called Powis at a construction shack in the Elmworth gas field in Alberta to tell him about the deal and that Brascan intended to acquire up to 20% of Noranda. The next day, a stunned Powis was back in Toronto for an emergency meeting with his top executives on the forty-fifth floor of the Commerce Court, just three floors below its new largest single shareholder.

Later that week, at dinner, Eyton assured Powis that Brascan only wanted to participate in the decision-making and to gain recognition of its investment; Brascan would not alter

Noranda's course or its management. Brascan sought two seats on Noranda's board of directors and one on the executive committee of Noranda.

But Powis was not the type of executive to leave himself defenceless. Dismissing Eyton's assurances, he said, "There is always soothing talk at the beginning of these things." In November 1979, in an effort to stop Brascan from gaining control, Noranda issued an additional 14 million treasury shares at $19 a share. The buyer of the shares was Zinor Holdings, a holding company controlled by three Noranda subsidiaries and two affiliates. The share reshuffling, which raised $266 million, diluted Brascan's 16.3% equity in Noranda to 14%. This, in turn, made Brascan's declared bid for a 20% threshold in Noranda more difficult — and more expensive. Brascan owned 14.2 million of Noranda's 101.5 million shares; it would cost the company another $120 million to buy the additional 6 million shares needed to reach 20%. At the same time, Noranda's board turned down Brascan's request for seats on the board. Then in May 1981, Powis took another step to stave off Brascan by purchasing for $629 million, half of the giant B.C. forest company, Macmillan-Bloedel Limited.

Undaunted, the boys at Brascan came up with an unlikely — but successful — vehicle for a major takeover thrust on Noranda: they checked Noranda's shareholder list and found a suitable ally in the Caisse de dépôt et placement du Québec, a provincial government agency that invests contributions from provincial pension plans and other social benefit programs. Brascan and the Caisse de dépôt pooled their 24.4 million common shares in Noranda to create Brascade Resources Incorporated, which was thirty per cent owned by the Caisse de dépôt and seventy per cent by Brascan. Brascade owned 21.5% of Noranda's 113.4 million shares, edging out Zinor, which held 21.1%.

In August 1981, after an acrimonious two-year battle, Brascade Resources finally acquired a control position by buying 12.5 million treasury shares for $40 each. Noranda and Brascan had come to terms; Brascade acquired thirty-seven per cent of Noranda and agreed to keep its ownership position at less than fifty per cent. Powis, Zimmerman and Noranda senior vice-president Kendall Cork kept their jobs and their independent frame of mind. When peace was restored, Powis said that while the $40 Brascan paid for shares was "not overly generous, it is still a reasonable price."

Noranda's management — long accustomed to working in an informal style with minimal bureaucracy — emerged from the takeover with day-to-day control of corporate policies (guaranteed as part of a secret letter of understanding) plus a $500-million cash infusion from the new shareholders. Noranda had maintained many of its chiefs of staff for a generation or more; but the threat of the Brascan boys at the table was very real. In November 1981, Noranda's board was expanded to eighteen members from twelve to make room for the new major shareholders. Brascade received four seats on Noranda's board. The seats were filled by Eyton, Cockwell, Paul Marshall, then president and director of Westmin Resources, and Harold Wright, chairman of Wright Engineers in Vancouver. The Caisse de dépôt placed two representatives on the board. Relations between Noranda's management and Brascan began to be described as "cordial."

But in 1982, just a few months after Brascade's costly control purchase, the share price dropped to $11 3/8. Before commodity prices plummeted, Noranda had earned a record profit of $408 million. Even in the depression years of the 1930s Noranda made money. But in 1982, resource prices dropped to such dismal lows that for the first time in its fifty-nine-year history Noranda suffered a loss of $82.9 million. Noranda's earnings couldn't take care of the company's indebtedness. Two new mines had been costed out at metal prices the world has yet to see; a pulp mill had gone $75 million over budget. Says Zimmerman, "I was made president just at the beginning of this decline and the Zimmerman years as president are hardly glorious, but if I had gone to the board at that time and said, 'Look this copper business is for the birds. It's going to go off the cliff, we're on a high right now. Let's sell it.' I might have been right as rain but I would have also been dismissed as crazy."

During the early 1980s, Brascan began to accumulate huge tax losses from its Noranda subsidiary. By 1984, Brascan was, in the words of one financial analyst, "a cash-flow-deficient company."

Because Noranda was a blight on the Edper landscape, for years people expected Alf Powis, a blue-chip powerbroker of the old school, to land outside the door. But it never happened. In spring 1986, Bay Street denizens bought Noranda stock merely on the rumour that Mike Cornelissen, who had left Trizec to turn around Royal Trust in 1982, was moving on to Noranda to replace Powis. He didn't. Instead, in the winter of 1987, Hees' David Kerr moved to Noranda as president to begin what boiled down to a workout of the Noranda problem. Powis remained as an elder statesman, and Adam Zimmerman, the company's extremely popular president, was given the new Noranda Forest subsidiary to oversee. Says a none-too-sympathetic Zimmerman, "The Noranda investment must have been close to a disaster for them because it was a very big one."

It was a different story at Labatt's. There, after the taking of Brascan in 1979, a strong operational structure was already firmly in place as was a man who was his own man. Ontario Premier David Peterson, as an old Londoner, still has the chauvinistic opinion that Brascan "stole" London Life years ago. But he has some praise for them. "They've really done a very good job with London Life and Labatt's. And they sort of run an arm's-length operation. These guys run their own ships. They [Edper] pick management, they invest in management, in both [Earl] Orser and [Peter] Widdrington. They are very able chief executive officers."

Widdrington is a particular favourite of Peterson's, as he is with just about everyone. Peter Widdrington has his own way of thinking. He is the consummate charmer, the marketer who knows he can step outside the bounds of his own sales pitch and still win. At times he has even gone beyond the bounds of good taste and emerged the hero as few can. Once, at a meeting of the Toronto Society of Financial Analysts, a group that takes its monthly lunch-time grillings of corporate execs very seriously, Widdrington was being berated about poor results. What was he going to do about it, one food and beverage specialist demanded. He began to outline his long-term strategy, but was interrupted. Didn't the results bother him now? What was he going to do about it that very afternoon? "I don't know what you're doing this afternoon" responded Widdrington with a little-boy grin. "But I might get laid."

Politic is the word to describe Peter Widdrington. His is almost a calculated outrageousness; he relishes the role of the eccentric surrounded by buttoned-down money men. Self-described child protégé of the old Brascan guard, Widdrington likes to distinguish the Moore and Edper regimes as Brascan One and Brascan Two. Brascan One had more day-to-day involvement, including a joint venture in the beer business in Brazil. "It was rather a difficult working relationship," says Widdrington. In fact, Brascan One at one point thought of buying compete control of Labatt's as a way of soaking up some of the Brazilian cash. Widdrington, who was on the board of Brascan, opposed the idea and used it as an excuse to remove himself from the battle that had begun with Edper. "I personally stepped to the sideline," says the canny Widdrington. After Edper's triumph, four of them joined the Labatt's board and, he says, "They were far more clear cut in their ideas of what they wanted to do, where they wanted to take the business."

Under Widdrington, Labatt's has changed from a Canadian company to a North American one — 40 per cent of Labatt's sales are now generated in the U.S. — and Widdrington continues to lay the groundwork for further international expansion. Labatt's has more than 40 per cent of the beer business in Canada as well as a lion's share of the milk, flour and pasta sold in Canada. Because of that, the limits of expansion within Canada are reached. "It's pretty tough for us to expand in Canada," says Widdrington. But from that base there are plenty of opportunities. One small operation, Olmstead Foods, which is based in Wheatley, Ontario, supplies between 50 and

60 per cent of the Lake Erie smelts consumed by Japanese. In another ten years, a major company in any part of the world has to be international in scope.

Just as Labatt's is markedly different in character from the financial businesses in the Edper empire, so are businesses within Labatt's different from each other in management style. Beer, a high-margin business, is run differently than milk, where the profit margins are slim. The show-biz nature of The Sports Network attracts a different type of executive than the flour operations do. And it is at Labatt's that Peter Bronfman plays the role of dilettante manager, poking his nose into whatever strikes his fancy. Widdrington attributes at least some of Peter's interest to the fact that beer is a high-visibility business. Edward's favourite operation is The Sports Network.

But there are definite links on the financial side of the business these days. "We're operators, we make beer, we process milk. Finance is not our business," Widdrington adds. For that, the people at Labatt's talk to Ken Clarke at Great Lakes, Cockwell, Eyton, Bob Dunford, and Bob Simon at Brascan. "We respect their expertise and we've made use of it. And we've done well by them."

The Edper group is usually depicted as a unit that will not take no for an answer. But in dealing with their most important U.S. acquisition to date, they definitely decided that sometimes it's best to take the money and go home.

Soon after the takeovers of Brascan and Noranda, Jack Cockwell decided he wanted a cash-generating acquisition, and he found one in a Philadelphia-based consumer-products concern, Scott Paper Company. It sold almost $2 billion worth of personal and household paper products annually, and it owned vast tracts of forest in Canada, the United States, and Brazil. By December 1980, Brascan owned four per cent of Scott. Then, in March 1981, Brascan announced it was raising its holding in Scott Paper Company to 20.5%. The

101-year-old company had always been independent and had no large shareholders. Scott's scrappy chairman, Charles Dickey, responded to Brascan's announcement by underlining the company's desire to remain independent.

Eyton did his best to mollify Dickey; he sent him a copy of Brascan's red-covered corporate credo and the home telephone numbers of the company's board members. But the sixty-three-year-old Dickey, a former Marine, would not be placated. Meanwhile, Brascan was able to secure more stock, and brought its stake in Scott up to twelve per cent. Eyton and Cockwell flew to the company's unassuming six-storey head office, near the Philadelphia airport. Their trip was an attempt to reassure Dickey that they had no interest in taking over Scott, although they wanted a larger stake in the company. But Dickey had secured the services of New York-based Skadden Arps Slate Meaghen and Flom, a noted merger and acquisition law firm, because Scott's board had told him to find a solution to Brascan's requests or to get ready for a battle in the courts. Dickey and Scott president Phil Lippincott visited Brascan's office in Toronto a number of times and a deal was finally struck. The two companies signed a five-year stand-still agreement to avoid a costly takeover battle. Brascan agreed to buy $102 million of Scott's treasury shares and receive four board seats, and agreed to limit its increases in its Scott holdings. Brascan was worried about its rights under Pennsylvania law — and the spectre of facing Scott and their battery of Philadelphia lawyers. "Particularly in the United States you've got to be careful before you take on someone in the courts. You can tie up your whole organization for several years," says Peter Widdrington, a Brascan board member and one of the four — along with Peter Bronfman, Eyton, and Cockwell — who joined the Scott board.

In 1986, several months before the stand-still agreement was to expire, Brascan sold its twelve million common shares in the Scott Paper company back to Scott. The sale netted Brascan $186 million. Eyton said the sell-out to Scott was the result of a "conflicting notion" about the desirable level of Brascan's holdings. "Brascan's a bloody big company," Widdrington says. "I don't think people in the American business community are too enamoured about Canadian companies doing all that well."

For Brascan, the message was clear. "If you can't work out a reasonably friendly arrangement with somebody like Scott, then go spend your time on something else, because it's just not worth it," Widdrington says. Even now, Widdrington and Eyton are quick to point out that the investment in Scott produced a profit when Brascan sold. But they also invariably refer to the warrants Brascan still holds, which are convertible down the road. And Scott continues to be included in organizational charts depicting Brascan, Labatt's, and the consumer-products holdings of the Edper empire.

As part of the pull-out, three of the four Brascan representatives had to step off the Scott board. The question was who would stay. It was clear from the Scott people that they preferred Peter Bronfman, perhaps for his cachet, perhaps for his mild manner. Equally clearly, they preferred not to have Trevor Eyton remain on the board. Eyton, who prefers getting even over getting mad, volunteered to stay.

Any future consumer-products acquisition will be made by Labatt's, not Brascan. And Widdrington's distancing from the Scott attempt perhaps portends that things will be done differently by the operators than they have been by the financiers.

In August 1980, Royal Trust Company was threatened by a takeover led by Canadian developer Robert Campeau. That attempted coup failed. But it took all the ammunition the old guard could muster to fend off the upstart Campeau, and led to changes that would eventually sweep out the old guard and forever alter the company and the industry.

To defeat Campeau, a small group banded together and bought stock in Royal Trust. After the takeover bid was over, that stock ended up in only a few hands. The billionaire Reichmann brothers had purchased ten per cent of Royal's stock as part of the defensive manoeuvre; by 1981, they had secured twenty-three per cent.

Brascan also bought seventeen per cent of Royal in the spring of 1981. Eyton claims it was a favour to the Reichmann brothers, who wanted to shake up the company. They had naturally turned to their partners in Trizec, Edward and Peter Bronfman. The Reichmanns offered Brascan up to eighteen per cent of Royal stock. It was a nice fit for Brascan, because they already owned London Life. The idea was that the insurance company and the trust company could add to each others' product lines.

The Brascan boys arrived at Royal with their usual request for proportional board representation. They felt Royal needed some basic planning, which management was not providing. That meant Ken White, Royal's feisty president, had to go. As well, the new shareholders didn't like the company's Florida banks or the rapid expansion Royal had undergone in the 1970s. The company's strategies weren't reaping a high enough return. But things changed dramatically when Mike Cornelissen, who had restructured Trizec a few years earlier, was parachuted into Royal. He made the jump from board member to president in August 1983, when Royal's president, John Scholes, left for health reasons.

Cornelissen pulled together a management team to create a new vision when he arrived at Royal Trust. He wasn't interested in hiring management consultants, the usual approach, because they cost too much, and they left with too much precious inside knowledge. "Consultants can represent an abdication of responsibility," Cornelissen says. Instead, one of the first things he did was bring more of the decision-making power to the upper echelons. As he explained it, they would "suck it all up, take a close look at it, then let it back down again." The new executive could find out which middle managers made which decisions and pinpoint exactly who was responsible for what. Moving operational decisions up to executive levels "resulted in decisions that were better by several hundreds of thousands of dollars." Closer control paid off.

Cornelissen and his team spent six weeks expanding their

ideas. The result was a company that was "destructured," to Cornelissen's way of thinking. They created four divisions, which would interact through the board of the central holding company. The board was responsible for company management.

The first senior person Cornelissen hired was Courtney Pratt, a Touche Ross human-resources expert and someone Cornelissen had used at Trizec.* The two had become friends in Calgary. Pratt became the architect of the change at Royal Trust. Pratt chose senior executives who were either already prominent managers at other financial institutions — like Bill Harker, who was lured away from the Bank of Montreal — or promising recruits from alien businesses, such as newspaper publishing and law. Although human resources is usually accepted as a cost of doing business, Cornelissen changed that. "If the quality of our people isn't up to scratch, Courtney is accountable. When he achieves a culture change in four years that normally would take ten years to achieve, he gets the credit," Cornelissen says.

Cornelissen took what he calls "the normal steps" to convince managers at Royal Trust to embrace group values. Aside from those senior people who "found they couldn't keep up with the new pace we set for ourselves and retired gracefully," Cornelissen claims universal acceptance of the Edper creed. He lists those "normal steps": "Tell them where you want to go, individually and in groups. Write them letters, cite examples, question them, encourage them, threaten them. You name it." As well, he brought in a share-holding program for employees. Half the staff took the company up on its offer.

At Royal Trust, Cornelissen sits at his desk and punches new-product suggestions with a triangular red stamp that bears a pointed message: "Where's the wealth?" Cornelissen says his priority is to "make our clients wealthier every day." He arrived at Royal Trust thinking the company had "hidden values," which the group could use to make new profits, and he wasn't thinking only of buildings. "The company has hidden values in people," he declared in 1984. Some money-

---

* Pratt moved on to work with David Kerr at Noranda in 1988.

making attributes could be brought out by closer association with senior management; interest in the work would increase as loyalty increased. As well, managers would work toward a common goal. "Everybody has to have a sense of ownership," Cornelissen explains.

Under Cornelissen, Royal Trust drew up a business plan with stages. First, they would match assets and liabilities. Then they would institute tight financial controls and reporting procedures; raise money on the stock market and through the debt markets; upgrade the company's credit rating; reduce loan-loss ratios; and, underlying all this, they would reduce the number of reporting layers. The company almost tripled its assets, from $8 billion to $21 billion, in four years. It now manages $60 billion in estate, trust, and agency funds, and it is expanding the fee-producing advisory side of the business — what Cornelissen calls "value-added services." At the same time, Royal Trust has become very picky about its lending business; it turns down eighty per cent of its mortgage applications. Cornelissen isn't interested in building assets; he's interested in building profitability.

Cornelissen likes to use the 1986 acquisition of Dow Financial Services, which gave Royal Trust an entrée into the European and Asian markets, as an example of their ability to get things done quickly and effectively. Within six months of getting regulatory approval on the purchase, three Royal Trust executives had culled out the dogs — they amounted to one-third of the assets — and sold them off at handsome premiums. Royal Trust ended the year with an eleven-per-cent after-tax profit on the $235 million purchase.

Michael Cornelissen is from the Cockwell school of financing: Royal Trust has $1.8 billion in outstanding stock. "I don't think one can be too conservatively financed," Cornelissen says. In 1987, Royal Trust signed a deal with Great Lakes Group, the Brascan subsidiary that provides backing for group securities issues, for a special $1 billion five-year standing line of credit. "One of the business standards that we have is to be very strong," Cornelissen says. "You achieve that by actively entering into financial transactions and being active in the marketplace and issuing new types of securities."

He has used much of the new equity to invest in securities; Royal Trust's investment portfolio grew from $500,000 to $1.8 billion between 1982 and 1987. Cornelissen insists that, contrary to old industry rumours, Royal Trust has never bought much of the group's own issues. And the numbers in 1987 show that the firm's holdings of group stocks are relatively insignificant: $98 million in common and preferred shares in twenty-two related companies, or one-half of one per cent of the stock portfolio.

Royal Trust was the second offshoot of Brascan's financial services operations; the first was London Life. In 1983, the group decided to formally structure a financial-services group under an umbrella. The Reichmanns and Toronto-Dominion Bank, Brascan's partners at Royal Trust, joined Brascan in setting up a holding company called Trilon Financial Corporation, and the group placed both Royal Trust and London Life under the Trilon umbrella. In the next few years, other acquisitions went under the umbrella: Royal LePage real estate, Wellington Insurance, a new merchant bank called Trilon Bancorp, and a leasing company called CVL. Then the insurance companies were placed under a separate holding company called Lonvest.

The purpose of marrying the diverse financial services was to create what businessmen like to call "synergy": common computer systems, master lists of prospective clients, and the natural business fit of, say, mortgage lender and real-estate broker. Says Cornelissen: "Ten to fifteen per cent of our bottom line would be generated as a result of our affiliations." At least a hundred Royal Trust employees contact employees at other Trilon or Lonvest companies on any given day.

In 1982, Royal Trust began to discuss a merger with the giant real-estate company A.E. LePage. But the senior executives at Royal couldn't agree amongst themselves, and the deal fell apart. Then, in 1984, the chairman of A.E. LePage, Gordon Gray, bumped into Trevor Eyton at a tennis camp. The two again discussed a merger. Bill Dimma, vice-chairman of Royal, followed up their chat by meeting with Trilon's Mel Hawkrigg and then with Mike Cornelissen. "The second time around, the people we were dealing with were quite clear on what they wanted, and as a result there wasn't much waste motion," Dimma said.

The merger of Royal Trust and A.E. LePage was a marriage of balance sheets rather than physical assets. The new company is 50.1% owned by Royal Trust. But Royal LePage is regarded as a separate entity under the Trilon umbrella. In 1987 Royal LePage went public. There is still a separate Royal LePage board, with fourteen original members and six new members, three from Royal Trust and three from Trilon.

With all this cross-reporting, there were what Dimma calls "efficiencies and conveniences," such as "dealing with the same accounting firm, the same law firm." For example, A.E. LePage had always used Price Waterhouse as auditors. Within six months of the merger, Royal LePage used Clarkson Gordon. "Clarkson Gordon has been the auditors for pretty much the whole group right from Brascan down," Dimma says. He was happy with his old firm, Price Waterhouse. But, he explains, "in accounting there is often more than one way to handle an issue. So if you are dealing with Clarkson Gordon, you know that it's more likely to be consistent at London Life, Royal Trust, and Royal LePage."

At Royal Trust, Mike Cornelissen emphasizes the human side of his hard-running team. Shortly before Christmas every year, the fifty-odd vice-presidents set aside an afternoon and evening to evaluate their year. Each manager must stand up and list his or her three major accomplishments, worst failure, and the funniest things that happened all year. They have prepared stand-up comedy routines, group videos, and slide shows to tell their stories. Cornelissen cites Bill Inwood, who even the serious and acutely sincere Cornelissen considers dry, as an example of how funny these guys can be. Inwood, whose responsibilities include government relations and corporate communications, described his dealings with the board and the chief executive: "March 17, made my presentation. Was fired. June 30. Fired again. September 19. Fired repeatedly."

Says Cornelissen of the festivities: "You feel very good at what you've achieved. At the same time, you just weep with laughter."

There was a time, not so long ago, when Jack Cockwell ran Hees International out of his back pocket. In 1979, Cockwell was engineering the fortunes of newly purchased Brascan and watching over the freshly minted partnership with the Reichmanns at Trizec. Then he took a hard look at the almost dormant Hees and decided to use it as a tool to finance the group's burgeoning load of companies. Within four years, Hees took on part-ownership of Brascan and became, in Edpergroup parlance, the branch of the empire that sits at the top of the heap, closest to the family. Hees, like Trilon, is part of the group's third sphere; it marries merchant banking and management consulting, and helps turn around any companies the group picks up along the way. Cockwell also established a huge stock-trading portfolio and set up a market-making activity for preferred shares. And all this was done on the side; for quite a while, few people even noticed.

Hees had been around for about a decade as a corporate holding when Cockwell began to make it over. It had been purchased by Neil Baker in 1966 from Toronto promoter Dutch Holland as a side benefit of the Great West International Equities deal. In 1980, Cockwell decided to use Hees to help one of his Montreal ventures, Mico. Mico, which had started life as Marigot Enterprises Limited, owned real estate in Marigot Bay, in St. Lucia; Mico also owned a trading company and the West Indian Stock Exchange. But Cockwell thought Mico needed more stock-market exposure. Mico was a public merchant-banking company, but it only traded in the Montreal over-the-counter market; Hees had a real Toronto Stock Exchange listing. In 1980, Cockwell combined Mico and Hees. Immediately, Hees became revitalized. It gained a stock portfolio; it gained the Mico management team, including the core of Montreal Edper guys, Tim Price, Tim Casgrain, and Bryan McJannet; and it gained a merchant-banking mandate.

These days, Hees is clearly the company nearest to the heart of Edper. In 1983, Hees purchased the Patino family's interest in Brascan, and thus became a major Brascan shareholder. In 1987, Hees traded its holdings in natural-resource company North Canadian Oils to Brascan-controlled Noranda Incorporated, in return for an even tighter clamp on Brascan. And Hees bought Conrad Black's Norcen for Brascan, then traded Norcen within a year for a chunk of Brascan subsidiary Great Lakes Group, a company that had already assumed some of the Hees financing duties, and that even expert observers at times confuse with Hees.

Hees and Carena Bancorp are the holding companies in which Cockwell has most of his investments, and Carena is in many ways tied to Hees' apron strings. Partially shared management means that Hees executives often mix Carena companies into their spiels about Hees. Lawyer Bill L'Heureux, hired as a corporate spokesman in the Trevor Eyton mould, says that Carena "is virtually run out of the Hees boardroom." Hees flaunts a corporate chart that rates Brascan as a corporate investment. And, through Hees, vice-chairman Jack Cockwell can dictate to Trevor Eyton and Brascan, should he so decide. Hees is an active merchant banker, a deal company. But the main business of Hees is to oversee the group's health. Along the way, it produces extraordinary profits for its shareholders.

To understand Hees is to understand the empire. Hees is not an operating company, but its executives insist that it is not a holding company, either. They do not take the Brascan approach of influencing subsidiary management through board meetings. Instead, when they do a work-out, they do it merchant-banking style: drop in an executive or two and see how the company can be turned around. And instead of charging fees, the way an ordinary management consultant or liquidator would, the guys at Hees figure out a way to take a stake in the company as payment for the work-out. L'Heureux likes to call the assets gained from these work-outs "our private pension plan." It might take twenty years to make a gain on some of these assets, L'Heureux points out, but the assets — real estate, natural resources, beer plants — will always be there.

But it is definitely not the role of Hees to ensure that Labatt's makes better beer or that Noranda has better miners. The Hees people are financiers. They provide the financial framework and attempt to instil a management philosophy that will allow managers to create better beer or drill more or market mortgages more aggressively.

Hees is Jack Cockwell's favourite kind of business. It exists to make money from financings and refinancings. And its executives can, at times, be mistaken for computer programmers. Every year, they set up computerized profit objectives. If the company makes more than the objectives, they take the "excess" — all that hasn't been pre-programmed — and use it to write down slightly questionable assets to more realistic values. If the company doesn't achieve the expected profits, they try to find the money somewhere. They like to always arrive right on projections, to manage the company's results to the last nickel. In the past, some Bay Street types have joked that "those results are created on the computer." But Hees' Manfred Walt would say the same thing — and fail to understand why the concept disturbs people.

Indeed, at Hees the main beef is why the company's stock price isn't higher. They don't acknowledge the classic argument that a holding company's price is always discounted because it is really a basket of assets without ultimate control over management. It is more like a pension fund than Bill L'Heureux might like to admit. And they refuse to accept the valid complaint that, because all Hees' profits are created by specific deals, the shareholder has no real guarantee that this year's performance can be equalled, that there will always be another good deal down the road.

Price, L'Heureux, and the other managing partners at Hees feel their track record says it all. Certainly, the facts are impressive, almost staggering. At the end of 1987, Hees' merchant-banking function ranked fourth in North America, with $1.4 billion in assets, behind only Salomon Brothers, Merrill Lynch, and Goldman Sachs and Company, and ahead of Prudential

Bache and First Boston. Before the stock-market crash, Hees common shares had doubled in value in ten years. Assets had grown by forty-four per cent annually in the decade between 1977 and 1987, from a base of $65 million to a total of $2.5 billion, and shareholders' equity had grown by sixty-one per cent annually. The group investments controlled by Hees had a stock-market value of $1.7 billion. The big question in 1987 was whether Hees could stand a major market crash. The answer was a resounding yes. Every growth target for the year was met, except the stock price. And while the stock price dropped in October 1987, it rebounded, by year end, to its 1986 level. The ten-year compound growth of the stock price was thiry-nine per cent annually.

Hees corporate work-outs have included Jimmy Kay's private oil and gas and restaurant interests, reincarnated as Dexleigh and North Canadian Oils; Carma Limited, the western Canadian land-banking and house-building company; Coscan, a Toronto home builder; Versatile, the Vancouver-based shipbuilder and natural-resource company; and, most recently, National Business Systems (NBS), a credit-card manufacturer whose financial results didn't reflect the company's real situation at the end of 1987. Tim Casgrain and Bryan McJannet worked on the books and negotiated with authorities while the RCMP looked for missing money.

The names change and the circumstances differ, but the formula remains the same: parachute in executives; closely scrutinize operations; involve existing management whenever possible; work a deal with the creditors that involves an investment by Hees and management or other owners; provide financial stability; then let management run the business. The name could be Trizec or Noranda or Royal Trust. Tim Casgrain was the Edper point man on the original Mico work-out; more than a decade later, he was the Hees point man at NBS. It is Cockwell's stamp.

Because Hees is the ultimate Cockwell company, it is natural that Tim Price is Hees' chief executive. Cockwell writes the program and Price runs it. Price (who backed out of an interview with us because his version of Mico and Hees history might be "a different view" — however slight — from the

packaged version) is down-to-earth, a regular guy. Young
Manfred Walt, on the other hand, is so earnestly sincere that
he is frightening. Walt, a South African import with Afrikaaner
roots, has a manner that unconsciously mimics Cockwell's.
Manfred Walt and George Myhal, who makes the Hees
preferred-share market, are the next generation of Hees. Walt
is also a junior advisor to Peter Bronfman and his children.

This linking of the public company to the major shareholder
is more obvious at Hees than anywhere else. The blurring of
the lines that separate the empire's three spheres is almost
obvious here, since part of Hees' *raison d'être* is as a holding
tank for all the other Edper investments. This brings home
Cockwell's dilemma in viewing his creation. For the family
is always a volatile unit. In spring 1988, an article in the *Globe
and Mail*'s Report On Business magazine stated that three-
quarters of family businesses "detonate" by the third generation, that the average life of a corporation is twenty-four years.
Cockwell has now been working for the Bronfmans for twenty
years; they are in the beginning stages of a transition to the
third generation.

His plan was that the family should be eased out of their
pre-eminent, dominant position at Hees and Hees would take
over share ownership of companies previously held by Edper,
which was a private company. That would put more of the
Bronfman assets into a publicly traded vehicle — and, as it
happens, the company where Cockwell has his largest stake.
"Hees, the central company, is now so big that Peter and
Edward no longer control it," says Ira Gluskin, an investment
consultant. "Cockwell is worried that Peter and Edward's kids
could wake up and decide they didn't like the empire."

Certainly now, the group is more than the Bronfmans —
but it is also more than Jack Cockwell and Trevor Eyton.
Lionel Schipper, Peter Bronfman's close friend and personal
advisor and a director of Edper, says, "Would the Edper
organization crumble if they quit? I don't think so. Would
it be different if they quit? No question. Can you replace a
Jack Cockwell? I don't think so, but there are a lot of other
successful businesses that don't have Cockwell at the head.
Can you replace Trevor Eyton? Not easily, maybe not, but

again, there are other combinations of people running businesses. Would it be painful? I'm sure it would be, because they are more than just business managers."

Ira Gluskin also thinks Bay Street would accept the group without Jack Cockwell. "If Jack ran away to Brazil, I wouldn't sell my Trizec shares; maybe I'd sell my Hees shares, but I probably wouldn't sell my Brascan shares."

Lionel Schipper says, "I don't think one or two people can actually build what they've built over the past fifteen years." He credits others who have come on board, either hired by Cockwell or gained as part of a merger or acquisition. This is the standard company line these days. Gluskin agrees, but points out that only recently has the Edper group reached that safety point. "What he has created, I'd say it has a life of its own now. But to get to this stage, you have to have somebody who wants things to grow. Who is that force? Jack Cockwell."

CHAPTER SIX

The Priestly Caste

All great civilizations have had their priestly caste.
Our priesthood will be those who occupy positions
of great economic power.
— from an inscription on a plaque in the head office
of Brascan Limited

Brascan headquarters is on the forty-eighth floor of Commerce
Court West in downtown Toronto, one of the tall and
characterless bank towers that Torontonians like to think
makes theirs a world-class city. The reception area is a tasteful
plum and taupe. One wall is dominated by enormous brass
doors — the palace gates — that whisk open and shut, controlled by a button at the receptionist's desk. Just outside the
doors is an ironic palace guard. A portly fellow, clad in an
overcoat and carrying a briefcase, he stands cast in brass.
Beneath him is a brass plaque, which describes him as raising
his eyes "in pious reverence, seeking divine inspiration
necessary for the consummation of the Big Deal."

Visitors to Brascan almost always notice and comment on
the statue. Some remember that it was that old capitalist Jake
Moore who put the statue there; it is Trevor Eyton who keeps
it there. "It's great fun," he tells visitors. "If you read the

inscription, you see that the artist, I think tongue-in-cheek, says the new priestly caste are the businessmen." But he doesn't agree with the artist; he thinks businessmen are too human and too candid. Humanity and candour notwithstanding, many people see in the Edper group a theological bent, a predisposition to dogma. There are articles of faith that form the way Edper people do business.

They call them "shared beliefs and corporate values." They have a Jesuitical approach to business, a disciplined, ascetic, no-nonsense, suffer-in-this-life philosophy. First among the sacred beliefs is the rightness of low salaries and huge compulsory stock-purchase plans. Top managers at Hees, Brascan, Carena, Trilon, and the operating subsidiaries, such as Royal Trust and Trizec, receive salaries well below comparable industry standards. Jack Cockwell, for example, the single most important individual in the Edper empire and a twenty-year veteran, earned a salary of $135,000 in 1986. Bill L'Heureux was paid more than $250,000 as a partner at Tory, Tory, Deslauriers and Binnington. He moved to Hees, where he earned a salary of $100,000. As Edper managers move up the ladder, the salary gap between them and their peers widens. A junior group manager might earn up to ninety per cent of the going rate, but a top manager like Eyton earns about a third of what he would be paid elsewhere.

The Edper group also believes in minimal staff. Hees has "partners" and other support staff. Throughout the group, senior officers, but particularly at Hees, are expected to work "long hours, although every effort is made to keep weekends free to spend with family and friends. Senior officers are expected "to put their business interests ahead of their personal interests when they are involved in a major initiative." This is actually written down. At Hees, senior people "acknowledge the fact that regular office hours will be required for day to day decisions, transaction settlements and general enquiries. The evenings and weekends are reserved for personal development reading, to do basic research and to plan new initiatives." Mel Hawkrigg, the ebullient president of Trilon, arrives home most nights around eleven o'clock. On Fridays, he tries to make it for dinner by seven-thirty, but he brings home plenty of reading. "Family time is weekends. I'll go to just about any length — as will just about anybody else in this office — to make sure Saturday and Sunday are private." Peter Bronfman, who does not work the long hours demanded of his staff, says that it is very rare that one Edper executive will phone another about a business matter on the weekend. Still, says Hawkrigg, "It's longer hours than I've ever had before."

The motivation to put in a superhuman work week is underscored by another principle at Hees: the company expects its senior officers to contribute $2 million a year to the company's earnings, after financing and overhead costs, within one year of joining. And each officer, whether he be a finance person, a legal person, or whatever, is expected "to be a leader in one or more business discipline and have a good general knowledge in the other business disciplines" required by Hees.

Group managers at Edper don't receive many of the perqs that are part of the package for most senior executives. "Limousines, corporate aircraft and other such perquisites are considered inappropriate and an improper use of shareholders' funds," wrote Jack Cockwell in the 1986 Hees annual report, where the Edper creed was articulated for the public for the first time. Also on the list are lavish premises and long lunches — particularly with other group managers. Outside board director appointments are discouraged unless there is a "meaningful direct benefit to the group." If someone wants to sit on a board, he'll be appointed to a group company. And if an exception is made, any director's fees must be turned over to a manager's parent company or the company for which he works directly. If that is against the outside company's practice, then the director's fee is taken into consideration when the manager's salary is set.

Breaking any of the Edper commandments can have serious consequences. A dispute over long-time Edper lieutenant Harold Milavsky's use of the corporate jet showed that anyone can be brought to account. One close observer says that the Edper group contrasts sharply to one of the country's other great personal conglomerates, Power Corporation, owned by

Paul Desmarais. "Paul is in it for power. He can see that by diversifying his eggs and doing these reverse takeovers, he can consolidate his wealth position and lead the life he wants to live — his personal jet, France, the internal connections, shooting in Texas, having your own island, all that kind of stuff. Paul's ambitions, while for the ordinary person rather breathtaking, didn't really extend to rolling up his sleeves and getting in and making Great West Life a good life-insurance company." In 1969, when he took control of Great West Life after the Bronfmans backed out, Desmarais raised $100 million by telling investors that he planned to integrate the insurance company with his trust company and mutual-fund investment company. It was a great concept, but insurance executives told him that the plan was next to impossible and Desmarais abandoned it for more than a decade because it was too difficult. But one insider says it was more than that. "He had already achieved just by taking over most of what he had set out to do. The Edper guys, once they take that first step, it's not the end. There are thirty steps to come. And they are implacable, they don't stop."

The Edper boys are in the game for power, but they are also in it for their own financial health. While they don't make much money in salaries, they make plenty on stock holdings when their companies do well. It is called "pay for performance." To foster an owner mentality rather than a manager mentality in their senior officers, Edper companies demand that senior people take a large portion of their remuneration in share ownership. It is not, strictly speaking, compulsory, but when asked what would happen if a new recruit chose not to invest in company stock, one group officer suggested that individual wouldn't last long. Under the group's executive share plan, senior officers are expected to purchase shares equalling up to ten times their salaries in the company they work for; later, they purchase stock in other group companies.

Executives can usually buy stock at below-market prices, and the interest on the loans is equivalent to the cash dividends paid on the stock. An Edper executive is expected to pay off the loan in five years. Trilon president Mel Hawkrigg says,

"When I think of my own personal situation, the amount of assets I've got tied into the companies with which I'm involved, I tell you it's très significant. We all recognize we've got a lot of personal risk out there. If we screw up, that's a problem. I go home and say to my good wife, 'Well, we only owe a few million this week.' We had to leverage ourselves a bit to buy more stock. From the old Anglo-Saxon tradition — that is, you owe a dollar, you work your butt off to pay it off — the wife had a little adjustment to make, but she's okay."

Because of the way the remuneration package is structured, each officer (except perhaps for someone as wealthy as Royal Trust chairman Hart McDougall, a scion of the Montreal Molson family) must go through a period of servitude before receiving any just reward. "The kind of heavy commitment they make in terms of the stock they have to buy, they can't buy any other stock, and they have these five-year performance contracts," says Unicorp Canada Corporation president Jim Leech, drawing on his knowledge of his close friend Tim Price. "It's tough stuff. You sell yourself to the organization."

When the reward comes, it is not in the form of a sinecure. Alan Hockin, dean of York University's business school, describes the reward system as a total reversal of traditional mores. He is now on his third career, after stints as a senior banker and a federal bureaucrat. (When Hockin was senior vice-president of Toronto-Dominion Bank, he stunned the financial world in 1983 by moving the bank into the world of discount stock brokerage.) Hockin turns to the world of his businessman father to illustrate how attitudes differed in the past. "You did what you were told until a certain stage, and then you would be rewarded by being made a manager, director, whatever. And then you could relax. You could go and play golf, go swimming, go fishing, and all the minions who were serving their apprenticeship would carry on, while you had this nice big salary. And this I think is a problem that has dogged not only Canadian business but all western business for a hell of a long time."

Hockin is also an outside director of Trilon Financial. There, he says, a very different philosophy is practised: "The more senior you get, the harder you work. And don't expect to live high off the hog." Whereas the executive of old demanded his reward, at Edper, company executives are told they must build their own return. Hockin says they are told by the board of directors. "We want you to build, and you don't get a big salary, you get a lower salary than most people. But what you do get is not only an option to buy stock — you are expected to buy stock. They push it at you." The group has grafted onto the role of manager the mentality of the owner, the stockholder. "Our operating philosophy of making our key executives part owners of their companies unlocks their entrepreneurial flair," says Trevor Eyton, "and enables them to realize their full potential. We don't believe in employment contracts and golden parachutes, but we are happy to see group executives achieve financial independence." In 1985, Eyton owed $3.3 million to Brascan under the executive share-purchase plan; Jack Cockwell owed $2.2 million; Bob Dunford, Brascan's executive vice-president and chief administrative officer, was in debt for $1.6 million; David Kerr, vice-chairman of Hees and then president of Noranda, owed a little more than $1 million; and Gord Cunningham, chief operating officer at Trilon, owed almost $1 million for Brascan stock he had bought, as well as loans under the Trilon share-purchase plan. In 1985, Brascan spent a mere $1 million on salaries for its nine most senior officers.

"I'm very interested in what's happening to shareholder values," says Mel Hawkrigg. "I don't want to sound like it's straight profit-motivated. I guess it is, to a degree, but because you have ownership, there is a much different approach and attitude than you have when you're salaried." An outside director like Hockin, who is on the board to represent the interests of minority shareholders, knows that when results are bad an executive can't cut and run.

The group had to re-think its rigid rules slightly after the sudden market crash. But the solution proffered to managers worried about big loans and low stock prices was in line with the creed: managers were lent even more money to buy more stock at the lower price. Their investment cost perhaps was lowered, but they were, of necessity, more committed than ever.

Not everyone is thrilled with the corporate creed, however. Peter Widdrington, the man who runs Labatt's, has become Peter Bronfman's personal advisor and Trevor Eyton's close friend since Brascan, Labatt's controlling shareholder, was taken over by Edper in 1979. He maintains that he hasn't changed the way he operates under the new owners, and he knows little and cares less about the way the Hees boys practise their creed.

Widdrington sees his role as a manager, not an owner, although he does admit that the share-ownership plan "certainly gives you a little incentive! I mean, who is kidding who? Jesus!" But he sees the downside of share incentives, as well. "The only danger is, in any kind of bonus, commission, stock-option plan or whatever, management could take short-term decisions or short-term gains at the expense of longer-term potential in order to achieve. In every system there are always plusses and minuses, and that's the thing you've got to watch about that system." He emphasizes that, in the group's system, he doesn't think there is this style of management-by-quarterly-reports. "I don't think it happens. But that's what you've got to be aware of."

In the beer business, Widdrington says nonchalantly, sumptuous lunches and perqs are the norm. No one at Brascan has objected, either. Widdrington cannot contain his laughter as he contemplates the Brascan boys trying to stop the Labatt's executives from taking lunch. "I have honestly never heard of a policy that says don't take lunch with somebody. They don't get down to the lunch level." Eyton and Cockwell have casually pointed out to him their statements of beliefs, but, Widdrington says, "I'm not familiar with a bunch of guys from Brascan running in here intercepting guys on their way to lunch." It may be amusing to Widdrington, but it is hard to believe that Cockwell could take his beliefs so lightly. In 1986, in an unusual move for Cockwell, who prefers financial companies, he joined the Labatt's board.

Another iconoclast is Adam Zimmerman, Noranda's president for years and now head of the company's new forestry spin-off subsidiary. His independent turn of mind has remained intact, despite eight years of working with Brascan-style theology. "Everybody has [his] personality and I think Brascan are pretty clear about their theology. You'll see that in this year's Noranda annual report," Zimmerman said during an interview in the spring of 1987. "It appeared suddenly in there and it appeared throughout all their various companies." While Edper has successfully grafted its theology on to some of the companies it has acquired, for example Royal Trust, at Noranda it has not worked well. "I don't think you can impose a corporate culture on anybody. It's something that's organic and develops. In the end, though, if they set certain rules, you're going to get people who want to play by those rules. [Those that don't] all go into the sunset quietly over time."

Zimmerman is scornful of the Edper creed as it relates to executive compensation through share ownership. "I gather something is going to be pushed at us in that regard," he said. He and Alf Powis, Noranda's chairman, have invested heavily in Noranda over the years on their own. They have held their stock through thick and thin, often at great personal cost, instead of trading for millions in profit. During a Noranda common-share issue in 1985, Zimmerman was the only director to buy ten thousand shares; he financed the purchase on his own. "I don't need to be given any theology about the virtues of owning shares," he says. "I believe in it and I always have. Their theory is that that's incentive for remuneration and I think it would be a very difficult thing to control in a cyclical business."

During Noranda's lean years, the company cut out a number of internal boards of directors for which senior managers received fees. "None of that has been recognized at this stage," says Zimmerman, "but nobody needs to hold a tag day for me." For Zimmerman and Powis, the clash of cultures could be held at bay for a long time but never entirely resolved. Finally the group put its own man, David Kerr, in as point man in 1987. "I don't really know what kind of world they are looking for, but my world is building and running things. I'm more interested in that, so I feel quite detached from the other. I think it's a mistake in the end to try and. . . .'' He pauses and changes direction. "You can't make anybody be part of a family.''

The high priest of the Edper family is Jack Cockwell. A slightly built, trim man who almost fades into the landscape, he is the supreme arbiter of right and wrong within the empire. Here is the ego he hides from the world. He wrote what became the Edper creed in the early 1970s as a reaction to the chaos of the Bronfmans' holdings and the self-serving practices that were standard in the real-estate and investment industries. It was a natural thing for the young accountant to do, given his philosophical, reformist bent and his immigrant's reaction to a closed society.

He has a righteous indignation, a pure, clean fire in his breast. "There is a sort of spartan discipline about it,'' says Jim Leech of Cockwell's philosophy. "It's almost the Trudeau Jesuit thing; you know, you get it in the face every morning and it wakes you up.'' Outsiders agree that Cockwell's vision is rigid and narrow. It's his way or the doorway. He is impatient when people don't follow him, and contemptuous when they don't agree with him. In the Hees annual report for 1986, Cockwell typically rails against society's rules in defending his own system of management accountability: "Unfortunately, our legal system and the general public are more concerned with the rights of shareholders and managers than their responsibilities to perform and be held accountable.'' He doesn't believe in differences of opinion, and he usually doesn't have to. His technical skill is supreme, and others don't usually question the way he implements his ideas. According to Tom Kierans, president of Toronto brokerage firm McLeod Young Weir, "Jack invariably gets his own way.''

But funnily enough, one of the articles of faith Cockwell holds most dear is management by consensus. At Hees, the senior executives operate as a partnership, and investment decisions are made through consensus. It has been that way since the early days on Peel Street, when the "original five or six guys" operated out of the Edper office and each had a particular role in the great scheme of things. Don Wells, Jack's mentor at Touche Ross and a long-time friend, says the organization reminds him of a scene from the movie *The Great Escape*, where each member of a group of prisoners of war had a specific role that ensured the success of the group's escape from a German prison camp. "Tim [Price] is a negotiator, Dave [Kerr] is a closer, although now apparently he is a manager," Wells says in reference to Kerr's elevation to the top of Noranda. "Donnie [Marshall] looked after Edward." They worked on different aspects of a deal, but they had to agree on the result, because the result determined each person's financial compensation. When timing is crucial, three senior officers can commit Hees to a deal, even if it involves several hundred million dollars, provided they inform the remaining Hees partners and are confident they can win their approval "before the day is over." If consensus is not reached, the Hees rule is to get rid of the deal as soon as possible. "Senior officers of Hees act as a united force and speak with one voice to shareholders, bankers, and third parties," Cockwell's creed dictates, although it is also written policy to maintain a low public profile (except when issuing stock, it seems) and to operate in a "discreet manner beyond the immediate public eye."

That style of operation runs through Brascan and Trilon, as well. "We're strong people and we have our own opinions to put forth, but once a decision is taken it's a team decision," says Mel Hawkrigg. "There's none of that pride of authorship, none of that turf protection you find sometimes in other organizations." One story makes a telling counterpoint to the written creed. Upon reaching a tentative agreement during negotiations on a big deal, a senior officer from Hees told the other side he would have to seek approval of the management committee. He walked down the corridor to Cockwell's office and returned minutes later with approval. "*He* said the deal was okay," the Hees officer said with a wink. "Obviously," concedes Hawkrigg, "Jack and Trevor are the final authorities. They're the senior partners, where you ultimately go for full and final endorsement. We go to them as our mentors and our consultants.''

Within the tight-knit Edper group, there are two species of executive: the Cockwell people and the Eyton people. Wendy Cecil-Stuart calls Cockwell's young protégés at Hees "a whole different set of animals.'' Harold Wolkin, a financial analyst with Nesbitt Thomson, describes the scene at Hees: "When I go in there, they take off their jackets, we'll grab a sandwich and a Coke from the fridge, and we find a boardroom or just a couch to sit down, and we talk for half an hour or an hour, two hours.'' Adds Barney Finestone, a long-time Edper groupie who likes to have a sandwich with the Hees boys whenever he is in Toronto, "That's where they chew it up with each other. It's the most informal network you've ever seen in your life.'' Coffee meetings are enshrined in the Hees bible: "Hees senior officers are also encouraged to seek out and meet knowledgeable members of the business community to exchange views, preferably through short and to the point 'coffee meetings' rather than extensive lunches or other social engagements.'' Wolkin is pleased that he "can even get them out for a squash game.'' He says, "You can't do that with Trevor, Jack is too busy, Dunford is not that kind of person.'' He might have a discussion over coffee at Brascan, but the meeting must be set up weeks in advance and the tone is formal.

At Hees, says Wendy Cecil-Stuart, "They are not as interested in publicity. They want to do a good job, make money, change things, show that their values work.'' And there, Cockwell has his own apostles. Shared beliefs are a constant, if muted, strain at all group companies, but the strictest adherents within the Edper empire are at Hees, the company in which Cockwell's influence is most apparent. Cockwell is vice-chairman of Hees, and it is in Hees that Cockwell has most of his stockholdings. Hees officers are expected to be "positive and constructive in their approach to business and life in general.'' They have a do-it-yourself approach; they rarely employ outside consultants. Mike Cornelissen has said in the past that consultants "borrow your watch to tell you the time.''

Officers are held directly accountable for results at quarterly management meetings, where performance is judged and

futures are planned. Deals are not based on personal friendships, but on sound business principles, and Hees people are
reminded of their "special loyalty to Edper," which "entails
the absolute dedication of Hees' management and financial
resources to the support of Edper's strategic initiatives." As
well, like the crack squad in some corporate army, Hees executives are trained to be used by Edper "should the performance of a group company be below standard, or should the
management of a group company fail to conform to group
values." Hence the appearance of David Kerr at the helm of
Noranda in March 1987.

In its investment partnerships, Hees "looks for partners who
keep their word, who seek a fair sharing of rewards and do
not require written agreements to remind them of their commitments." Those entering into partnership deals with Hees
are expected to subscribe to the company's theology, and in
particular the fair-sharing principles. The fair sharing is crucial: the party initiating the deal is expected to ensure its success, and the profit share is divided so that the one at full risk
gets eighty per cent; the one at low risk gets twenty per cent.
Any more profit than expected is regarded as the fair share
due the side whose idea it was in the first place.

Finally, Cockwell exhorts his people to promote the Hees
team "in a friendly, professional manner" and to ensure that
Hees' actual performance always exceeds a client's expectations. The people are required to be punctual for meetings,
to return telephone calls, and to be as cost-conscious with the
funds of clients and partners as Hees is with its own funds.
They are urged, in short, to be immaculate in thought, perfect
in deed.

Cockwell prefers to draw his people from familiar sources.
He has hired a number of group executives from Touche Ross,
including Tim Price and Michael Cornelissen. Cockwell also
displays a chauvinistic appreciation for South Africans; Cornelissen, Manfred Walt at Hees, and Kevin Benson at Trizec
are fellow countrymen. Walt worked with Touche Ross in
Johannesburyg; Benson worked with Cornelissen at an
accounting firm in Durban. Cornelissen, who works in
Brascan-controlled Royal Trust, is still the closest to Cockwell

in style and manner; Hees partner Bill L'Heureux once confided that Cornelissen wished Royal Trust was part of Hees rather than Brascan because Cornelissen was at heart a Hees person. Accountants are also part of the Cockwell specialty. Great Lakes president Ken Clarke, a Brit, is an old friend of Cockwell's from Touche Ross. Later Clarke was the point man for the group at Merrill Lynch before joining Edper. Trilon's Mel Hawkrigg, once president of Fuller Brush and an executive at Canada Trust, started at Clarkson Gordon, the group's second-team accountants.

But although he is an accountant, Hawkrigg is a Trevor Eyton person. Eyton has his own loyal coterie. He remains an honorary partner at the Toronto establishment law firm of Tory, Tory, Deslauriers and Binnington, and has plucked several partners from that fold, including Trilon's Gord Cunningham and Hees' Bill L'Heureux. L'Heureux is an anomaly at Hees, but he serves a purpose: he is the spokesman, the Eyton-like lieutenant in Cockwell's favourite company. Tory, Tory, Deslauriers and Binnington continues to be Brascan's corporate counsel; Eyton's personal lawyer at the Sinclair Stevens hearings was Tory, Tory partner Lorne Morphy, a close friend from University of Toronto days. Touche Ross retains the account of many of the group companies. "There are two sorts of people there," says Jim Leech. "They are the Touche Ross accountants and the Tory, Tory lawyers. And they've got this corporate culture they instil in you." Other people are chosen for their track record or their promise. George Myhal joined the group after emerging as a star pupil in York University's finance program. In 1987, at age thirty-two, he was promoted to become one of six managing partners at Hees. Frank Lochan has risen steadily through the group ranks. At one point, he was the treasurer at both Brascan and Trilon. On the other side of the ledger, Trevor Eyton has proven himself adept at spotting good public-image talent. He hired the smooth-talking Mel Hawkrigg and convinced Hart McDougall — "his blood is a special kind of blue," Eyton once said of McDougall admiringly — to move from vice-chairman at the Bank of Montreal to be chairman of Royal Trust. Eyton also scooped up Allen Lambert, former chairman of the Toronto-Dominion Bank, and made him head of the board of a number of Trilon-sphere companies. When Lambert turned seventy-five in 1987 and had to, by law, give up some of his board directorships, he was brought onto the board of Labatt's and Brascan. He is considered sacred, both for his stature in the community and for his independence of thought; insiders insist he is still active in decision-making. Don Wells says the group's care in choosing and using its executives is at the heart of the corporate creed, which "is all about the development of people."

Many of the accolytes take their lead from Jack Cockwell and avoid ostentation. Senior people live in Rosedale or in Moore Park, a kind of Rosedale-in-training located nearby. Edward and Peter Bronfman live relatively simply, given their immense personal wealth and family background. Peter's home, in downtown Toronto, would be a Yuppie's pride and joy, but it is certainly not the usual billionaire's home. Aside from the designated social butterflies like Eyton, Royal Trust's Hart McDougall, and Wendy Cecil-Stuart, group executives don't throw big parties. "I guess they just don't get off on those trappings of power necessarily, that maybe we all did or our bank managers still do," observes Unicorp's Jim Leech caustically.

They network and they head charitable organizations with unsurpassed zeal. "The first social responsibility of the business [at Hees] is to create capital," according to the company's written corporate values and shared beliefs. After that, and after they achieve personal financial independence, Hees officers are free to support educational, athletic, and philanthropic activities — on their *own* time. "Hees' basic belief [is] that philanthropic giving is essentially a personal matter rather than a corporate issue," the literature says. However, an exception is made when "senior officers or valued business associates have dedicated a meaningful amount of personal time or contributed personal resources to a cause [that] has meaningfully increased the community's respect for the Hees Group." In 1984, Michael Cornelissen chaired the Metro Toronto United Way campaign with unprecedented success. In Hees' view, that "brought considerable goodwill and honour to Royal Trust."

In 1985, Hees made a corporate contribution to the United Way that was equal to the total donations of its senior officers and employees.

The Edper group is a family rather than a social set. When Mel Hawkrigg talks about expansion into the United States, he says, "I'm talking about family going and doing a job in the States like we've been doing here in Canada." And, as in any family, it is difficult to break away. Only one member of the holding-company team has quit since Edper took over Brascan and began setting up its current corporate apparatus. Ian Jamieson, a highly respected, no-nonsense Scot who runs the huge Dofasco pension fund, was hired in the summer of 1981 to bring the financial-services companies controlled by Edper under the Brascan umbrella. Jamieson, then fifty, was wooed by Cockwell, whom he had known for some years. Jamieson found the Edper environment very comfortable, free of the usual office politics, and he liked the analytical rigour the group applied to everything it did. "It wasn't a case of struggling to overcome antagonisms," he recalls. "Everyone knew everyone, it was a tight group, and you didn't report to this guy or that guy." But that very quality eventually drove Jamieson away, because he grew frustrated with the management-by-consensus doctrine and the cautious approach that Edper's partners, the Reichmanns, were urging in dealing with the Ken White old guard at newly acquired Royal Trust. Jamieson's departure opened the door for Earl Orser to expand his activities beyond London Life and Mel Hawkrigg was hired by Eyton to co-ordinate Trilon. "The turnover has been just about nil," says Mel Hawkrigg, "because of the whole package and how close-knit we are as a group. We're very careful and very selective when we hire."

Instilled in the family members is a belief that they are chosen. Sprinkled throughout the conversations of almost every Edper executive are words like "superior" and "exceptional" to describe themselves and their colleagues. "I'd like to have the house lights up so that we can see this exceptional group," Trevor Eyton said at the Brascan annual meeting. "It's once in a lifetime to get involved with some very superior people," said Hawkrigg during an interview. When explaining that he was complimented that a Cabinet minister had asked for the group's help to privatize Crown corporations (see Chapter Twelve), Eyton made sure to tell a government inquiry that his colleagues were "people that had special qualities," and added, "I am proud of the quality of the people that I work with."

The family that plays together stays together. "We've got a formula of success, not only for rewards for each of us individually, but also a formula for personal relationships," said Hawkrigg. The group believes in sport. It instils "the right values" through good, clean, hard fun. Eyton's days as a football hero have stood him in good stead in business, and his passion for Toronto's domed stadium is something only a jock could muster. Cockwell was a rugby player and an amateur boxer in South Africa — his ears still bear the scars — and he relishes an aggressive game of soccer. At the group's annual summer picnic one year, the soccer game was so rough that Cockwell broke his collarbone and another enthusiastic company athlete broke an ankle. Mike Cornelissen's passion is for sailing; he sails out of the Oakville Yacht Club near his suburban Toronto home, and is organizing the financing of Canada's entry in the next America's Cup. Ken Clarke loves nothing more than to beat his chief operating officer, Sandy Reilly, in a sailing race. Wendy Cecil-Stuart is an accomplished marathon runner. Peter Widdrington loves to play hockey with the boys from the plant; Hart McDougall's "tennis-anyone" training is woven into the tapestry of happy men on the playing field. Edward Bronfman is an expert skier and his brother, Peter, while mediocre at many of the sports he attempts, is a committed hockey fan. Gord Cunningham played college hockey against Montreal Canadiens' goalie Ken Dryden, who still remembers Cunningham's finesse on the ice. For the Edper family, a high energy level is as necessary as slide-rule precision in upholding their special brand of belief.

While Jack Cockwell is the high priest of the Edper creed,

Trevor Eyton, like any convert, is more holy than the holies. He is the public preacher; he immerses corporate Canada in the sacred teachings. Trevor told a public inquiry in 1986, when describing the group's beliefs, that they are "more" than mere words on paper. "While the heading in the reports is 'Business Principles,' they are also invariably our practice."

Behind the united front, however, fundamental changes have occurred. Cracks had been forming for some time, under the pressure of corporate evolution; then a personal drama, played out in the offices of Brascan, accelerated the process. Wendy Cecil-Stuart was a central figure. She is a dynamic woman who first joined Brascan in 1974, when Jake Moore still ruled the roost. Born in Stratford, Ontario, in 1948, she had arrived at Brascan with a B.A. from the University of Toronto and three years' experience at the Toronto Stock Exchange as a public-information officer. At Brascan she began to move up the ladder in the public-relations department. She took an executive-management program at York University in 1977. She proved her political mettle when she survived a changing of the guard in 1979, when the Edper forces moved into Commerce Court. She began to learn about other areas of the business, and became involved in issues and public policies at the company. By 1987, she sat on the boards of several Edper holding companies: Great Lakes Group, where she was also a vice-president and corporate secretary; Brascan Holdings; Brascan Resources; Brookfield Investments; and Carena-Bancorp.

As a vice-president of Brascan, Wendy Cecil-Stuart was the highest-ranking woman in the group. In a candid 1984 interview, during which he expressed genuine surprise at the suggestion that she could head a company, Eyton admitted that he didn't spend much time thinking about having senior women in the group's companies. He explained why there were no female board directors: "First of all, it's habit. That's the way things are and it's perceived that way. When most senior management on boards are looking at successon, they tend to be male and they tend to try to carry on the male process."

He added that "there is a kind of a structure to corporations that I think makes it more difficult for a woman to achieve the highest office." Attitudes also play a part, Eyton offered. "It's aggressiveness and just a desire and a commitment." He hasn't met many women who would tell him they want the job, that they're willing to sacrifice their personal lives and prove they deserve the job. "It's possible for a man to be one-sided, to be macho and masculine and to have that overriding commitment. I think it's harder for a woman to be feminine and attractive and function with that same commitment. More is expected of a woman. In fact, they demonstrate a better balance, but it still means it's harder for them."

It's not a risk, he added, to place a woman in a senior position, but it would be to place her at the top. There is the worry of community reaction; the worry of whether a woman will "be able to command." "Dealing with subordinates is the biggest single challenge the woman will have to face," he declared. "She's got to be tough enough to deal with recalcitrants that aren't giving their full cooperation."

Since then, in 1985, Brascan plucked American Jill Conway, president of the women's university Smith College, for its board. Jo-Anne Chang stands out as the other female incursion into the group ranks as associate treasurer at Hees. At Royal Trust, Sheila Robb holds the more traditional woman's post of vice-president, public affairs — but reports to another male vice-president, while the other VPs all report to the president. In the summer of 1987, Robb plunged into a personal nightmare when her husband was charged by British police with killing her lover, a senior executive of the London office of international public relations giant, Burson-Marsteller. In January 1988, he was convicted and sentenced to three years in a British jail. Royal stood behind her during the crisis, and she continued in her job there.

Wendy Cecil-Stuart has worked for her laurels. Yet her greatest coup was in working her way into the macho world of Edper-Brascan by taking up the gruelling sport of long-distance running. She became extremely good at it, winning the Toronto Marathon as well as foreign long-distances races. Doing so well at running, she liked to say, showed the men at Brascan that she could apply herself to something and conquer it. And it was something the jocks at the office could relate to. She scorns equal opportunity initiatives, feeling success must come by working from within the system. In a 1984 interview, she cited a *Fortune* magazine article about how executives are chosen: "The biggest hurdle is a matter of comfort, not competence; someone who fits, someone who gets along, someone you trust." She crossed that barrier. By 1986, she was vice-president of business development at Brascan. But she was still responsible for the group's — and Eyton's — public relations.

In the pressure-cooker atmosphere of Edper, where a small group of people work together for long hours, personal relationships are intense. As his aide-de-camp, Cecil-Stuart travelled extensively with Eyton and worked closely with him in the office. When Brascan held a reception as, say, a sponsor of the National Ballet, it was Cecil-Stuart who co-hosted with Eyton, rather than Eyton's wife Jane. The situation was unusual and the result was predictable, particularly on macho Bay Street. Rumors spread of an affair between the two. Cecil-Stuart over the years became all too aware of the rumors, which some people in the group's orbit enjoyed parading as fact. They hung like a cloud over her reputation; she couldn't stop them, although she denied them. There is reason to believe that Jane Eyton accepted the rumors as truth. Cecil-Stuart recalls that Jane ran hot and cold with her; at one meeting she would be friendly, the next she would snub her husband's close colleague.

Cecil-Stuart's role within the group — and her relationship with Trevor Eyton — shifted dramatically, however, after her life took a significant turn in 1985. With one marriage and some relationships behind her, the thirty-six-year-old entertained thoughts of becoming a single mother. The group's theology includes full disclosure of personal finances and intimate personal goals — a corporate confessional. At a formal career-planning session with Jack Cockwell, Cecil-Stuart raised the idea of single motherhood. Some time later — Cecil-Stuart says it was a year later — Cockwell, who was separated from his second wife, asked her, "Why not give me a chance?" At the Brascan annual meeting in 1986, she was happily and visibly pregnant. On July 30, she gave birth to a daughter, Tessa, named after a journalist acquaintance at a financial newspaper.

After a trip to South Africa, where they were married under that country's law, Wendy changed the name she used publicly to Cecil-Cockwell. She and Jack bought a comfortable house in Rosedale from Michael Sanderson (chairman of Merrill Lynch Canada). Insiders say Cockwell's substantial personal wealth, estimated at about $50 million, complicated his divorce. Under Cecil-Stuart's influence, he began attending more social events; he hosted a gala reception for opera star Joan Sutherland and her maestro husband, Richard Bonynge, at their new home in April 1987. But his alliance with Cecil-Stuart caused tension within the Edper empire, because it attracted unwanted publicity. Cecil-Stuart's proclivities for media relations had also triggered concern among some people in Edper about Cockwell's rise in the public conscience. Cecil-Stuart happily posed in her new kitchen with her baby for a show called "Successful Career Woman," a half-hour program aired on the CTV network in late January, 1987. During the show she talked about life with Cockwell. Then, in April 1987, the *Wall Street Journal* ran an article that focused on Jack as the group mentor, strategist, and back-room genius, and gave details of Cockwell's and Cecil-Stuart's relationship. Certainly for some in the Brascan circle, the spectre of a prominent executive such as Cockwell moving from a marriage to a new relationship with an attractive colleague such as Cecil-Stuart was tremendously disturbing. By the summer of 1987, the tension caused by the relationship between Cockwell and Cecil-Stuart proved too much for even the broad-minded Bronfmans. Cecil-Stuart resigned her position at Edper and set up a public-relations business, which she runs from her home, and became pregnant for a second time. The relationship created a permanent rent in the Edper fabric. Said Cecil-Stuart of Cockwell's and Eyton's relationship, "Two or three years ago, they were more of a package."

Until recently, Trevor Eyton was the public face of the Edper group, "the statesman who took the public flak and glory," as Cecil-Stuart described him in 1984. Brascan, for example, was known commonly as "Trevor Eyton's Brascan." In the early 1980s, recalls Tom Kierans, high-finance types knew that Cockwell was "seriously smart and very determined," but for most outsiders, "the gap between Cockwell and Trevor Eyton was like night and day. Trevor was not only the front man, he was *the* man."

But by August 1986, the media had at last fixed on Jack Cockwell as the centre of power. *Globe and Mail* reporter Paul Goldstein identified Cockwell as the chief strategist for Peter and Edward Bronfman, as a living legend on Bay Street, and as a secretive genius who preferred to let smooth-talking lawyers Eyton and Bill L'Heureux speak publicly for the empire. Now, says Harold Wolkin, the companies have issued too much stock to hide under Eyton's mantle. One of the things that particularly irked Eyton about the *Wall Street Journal* article was that, before an élite business audience across North America, his share of the spotlight was partly obscured by the public emergence of Jack Cockwell. Cecil-Stuart says that Eyton is scared; he wants to keep his image but he believes he is "in danger of being overshadowed." As for the new corporate line that emerged during 1987, of a core group of twenty-five indispensable group officers, Eyton "would be happy not to say it," says Cecil-Stuart. At an annual meeting in the spring of 1987, held at the luxurious Four Seasons Hotel, Eyton dutifully told assembled shareholders that their thirty-per-cent annual rate of return from share-price appreciation and cash dividends over the preceding five years "is due to the collective and individual efforts of more than twenty-five key executives."

Equally bothersome to Eyton was the Hees annual meeting, which had taken place several weeks before in a small hall at Commerce Court. Tim Price, David Kerr, Tim Casgrain, and Manfred Walt had explained to an overflow crowd the Hees partnership arrangement and unusual corporate beliefs. It seemed to observers that the company had finally come into its own and blossomed as a spectacular corporate flower. Cecil-Stuart said that, after the meeting, Eyton and Peter Bronfman were struck by the sudden notion of Hees as a world unto itself. In fact, when Eyton saw an organizational chart depicting Hees on top of Brascan, he became angry and said, "This is a financial chart, not a management chart."

In contrast, Manfred Walt publicly stated some months later that, within the group, Hees had been acknowledged as the senior group company since 1983. Harold Wolkin says: "Four years ago, Hees was not even a known factor to most public companies, but [now] Trevor Eyton doesn't speak for the group any more than Cockwell or Tim Price or David Kerr or Bill L'Heureux or Manfred Walt. There has been a major transformation of the group over the last couple of years." That transformation includes managerial succession, which is best demonstrated by the appointment of the Hees management partners — of which much was made at the Hees annual meeting in March 1987 — and the move of David Kerr out of Hees to Noranda. Says Wolkin, "The opportunity and the ability for them to move him out completely into Noranda shows a strength, not a weakness. They were ready to give his responsibilities within Hees to other individuals and let him bring a new generation of thinking and management to Noranda."

There is no doubt that the Bronfman brothers had hired some good people in the sixties, and they had the wisdom to give Jack Cockwell a free hand in developing the theology of the group. Paul Lowenstein, a former Edper manager and board director, says, "They had in Jack more confidence than they had given to any other person that they had hired." But that confidence was not a reflection of any particular philosophy. Says Wolkin, "I don't think there is a particular moral or business ethic that the Bronfmans expound." Leonard Spilfogel, who maintains good relations with Peter and Edward Bronfman, was asked if the corporate theology is Peter's. He replied, "I don't think so. You have to understand what's happening here. There are multiples of rings going on. A lot of what you see is real and a lot of what you see is fictitious, and I'd say very few people really understand. But I think when you see things that are in public, that are written, that's not Peter and Edward; those are Jack and maybe Trevor. Peter is more interested in where is the boat going? Are we [going] in the right direction? Are we making progress?" The most important decision the Bronfmans made was in trusting Jack Cockwell. "As for all that philosophical stuff, well, it keeps Jack happy."

Cockwell began shaping his beliefs and theology soon after joining Edper, in 1968. In 1974, Cockwell borrowed $1.2 million to buy shares in Mico. His salary that year was $20,000. In 1979, in a rare interview, Peter Bronfman told Amy Booth of the *Financial Post*: "We encourage our guys to have a stake in the companies we invest in; we facilitate it sometimes. As a result they have a stake in their own future and we're all pulling in the same direction. . . . We like the top officials in the companies we control to have stock in the companies we control, too. Then it's like their money they are operating with. We don't want to be looking over their shoulders all the time. Our interest is in the bottom line."

Ten years later, the principle of ownership has, in effect, given the managers leverage over the Bronfmans. Collectively, the managers own millions in common equity in the group. Managers move up the ladder not through operational restructuring but through the creation of satellite companies. Wolkin calls Dexleigh, a company that was created to bail out Jimmy Kay (see Chapter Nine), "Son of Hees" because of the role of Bryan McJannet and other Hees boys in its re-creation. "Even Great Lakes is a spin-off with a whole new group of managers, Ken Clarke coming over from Merrill, there's seven other guys that have come in. There's plenty of management to draw on." He calls them the farm team, in which they groom executives within a company to be interchangeable. Jim Leech at Unicorp says, "The numbers of good, solid people are absolutely incredible. If there is a meeting with one person and he can't make it, they've got another ten guys they could send into that meeting and it won't make any difference. They can pull guys off the bench. The rest of us don't have that depth."

In setting up new rules of behaviour, the Edper group has rejected the standing rules. They have engaged in some of the most hostile takeovers in Canadian corporate history; they have gone head-to-head with the establishment; they have rewritten the rules for stock underwriting; and they have proven that control of an empire does not dictate one-hundred-per-cent ownership. When Jack Cockwell arrived, the Canadian business community received a kick in the pants. Alan Hockin says the lessons were needed. "They are bringing, into Canadian business, thinking and management and concepts that I think should be of benefit, not just for that company [Edper] but to the whole country. Because that is building for the future, it's not taking a quick high return now. It's working hard. All of these things which I think Canadian business needed to learn." Even people who had serious questions about the Edper group's actions in the past now hold it up as an example of a new business philosophy. Says Tom Kierans: "We have new standards of operating businesses to work by, and these guys have been part of the catalyst for change."

Such a drastic change in business philosophy must arouse controversy. Some business people believe in the new Brascan-style management, and others disapprove. Says Jim Leech, "It's that owner-manager mentality versus just a manager where a lot of companies grew up and were allegedly successful, but had built in so many layers of fat and extra perqs that they lost perspective. There is the famous story about Massey Ferguson, when somebody asked how much it cost to make a tractor, and nobody could answer the question." That clearly could never happen at an Edper company.

Canadian businesses have become lean and mean, but few have adopted the entire Edper theology. First-class airfares have been replaced by executive class, but executives still travel to meetings in cars rather than on the subway. Cockwell takes the subway. Even Jim Leech, who subscribes to the shareholder-manager theology, sees the Edper group as an extreme form of the species. "They've been the epitome of it, but [you can't] accomplish what they have done without being really disciplined, setting out single-mindedly with the purpose of getting from A to B."

What alienates ordinary mortals from the group are its intolerance of other styles and its arrogance, which are reflections of Jack Cockwell. One friend of the Edper group tells the story of John Scrymgeour, founder of Westburne International Industries and its chairman from 1959 to 1987. Scrymgeour's company paid for a 727 jet, a flat in London, a place in Barbados, and a cottage in the ski resort of Windemere, British Columbia. Scrymgeour sat on the board and executive committee of Brascan, and is a friend of the Bronfmans. When Jack Cockwell learned of Scrymgeour's extravagant ways, he refused to talk to him and called him unprintable names behind his back.

The Canadian government could enshrine the rules it wants Canadian businesses to use. "If you don't want a France system, in which all the rules are written out for the reasons of a market economy, you have to have unwritten rules," says one observer, who feels the Edper group has done "violence to the system" by breaking the existing rules of behaviour. The group, meanwhile, would like its own beliefs incorporated into the system. Says Harold Wolkin, "There is no group of managers that feels more pressured to make clear to the investment public what their moral principles about business are." Alf Powis, now elder statesman at Noranda, studied free trade for the group; Manfred Walt at Hees prepared a group paper on how tax reform would affect the group, the market, and the business community. The Trilon boys were immersed in the future of financial institutions; they wanted to set Ottawa's agenda for the decade. The group works together on these issues. Says Wolkin, "Any major initiative is a group effort." Trevor Eyton co-ordinates this public-policy agenda.

This accommodation of the beliefs of the public is a major change in the group's way of thinking. They have always asked their shareholders to trust them. Group executives have been shocked by open questioning of their values. Hockin, an admirer of the group, still agrees that they have, in the past, viewed dissenters as troublemakers who should be avoided and ignored. He doesn't agree. "Anyone who had been really sensitive to the outside environment shouldn't have been shocked. This is the way the world is today. The public is extremely sceptical, not just about Trilon or about Brascan. . . . It doesn't matter what it is, and it's a fact of life. You've got to live with it."

One Brascan-watcher speculates that Trevor Eyton, the collegiate football centre, "sensed changes in the field" after Jack Cockwell vented his righteous indignation when the group's methods were publicly questioned by the House of Commons Finance Committee in the summer of 1986. When asked to account for itself by politicians, the group lost control of the way it presented itself. Eyton is reasserting that control. Other aspects of the group are being opened for scrutiny; the investing public and the public at large want to know exactly how they work. Harold Wolkin cites the 1986 Hees annual meeting, held in April 1987, as a good example of this new openness. "They came clean on a number of issues that they hadn't before. In fact, anyone who was there had to chuckle a little bit for George Myhal, who seemed to get cornered into answering a couple of questions he didn't know if he should or could answer. But he answered them anyway, and no one seemed to care."

When Brascan group people want to show that their theology is in the vanguard of change, they cite their Business Conduct Review Committees. These committees are supposed to review all significant deals between group companies or individuals. But people at Brascan were talking as though the committees were established long before they were actually in place, which may have hurt their credibility. In 1985, Royal Trust made a $10 million stock investment along with several other group companies in Leech's Unicorp's stock, in what later looked like a Brascan-orchestrated conspiracy. Jack Cockwell admitted that the Business Conduct Review Committee had not been asked to review the investment. "The shares were purchased at the initiative of management, and they did consider whether there was any conflict with any other group company, and decided that there was no such conflict that needed to go before the Business Conduct Review Committee," Cockwell stated. Admits Alan Hockin, "They are still feeling their way as to how they will actually operate."

The committees are a crucial element in the drive for public acceptance of the Brascan way. They are meant to compensate for the fact that the managers are so close to the controlling shareholders, and to counter the perception that the managers care only about the Bronfmans and themselves. In

1984, Brascan owned fifty per cent of the shares of Royal Trust. Brascan sought to remove a long-standing bylaw that restricted voting to ten per cent, regardless of the percentage shares owned. Minority shareholders and non-aligned board members were understandably reluctant. Brascan's lawyers thought the bylaw could be defeated in court. A committee of independent board directors was charged with finding a solution to the impasse. The committee, which retained Eyton's old personal friend Purdy Crawford as its counsel, devised a constitution that would provide safeguards against conflicts of interest and self-dealing abuses, including the Business Conduct Review Committee. Says Jack Cockwell, "If at any stage one of the senior companies tried to impose a transaction on a junior company, the management of that company or the independent directors have a ready audience to blow the whistle."

These actions by Edper are, most of all, meant to squelch all the talk about conflict of interest arising from transactions between the group's companies. Says Harold Wolkin, "I think the group works as hard at credibility as it does at getting its earnings to come in as expected, or raising new financing for a new deal, or anything else." Alan Hockin says the committees are "no rubber stamp or pretty front. There is reality behind it." Hockin is on the Trilon committee. Trilon couldn't set up a business conduct review committee of outside directors when it wanted to because "it didn't have enough outside directors." Hockin was "a committee of one" for a while, the only outsider; he brought in public thought. While Trilon doesn't always like his perspective, Hockin insists they listen.

It would be easy to dismiss the Edper gospel as so much window-dressing, designed to cover up a bullying, secretive corporate style. Certainly Cockwell and his patrons, the Bronfmans, are inclined to secrecy and anonymity. But for Cockwell, it is a logical personality for a private family fortune. And for Cockwell, who is so sure of himself, so certain that he is right and that he does right by those who trust him, it is untenable and outrageous that outsiders should question his methods and his motives. In an interview in 1986, Bill L'Heureux observed that Cockwell has high moral standards. L'Heureux says,

"Cockwell will declare to anyone who will listen, 'They are not principles that are hidden away, they are published for the whole world to see. We are confident that we can match them against any practised elsewhere that we are aware of. And we are comfortable having our behaviour measured against those principles.'"

Cockwell's strength of character in the old-fashioned sense is best demonstrated by his penchant for staying in the background and for eschewing fancy titles and trappings. His ego doesn't need them. But his ferocious temper and his legendary impatience erupt when people fail to see how utterly right he is, when they fail to acknowledge the pre-eminence of the group's theology. "He is," wrote *Globe and Mail* reporter Paul Goldstein in 1986, "almost evangelical on business morality."

The test of true morality comes at the moment the end justifies the means. For some who have come up against the Edper Goliath, it is a test Cockwell, a mere mortal, has failed. For Tom Kierans, Cockwell is like many other businessmen. "The group's theology," observes Tom Kierans, "is a combination of common sense, good intentions, religion, and personal greed. It's the usual mixture."

CHAPTER SEVEN

The Front Man

If there were phone messages on your desk from Trevor Eyton, Paul Reichmann, John Bassett, and Peter Bronfman, whose call would you return first?
— from *Toronto Life* magazine, which, in May 1986, ranked Trevor Eyton as the most influential man in Toronto.

When John Trevor Eyton talks to the press, he always runs over the allotted time. He might start by stating bluntly, in the impersonal mode he favours and with a glance at his watch, "I have something less than half an hour." But after the coffee and the chocolate-chip cookies have arrived, he is caught up in stories of his own weaving, and the interview stretches on, past an hour, beyond its original purpose. Eyton lingers at its finish, edging the journalist into a tour of the Brascan art collection or an introduction to a guest who has been left waiting in the lobby. Eyton's cautious lawyer's mein has been replaced by a painful eagerness to close the deal. There is a plea for approval in the smile of this middle-aged man with the balding, sandy pate, a tension in the pasty face, and a defensiveness in the awkward slope of his shoulders. In the intricate dance of words between raconteur and scribe, Eyton is both master and victim of his own choreography.

171

Eyton's relationship with the press cuts both ways. This has been his most controversial role since he joined the Brascan empire and exchanged the persona of advisor for that of front man for the group. At first, the business community was leery of Brascan, and Eyton jammed his evenings with two or three parties, the better to gladhand. Yet he did an admirable job of soothing the media. An unlikely candidate, with his permanent-wrinkle suits and steel-rimmed glasses, he became a media star, titillating business writers with naughty stories about the big banks, always a favourite target. He became a valued source, an amazingly open chieftain of a very closed-mouthed empire.

The media believed for a while that talking to Eyton was the next best thing to talking to Peter and Edward Bronfman. Eyton revelled in the attention. In 1979, as he began to ascend the ranks at Brascan, he also began collecting clippings for an authorized book on the Edper group. After Peter Newman portrayed Eyton's buddy Conrad Black as the epitome of the Canadian establishment, Eyton began to court Newman to write the Brascan story.

But the jackal press is fickle. It values its reputation for judgement; it is ruthless when it feels it has been taken. For a journalist, the reward is a reputation for savvy, for knowing the right people and pegging who is and isn't worth cultivating. There are two particular sins the media will never forgive: a source who is puffed up in admiring pieces, then later suspected of abusing the media system; and a source who is not as powerful as he initially sets himself up to be. When Trevor Eyton appeared on the cover of *Toronto Life* magazine as the most influential person in the city, his image as the eyes, ears, and brains of Brascan was already unravelling. Eyton was so upset at the *Globe and Mail*'s coverage at one point in the mid-1980s that he paid a visit to the newsroom in an unsuccessful bid to remove a reporter from the Brascan beat. In fact, beginning in late 1985, Trevor Eyton was being judged by the paparazzi and found wanting.

After the *Toronto Life* article was published, Eyton denied that he was Toronto's most influential man, with what was, for him, a surprisingly simple declaration: "I don't feel like it." He even agreed that Jack Cockwell was the back-room boy, Eyton the front man. Eyton added, "I'd like to think that he's also a spokesman, and that I'm a little bit inspired now and then. But we're very much a team and have been for a long time." To the media, with its need for black-and-white reality, Eyton's statement was prevarication — they only wanted to talk to the powerhouse. If Cockwell was the real puppeteer for the group, he was the one they would seek out. But such an attitude was as nearsighted as their earlier fad of lionizing Eyton. To understand the empire, it is necessary to comprehend the front man.

At the turn of the century, Trevor Eyton's paternal grandfather arrived in Nelson, British Columbia. Nelson was a mining town, reminiscent of Grandfather Eyton's home in North Wales, where he had been that rarest of personages, a well-off man in a poor mining community. "I doubt if my grandfather had worked nine to five very long," says Eyton's cousin Rhys Eyton. He was "the local gentry." He and his Welsh bride had three children, a daughter and two sons, Jack and Geoffrey Tudor. The daughter and one son moved to Vancouver; Jack moved east, to Quebec, where he worked for Abitibi Paper. Trevor was born in Quebec City on July 12, 1934; his father's job took the family to Toronto a few years later.

With his elder sister, Marion, and baby brother, Tony, Trevor lived with his parents in a modest home north of Danforth Avenue near Broadview, then a middle-class Anglo stronghold. He was a star football player at Jarvis Collegiate, although friends teasingly referred to him as "the oaf." His future wife, Jane Montgomery, lived in Rosedale and attended private schools. They married while she was nursing and Eyton was in his second year at the University of Toronto's Victoria College. Some old friends credit his father-in-law, Dr. R.C.

Montgomery, the chief medical officer at Crown Life Insurance, with an enormous influence over Eyton's early career. Montgomery's encouragement and Eyton's new role as a husband helped him to overcome a shaky start at university and graduate with a gold medal in 1957. Then he gained top honours at the exclusive and demanding University of Toronto Law School.

Through university, through law school, Eyton played football. Even today, the way Trevor Eyton presents himself and the terminology he uses are influenced by the fact that he was a university football star. Eyton was a centre — one of the guys who keep their legs open to receive the ball. Eyton still walks with that funny, sea-legs style. Toronto politician and lawyer Julian Porter, a friend of Eyton's for three decades, remembers playing beside him on offense at University of Toronto's Victoria College. "He was a hard-working, disciplined athlete. . . . He was essentially a better player than I was, but we played the first string together in the last year, when we won all the games." Eyton was captain of the team that year. "He was not the fellow that you would have the concept of being the leader," reflects Porter. "But he was the leader, very quiet, with a good, droll way about him." As would be his pattern in his business life, Eyton traded off the strengths of others on the team: "He had a couple of people around who happened to be the world's best linebacks."

Rhys Tudor Eyton, Trevor's first cousin, has built a career from the family's Western Canadian base. Only a year younger than Eyton although he looks several years his junior, Rhys emerged as a business star in 1987 after his Western Pacific Airlines was a willing participant in a reverse takeover by Canadian Pacific Airlines, to create Canadian Airlines International (CAI), a strong number two to Air Canada. Rhys didn't meet his Central Canadian family until high school; he became well acquainted with Trevor only when he attended the University of Western Ontario between 1955 and 1958 and visited with his uncle, aunt, and three cousins in Toronto. Even that far back, Eyton was well connected, Rhys recalls. "He has a very close network of friends in the Toronto area who have always been high achievers. . . . Trevor has a very unique talent, he is so affable and has the appearance of being unassuming."

Eyton's friends point out that the friendships that have been at the base of his career were cultivated particularly during university days; he left many of his Jarvis Collegiate friends behind, although he is still close to Lorne Morphy, a Jarvis graduate who worked with him at Tory, Tory, Deslauriers and Binnington. A few years after graduation, Eyton urged his university friends to take a little flyer on an investment club. Each member could contribute a bit of expertise and have some fun at an annual dinner paid for by the club's profits. Members of the Canyon Beauport Club include Julian Porter, Lloyd's Bank of Canada president David Lewis, Fred McCutcheon, Allan Slaight, and a cast of other bright young (and often wealthy) men who have become major players on the Bay Street stage.

In a strange way, it's the ability to connect that has created a successful diplomatic career for Eyton's younger brother, Tony, according to Rhys. Tony, who spent five years as ambassador to Brazil, where Brascan still is Canada's largest single corporate presence, returned to External Affairs in Ottawa in 1986. The two brothers' roles differ, Rhys hastens to point out. "Tony is really representing various political views, Trevor is really shaping those at Brascan. . . . They are both equally talented at being able to put them across in a saleable way."

Trevor Eyton's network resembles that of another lawyer, Brian Mulroney, who is a recent but warm acquaintance. Like Mulroney, Eyton has found that the penchant for networking that made a good fraternity type was a natural for the practice of law. Lawyering is, after all, a service business. Despite the gold medal in university, Eyton has never been a stickler for detail. He is an ideas guy, not a details person. Eyton says his skills lie in "rules, regulations, and the written word." Andy Sarlos, a long-time friend, credits him with "a knowledge of how business is conducted." And for Jim Leech of Unicorp, Eyton's value is as a conciliator. "He did a very good job at endeavouring to try and bring temperatures down," Leech says of the post-takeover meetings between Union Gas and Unicorp directors. Eyton is a manipulator of words, ideas, stories, people. "His forte in the old days," recalls Porter, "was always talking, sitting and talking, controlling."

While the approach is understated, it is carefully designed to elicit the right reaction from the listener. Eyton likes to tell stories; some listeners say he has a tendency for the dramatic, the apocryphal tale. Bronfman family friend Barney Finestone calls it a native instinct, the kind a good politician has. "He instinctively has the feeling of how one has to reassemble the data," says Finestone of Eyton's clear memory for detail in story-telling. "If you are honest, you never lie, but you sure can reshape facts so as to reach a more agreeable conclusion."

His controlling approach can be attractive to clients. "He's smart, and he has a nice way of unravelling whatever he is talking about, and he's very persuasive," says Porter. "That's our business, one way or another. Forms of persuasion."

David Dennis recognized just that element of confident persuasion in Eyton. Dennis is the son of Reuben Dennis, who, during the 1950s and 1960s, was one of Toronto's largest apartment developers. David Dennis calls his company Third Generation Realty, but despite his father's portfolio in the 1960s, Dennis was unsure about how to move into the big leagues. He graduated from the Osgoode Hall law school three years before Eyton obtained his law degree from the University of Toronto. The two met while Dennis was working with his father; the Dennises were negotiating with Roy Thomson to build a headquarters in downtown Toronto for the international media chain owned by Thomson. Eyton's law firm, Tory, Tory, Deslauriers and Binnington, handled the giant Thomson account. Co-founder John Tory usually represented Thomson at the negotiating table, but at times he was seconded or even replaced by Eyton. Dennis was acting as the lawyer as well as a co-owner of the property; he and Eyton finalized the deal.

After the deal was signed, Dennis hired Eyton as his own personal lawyer, as well as the lawyer for the family group of companies; over the years, the two have become friends. Dennis wanted a lawyer who understood how business is done, not some academic worried about the structure of the document. "The job of lawyer is not only to protect clients but to make a deal. It makes little sense having a perfect contract that never gets signed." He also chose a lawyer who would project the right image. "Trevor is bright, but more than that he is very personable. That part of his characteristic was very important to me. I was then emerging as a business person, feeling my way . . . it was a very personal kind of decision."

A number of Eyton's clients were entrepreneurs, people pleased with the cachet Trevor Eyton could provide. One of his biggest clients in the 1970s was Bruce McLaughlin, whose development company, S.B. McLaughlin Limited (later Mascan Limited) helped to create the building boom in Mississauga, Canada's ninth-largest city. McLaughlin was a member of Eyton's Canyon Beauport Club. But he became quite bitter toward Eyton after Edper withdrew its backing from his company in the mid-1970s. Still, his was a lone voice amid a chorus of fraternal approval, and most people blamed the split on McLaughlin.

When Peter Bronfman approved hiring Trevor Eyton as an advisor to Edper in the late 1960s, he was looking at many of the same qualities that had motivated David Dennis and Bruce McLaughlin to choose Eyton. The Bronfmans had originally turned to Tory, Tory, Deslauriers and Binnington when Austin Beutel and Ned Goodman were managing their portfolio. Eyton acted as the lawyer for a small chemical company, which was being refinanced by Toronto stockbroker Chuck Loewen. (Loewen was later a founding partner with Eyton's friend Fred McCutcheon in the brokerage firm of Loewen, Ondaatje, McCutcheon.) Edper was an investor, and Eyton negotiated with Beutel and Goodman. He did bits of legal work for the group in Ontario after that, and was eventually put on retainer by Neil Baker and Paul Lowenstein to be Edper's Ontario man. During the 1970s, Eyton became an increasingly important element of their corporate team.

It was really Jack Cockwell's idea to bring Eyton into Brascan as chief executive, but Peter broached the subject; he treated it as a bottom-line backing for Eyton's recommendation that the group buy Brascan in 1979. If they did buy it, Eyton must be prepared to commit himself to the company for two years. Bronfman agreed with Cockwell that this was a crucial time for the group, and its takeover of Brascan gave the group a presence in the strange, introspective, corporate world of Toronto. The group needed polish; they needed standing; they needed image. And they thought Eyton could help them acquire all those things. Kierans, of McLeod Young Weir, calls him "the vehicle." Says Kierans, "They [the Bronfmans] had the desire, and that was what Trevor Eyton tapped into." Peter Bronfman publicly puffed up his new boy, and the rest of the group fell in line behind him. Eyton didn't need any more of a signal as he set out to make himself a name. "In many respects, Trevor was given a history in 1979," says Wendy Cecil-Stuart.

Eyton downplays his eagerness to grasp the brass ring. "I had no choice to respond to the call when in fact it was made," he says of Peter's request that he join Brascan, "although it did come as somewhat of a surprise." Bronfman is equally eager to make it clear that Eyton was not forced to join the group. "Trevor was not lured out of Tory's, nor did he leave reluctantly," Bronfman says. "He agreed to come with us for a two-year trial period. The rest, as they say, is history."

David Dennis recalls how excited Eyton was about the move. They met to discuss it over drinks after Eyton told his client he would be leaving the firm. Dennis recalls that Eyton felt he could bring a new view to the group; after all, he was so involved already that he had become a "surrogate executive" at Brascan. The move was a natural one. Eyton says, "I do not feel that my role shifted markedly during the takeover of Brascan, although it clearly became more public."

When he arrived at Brascan as a real executive, Eyton took his black "Daytimer" diary out of his jacket pocket and set to work, organizing meetings with a pragmatic view to the group's strategy for conquering Bay Street. He had been an advisor before, but as a lawyer, he had had to remember his position. "They really wanted Trevor to take the lead in the public arena," says Dennis. And for a few years, it worked. In the early eighties, top executives on Bay Street thought Trevor Eyton was Brascan.

Eyton has always seen his role at Brascan as an anointment.

"I was formally designated as the senior spokesman for Edper," he says, with the emphasis on "senior." He feels he has been chosen to preach the gospel. His two-year term has stretched to nine years. Barney Finestone recalls calling Eyton in 1981 to tease him about his two-year commitment to the group. "I said, 'Trevor, I didn't see any announcement.' He said, 'No, well, we postponed that decision.' I said, 'You've been corrupted.' He said, 'I'm having such a good time.' " In fact, Eyton is now clinging to the role of Mr. Brascan, although the job has outgrown any one spokesman, and the corporate philosophy has changed to include other executives in the limelight. "At base," he said recently, "I don't think my role has changed."

In the decade since he became the front man, Eyton has weathered challenges from the media, politicians, and opposing business factions; the public ascendancy of Jack Cockwell; and the move to broaden the group's exposure to the public. At the same time, his role as Brascan ambassador to the country's élite has made him a public figure whose name is synonymous with the 1980s version of the cigar-chomping deal-maker. His foibles have been exposed to public view, as well. A 1987 fund-raising dinner for one of the charities to which Eyton lends his name was billed as an opportunity to roast him. Former Ontario Premier William Davis emceed the gathering of five hundred Torontonians who paid $250 a plate to poke fun at Eyton. Conrad Black entered in a veiled sedan chair carried by six cronies, including Julian Porter, Allan Slaight, and Trilon's Gord Cunningham, while Eyton was brought in through the back door. Halifax lawyer Brian Flemming, an old Liberal chum, poked fun at Trevor's relationship with Sinclair Stevens. And Peter Bronfman, in classic fashion, delivered a two-step punch: Eyton, he said, was the most intelligent, charming, stylish, handsome, insightful, and humble man he had ever known. "I'd like to continue, but I am having trouble reading Trev's handwriting."

But the earthiest comments were delivered by Liz Tory, wife of Eyton's friend and former law partner, John Tory. When Eyton was a classmate at Jarvis, Tory said, he was no academic, but he graduated as a four-letter man. "However, I cannot use those four letters here tonight." Tory also said that Eyton was like Adam, because he could get excited about an apple when sitting in a garden with a naked woman. Eyton met his wife, Jane, when Jane was caddying at a golf course. Tory added: "It was good practice for the burden she has had to carry ever since."

Jane and Trevor Eyton have five children, two sons and three daughters. Like any family man, Eyton watches his children make their own way. One daughter is married to the son of Silcorp chief executive Eric Findlay, whose board Eyton recently joined. Another worked at John Bassett's CTV for a few years, then attended journalism school at King's College in Halifax, and then began working with Arthur Vaile, the business editor at Toronto CTV affiliate CFTO, on a television special about Canada's most influential people. Eyton's relationships with women and Jane's reaction have been public at times. Neighbours in Caledon say it has been hard on Jane to see women ogle Trevor. Some people interpret his position, his wealth, and his bawdy humour as an open invitation. He maintains an apartment downtown instead of travelling home to Caledon every night. Jane Eyton does not organize for her husband in the city's social scene of opera and symphony and ballet. However, she did arrange a gala surprise party at the Caledon Trout Club for his fiftieth birthday four years ago; the party is still mentioned by his cronies.

The family has investments in a bicycle shop and in Jane Eyton's Yorkville copper and brass retailing business. These are family ventures, but Eyton has other personal investments. He keeps dropping his pebbles, watching the waves spread in ever-widening circles. In 1986, he was part of a group of people who bid to buy the largest single group of apartment buildings ever sold in Toronto. The buildings were under the stewardship of a court-appointed caretaker because their original sale four years earlier had touched a public nerve and led to the discovery of a series of mortgaging frauds. Any resale would be politically sensitive. Eyton saw a role for himself, for Brascan director and one-time part-owner Pat Keenan, and for David Dennis in the purchase of the buildings. He called Keenan and Dennis and together they devised a plan that combined rent increases for the buildings with promises to build new rental units. Then Eyton discussed the idea with real-estate deal-maker, Eddy Cogan, over lunch at Chiaro's in Toronto's King Edward Hotel, Eyton's favourite dining spot. The bid didn't win; the court dictated that the highest bidder, not the one with the most politically palatable plan, be the winner. But Eyton, Keenan, and Dennis saw their ideas echoed in the Ontario government's later plans to tie new construction and rental increases to a new rental-housing policy. When he was forming the private deal, Eyton called himself "a friend of the acquirer." But, had his bid won, part of the ownership would have been his.

Eyton was one of the original investors in Hume Publishing, a firm specializing in personal finance manuals, including the well-known *MoneyLetter*, which advises annual subscribers, for a $95 fee, on "hot" stocks and other market plays. Among the high-profile columnists featured in the semi-monthly publication are Dr. Morton Shulman, the one-time coroner, NDP member of the legislature, and TV talk-show personality; and until recently Andy Sarlos, a long-time Brascan advisor, whose company, HCI Investments, rode the stock market in the late seventies and early eighties and was bailed out by Hees International in 1982. One wag suggests that Eyton makes more money from his investment in Hume than from anything else.

Perhaps because of his incredible business successes, Eyton sees himself as a potentate for other high offices from whence he could sprinkle his particular brand of magic dust. Like so many businessmen before him — Mr. Sam Bronfman springs to mind — Eyton has a yen to sit in the Red Chamber as a senator. After years of belittling the role and motivations of politicians, he might think he can do a better job. But he's not interested in an elected position; he wants a nice little appointment to round out his career. It is a dream Eyton mentions over a drink. David Dennis calls it a "very likely possibility" that Eyton would like to end up in the Senate. "It may be that this would round out for him his life achievement, to be a leader in the national sense, as a statesman, as a patrician." Wendy Cecil-Stuart says it is what he wants more than anything else.

With all the conflict in the mid-1980s between the Edper group and the House of Commons, and the painful public exposure caused by Trevor's involvement with Sinclair Stevens, it seems ironic that Trevor would care so much about a Senate seat. Eyton sees a Senate appointment as his destiny; he wants to be his generation's ultimate business voice. At times, Eyton sounds a bit like Senator Wally McCutcheon, who remarked at the 1965 Conservative leadership convention that he could feel the public mood as he visited "the boardrooms of the nation." Barney Finestone says that for Eyton it's a very natural, forgiveable failing. "Most people like this are élitist. I hope you don't think I'm faulting Trevor Eyton. He's a very good responsible citizen and somebody who, if I were in Toronto, I would be very proud of. And he's very typical of what he is and where he comes from."

But Eyton's métier is holding court for a small group; he does not shine when speaking on the public stage. His droll asides do not amuse a large audience; his famous rapid mumbling loses listeners. He appeared at a *Financial Post* conference in Britain a few years ago; his buddy, Eddy Cogan, dropped into the conference to mingle, and was on the same plane home as a number of conference participants. Cogan did not mince words when he talked to Eyton on the plane, according to one observer. "Cogan said, 'Why did you give that speech, Trev? That was the fuckin' worst speech I have ever heard you give!' And you know," the observer added, "the really funny thing was that he was right."

Still, it doesn't matter to anyone but Eyton that he is a less than inspiring public speaker. In early 1987 Eyton made a crucial distinction between the Brascan group's image in the press and its image in the business community. There had been some trouble with business leaders in the early years, he conceded, but that was dismissed by those who knew the group long before the media began to raise a fuss about concentration of ownership and self-dealing. Those were non-issues for the business community. His subtext was clear: he had done his job.

In one sense, he was right. There are different rhythms for the business élite and for the public, as represented by the press and politicians. The business élite did not like the Edper group pushing its way to the centre of action, but it had allowed the Brascan boys into all the right clubs. In the end, the group had earned or taken its place at the centre of Canadian business. While for years it didn't always have true acceptance, it gained a close enough approximation so that it could go about its business. Eyton has succeeded, then, in his mandate to create a public image for the group. At times he overcame open criticism of the group's tactics. But he has succeeded because others in the group have now been doing business with Bay Street for years. After the crash of 1987, there is no reason to doubt the group's long-term commitment, to question whether it is a mountain of paper. Yet the very strength of the other group members means that Eyton is not as secure in his position within the group as he was half a decade ago.

The choreography behind the building of Toronto's domed stadium is typical Trevor Eyton. He thought up the idea of a group of private-sector partners helping to fund the domed stadium; he approached former premier William Davis and former Metro Chairman Paul Godfrey, both old friends, with the concept; he found eighteen partners, including two group companies, Labatt's and Trilon. The Reichmanns and Merrill Lynch Canada's Michael Sanderson wrote out cheques for $5.3 million just because Eyton thought the stadium was a good idea. Each of the eighteen partners would put $5.3 million into the kitty; the first twelve cheques, delivered at the end of April 1986, were photographed in a group shot that was pasted in a Stadium Corporation scrapbook and proudly displayed in the corporation's reception room.*

---

* The original private-sector partners in Stadium Corporation are: Abitibi Price, a subsidiary of the Reichmanns' Olympia and York Developments Limited; the Canadian Imperial Bank of Commerce; Canadian National Railways; Coca-Cola Canada; Cogan Corporation; Ford Motor Company of Canada Limited; IBM Canada; Imasco Limited; John Labatt Limited; McDonald Restaurants of Canada Limited; Merrill Lynch Canada Incorporated; Trilon Financial Corporation; Hiram Walker Limited; George Weston Limited; Xerox Canada; and York County Foods. Competing beer companies Molson and Carling O'Keefe joined the team in an eleventh-hour cave-in, while Labatt's was in from the start. Eyton continues to sign new recruits.

Each participant will receive a ninety-per-cent tax write-off over ten years and exclusive advertising rights, some for more than ninety years, including use of the SkyDome symbol. They will have their names emblazoned over stadium entrances and rights to advertise on the stadium board, which will be flashed onto TV screens. They benefit from reserved parking and a decade's free use of private boxes, which will be worth as much as $200,000 annually. As well, each investor was awarded the right to a particular concession. For the Bitove family, whose York County Foods caters the airport cafeteria, the reward is a fast-food contract shared with George Cohon's McDonald's. The concession will serve Coca-Cola and Weston candy and ice cream, which will be transported in Ford trucks. For Xerox and IBM Canada, the reward is more ephemeral. They received advertising rights, and the stadium will use their products exclusively. As well, they bought a seat on the prestigious board — and, of course, the approval of Trevor Eyton. The stadium deal is vintage Eyton, a football captain handling the road blocks, the conflicts, and the public nay-sayers and winning through sheer determination. He oversaw the contract negotiations; he was the only one who could pro-vide access to the details; not even Premier David Peterson's office had a copy of the contract a week before construction began at the stadium.

For Eyton, the day the sod was turned for the domed stadium was "the happiest day of my life — well, my wife wouldn't like that, make that one of the happiest days." After the ceremony, Trevor Eyton posed, spade in hand and con-struction hat perched atop his pate, his glasses misted by the rain as a photographer shot a roll of film. He knew reporters were asking questions about his efforts to raise money to build the stadium; they were critical of the deal he negotiated and the way it was negotiated. They were critical, in fact, of the philosophy and machinations of Trevor Eyton.

The reporters wanted the right to question Eyton's motiva-tions. Before striking a pose for the photographer, Eyton told one journalist that, while some more important issues might merit discussion and allow for opposing views, his efforts for the domed stadium were beyond question. There wouldn't be such criticism in the United States, where there is some understanding, some respect for business. The journalist asked for the document outlining the details of the deal for the private-sector participants, saying that, in the United States, the document would be filed at a public hearing. Both Eyton and the journalist were fired up about the issue, but each had a larger issue in the back of his mind: Eyton's deteriorating media image. Could the front man stand the probing, the challenge to his carefully crafted public persona? In the photograph, he stands ramrod straight, a smile stretched across his face. It is a tense smile.

CHAPTER EIGHT

The Right Parties

*I expect that a year or two from now, I'll be part
of the old guard, too. Times change.*
— Trevor Eyton, 1985

Scene: Toronto, a public place. Enter two men
in formal garb.

The ticket is for 7:00 PM, Friday, October 24, 1986. But at
seven, only the anxious sponsors and the hired help are in
attendance at the fund-raising event especially scripted for big
money and big men. H.N.R. (Hal) Jackman and Murray Frum
are awkwardly chumming in the sparkling foyer of the Inn on
the Park's Centennial Ballroom. Jackman wears a bow tie
clipped on to his carelessly elegant suit; his wing-nut eyebrows
are working overtime as he hungrily spears Swedish meatballs
in tandem with Frum. Dr. Frum, a sandy-haired, bearded
dentist-turned-entrepreneur of fifty-five, with friendly, slightly
watery blue eyes, smiles around the room, flashing diamond
studs. He is a Stratford director and he has a serious commitment to the occasion.

Jackman is a member of the evening's featured sixteen-
member society entertainment troupe, the Guilt-Edged Players,
which will be presenting a tailor-made farce, *Much Ado About*

Something. This very private dinner-theatre performance has a $200 entrance fee — tax deductible, of course — and has been orchestrated by Shirley (Mrs. Conrad) Black and Hal Jackman's younger brother, Eric, to raise money for the Stratford Festival. Jackman has devoted his very considerable Thespian talents to the evening's play, but right now it seems that Jackman doesn't care about the performance in which he will naturally be starring.

Hal Jackman is angry. Earlier in the day, the Ontario Liberal government announced that it would be making a special, one-time grant of $1 million to the Stratford Festival. The favour renders tonight's fund-raiser a comedy of an entirely different sort. Jackman professes outrage that Stratford has been singled out for the grant, and he vents his spleen at Festival director Frum. "I've given a lot of money to Stratford. I wouldn't have given it if I'd known you were going to get the grant!"

For the past couple of years, Jackman has been lobbying for support to build a ballet and opera hall in downtown Toronto. Frum needles him now, suggesting that Jackman's Big Blue Machine connections have hampered plans for the opera. They agree that the Stratford grant didn't get approval through the usual route — the Ontario Arts Council. That it is a political decision goes without saying, and ordinarily wouldn't need to be discussed among friends. But Jackman is taking a perverse enjoyment tonight in calling a spade a spade: the grant went to the Stratford Festival, he insists, because the chairman of the Stratford Festival was Ontario Premier David Peterson's campaign manager in the 1985 election.

Who is this political power-broker, the target of Jackman's abuse? It is Bill Somerville, long-time Liberal back-room boy, although "boy" is definitely not an accurate term to describe the august Somerville. Somerville is also Jackman's own corporate lieutenant; he runs National Victoria and Grey Trust for Jackman, its controlling shareholder. Tonight's story is the latest in Jackman-Somerville politicking, a new twist in a joke so old it is taken for granted by those in the know. And the funniest part is that it's all true.

Jackman and Somerville begin to work the crowd as it

streams in; there is a glittering display of sequins and precious gems, black tie and gold lamé. Bank of Nova Scotia chairman Ced Ritchie, with wife, Barbara; Gil Newman, the Reichmann's right-hand man; Roy MacLaren, the politician as businessman; Bob McGavin, a former diplomat who, as head of public affairs at the Toronto-Dominion Bank, is in the middle of Conservative party fund-raising in Jackman's favourite riding, Rosedale. Somerville leaves his wife, Jean, who is tastefully dressed in blue-grey crêpe, and bounds over to one circle of people, pulling aside his closest political ally, John Turner's former law partner, Bill Macdonald.

Not everyone in the room, however, is a Somerville ally. Here's Jack Cockwell and his very charming lady, Wendy Cecil-Stuart, resplendent in a beribboned, puffed-sleeved dress with a V-back and wearing a five-strand pearl choker. Trevor Eyton walks awkwardly through the crowd, an almost-empty glass hanging from his hand. One of his daughters, in a calf-length silver-threaded lace creation with silver shoes, mingles nearby. Michael Sanderson sidles up to his Brascan chums, while Cockwell's protégé at Royal Trust, Michael Cornelissen, serious and greying, puffs his pipe by the bar.

The charmed inner circle is complemented by people who orbit around the powerful. Book publisher Anna Porter, with her husband, Julian, join close friends Murray and Barbara Frum. Known to nightly viewers as the egalitarian interviewer of CBC's *The Journal*, Barbara Frum will be performing tonight for a more select set. With them are one of Anna Porter's partners, Roy MacLaren, and the Porters' buddy David Lewis. Lewis has rushed back from a day in Ottawa, where he testified, before the House of Commons Finance Committee, that his Edper-controlled Continental Bank could not survive without a bailout takeover by Britain's Lloyd's Bank. He deserves an evening off. Sprinkled through the panjandrums are celebrities from foreign spheres of influence: author Pierre Berton, film-maker Norman Jewison, singer Catharine McKinnon, and her husband, Don Harron, the evening's script consultant and also a Stratford director and Canadian comedian. Toronto's Mayor Arthur Eggleton and his wife, known in these circles simply as "Art and Brenda," must settle for a table two rows back from centre stage. There are other measures of importance in this room.

Cockwell and Eyton seem to have a lot on their minds. They huddle together, talking intently, as the room buzzes. Bill Somerville takes the mike to announce that the fund-raisers have managed to net $112,000 for the night; his raspy whine is drowned out by applause. Sir Derrick Holden-Brown, with wife Patricia, arrives as patron of the evening's event. He wears his prosperity like a velvet mantle. It is another private irony. Holden-Brown is chairman of Allied-Lyons PLC of Great Britain, and the undisputed victor in a nasty little war waged earlier in the year against the Reichmann brothers of Toronto. The weapons used in the war were public relations; the prize was control of Windsor, Ontario distillery Hiram Walker. Holden-Brown, suave, charming, and upper-class, won hands down in the corporate arena. Tonight, the more-British-than-Tetley's businessman, with milady by his side, is a clear favourite among Canada's corporate ruling class. Displaying a natural public-relations acumen, Holden-Brown puns on his firm's fixed place at centre-stage of Canadian business in 1986.

The evening is an occasion, above all, for punning and magnanimity. Not all the Guilt-Edged players are as unconcerned as Hal Jackman. Conrad Black, Jackman's intellectual sparring partner and still this crowd's *enfant terrible*, although the grey is inching past his temples, is sweating just a little before he noses his way to the dressing room. "Jesus," he confides to an acquaintance, "this could be *embarrassing*." The night's entertainment is more important to some of the actors than it is to the audience. To Jackman, despite his anger about the government grant, the performance is a serious enterprise. He trod the boards in Shakespearean garb while he was at University of Toronto. Then his father, Harry, a stock-market guru who profited from the Depression, steered Jackman into law, to the London School of Economics, and then to the family investment business. Tonight's play is an opportunity to recapture some of the magic of performing centre stage, which has been sorely lacking from Jackman's life since his support of former Prime Minister Joe Clark cut him off from the wellspring of political power.

Conrad Black has also thrown himself into the spirit of the night; although he could not be at the final rehearsal, held at his lavish home on Park Lane Circle, he revised a portion of his script even while travelling back from London, England, on the Concorde. The new lines poke fun at his own Margaret Thatcher-style Conservative philosophy. The lines are a private joke with the more left-leaning Don Harron, scriptwriter.

By contrast, Trevor Eyton, drafted into the troupe by Wendy Cecil-Stuart, an erstwhile member of the ticket-selling committee, did not attend rehearsals or learn his lines. Eyton is always willing to lend a hand to a worthy cause, but he *is* a busy man. Tonight, Jackman and Black will carry the laurels. But Eyton's casual treatment of his role proves that he has earned his place on a different stage.

Performing community works is a tenet of the Edper corporate philosophy. Charity is one of the business principles Trevor Eyton has on his mental cue cards for use whenever the group's place in the Canadian kaleidoscope is questioned. He holds up the good-works card as a talisman, to show how benign are the group's intentions towards the city, the province, the country. Eyton is the chief publicist of Edper's community works. He is the hero of the University of Waterloo for his fund-raising finesse; he graciously agrees to speak, to write, to lend his presence. His good works, which fill almost half of his sixty-eight-line listing in *Who's Who in Canada*, are almost awe-inspiring in their scope. For example, in autumn 1986, he headed a fund-raising campaign for the Ontario branch of the Arthritis Society; he also was the first speaker at a special three-part "business and dance" series created by the National Ballet of Canada to draw young executives to the ballet by offering them first-course dinner speeches by the captains of Canadian industry. While he was plotting the funding of Toronto's domed stadium, he also did some work for the Canadian Centre for Advanced Film Studies, Norman Jewison's tutoring program in film production on the grounds of E.P. Taylor's Windfields estate, on Toronto's Bridle Path.

In contrast, Jack Cockwell's listing is *Who's Who in Canada* is bereft of personal detail. Cockwell does not claim to be a corporate do-gooder. David Lewis, the former Canadian Imperial Bank of Commerce executive who joined the Edper group's Continental Bank in 1981, affirms that this is part of Cockwell's definition of his partnership with Eyton. Lewis also believes that this could be altered by Cockwell's 1985 domestic alliance with Wendy. Like Eyton, Cecil-Stuart illustrates the importance of being ubiquitous. She has helped to raise money for her alma mater, the University of Toronto; she is on committees or subcommittees to raise money for Hal Jackman's opera house, Bill Somerville's Stratford Festival, and a clutch of other artistic endeavours. For years, she was the person to contact if a group wanted the co-operation of the Edper hierarchy — be it a speech by Eyton or his role in *Much Ado About Something*. Lewis says Cecil-Stuart sees no reason that Cockwell shouldn't take a role in this aspect of group life. But it is doubtful that Jack and Wendy's deal extends that far.

The Brascan creed demands that everyone else play on the community teams. They know the other players in the league; in fact, during the past half decade, a number of charitable organizations have come to look like they are dominated by the Friends of Brascan. Toronto's United Way, a blanket organization for charity fund-raising, is a classic example. When David Lewis was chairman of the board of the United Way of Greater Toronto, he hired Gordon Cressy, a former alderman and mayoralty candidate, to be president. (Cressy moved on, in late 1987, to head a major fund-raising campaign at the University of Toronto.) Lewis also takes pride in the way he suggested that Royal Trust's Michael Cornelissen, not a natural mixer, be head of the 1984 fund-raising campaign. Lewis, Cressy, and Lieutenant-Governor John Black Aird, whose son Hugh is an executive at Great Lakes, impressed on Cornelissen his duty to the good citizens of Toronto. Cornelissen, following in the footsteps of Royal Trust presidents, accepted, albeit with reluctance. His training in the Cockwell school of thinking was overwhelmed by his new environment.

When Cornelissen moved off the board, one of his executives, Courtney Pratt, moved up to serve as 1986 board chairman in tandem with fund-raising chairman Michael Sanderson. Also part of the United Way was David McCamus, president of Xerox Canada (he was fund-raising chairman in 1983), and Neville Kirchmann, president of Coca-Cola in Canada, who was fund-raising chairman in 1986. McCamus and Kirchmann were also involved in the domed stadium. Each of these men has a different style, according to United Way's Gordon Cressy. McCamus, a salesman, sold the idea of the United Way. Cornelissen, a manager, organized the finances and made sure his team delivered the funds. Broadcasting mogul Allan Slaight, who filled the fund-raising spot in 1987, before moving on to do the same for the Shaw Festival, is a communicator, and he improved the agency's profile. Michael Sanderson served as a cheerleader, with a team to overhaul the United Way's advertising campaign and special events.

Cressy does not apologize for the predominantly white male character of the fund-raising board of an organization that serves the broad, multi-racial, multilingual spectrum of Canada's largest city. Another board better represents the group the United Way serves; the fund-raising cabinet is for finding money. And thirty per cent of the United Way's money — $10 million in 1986 — came from corporate donations; sixty-two per cent came from individual employee donations pushed by large employers. When a company head is chairman, that push is very successful. Royal Trust's employee contributions rose from $12,000 to $78,000 the year Mike Cornelissen chaired the drive; with Sanderson as their chair, Merrill Lynch's rose from $38,000 to $141,000, with the company matching that. The companies involved get a big emotional boost. One day, Cressy recalls, Cornelissen chaired a particularly successful meeting of his "campaign cabinet." The year before, a similar meeting raised $15,000; Cornelissen's meeting raised $25,000. Everyone at the meeting had delivered at least $1,000. Later that day, Cornelissen closed a very large business deal. Cressy says: "I remember him calling me that night, and saying, 'You know, the thing I feel best about today is the contributions I got from the cabinet.' "

The general trend in society for the past two decades has been not to give, Cressy says. People don't have the push from the pulpit, and they look to government to take care of the disadvantaged; they won't delay their own purchases to give money to charity. Cressy's mandate at the United Way was to reverse a fall in donations; he and a few board members actively recruited a tightly knit group of younger, more aggressive executives to do just that. They succeeded, he says, by changing donors' attitudes. Instead of doing a favour, donors are taking on a responsibility. Instead of paying an ad agency, for example, the United Way asks agencies to volunteer their services. Notes Cressy: "Philanthropy, in its broadest sense, is not just giving of money; it is giving of time."

Yet while individuals are giving less, they are expecting businesses to give more, according to Christopher Newton, artistic director of the Shaw Festival in Niagara-on-the-Lake. "Government is demanding, and the people are demanding that business has a social responsibility. It is not just there to make money for the shareholders. These corporations have a responsibility to the country." Businesses receive a payback for supporting the arts. After all, Newton says, who could live in Toronto without the arts? "Unless it had the National Ballet and the Toronto Symphony, Toronto would have no style. If you have to think at the pace that most of us do these days, you need style. The arts supply the style that stimulates the economists to come up with the ideas."

Newton has been working hard to make the Shaw Festival into a theatre with an aura, a place to see and be seen, where people from the social and corporate élite mix with afficionados. "At Shaw, we are very consciously trying to make ourselves glamorous for the audience. At the theatre, you are likely to be sitting next to Victor Rice [the head of Varity, formerly Massey Ferguson] or Trevor Eyton, because they come here. And they are likely to be sitting next to the president of Pepsi Cola. You not only see great art, but you are also in a position to be able to further your own needs. So there is both an immediate return for your money, and a long-term return."

Networking is a draw for the theatre crowd, but Cressy turns the notion of networking on its head when he offers a justification for the plethora of blue-suited fund-raisers for the underprivileged. Here, if nowhere else, Big Business meets other representatives of city life. For example, businessmen and labour-union leaders might sit together on a board of directors. Cressy claims that strikes have been averted in the city because these people had built a level of trust through the agency and could call one another to discuss tensions in their negotiations.

Certainly, Mike Cornelissen learned a valuable lesson about dealing with people whose reactions didn't fit his precise flow-chart approach to labour management. When he took on the job as United Way fund-raising chief, his strength was his financial acumen, not his speaking skills. Cressy tells of Cornelissen's first fund-raising appeal, to a labour meeting in a union hall. Cornelissen arrived nervous, his speech raw; it was typed on a series of prompt cards. His halting dialogue was lost on the listeners. His speech was followed by the rousing, natural oration of the spell-binding union types. Cornelissen knew he had fallen flat, and told Cressy so. Then, in the washroom, Cornelissen was approached by a union chief, who put his hand on the Royal Trust president's shoulder. "Brother," said the union chief, "when you come to a labour meeting, you don't speak from cards." Crushed, Cornelissen left the washroom with a fierce determination to master the art of rhetoric. A series of speech lessons and hard effort made him a star at his own annual meeting within a year. "He would credit that year with the United Way," says Cressy, "with teaching him how to speak in groups." Cressy and other United Way workers have joined Cornelissen at the company's annual meetings in recent years; Cornelissen has earned his good-citizen badge.

Despite the lessons learned from the odd brush with other segments of the Canadian mosaic, charitable fund-raising is usually just a few businessmen talking to each other. In fact, corporate rivalries can be brought over to the charitable sphere. Ken Clarke, president of Great Lakes, wanted to move

Toronto's Princess Margaret Hospital to University Avenue. Clarke wanted government approval to rebuild the outdated cancer hospital near Mount Sinai Hospital and the Toronto General Hospital. But its relocation would hurt Wellesley Hospital. The Wellesley board had its own heavyweights, including Edward (Ted) Medland, head of Wood Gundy Incorporated. Clarke and Medland each lobbied for his pet cause; hanging in the balance were the people whose lives would be bettered if the research and treatment facilities at the Princess Margaret were improved. In the end, Clarke and the University Avenue site won provincial approval.

Why do they try so hard, these men who dominate the country's boardrooms and the back rooms of political campaigns? What is the appeal of being a good corporate citizen? There is, of course, a real belief in the good of any particular charity, such as Clarke's commitment to cancer research. And there is the basic adherence to a code of ethics that insists on charity towards others. Peter and Edward Bronfman demonstrate such a code. When Gordon Cressy was asked which group executive cared most about the United Way, he mentioned Peter Bronfman. "Actually, of the whole list, he would seem to be the most deeply, fundamentally committed to the non-profit sector, to the point where an extraordinary part of his life is devoted to it," Cressy said.

A basic belief in philanthropy was instilled in Peter and Edward Bronfman by their father, says Sheila Zittrer, who is in charge of the Edper Foundation in the Montreal office. Allan Bronfman was, in Zittrer's words, "a professional philanthropist"; his trips out of town in his later years were often connected to charitable work, particularly the Hebrew University in Jerusalem. "It's an inheritance. Just as you're brought up to have manners or be respectful or eat properly or brush your teeth, Edward and Peter were brought up with a sense of responsibility to sustain a charitable outlook to everyone around them."

The Bronfman boys started out early in the corps of charity workers. Barney Finestone, a long-standing friend from Montreal, remembers being asked to take them under his wing when they were teenagers and he was a twenty-seven-year-old division chairman at the Combined Jewish Appeal. Finestone hadn't met them before, and while he admired their father, he didn't much like having two rich kids foisted on him. They would be next to useless, in his opinion. They told him they were there because they "thought they ought to work." So Barney decided to play a little trick on them. He gave them pledge cards for some of the poorest streets in Montreal; the people who lived on those streets could afford to give only about two dollars annually. "I said, 'Here are two kits of cards.' And they looked through them, and they said, 'Do we have to tell them who we are?' I said, 'Not necessarily, why?' They said, 'Gee, if we walk up to one of these houses and say to Mrs. Schwartz, you gave two dollars to the Combined Jewish Appeal last year, could you give me three dollars this year, if we said we were Bronfmans, wouldn't that be awful?' "

Finestone thought they would balk at the job, but within a week, they were back. "They had climbed every one of those stairs and they had got a contribution on every one of those cards," he remembers. By the campaign's end, they had finished thirty-five cards, or three and half sets; the average campaign worker managed one set. Finestone says: "When I finally got them up to the $25 cards, they brought some of them back at $100 and $150. There they used their name."

For more than three decades, Peter and Edward have played their part in major charities, particularly during the years they lived in Montreal. Edward was involved in the Hebrew University; Peter played a role in a number of Montreal charities. He was president of the Jewish General Hospital from 1976 to 1978. Now, although Edward is still involved in large-scale fund-raising, they concentrate on efforts that better reflect their personal predilections. Edward is involved in Jewish community projects; he shines as a speaker and a mixer. He is comfortable in this world, and secure in his role. As well, he is actively involved in the Canadian Council for Native Business and the Canadian Psychiatric Research Foundation. Peter prefers projects that are based on causes rather than religious or cultural ties. He is involved in Planned Parenthood, and also in small half-way houses for battered women, shelters in Toronto such as Jessie's, and the Barbra Schlifer Commemorative Clinic.

For years, Peter refused to join the board of directors of the United Way. Then, in early 1988, he finally did. But he used to drop in on Gordon Cressy to discuss the needs of a particular charity. And he always answered Cressy's phone calls, something many executives who profess a commitment to the organization don't do. "I sometimes wonder," says Cressy, "if I call a CEO and they come out of a meeting, and they have ten calls, what level do they rank me in their callbacks? I always get a sense from Peter that I am in the top two or three."

But neither Peter nor Edward wants acknowledgement for their gigantic donations. In fact, they funnel many of the cheques through an Edper company, so that anyone searching the foundation's records, which are publicly available because of the foundation's tax-free status, will not be able to discover the extent of the Bronfmans' gifts to charity. When they endowed a new wing at the Jewish General Hospital in Montreal, they resisted for many weeks Zittrer's and the hospital board's pleas to make the donation public. They didn't even want their names on a plaque. They finally agreed that some acknowledgement of their donation could be made — without revealing how much money was donated — to encourage others to donate. "That is part of Maimonides [a twelfth-century Jewish philosopher] — that the donor and the recipient should not know each other," Sheila Zittrer says. "But very few people adhere to that today, because our society is built on what people know about you, and we all want to be loved and adored by as many people as possible." Although the Bronfmans are not particularly religious people, Zittrer says, sharing and giving and caring are part of their legacy.

Sheila Zittrer has seen the way fund-raising works in her decades as a volunteer as well as in her work at the Edper Foundation. She thinks most people don't approach giving the way the Bronfmans do. "In my experience, most of the people in Peter's situation, who have achieved a level of financial success, have a tremendous need for a continual reaffirmation of their success and their fame, and will seek out philanthropic endeavours that will enhance their prestige. There is an insatiable need on the part of many successful men to always be up there, to always be front and centre."

Peter does not need to be reassured about his place in the social sphere; he is a Bronfman. But for Trevor Eyton and others who adhere to his philosophy of social service, doing good establishes one's place in life. In his charitable work, Eyton is with friends, and friends made in one sphere carry through to another. So his partner in Toronto's domed stadium, Neville Kirchmann, becomes a Brascan board member. This is Eyton's indication that he is a man of influence.

That doesn't mean that Eyton doesn't work at his commitments: he does. And he works a certain kind of magic for grateful charities and arts groups. To Ross Morrison, executive director of the Ontario division of the Arthritis Foundation, Eyton's several years on the board have been invaluable. As campaign chairman, Morrison explains, Eyton had "a very limited amount of time. [But] he makes certain calls, and his clout carries. And then somebody else follows up." Eyton sent out two hundred invitations to a celebration breakfast that ended his term. When he is needed, he delivers. Three major corporate donors pulled out unexpectedly late in the Arthritis Foundation's 1986 campaign. "It took him two days to raise [the money]," says Morrison, "and he did it on a hands-on basis. He made three or four phone calls and he said, 'I need a favour.' "

This is the kind of return Trevor Eyton treasures above all else. His ability to collect money for charities shows the importance of Brascan to Canadian corporate life, social life, the life of the community. In five years, he has ensured that Brascan is as predominent in charity work as it is in other realms of business. His success allowed him to say with pride to the House of Commons Finance Committee, when explaining the Edper group's approach to doing business: "We believe strongly in corporate responsibilities. We do contribute, and we expect our senior people to contribute to the quality of life in the different communities — or, for that matter, on a national scale, where they can."

Mike Cornelissen's place on the United Way board is natural in the chain of being for the president of Royal Trust. In 1958, when the United Way was only three years old, Conrad Harrington, senior vice-president of Royal Trust, was chief of fund-raising. Harrington is a representative of the old way of doing business — in the clubs, among gentlemen. He never really approved of Brascan, but he remained on Royal Trust's board of directors after the group's takeover of Royal, retiring in early 1988. And Eyton was flattered by his patronage. Eyton likes to think he has taken up the mantle from the Harringtons of Canadian business. In 1985 he said, "I expect that a year or two from now, I'll be part of the old guard, too. Times change."

Those times, and those perceptions, have been helped along by Eyton's all-pervasiveness on the Canadian charity scene. Trevor earned his featured billing in the evening's play. Only one corporate family sponsored more than a single Stratford production in the 1987 season — Brascan and its subsidiary, Wellington Insurance, acted as corporate sponsor for Sheridan's *School for Scandal*, and John Labatt Limited hosted Ingmar Bergman's *Nora*, based on Henrik Ibsen's *A Doll's House*.

An emphasis on a particular cause is typical of the Edper group's creed. When Ken Clarke was working for the Princess Margaret Hospital, the executives at Great Lakes had to agree that the Princess Margaret was important enough for Clarke to devote time to it. The others would be picking up Clarke's slack at the office, so they had to feel as committed as he did. When that type of decision has been made, other companies in the group are informed. Royal LePage's deputy chairman, William Dimma, says that each year each group company receives a list of the charities and causes the other companies are supporting. When they choose their donations, the companies try to include as many "group" choices as possible. If a cause is good enough for one member of the group to approve it, it is worth a lot of support. The structured approach to the charitable sector is typical of the group's no-nonsense style. For the favoured charities, Edper's approach is manna from the heavens. Stratford's Jeff Murta, who organized *Much Ado About Something* for Bill Somerville, says, "They [Brascan] are one of the more generous companies around when it comes to charitable donations. They're tremendous people."

It is almost eleven o'clock when the Guilt-Edged Players, so prompt when performing in the boardroom, trickle from their makeshift dressing rooms. First there is a variety-show chorus: "Brush up on your Shakespeare and they'll all bow down." Next, the audience endures Valerie Rosedale, one of Don Harron's stock characters. It is clear from the beginning that Harron's portrait of Old Toronto, dear to many Canadians who have never viewed the real goods, is merely a crude rendition of an outmoded model.

It is power that is really on show tonight. Every joke, every nuance is a jab at a member of the audience or the troupe — the Toronto that counts. Harron demonstrates how much events have changed Toronto's establishment since he created Valerie Rosedale as she utters some of her opening lines. "Bobby" Campeau, Mrs. Rosedale explains, had to drop out of the play because he was "in New York buying out Brooks Brothers." Five years earlier, Campeau couldn't crack the Rosedale clique when he attempted to buy Royal Trust. Since then, he has reached for a place on a wider stage: in 1986, he bid for Allied Stores of New York. It was the largest-ever takeover of an American company by a Canadian — until early 1988, when he successfully purchased Federated Department Stores. When Campeau gave up on Royal Trust, Brascan moved in to pick up the pieces — and majority control of the old-guard company. Tonight, because Campeau isn't here, Eyton's role in the corporate morality play has been enlarged. Mrs. Rosedale explains the shift in power with a titter: "Trevor Eyton has taken over and he's always one to take over from you, in every sense of the word."

The play, which Harron crafted with plenty of advice from Shirley Black and Eric Jackman and rewriting by Conrad Black and Hal Jackman, is meant to be corny and cute, and it is. Its layers of gossip-mongering are fascinating stuff; the audience enjoys witnessing the Jackman brothers open old sores, seeing failed political candidates cruelly reminded of their shattered dreams, hearing taunts hurled at those gods of commerce who, on the cocktail-and-golf circuit, are much discussed but served only smiles and handshakes when they grace an occasion. But the play's most titillating scene had to be cut: John and Sherri Eaton were scheduled to play a love scene, but they separated shortly before the event. Harron was about the only one in the room who did not know why they were not appearing.

Scene One opens with media lawyer and Toronto Transit Commission chairman Julian Porter in tights and a sparkling gold robe, his chest exposed to the elements. He spars verbally with Mrs. Latham (Paddy) Burns, a beautiful and formidable society doyenne whose husband is a partner at the brokerage firm founded by his family, Burns Fry. (In September 1987, Burns partners sold thirty per cent of the firm to a U.S. bank for $100 million.) Julian intones in a garrulous way, "All of my world is a stage, and the men and women merely exits and entrances." But the courtroom thrust and party-room finesse is missing: Julian is forgetting his lines.

With the entrance of Royal Prince Hal, the audience sights a popular favourite. Indeed, Hal Jackman is familiar with the role of the slightly mad but brilliant crown prince of business who is frustrated by fate; he has been playing it on the lecture and interview circuit for years. He wears a fur-trimmed green plush cape and berates the audience for its lacklustre applause. "Thousands of friends, maybe one or two claps."

Eric Jackman, long ago snookered out of his share of the family business, arrives on stage as Hal says, "Here comes my brother, a dull fellow." It seems that we are to be treated to a bit of Canadian business history. In the mid-seventies, Hal Jackman was a king-maker, when J.L. (Bud) McDougald died and Conrad Black snatched control of Argus Corporation, a holding company that had a central role in establishment Toronto. Hal intones, "I do fear the people choose Conrad to be their lord," and Eric agrees: "By McDougald's death he is fain of Argus."

The central morality tale is sidetracked, however, as one by one other notables parade across the stage, some with little pretence to furthering the plot. Peter and Katie Hermant (he the head of Imperial Optical and she notable for her fundraising role at Toronto's Centrestage Theatre as well as her management of the 1984 election campaign of federal Cabinet minister Barbara McDougall) make a quick and sassy swipe at Shakespeare. George Cohon plays himself, the master burgher, in a commercial for McDonald's. Allan Slaight, representing the Shaw Festival, sets off a puzzling medley of fund-raising puns. Then there are appearances by stockbroker Duff Scott; former United Way chairman Janet McInness (McInness is the sister-in-law of Roy McMurtry, who once wanted to be Ontario Tory leader); and Barbara Frum, who is making an appeal for the Mother Corporation.

Finally, a semblance of a plot reasserts itself: Black enters, crowned with laurel leaves, with his wife, Shirley, dressed as a Valley Girl. Then Trevor Eyton enters in pilgrim's hat and green cloak, his face obscured, on the sparsely lit stage, by shadows thrown by his glasses. Lord Black lets the audience know what he thinks of the threat of the Brascan empire: "'Tis my nearest and dearest enemy, the lean and hungry Brassius," he mutters, adding, a few lines later, "My little body is aweary of this new world."

Eyton is stiff, particularly in comparison to Shirley Black, who has the pleasure of telling him, "Get serious, dork!" and "You barf me out." Still, the crowd is forgiving; these people are familiar with the anecdotal Eyton, who thrives in more intimate settings. He manages to camp it up a bit as he moves to the prop chest, dons a gold domed stadium hat, and blurts out, "Dome wasn't built in a day." Eyton's favourite fund-raising exercise rates a torch-song serenade, penned and performed by Paddy Burns, with the chorus, "Trevor, you've got to build a Dome for me." The Blacks stand, still unimpressed, as Eyton explains his need to sell beer at the stadium, "Or I will be cut off by the Brothers Bronfman, the choice and master spirits of the age." Finally, Black bursts out: "He is as tedious as a tired horse. I had rather live with cheese and garlic in a windmill than have him talk to me."

Eyton takes the abuse with an awkward shuffle and a smile. The play's climax is an attack on Black. Jackman wields an axe, Eyton a sword. The playwright has taken poetic licence: Black defeats his attackers and knocks them to their knees with a wave of his mighty arm. But the audience knows the reality. In 1982, at the age of thirty-eight, Black was crowned as "the establishment man" by Peter C. Newman, chronicler of the mores of the Canadian establishment. But Black had concentrated too much on cementing his lines of power and too little on the management of his companies. In early 1986, he picked up his marbles and headed for England, where he placed the London *Telegraph* at the head of a small, western Canadian newspaper chain. He sold the last remnant of his Argus legacy to the Edper-Brascan group, and is now a board director at Hees International. By 1987, Black was glorying in his new role as international media mogul; he bought Toronto-based *Saturday Night* magazine and was the fifth business and partial shareholder in the *Toronto Sun*'s purchase of the *Financial Post*. Still, he has moved from many of the central power plays of Canadian corporate life. and while the play was being rehearsed, Hal Jackman, a lifetime Tory bagman, played a secondary role to Eyton as the Brascan boys, who had better connections in Ottawa, were lobbying to ensure the legislative affirmation of their vision of the financial marketplace. It is small wonder Eyton had no time to practise his lines.

At the play's end, the business leaders and social divas bow and scrape to Ontario Minister of Culture Lily Munro, who gives largess on behalf of their pet charities. Dressed as a fairy godmother, Munro jokes about the grease paint that turns the wheels of political fortune. "Following such instances as UTDC and Minaki Lodge, it is with great pleasure that I call up Bill

Somerville." (The Urban Transit Development Corporation, a provincial Crown corporation set up by Bill Davis's Tories, cost the government $228 million after the Liberals sold it for $30 million in 1986. Minaki Lodge, a luxurious but inaccessible northern Ontario hideaway renovated by the Tories at the cost of $50 million, lost money; it was sold by the Liberals for $4 million.)

Somerville's face crinkles like crêpe paper as he happily accepts the cheque, and Munro waves her magic wand to dismiss her supplicants. The evening has been Somerville's; the play has been a success for the Jackmans and the Blacks. But as the orchestra swings into a gentle tune and many in the audience begin to exit, stage right, Trevor Eyton is exactly where he wants to be — centre stage, as the defender of the old guard.

CHAPTER NINE

Friends and Enemies

*This is an amazing business. You compete, and then
when you've got the business, you go back and say,
"Why don't you be our partner?"*
— Jimmy Connacher, president of Gordon Capital
Corporation

In Edper group business deals, as in the charitable spheres the
group dominates, it is important that friends help each other
out. But with businessmen, there is often a particular edge to
friendship. Ontario Premier David Peterson, who did a little
personal negotiation with Trevor Eyton and his buddies on
the SkyDome, says there is one big difference between cutting deals in politics and cutting deals in business. In politics,
everything is — or could be — open to scrutiny. Public opinion is a factor in any political decision. In business, as the
domed stadium deal demonstrated, public scrutiny is anathema. "They are used to picking up a phone and saying to
their old buddy, 'Hey, let me do this,' and they will answer,
'Okay,' " chuckles Peterson. "And nobody knows about it."

Privacy is one traditional business value that Jack Cockwell
espouses and Trevor Eyton practises as a true believer.
Cockwell is past master of the quiet agreement; Eyton has spent
a lifetime building contacts in a world of favours granted and

owed. For those who have become part of the Brascan sphere of influence, there are powerful incentives to play the game of *quid pro quo*. Some people are clearly in the Edper group's debt; others are adept at seizing the main chance when they see it. A smattering are attracted into the orbit just as any political junkie or musician's groupie is drawn to a charismatic, successful star.

Jimmy Kay, co-founder of Dylex, the largest retail clothing chain in Canada, has been called one of the most grateful friends of the Brascan group. Kay is a controlling shareholder of Dylex, which he started in 1966 with two brothers, Irving and Wilfrid Posluns. Kay, whose sharp features dominate his slight frame, is a garrulous man, a bit of a gambler, a consummate schmoozer. "Dylex" is a kind of an acronym for "damn your lousy excuses," and Kay invented the name for a collection of holdings he bought after he sold his father's manufacturing concern to C-I-L. The holdings included a clothing store called Fairweather. The Posluns family had an interest in men's clothing. The Posluns' interests combined with Fairweather to form the basis for a conglomerate of eighteen retail store chains that by 1987 had more than $2 billion in sales, or one-tenth of all Canadian clothing sales.

But Kay kept his own little investments on the side. In the early eighties they included an oil company and some restaurant chains that were unable to weather the recession of 1982. Kay turned to Hees for help in rescuing two companies, Foodex Corporation, which had an eclectic collection of businesses including Frank Vetere pizza restaurants and some U.S. racetracks, and Hatleigh Corporation, a real-estate and oil-and-gas concern. Both Foodex and Hatleigh had severe management problems and unmanageable debt loads. Hees sent Bryan McJannett to straighten out the mess, and he amalgamated the two companies to form Dexleigh Corporation. Kay's stock was part of the deal; Hees wound up with thirty-three per cent of the new company after buying $22 million in loans from the Bank of Montreal at a discount. It was a classic Hees workout.

Until Dexleigh was turned around, Kay placed his shares

in the Dylex empire as security for the Hees money. This move landed him in hot water with his partner, Wilf Posluns. The pair had made a deal years earlier that neither would ever do anything that would place the company in danger of a potential takeover bid. Posluns was worried that, if something went wrong, Kay would lose his shares to the Brascan boys. Relationships between Kay and Posluns remained strained, although by 1986 Kay had regained control of his shares.

Some people think Kay has shown his gratitude to the group by doing them favours. Anonymous Brascan-group aficionados claim that Kay has acted as an "accommodation account" for the Brascan group. An accommodation account is a polite term for a shill who buys something as a front for an interested party. This isn't allowed in stock-market transactions, where there are strict rules about how a company making or supporting a takeover bid or possessing insider knowledge can act. There were at least two occasions where the Ontario Securities Commission investigated Kay's involvement in purchases of stock that seemed to coincide with Brascan group deals. In 1985, Kay's North Canadian Oils and a slew of Brascan-related companies bought stock in Union Gas. Still later, they all tendered the stock to Unicorp Financial Corporation in return for preferred stock in Unicorp. Still later that year, Kay bought, through Gordon Capital, a stake in Canada Development Corporation, a government-controlled corporation, driving up the price just before Noranda Mining bought a ten-per-cent holding in CDC (see Chapter Twelve). In neither case did the OSC decide that there was anything out of line. But the purchases caused a lot of speculation about Kay's motivations.

Unicorp's George Mann and Jim Leech benefited from Brascan's support on the Union Gas takeover. Leech is a Royal Military College graduate and his father was a brigadier general in the armed forces. Leech fits in well with the brethren at Hees. But he says it is not a closed circle. At one time, Leech lived beside Bill L'Heureux in the Moore Park area of downtown Toronto. (Gordon Capital's Jimmy Connacher lives two blocks away.) Leech says, "L'Heureux wasn't over every night. But then, he was probably at the office. My wife and I went to

Tim's place [Tim Price, of Hees] for dinner. It wasn't just Hees people. If there were twelve people, there might have been one other Hees person.''

Through Hees, the Brascan group has bailed out many companies. Andy Sarlos, the stock-market maven, made all the wrong moves at the end of the bull market in 1982. Hees stepped in and restructured his company. But a much bigger fish landed in 1985, when Conrad Black knocked on the door at Hees. His Norcen Energy was dragging him down, burdened with debt and unravelling with the low price of oil. Black sold Norcen Energy to Hees, with the understanding within the group that the company would eventually end up in Brascan's new oil subsidiary. Black, arguably the most egocentric mogul in the country and certainly a legend in his own mind, had given up on the last portion of his 1976 Argus heritage. Deciding he'd rather stick to newspapers, Black sold the Hees shares he had received in payment only months later, but remained on the board of Hees. He added George Mann's name to the list for his annual black-tie Argus Corp. dinners at the Albany Club. And, to Black's delight, Peter Bronfman became the group's representative on the board of Black's Hollinger Incorporated.

A few acolytes have nurtured their careers by associating with the group, or copying their methods, or investing in the group over long years. Christopher Ondaatje, aged fifty-four, was born in Ceylon (now Sri Lanka). His father lost his entire family fortune to a socialist government. Ondaatje arrived in Canada from England with a bit of banking experience at the age of twenty-one. After working as a clerk and at publications, including the *Financial Post* as an ad salesman, Ondaatje became a stockbroker at Pitfield Mackay Ross. In 1970, he was a founding partner in a brokerage firm with Charles (Chuck) Loewen and Fred McCutcheon, both friends of Eyton's and founding members of Eyton's Canyon Beauport Club.

He held this interest until 1988, when he decided to concentrate on his other business. For on the side, Ondaatje had built a strange and wonderful merchant bank. He made investments in resources, financial companies, and technology, starting with a successful art gallery and publishing business called Pagurian Corporation. His younger brother, Michael, is one of Canada's foremost poets. Ondaatje has called U.S. moneyman J. Paul Getty his "single, most influential guide." Ondaatje is a man of eclectic tastes. He has had Prince Andrew at his office for lunch; he is obsessed with his collections of rare, historical maps and Canadian art; he was a member of the other Canadian bobsled team that competed alongside the gold-medal winners at the 1964 Innsbruck Olympics; he funded a climb of Mount Everest by one of Pagurian's directors, Norwegian financier Arne Naess, who is married to singer Diana Ross. In 1987, at its annual meeting, Pagurian began a strange public-relations practice: it handed out three "non-official" $25,000 awards to individuals Ondaatje decided deserved to be honoured for achieving that beatific state known as "excellence." For statesmanship, he chose former prime minister Pierre Trudeau, who came to the meeting to pick up his medal and cheque. The late Erik Bruhn, director of the National Ballet of Canada, was chosen for artistic achievement. For achievement in business, Ondaatje chose the man whose firm handles some of Pagurian's stock business, the head of Merrill Lynch Canada, Michael Sanderson. Ondaatje didn't see any conflict of interest; Sanderson deserved the award, he said, because of his success at Merrill Lynch and his work with the United Way.

Pagurian has a sizeable investment in Hees; it has ranged as high as twenty per cent at times. In early 1984, Pagurian bought out the Patino interests in Edper and traded them for cash and Hees shares. A pagurian is a type of crab that makes its home in the shells of other crabs. Ondaatje starting by using the resources of other book publishers to produce and distribute his books. He has since applied a symbiotic approach to his complicated financial holdings. Just after the Hees deal, he said that he learned so much negotiating to buy into Hees that "the effort involved has been repaid, even if I don't make one nickel. I've learned how the Bronfmans operate, how a merchant banking firm should operate." In fact, much of

Ondaatje's complicated financial arranging and rearranging of his empire's stockholdings in recent years can be deciphered by thinking the way the folks at Hees do.

Aside from those who have been bailed out by the group, and those who have bought in or copied the group's style, there are those who simply lend their presence to the occasion. A directorship is one signal that a new star has entered the orbit. In February 1984, then Minister of State for Finance Roy MacLaren appointed a blue-chip business committee to examine the future of the country's financial institutions. To chair the committee, which was an amalgam of interest groups, he chose Bill Dimma, then president of A.E. LePage Limited, the country's largest real-estate broker, and a long-time Liberal. By the time Dimma's report was ready, later that year, MacLaren had lost his seat in a federal election. Then, 1985, LePage merged with Royal Trustco's real-estate sales arm. For Dimma, a former academic and one-time executive at the Toronto *Star*, the merger would eventually mean a move upstairs and out of the decision-making circle.

For MacLaren, it was a natural step to become a director of London Life's holding company, Lonvest Corporation, in 1986. Allen Lambert made the approach; MacLaren, long an admirer of Lambert, the former head of the Toronto-Dominion Bank, declared he couldn't have Lambert coming over to his offices; he'd drop in on Lambert. MacLaren was happy to take the post; in fact, he already had other connections with the group. His good friend David Lewis, then president of Bronfman-controlled Continental Bank of Canada, had purchased a chunk of Key Porter Books in 1985, making him one of its largest shareholders, along with MacLaren and Anna Porter.

MacLaren wasn't the only politician wooed by the group after leaving public life. Ontario's William Davis and Alberta's Peter Lougheed, a personal friend of Peter Bronfman, became directors of group companies after more than a decade of disagreeing about almost everything as czars of provincial politics.

Davis's place in the Brascan pantheon is perhaps the best illustration of how the lines of allegiance can become very quickly tangled in the small world of Canadian business. Two of Davis's most loyal and crucial political advisors during his fourteen years in office were Eddie Goodman, senior partner in the law firm Goodman and Goodman, and Tom Kierans, president of stockbrokerage McLeod Young Weir. Goodman is a long-time director of Labatt's. His former law partner, Lionel Schipper, is Peter Bronfman's closest personal advisor.

Schipper, a founding shareholder of the *Toronto Sun*, has quiet but lucrative business interests. He was chosen by Bill Davis in 1984, when Davis was premier of Ontario, as one of three people to head the domed-stadium site selection committee. When Davis left office a few months later, he joined Trevor Eyton's alma mater, Tory, Tory, Deslauriers and Binnington, as a counsel. He had incredible connections. The offers of board directorships soon arrived, and Goodman was one of the people who advised Davis which company board appointments to accept. He accepted a board seat at the Montreal Bronfmans' Seagram's. He chose the Brascan group as a favourite: he was a director and, in July 1987, became chairman of Trizec-controlled Bramalea Limited. The posting fit perfectly with Davis's image as the boy from Brampton. Real-estate developer Bramalea had built the town of Bramalea, Ontario, from scratch during the time Davis had been politicking to bring industry, residents, and "progress" to the area. It was a more active role than any of his other board appointments.

But there are important breaks in the Brascan chain of relationships. Tom Kierans, Jack Cockwell's old sparring partner, is as close to Eddie Goodman and Bill Davis as they are to one another; he is part of the group of Davis's private advisors who helped form public policy under the banner of the Big Blue Machine during the glory days of Tory power in Ontario. Yet Kierans and his partner, McLeod Young Weir chairman Austin Taylor, are two of the most prominent and public critics of the Brascan group. And Kierans has spearheaded the attack. He was the point man in the battle to stop first Brascan, then Unicorp Canada Corporation from gaining control of Union Enterprises in 1985. Union Enterprises was run by Davis's ex-Cabinet minister and Kierans's close friend, Darcy McKeough.

Kierans was on the other side of the issue when a judicial inquiry explored potential conflicts of interest by one-time Cabinet minister Sinclair Stevens in 1986, when Trevor Eyton's credibility as an honest businessman was being questioned by the government-appointed lawyers because of his ties to Stevens.

Personal friendships are even more interwoven than business deals. Gordon Eberts, one of the founders and a driving force at Gordon Capital, has been a friend of Jimmy Connacher and Tommy Kierans for twenty years. Eberts's co-founder, Monty Gordon, and Connacher tried to woo Kierans to their new firm in 1974, when Kierans was changing jobs. Back in the early sixties, Kierans recalls, "Jimmy Connacher, Gordie Eberts, Monty Gordon, Neil Baker, and I were all in Montreal. We all drank together, chased the same girls together, did the same things on Friday nights, and we all trusted each other. And still do."

After so many years, the connections begin to tangle. A close personal friendship has grown between Kierans and Peter Widdrington, Labatt's chief and one of Peter Bronfman's friends. Trevor Eyton revels in memories of New York weekends with Widdrington at the ball park; Kierans and Widdrington went trekking in Nepal in 1984, in a group that included Eddie Goodman; Ira Gluskin's partner, Gerry Sheff; and Cadillac Fairview Corporation's chief executive Bernie Ghert. However, it was Ghert who incited Jack Cockwell's public censure when he differed with the group's position on inter-corporate ownership. Another long-time associate of Ghert's is Toronto real-estate deal-maker Eddy Cogan, whose participation in the domed stadium is an example of his efforts to court Eyton's approval. Cogan travelled to London, Ontario, on a rainy September day to attend the 1987 Labatt's meeting and quaff beer with Eyton and Widdrington. But Goodman insists he is the only legitimate link between the worlds of the Bronfman cousins: "I claim I'm the only living person who bridges both sides, between Cadillac Fairview and Brascan and Labatt's."

At times, the Brascan boys find it hard to contain their feelings. Trevor Eyton must socialize with his Caledon neighbour, Austin Taylor, since they meet each other at local dinner parties. But on one occasion, Taylor, who was wool-gathering while Eyton was engaged in a heated debate down the table, was surprised to find himself suddenly pelted — hard — with a dinner roll. Some members of the group definitely divide the world into "we" and "they."

It is the most natural thing in the world, of course, that as its influence has grown, the Brascan way has spread from a small team to a larger corporate group, and from the group to a wider circle. The widening of the circle is the best example of Eyton doing his job. After a while the movement takes on its own momentum. Now that Brascan is the biggest game in town, the allies arrive daily. At times, group executives chuckle about the hangers-on who hover, waiting for the bits of power and influence and money that fall from the table. "They're like little birds with their mouths hanging open, chirping, 'More, more, more,' " mutters one insider in a moment of cynicism. But he's happy to have them there. It's much better than the old days, when the Canadian business élite was waiting for the Brascan boys to take a fall. It took years of Cockwell planning and Eyton networking, years of convincing people that the Brascan way is the right way, to create these valuable friendships. The Brascan people are fondest of the friends who were there when it counted. Two brokerage firms stand out. In the five years when the Brascan group issued more stock than any other single group of companies in Canada, their relationships with Gordon Capital Corporation and Merrill Lynch Canada Incorporated proved that, for both sides, alliances are essential.

It was raining the day the sod was turned for Toronto's domed stadium, but the rain wasn't touching Trevor Eyton. Another man sheltered the chief executive of Brascan under a white umbrella dotted with the sign of the bull. Merrill Lynch Canada's Michael Sanderson was making sure that his client was coddled. For Sanderson, whose aggressive smile says "I'm from the United States" even before his New England accent kicks in, it was very important to be by Eyton's side that day. Sanderson's company had dropped $5.3 million into Eyton's new sports stadium. Most of the private partners were gaining valuable concessions and tax write-offs, but not Merrill Lynch. Their investment was more subtle, but equally satisfying. Merrill Lynch executives up from the States always smile when they say they love Canada, and that the company will be here forever. But when Merrill Lynch says it loves Canada, it means Bay Street. And more than anything else, it means Brascan. From the time Michael Sanderson arrived in Toronto in the spring of 1984, one of his main jobs was to court Trevor Eyton and Jack Cockwell. Says Merrill Lynch's worldwide chairman, Bill Shreyer: "We wanted to have a relationship with one outstanding leader in the Canadian community, and Trevor was a natural." Small wonder. From 1985 to mid-1987, the group raised more than $6 billion in equity financing. Merrill Lynch had a piece of many of those deals; a very conservative estimate of its fees from Brascan business during that period is $20 million — one third of its capital in 1986. As well, it has been part of debt financings, and its merger and acquisitions group handled the sale of Brascan's holding in Scott Paper. Sanderson says of the Brascan connection: "It was like manna from heaven."

Sanderson met Trevor Eyton at Brascan's headquarters a month or so after he arrived in town in 1984. Sanderson arrived at the headquarters full of hope and *joie de vivre*. When Eyton walked in, Sanderson recalled, he immediately had a good feeling. "We both have an equal amount of hair, approximately speaking, and in those days I used to wear wire-rim glasses. He and I looked alike." Sanderson liked the shirt-sleeve tone of the meetings, the low-key atmosphere, and the high-range goals. "I left with the sense that in fact we could do a lot of business together around the world."

Merrill Lynch, a global trading company, sent Sanderson to Canada to build its dormant operations in Toronto — the world's fourth-largest securities centre — into an important outpost. Sanderson, the son of a diplomat, grew up in Tokyo,

Saigon, Sri Lanka, and Madras, where he attended a Baptist missionary school. Next came an international relations degree at Brown University in Rhode Island, then a degree in politics, philosophy, and economics at Oxford by the time he turned twenty-three. Merrill Lynch seized on the young, enthusiastic graduate as a perfect recruit while he was still in England. Sanderson rose through the branch system to a vice-presidency at thirty-six, when he helped develop Merrill Lynch's Cash Management Account (CMA). Merrill Lynch folk use the term CMA as a sort of mantra: say it often enough and everything will work. The concept, essentially a sales tool for one-stop financial shopping, certainly worked for Merrill Lynch in the United States, and Sanderson became a shooting star in the Merrill galaxy.

When he arrived in Canada, Sanderson had orders to build a brand-new Merrill Lynch. He instituted new reporting techniques, zero-based budgeting, and a large-scale management shake-up. But he needed something spectacular to change the position of Merrill Lynch, which had been sitting still since 1969, when it had swallowed Royal Securities, which had caused the regulators to order it to limit its growth. Merrill Lynch knew the restraining order couldn't last much longer. Sanderson planned to be ready for a new, deregulated marketplace. Brascan represented the single group that could bring Merrill Lynch into the front ranks quickly. In return, Merrill Lynch could take Brascan into other markets in the world. Sanderson spent his first two years in Canada building his bridges to Brascan and a few other key clients. Then he began taking their products abroad. The consummate American, he wears gold maple leaf cuff links — which continuously trip him up in airport security checks. "The only thing I don't do is wear these ties with the American and Canadian flags on them. They're polyester and they don't go with my shirts." He is only half-joking.

The first joint venture was Great Lakes Group, a new investment bank that Jack Cockwell thought up to help create financing for the group. Merrill Lynch became a part owner, and Sanderson thought the bank helped provide an international connection for the group. Great Lakes won't need foreign offices, Sanderson says: "They've got me in Tokyo. I've got forty people there. That's why our relationship works so well."

As well as doing business, close associates can exchange ideas and refine tactics together. "Jack and Trevor and I, we will talk constantly," says Sanderson. "How is the industry changing, what does deregulation mean, how do you position yourself in this new environment, what does Bay Street do well, what does Bay Street not do well that we need and that we could do ourselves." The ties between broker and client were never closer.

The ultimate symbol of the symbiosis is Merrill Lynch's International Advisory Council. The council includes the chief honchos at Merrill Lynch, as well as five outside members: chairman William Rogers, a Reagan advisor and a big Republican; Lord Weinstock, managing director of General Electric, representing Britain; Michel François-Poncet, chairman of Banque Paribas, from France; Dr. Saburo Okita, the chairman of the Institute for Domestic and International Policy Studies, from Japan; and Trevor Eyton from Canada. This august assembly gathered for three days in Toronto in late May, 1987, its second meeting in Toronto since it was formed in 1984. It holds three kinds of meetings during its stay in a country. There are public forums, with a select business élite invited. In Toronto, this included a panel on free trade with David Peterson and high-level Israeli and U.S. officials. A businessman's panel included Merrill Lynch's ex-chairman Roger Birk, U.S. Business Roundtable spokesman Charles Levy, Canadian lobbyist extraordinaire Tom d'Aquino, and Noranda's Alf Powis, Brascan's man on free trade. For the final evening, fifty people were invited to hear Secretary of Commerce Malcolm Baldridge speak on the U.S. perspective on free trade.*

---

* One of the facets of the U.S. politician that fascinated the crowd was his renown as a rodeo rider at age sixty-four. Baldridge died two months later, when his horse trampled him during a rodeo in Texas.

Among the guests was a healthy sampling of Brascan executives, including Alf Powis as well as Mel Hawkrigg and Allen
Lambert from Trilon Financial. In the midst of Merrill Lynch's
ultimately unsuccessful negotiations with Burns Fry, Latham
Burns was a guest of Merrill Lynch. John McNeil of Sun Life
was there, as was Jean Campeau of the Caisse de dépôt and
placement du Québec — a significant shareholder in Brascan-
controlled Brascade Resources — and Dave McCamus of
Xerox, who knows Eyton and Sanderson from working on the
domed stadium and the United Way.

Merrill Lynch New York executives thought Peter Bronfman was a prized guest, and they courted him assiduously.
One even stated baldly that he was trying to rustle up some
business. But Bronfman wasn't buying any of it. He turned
away advances, assuring the brokers he'd talk with them later,
preferring to chat about peach schnapps with a journalist. He
was too quick for them, and ducked out as they trooped to
dinner.

The most important meetings are the private sessions, where
the kings of commerce sit down and bluntly discuss the political
and economic situations in their own countries. This is where
the chosen panel has the most impact, both on Merrill Lynch's
decision-making and on the decisions made at high levels in
other countries. This is where Trevor Eyton's viewpoint is taken
as gospel for the state of affairs in Canada. This is where he
is closest to being a senator.

Merrill Lynch has introduced Trevor Eyton into the high
society of international business. Michael Sanderson has gained
an entire Canadian social set in one fell swoop. Aside from
the Brascan group itself, many of Sanderson's guests were in
the coterie. Sanderson compares the group to a family and says
they party as well as deal. It's even better when the corporate
family and the personal family can deal together. In 1986,
Sanderson sold his Rosedale mansion. Royal-LePage Real
Estate handled the sale; Royal Trust provided the financing
package to bring the buyer in. The buyers were Jack Cockwell
and Wendy Cecil-Stuart. "Like family," Sanderson says
breezily.

This extended family, a mixture of old-guard converts, new-style entrepreneurs, and sports and media personalities, is called the "orbit" by some business journalists. The term first came into common usage when it was perceived that "friends of Brascan" were buying shares of Union Gas and selling them to Unicorp during the 1985 takeover battle (see Chapter Eleven). But it is just as noticeable in the realm of charity and the social columns (see Chapter Eight). Sanderson has ensured that he shines in this orbit of stars. He is one of only a few Canadian chief executives who has a special assistant devoted to his public-relations strategy and all his corporate benevolence chores.

Jim Coutts, who at six feet two inches can never be mistaken for the former prime ministerial aide with the same moniker, trained in sports management before joining Merrill Lynch in 1982 as a stock salesman. He was soon promoted to Sanderson's right hand, and sits at all public functions so he can read the great man's wishes through his eye movements and hurry to his aid whenever he is needed. Coutts is point man on the domed stadium investment; he helped when Sanderson was head of the Toronto United Way campaign in 1985. Coutts, who was involved in supervising athletes at the 1976 Olympics in Montreal, is on Toronto's 1996 Olympic committee and organizes the annual Presidents' Night at the Toronto Symphony, which has, in the past, featured special guests such as Dyan Carroll and Andy Williams. Sanderson keeps a photo of himself and Carroll in his office. In 1987, there was a minor calamity in Toronto society when the Presidents' Night was held on the same night as the Stratford Festival's Champagne Express, where $250 buys a return train ticket and theatre seats, with dinner and champagne served en route. The Champagne Express included, among its organizers, Wendy Cecil-Stuart and the other Jim Coutts. But Coutts, who has filing cabinets at home filled with studies of leadership techniques, kept smiling. He is rarely seen with a frown; it wouldn't do for the smoothest executive assistant in town to be caught worrying. It may, in fact, be a code of conduct at Merrill Lynch these

days, for the only one who can rival Coutts's pearly whites
is his boss, Michael Sanderson.

It is rumoured that Jimmy Connacher also likes a good laugh,
that he has a ticklish rib, and that his bellow can be heard across
the trading room. But no journalist has ever seen him crack
a smile. Connacher is Sanderson's main competition for broker
with the inside track at Brascan. Connacher has been close to
the Brascan boys far longer than Sanderson. His company's
links, after all, reach back to the early days, when Neil Baker
worked for Peter and Edward Bronfman, and were solidified
when Connacher played a pivotal role in the Brascan and
Noranda takeovers. And while the diminutive Connacher
cloaks himself from the public view, he likes to shine in his
own right every bit as much as Sanderson. He moved to
Gordon Capital, a bare-knuckles company, when it was called
Gordon Eberts Securities, after founders Monte Gordon and
Gordon Eberts. They set up the company in Montreal in 1969,
then moved it to Toronto when the business shifted in the mid-
seventies. Connacher arrived in 1970 with the understanding
that he would head the company. Securities lawyer Garfield
(Gar) Emerson calls Connacher "the spiritual leader" of his
company, the one who provides direction, despite the important position still occupied by Neil Baker.

Connacher is a man who has never put up with pussyfooting.
He started his brokerage career at Wood Gundy, but left after
fourteen years when he realized that the firm wasn't aggressive
enough. Connacher would make sure Gordon Capital was the
most aggressive firm around. It announced a merger with
Wood Gundy in 1986, which was scuttled after the execs at
the staid Wood Gundy realized that they couldn't adapt to the
new world carved out by Connacher, who was promising (or
threatening) "a bottom line analysis of the talents of
everyone." The cancellation of the merger was helped by a

palace revolt at Wood Gundy. During the days after the announcement, in bars up and down Bay Street, Wood Gundy employees were taunted by Gordon Capital boys about how the merged firm would be "go-go-Gordon" all the way.

There was reason for Wood Gundy employees to expect that the Gordon Capital style would dominate. It was much more successful, much better adapted to the new, international brokerage business. By the early eighties, it had become renowned for its ability to make large institutions happy by buying and selling their large blocks of stock with particular finesse. Jim Leech, president of Unicorp Capital Corporation, calls Connacher "the consummate trader. He just has a sixth sense about the market." Gordon Capital's ability to scoop deals from other companies, Leech adds, is part of its trading mentality. Gordon Capital also trades agressively for its own account; it is rumoured the firm lost $25 million of its $40 million in capital when the bottom fell out of the market in 1982, forcing Neil Baker to pump millions into the firm and increase his shareholding. But Gordon made all the money back, doing $1.2 billion in deals in 1984 and 1985. In mid-1987, without Wood Gundy, Gordon was looking for a partner to bankroll it on Bay Street as it rode the peak of a five-year stock-market wave. It struck a deal with the Canadian Imperial Bank of Commerce to set up a new investment bank. When the crash of 1987 left some brokerage firms scrambling to cover losses from big securities purchases and trading losses, Gordon soon made it clear that this time it did not need to worry. Indeed, it took to running full-page ads in the financial press proclaiming its strength; Gordon, together with its investment bank joint-venture with CIBC, had become the largest investment dealer in the country by the spring of 1988. Its capital base was more than $500 million, a huge jump from $150 million the year before. And new partners in the investment bank include Canada Life and Hong Kong multi-billionaire Li Ka-shing.

Part of the trader's mentality is a belief that business is a game. Connacher has a ski chalet in Stowe, Vermont, and a yacht in the Toronto harbour. He exhibits a boys-will-be-boys demeanour. In the past, he has received a number of interesting presents, including a live piranha and a stuffed barracuda, both comments on his personal style. When fighting Canada's largest brokerage firm Dominion Securities, during a takeover battle, Connacher received a live turkey from his University of Manitoba fraternity brother, Jim Pitblado, head of Dominion. Connacher's answer: a dead duck. He also sent a dead fish to Howard Beck, a regular Connacher retainer, who worked at the law firm of Davies, Ward and Beck. A few months later, they were all doing business together again.

Connacher doesn't hold grudges, but he has made enemies. Fees are Connacher's business. Gordon Capital didn't hesitate to alienate a chunk of its long-time institutional clients by thinking up a ploy that could have excluded those valued clients from a very profitable sale of stock in Canadian Tire Corporation in late 1986. Connacher's clients in that case, the franchised Canadian Tire dealers, were paying Connacher's bills. Connacher is teased by his clients about being the ultimate hanger-on. "We always call him the bell hop, and tell him that he should buy the goddamned hotel, instead of taking the tips," says the president of Unicorp, Jim Leech. When Connacher turned fifty, Leech and his senior partner, George Mann, took the joke one step further: they sent Connacher a hand-made poster featuring Connacher in a bell-hop uniform standing outside a hotel door, while Leech and Mann smoked big cigars and drank champagne inside.

Whatever Connacher's motivations, Bay Street questions his methods. Conspiracy and Gordon Capital have often been whispered about, although little has been proven. The main complaint is that Gordon trades for its own account when a takeover is on; the other alleged transgression is that the company buys and holds, or "warehouses," stock during a takeover through accommodation accounts. It is said that Gordon will arrange for a friendly client to buy stock and park it in his account at Gordon, then resell it to another client who wants it — say, someone in the Brascan group. This is where Gordon becomes, according to some conspiracy theorists, a dark star in the Brascan orbit.

The reason people have been so keen to draw lines connecting moves by Baker, Connacher, Gordon Capital, and Brascan is that when Connacher fought to shake up the complacent world of Bay Street stockbrokerage houses during the early 1980s, he did it with Jack Cockwell whispering directions in his ear. Connacher was on the front line, but it was all part of Cockwell's master program for group financing. With help from their friends, the group became the most important force on Bay Street. And the shake-up Cockwell caused drastically altered Bay Street at a crucial time in its history. Jack Cockwell and the group spearheaded a revolution in the way business is done on Bay Street.

CHAPTER TEN

Revolution on Bay Street

You remember where you were when Kennedy was assassinated and when Paul Henderson scored his goal. And I remember standing by a quote machine and reading the tape. It was the Royal Bank deal that Jimmy Connacher did, and I remember saying to myself, my God, what has this guy done to us. . . . He revolutionized and demystified the business. It was the end of the investment business as we knew it in Canada.
— Chuck Winograd, president of Richardson Green-shields of Canada Limited, recalls the day Jimmy Connacher broke the Bay Street stock-selling groups.

It was the look in Jack Cockwell's eyes that made McLeod Young Weir's Tom Kierans realize there were going to be big changes soon in the way his business worked. Kierans, at the time the youngest president of a Bay Street stockbrokerage firm, was sitting through his umpteenth client-counselling session one day in early 1981; the head of another firm was explaining to the client the standard broker payment formula. The client, Westmin Resources, was issuing stock; Westmin's president, Paul Marshall, a white-haired, no-nonsense

Calgarian, was flanked by Jack Cockwell, chief operating officer of Westmin's controlling shareholder, Brascan Limited.

The broker leading the planned sales effort was explaining how the stock issue would work. The brokers were taking a risk in pledging to buy the stock, then resell it in the open market, so they would be paid a risk premium as part of their fee. Today the stock issuer was Westmin, but it could have been any company, any chief executive. Says Kierans, "The old, honed speech was the same thing that Deane Nesbitt or Mr. Chapman could have given twenty years earlier."*

Kierans felt bored by the song and dance, and he didn't pay much attention when Marshall queried the brokers' costs. His attention wandering, he glanced around the room. His eyes met those of Jack Cockwell. Kierans's hotshot financial guys had told him Cockwell was smart, but the two had not met before. "I looked at Cockwell, and realized that he knew that it didn't wash." For Kierans, the memory is vivid. "The look of scepticism, the frustration on his face was something to behold. I knew for the first time that the business was going to change."

Kierans was right about the way Jack Cockwell felt about Bay Street. Cockwell was contemptuous of the whole system: the stockbrokers who pretended to take risks to sell clients' stock, but really didn't take any risks at all; the high fees they demanded to sell the stocks; the small clubs or "selling groups" that guaranteed clients would be loyal to a particular stockbroker for life. To Cockwell, the stockbrokers just weren't working for their money. Every time one of his group's companies issued stock, it paid more money to the fat-cat brokers than it should. Grumbling from issuing companies was getting louder, recalls Garfield Emerson, an expert on securities law at Davies, Ward and Beck. "Guys like Jack Cockwell were wondering what underwriters were getting paid for. Why do you pay them five per cent when they don't take any risk?"

---

*These were the deans, the legends of the business in Montreal in the 1950s and 1960s. Nesbitt headed Nesbitt Thomson; Chapman lorded it over the industry at A.E. Ames.

Cockwell would only stand for that for so long. He planned to issue a lot of stock to restructure the Brascan-Edper-Hees companies, and he didn't see why, just because a system had always operated a certain way, it had to continue to operate that way. Neither did some of the Brascan group's key advisors, men like Jimmy Connacher at Gordon Capital. In the early 1980s, Cockwell and Connacher would begin to play by their own rules. By doing so, they would force Bay Street to change. Some pundits now say that if they hadn't forced the changes on the investment world, Bay Street would have had to change by the end of the decade in any case, in order to keep up with a vastly altered international financial landscape. But the moves Jack Cockwell made to ensure that his group obtained the least expensive financing, and those Jimmy Connacher made to show other corporations how they could gain the same savings, were among the changes that dictated that Canadian financial markets open up to new players in Canada and, ultimately, to the world. The old club fought the changes as long as it could; regulators held interminable hearings during the eighties, published reports, weighed testimony. And Cockwell and others like him simply kept changing the rules by cutting deals in new ways. By the time the altered rules were finally acknowledged as inevitable, many respected old brokerage firms hadn't made the cut; the others were kowtowing to the new power-brokers.

Connacher and his company, Gordon Capital, first grabbed the spotlight in 1983 when Connacher broke the cozy stock-selling groups that angered Cockwell. Gordon Capital scooped up clients by paying the stock-issuing company before it sold the stocks, eliminating costly selling teams and prospectuses. Like all moves of genius it was simple — in retrospect. At the time, recalls one broker, "It was, in the Canadian investment industry, the equivalent of the cave man inventing fire." Behind the scenes, providing Connacher with the financial muscle to play the new game, was Jack Cockwell. Gordon Capital needed some assurance that it would not be left holding stock; the company wanted a buyer of last resort. Hees International, Jack Cockwell's merchant bank, was that assurance. Later, another Cockwell creation, Great Lakes Group, would move into that role. But to some observers it didn't matter what the name of the company was. They likened it to a retail chain, operating under different banners with the same merchandising techniques. Said one observer: "All roads lead back to Jack Cockwell."

Connacher did what the other brokers had been professing to do all along: he offered to take the risk, to buy the stock issue and give the client a cheque. Then he turned around to sell the issue. But with big stock issues from solid, stable companies, Connacher knew — as the brokers had always known — that if the issue was listed at the right price, he'd have no trouble selling it at all.

The radical change in thinking came about in two steps. In the early eighties, Connacher knew the market for stock better than anybody. Gordon Capital, Connacher's company, was a small company that specialized in quickly buying or selling large blocks of stocks for companies, a practice known on the stock exchange as block trading. Connacher's people knew all the large buyers. "Connacher learned the names of the twenty largest accounts in the country," says Charles Winograd, president of Richardson Greenshields of Canada Limited. "He was the first guy to really isolate that end of the distribution channel. Connacher was doing deals with these guys every day."

Connacher had already broken traditional trading ties between clients and old-line brokerage houses. But while he knew all the players, Connacher and his company were not allowed to play the game. Selling groups were limited to a few brokers who closed ranks to newcomers. At the end of 1982, when institutions were buying stock as if there was no tomorrow, Connacher was making big block trades, but he wasn't allowed to deal in new stock issues.

Connacher wasn't going to put up with that. So he simply took his usual deals one big step further. He found companies that wanted to issue stock, rather than waiting for the stock to appear on the market. Then he made his usual trades for his usual clients. "The key element was not the risk of capital but the idea that all you needed to do deals in Canada was twenty phone numbers. And they [the partners at Gordon

Capital] knew those numbers," adds Winograd. "Just because they weren't in the selling groups didn't mean they couldn't take out the best girls."

The prom queen was the Royal Bank of Canada. The bank wasn't Connacher's first deal, but it was his signature deal: in 1983, he walked in and slapped a cheque for $228 million on a senior Royal executive's desk. The bank would save more than $60 million on the preferred-share deal if it went along with Connacher.*

The bank cut its half-century ties with a selling group led by Wood Gundy and deposited the cheque. Wood Gundy had been preparing a prospectus, but Connacher's way was quicker and a lot less expensive. Connacher only charged a one-percent fee, while the old-line group was planning to charge four per cent. The bank's decision "was a significant departure," says Emerson. "[It] broke the traditional underwriting syndicate." Kierans echoes the common wisdom: "It was when the Royal Bank put its imprimateur on this process that the nature of the business changed." After that, other brokers would have to be willing to place their capital on the line.

Once Connacher invented the bought deal, stock-issuing companies realized it was just what they wanted. Connacher guaranteed the price of the stock from the day they signed the contract, not next week, when the prospectus was ready, or still later, when they were about to sell. Says James Pitblado, president of Dominion Securities, "It was the certainty of the pricing that was the key element in the move to the bought deal."

The entire broker-client relationship changed after that. For example, as Pitblado points out, traditionally brokers did work for clients and didn't charge them; the charge was added to the next underwriting fee. The official regulatory "unbundling" of commission rates occurred in Ontario on April 1, 1983. The reason for treating clients differently had already been demonstrated.

---

*The first "bought deals," as Connacher's manoeuvres were called, were for preferred-share issues; the larger, more risky common-share bought deals would not be done for some months.

Ironically, one of the keys to making the bought deal a marketable reality was the introduction in 1982 of the short-form prospectus or the Prompt Offering Prospectus (POP). Before the POP, bought deals could only be arranged for private placements of stock, and not for public issues. Private placements had to be held by the buyer for six months before the buyer could resell the stock. The idea of a short-form prospectus, one that would simply update the regular filings of well-known companies, was hatched by a coterie of established brokers headed by Ward Pitfield. His company, Pitfield, Mackay, Ross, and competitors Dominion Securities and Burns Fry Limited, all thought it was heck of an idea to simplify the stock-issuing process, and they hired Gar Emerson to counsel them on the idea. The old way was expensive and redundant and kept large companies from taking quick advantage of financing opportunities; they wanted to replace the old form with a financial postcard that could be pushed through the securities commission in five business days. Then, if a broker guaranteed a client the money within two weeks, he would have another week to guarantee sales of the stock before he had to pay the money. It made the market more competitive with Eurodollar debt financings, which could be arranged within days. The POP was approved in 1982. But the brokers weren't really thinking of doing bought deals. In fact, they were getting tougher on clients, pushing more and back-peddling more, becoming more averse to taking risk in touchy markets and more anxious to protect their capital.

In contrast, the Street believed that Gordon Capital didn't have to worry about capital; it had the Brascan group behind it. To some, that made it a creature of Brascan, and Brascan was, after all, a major stock issuer. Others thought the two companies simply had a close working relationship. "A large part of the Street believed that because of past associations of Gordon with the Edper group — including the Brascan takeover — Brascan was prepared to work with its friends," recalls Emerson. "They had developed a relationship in terms of trading. I don't think [Brascan] looked at Gordon as a captive or bought firm. But I think [Gordon] recognized that they had a friendly relationship with the Brascan group. I don't know if that is any different than a lot of other underwriting relationships that are created for other reasons," adds Emerson. But, because of the relationship, Connacher had an inside track on just how upset Brascan was with old-fashioned financings. Michael Sanderson of Merrill Lynch thinks there was cause and effect: "The bought deal environment was really started by Brascan, by their frustration at getting Bay Street to stand up to a commitment. That led to the demand for bought deals, which Connacher satisfied."

While they were lenders, however, the Hees folks never had a stake in Gordon Capital, according to Neil Baker, a partner in Gordon Capital and Jack Cockwell's old boss. "Just to set the record straight, Hees has never acquired one nickel of Gordon Capital's capital, debt or equity," Baker said in late 1984. In fact, Connacher didn't have a firm arrangement with Hees for every deal in the early days. Sometimes he arranged bank financing to make his deals work; it was easy in those days to get a bank guarantee, because he had buyers willing to move in immediately. Connacher went around "looking for nets," in the descriptive phrase of one banker, because he was operating without one. He was relying on his own innate judgement of the market and taking big risks. "I think that is the main difference between Jimmy and most of the established companies — he was prepared to take enormous risk," says Alan Hockin, a former executive with the Toronto-Dominion Bank. "He didn't always win; there were some occasions when he really got burned. But he was successful enough in his judgement of the market early on that he was able to make a hell of a lot of money and establish his position with people like the Brascan group."

The institutional acquisitors arrived in the market, ready to buy stock that might otherwise sit on a broker's shelf and wait for it to ripen. They were the fallback. And this was needed, particularly when the recession of 1982 to 1984 scared retail buyers away from the stock markets. Most of the stock issues during those times were bought by institutions. Neil Baker defended block buyers during the 1984 regulatory session on the future of the business: "They have the staying power in bad times and, in fact, did shore up the Canadian corporate sector when, in fact, the retail public, for whatever reason, wasn't there."

Many of the Connacher's clients didn't plan to hold their stock for long; they made a quick profit, then sold the stock. Institutions made money this way, and the biggest player of all was Hees International Limited. Hees began to make a bundle on stock-market turnovers. In consumer terms, what Hees did is called "warehousing" stock for resale to retail buyers. Hees ran the biggest warehouse. The group said it was acting as "purchaser of last resort," and that acting as such a purchaser was one of the tenets of their merchant-banking theology. Connacher liked dealing with the guys at Hees not just because they would put up the money, but because they would do it quickly. Connacher could walk into a meeting, strike a deal, make a phone call to Hees, and report within a couple of hours whether he had the financial backing to buy the stock.

But however closely the people on Bay Street thought he was linked with the Edper-Hees-Brascan forces, Connacher feared the arrangement wouldn't last forever. In what he termed "a bit of a smart-ass answer" to the Ontario Securities commissioners during one of their interminable inquiries into the securities industry in November 1984, Connacher said that his firm had been able to do every deal that had been brought to it that year, "so I don't know of any that have not been done because of the lack of capital." But he also said the industry simply didn't have enough capital, and that he was relying on "outside capital, which is at the whim of being with us or not being with us tomorrow. . . . I am not at liberty to tell you specifically what outside capital charges us, but it is fairly substantial, and at any given moment in time, they may not be there. So it is a bit precarious on a long-term basis."

While Connacher credited this "third party capital" with building his success in the past two years, he wanted to be his own man. The boys at Gordon Capital didn't want to be satisfied with "adequate" capital; they wanted to be able to build their capital and then see what they could do with it.

Boasted Connacher, "We have raised over a billion and a half dollars in the last year by having that capital available to us. [With more money] we can see all sorts of other avenues."

The securities regulators had already closed one of those "other avenues." In 1984, Gordon Capital attempted to form a joint venture with a Belgian holding company, Groupe Bruxelles Lambert. The move forced the regulators to rethink their policy on ownership restrictions. The Belgian group would have had forty-nine-per-cent ownership but only a ten-per-cent voting position in the joint venture with Gordon Capital. Neil Baker complained to regulators during the securities hearings that the Europeans didn't care that their voting was limited. "What is the difference between ten per cent and forty per cent when in fact the goodwill resides truly with Mr. Connacher and Mr. Baker? You are not buying bricks and mortar." Baker added that the Toronto Stock Exchange "couldn't quite comprehend that. They looked for a possible conspiracy to exist under the table." Gordon Capital would continue to hunt for potential partners.

By this time, the industry had caught up to Gordon Capital on the bought-deal pathway. Recalls Dominion Securities president James Pitblado, "We took a look at the changing system, and said, hey, what have they got that we don't have, or what have we got that they don't have? We've got more capital." As well, Dominion Securities had their own institutional contacts and a retail distribution system. "We're realists," Pitblado said. "The world is going to change around us. We're not going to stand idly by and let our competition do business with our clients. We're going to get in and compete."

Others, including the Brascan group, of course, had also seen those "other avenues" Gordon Capital was eyeing. And other companies had the money to explore them. They were working in a new market called the "exempt market," which consisted of big deals for big customers only. Because each deal involved only a few limited players, the players were not required to register the deals with the securities regulators. Neil Baker was frustrated because Gordon Capital had to watch this exempt market growing while his and other brokers' capital limits were stiffly enforced. The enforcement was at the urging of the main-line brokerage houses. "There is a horde of people with lots of capital sitting there waiting to participate in our industry," Baker said. Why was there excess free capital among some brokers, while other companies couldn't get into the business? Said Baker: "Obviously because the existing system has chosen not to use its capital the way the marketplace wants it used, because, by definition, had they done that, the exempt market would not be a problem today."

Jimmy Connacher pointed to debt financing done in Europe through the established Eurobond market. Only one in fifteen leading firms that sold Canadian Eurobond issues was a Canadian broker. Canadian brokers didn't have the money, the clout, or the expertise to compete in the Eurobond market, or in international debt financings. Aggressive American firms were building new markets and Japanese brokers and European banks were offering services Canadians couldn't offer. Finally, there was domestic competition in the exempt market and in the development of new products.

The Brascan group, in tandem with Gordon Capital, had developed a new market for preferred shares during the early 1980s; then in 1984 Brascan had introduced its own exempt-market player, Great Lakes Group, to replace Hees as a buyer of last resort on short-term market plays and to move into other securities deals. These two moves would be among the group's most high-profile and controversial; they were also key steps in Jack Cockwell's long-range plan to change the nature of the group's financing.

The popularity of selling preferred shares has ebbed and flowed with recession and boom and the political tides of the past decade. Traditionally, preferred shares have been widow-and-orphan stock, issued by companies like Bell Canada and the Bank of Montreal — providing safe returns, higher than bank interest with about as much real risk. Preferred shareholders receive tax-deductible dividends; they rank ahead of common shareholders and after creditors in the very unlikely event of default. For this measure of safety, the preferred shareholders sacrifice a voice in the company's fortunes: preferred shareholders don't vote. Preferred shares fell into disrepute after the market crash of 1929, when small investors were wiped out, but slowly regained an aura of respectability. They drew Jack Cockwell's attention when he went looking for a way to change his companies' debt to equity. They fit beautifully with the group's traditional words to investors: "Trust me."

In the late 1970s, a stockbroker named John Abell who worked at Wood Gundy noticed that all the traditional attributes of preferred shares could be used for a different purpose. Many companies were having trouble with rising interest rates on bank loans. Instead of borrowing money from the bank, a company might issue preferred shares. Then the bank could buy the shares and give them the money at a lower rate of interest, because the bank could deduct the dividend payments — which would replace loan repayments. In essence, the Canadian taxpayer would subsidize the loan. But the bank wouldn't want such an arrangement to go on forever; a bank is a money lender, not an investor in business. Preferred shares would be given a special feature called "retractability." The shares were usually retractable after five years. In essence, the shares were a short-term loan. And the banks, which were faced with the option in some cases of moving in on companies that couldn't afford to refinance at high rates, thought it was a grand idea.

One of the first preferred-share deals was arranged for the Toronto-Dominion Bank by Barry Zukerman, who later left the bank to start a stock-market investment business with his partner, Andy Sarlos. Zukerman, a recognized investment genius who was discriminated against at the bank for being Jewish, died of cancer in early 1987. Alan Hockin, the Toronto-Dominion executive who worked with the bank's "bundle" of preferred shares, says that banks set a pattern of investment in the late seventies. The banks, however, were too greedy; by 1978, they weren't paying any income tax at all, because of their enormous holdings of preferred shares. Ottawa couldn't accept the situation. What had started as a good financing ploy had become a public policy issue, and the banks were criticized by a Parliamentary committee.*

The pattern emerged again, this time with Edper-Hees-Brascan as the big market player taking advantage of the tax system. Two clauses in the Income Tax Act helped the group. First, related companies were not taxed on dividends from one another — called "intercorporate dividends." As well, the dividend tax credit provided a write-off against dividends. The tax-credit write-off was a public policy move to encourage individuals to invest in stocks. Canadians have traditionally been fond of bank accounts rather than stocks; only one in eleven Canadians invests in stocks, compared to one in six Americans. The government tax break on stock dividends was intended to reward people for taking an investment risk — after all, common-share ownership is a risk because common shareholders rank last when something goes wrong with a company. But a stock is a stock, and it was possible to use the write-off for a safer type of investment. "Preferred shares have become one of the major and significant beneficiaries of the dividend tax credit and non-taxability of intercorporate dividends," says James Pitblado of Dominion Securities. "More and more financing, both corporate and individual, was geared to preferred shares — which was not, I don't believe, the original public-policy rationale for the dividend treatment."

Alan Hockin comments, "As an issuer, you've always got to be thinking, 'What is the market telling me they want?' You get in and you tend to get in fast because you say, 'Well, maybe they will get tired of it and I'd better get the preferred share money before somebody else does.' " Jack Cockwell kept a

---

* The banks continued to use more traditional preferred shares to reduce their taxes. In 1984, Dick Thomson, the head of the Toronto-Dominion Bank, ranted in a speech about other banks and trust companies arranging to buy each others' preferred shares. He was upset because both banks and trust companies belong to the same federal insurance system, so their share-buying arrangement created an artificial hike in the capital bases of both buyer and seller. Thus there was double accounting, for the insurers' purposes. The Inspector General of Banks questioned whether retractable preferred shares could be classified as equity for banks. The Canadian Imperial Bank of Commerce and Royal Trust were big players in this market.

close watch on preferred shares. Because of preferred shares, Cockwell could switch from debt to equity ownership. Yet he didn't have to give up common-share ownership of companies that hadn't reached their full potential and value. In the early 1980s, many of the group companies were ready to climb the ladder to preferred-share financing. And there were buyers for the shares. After all, there was a contractual assurance that the dividends would be paid. That assurance doesn't exist with common shares. Just like the banks a half-decade before, the corporate buyers were more interested in five-year investments that would earn them twice as much as a government bond would; they did not want long-term investment in a company stock.

But Jack Cockwell's vision never stops with a simple financing decision. He began to envision an entire market for preferred shares, a special type of market composed of companies issuing the stock — dominated by Brascan group companies, but including others — and institutions eager to buy the stock. He could cut out the brokers and do the deals himself. He needed buyers for his own stock, and he had to be able to offer them a wide range of preferred shares to legitimate the product he was planning to flog. His ideal market would be an independent facet of group operations, a new sideline to the empire, built on the principles of merchant banking.

Cockwell told some senior brokers what he intended to do and why it would work. One broker who took a more active look at the whole idea was Cockwell's good buddy, Jimmy Connacher. Connacher didn't see anything wrong with his own firm moving to cash in on any potential market. He already had a network of institutional clients — those twenty vital phone numbers — because of his company's block trading and because of bought deals. Connacher chose to work with one of Gordon Capital's founders, Gordon Eberts.

It was an inspired choice. Eberts had only recently resurfaced at the stockbrokerage company. He had founded the original version of Gordon Capital with partner Monte Gordon in Montreal thirteen years earlier, but he hadn't been around for about ten years. Instead, the eclectic Eberts had wandered away from the world of brokerage, travelling and dabbling

at collecting art for clients such as Montreal food-store magnate
Arnold Steinberg and friends from Winnipeg and Toronto.
According to one friend, Eberts is not "a unidimensional Bay
Street jock idiot." By 1981, Eberts decided he needed to earn
money again, so he wandered back to Gordon Capital. There
was still a seat waiting for Eberts, considered brilliant by his
peers — as long as he understood that Jimmy Connacher was
boss. What was there for Eberts to do? His specialty had always
been bond trading, and he had been the best. Connacher wasn't
that interested in bonds — but he was very interested in Jack
Cockwell's ideas about these new preferred shares. Gordon
Eberts became Canada's first real preferred-share engineer.

At first, Eberts was not at all enamoured of the new product. He began to study it from every angle. How would it
benefit a financial institution to own these shares from a tax
perspective? How would the institution invest money? What
would the investment do for the company's earnings? How
could Eberts explain all this to Gordon Capital clients? While
Cockwell was perfecting his plan within the Brascan family,
Eberts began selling the idea to institutions. Eberts became
better at preferred shares than he had been as a bond trader.
"He really came into his own with preferreds," says the head
of a major Canadian financial supermarket. "He did his
homework. He spent a long time, a lot of dreary hours personally doing the kind of diligence that you do if you want
to be the king of the castle in that kind of area. He understood
the tax act and he knew where to go in Ottawa to get fast
answers." Eberts used the answers to figure out how to structure the share issues; that is, he made a blueprint for the
market. "He spent a lot of time with the decision-makers on
the buy side, and the decision-makers on the issuing side. He
moved in a circle of people on both sides of the table that kept
the time frame short and the puffery out of it and got action."

One merchant banker explained what happened next. "The
more successes you have, the more successful you become. If
you do one deal, you see another one, you see two more and
the next thing you know [there are] a couple on top of that
one." In fact, Eberts gained ground on Cockwell. He set up

a market for special shares no matter who the issuer was. This was the market Cockwell had been planning to control.

"Basically, Cockwell met his match," said one stockbroker. "Eberts didn't steal Cockwell's thunder, because from the corporation's point of view and from the tax-avoidance point of view, Cockwell conceptualized and achieved what he set out to achieve. But from the point of view of establishing the market, which Cockwell wanted to do within his own merchant-banking corporations, Eberts ran away with it." Eberts' success remained a sore point between Cockwell and Connacher for years. Cockwell was incensed because he had been bested by a man who had simply shown up at work one day after ten years out of the business. With characteristic bile, Cockwell complained privately about "that bum, who dug himself out of the gutter and came and pissed on my parade."

Cockwell didn't get all the glory, and he didn't get to control the preferred-share market, as he had planned. But Cockwell's new market was established, and his plans for refinancing the group were in place. Again, Bay Street had been shaken by Jack Cockwell's view of the world. Critics thought of the short-term preferred-share market as a more polite, Canadian version of the U.S. junk-bond market. Junk bonds were seen by some as simply companies papering over their cash-flow problems by offering high interest rates to buyers. Preferred-share issues gave the Edper group a reputation, in some circles, of being a paper mountain. But had this "paper" been purchased by the stable companies in the group, such as Royal Trust and Hees? If the stock market began to fall, could the "paper" shareholdings sink the big, publicly traded companies?

Even Trilon director Alan Hockin worried about the preferred-share financings. "Certainly, I used to mutter about this and look at it." He agreed that the group had issued and bought a lot of preferred shares. But Hockin draws a big line down the middle between the two types of transactions. "I think they [Edper] feel that the kind of preferred shares that they would want to issue are not the kind of preferred shares that they would want to own. In other words, if the market will take the kind of preferred shares which they can issue, they are selling to the market, they are not buying." If they bought shares to prop up their stock issues, it would be through Hees, the group's central bank, not through Royal Trust. Hees might hold the stock for a while, Hockin explains, but it would then be "sent out to friends, or whatever." Hockin adds that if he had been a Hees director, "I think there were times when I should have been worried."

After its systematic popularization by Cockwell and company, preferred-share financing grew; soon no firm could ignore it. "It's kind of like going to a movie premiere. It's a private show and only a few people see it," remarks a prominent merchant banker. "But after the premiere, then everybody has the chance to go see it, and it becomes the talk of the town for awhile. Once it [the preferred-share market] started to be publicized, participants identified with it and hoped to get more business." Once boards of directors began approving the purchase of the new kind of security, board members began to wonder how their own firms could use the preferred shares. Bay Street discovered technicolour financing.

While preferred-share financing took advantage of the tax system, this was, at base, a method of ensuring financial stability for the group. Andy Sarlos suggests that Cockwell might have used the tax motivation as a screen to his real motivation: survival of the group. But investment guru Ira Gluskin argues that Jack Cockwell could have structured the group's survival in a number of ways. "Their empire is founded on good companies," Gluskin said. "The paper shuffling in the preferreds have enabled them to [finance]. That has been technique one. They could have done technique two, three, four, five or six." By 1987, Ottawa had changed the tax rules, and preferred shares were passé. Cockwell, of course, had long since moved on to new financing wrinkles; he also began to publicly state that the group's financing structure was not motivated by taxes. He pointed out that the group paid $2.2 billion in taxes between 1984 and 1987. Still, he couldn't resist defending the preferred market he had fathered. He proudly told an attentive audience at Brascan's 1987 annual meeting that a recent European study had ranked Canada as the most sophisticated preferred-share market. Canada's resource base needed preferred shares during the early 1980s, Cockwell said, to provide the money banks wouldn't lend companies. The preferred share market was "a very useful buffer during the down periods.

"We have established the financial base of the group over the last three or four years," Cockwell proclaimed in the spring of 1987. To do that, he had used the bought deal, the merchant bank, and the preferred-share market. But his view of how to run the financial system spawned an even more important innovation. His plan had dual, interlocking aims: to help finance the group, and to change the approach of Bay Street to the group's public-share issues. The introduction of Great Lakes Group in 1984, however, went a step further: it established a Brascan group financing engine with more financial clout than the entire Canadian stockbrokerage industry.

Great Lakes Group was big, four times the size of the largest stockbroker in the business. The day Great Lakes was formed, it had $450 million in investment capital, more than half the combined capital of the other ninety-eight investment dealers. And looking at only equity, not debt, it had more permanent capital than the entire investment fraternity. Neil Baker didn't hesitate to mention this to regulators shortly afterward to help his bid for more industry capital, although he did add, "Mr. Eyton and Mr. Cockwell are going to love me for this."

The corporate shell of Great Lakes Group, a hydro-power utility, had been an orphan in the Brascan group for years. Jack Cockwell had tried to sell Great Lakes to Union Gas in 1982. But he soon realized he was stuck with it for a while, and he didn't want it to be sitting idle. He decided to place it at the base of his new financial company. As always with Cockwell, there were tax reasons. As well, he hoped the steady nature of the utility business would offset the more cyclical nature of the financial business. And the utility had the aura of a regulated company, a stamp of public approval.

Great Lakes Group was conceived as a way to provide "last-resort" financing for brokers, so the Edper group would not have to turn down a financing deal, or sell stock at a lower price than Cockwell and his team thought it should sell for because the broker was afraid to push the market. For a fee, Great Lakes Group would guarantee the broker a market for any unsold shares. Originally, the fee was to be paid by the selling company; later, the fee was paid by the broker. Beyond that particular goal, flexibility replaced strategy as the watchword for future company operations. But the real genius behind Great Lakes Group was that instead of trying to compete with banks and stockbrokers, Cockwell invited banks and brokers to be his partners, so he could draw on their resources.

Not everyone was interested in working with Great Lakes. At least one financial institution, worried about Great Lakes' potential role and the regulators' reaction to a deal, turned down the offer. But for Merrill Lynch, it was an offer that came at the right time. Michael Sanderson of Merrill Lynch first met Jack Cockwell when Cockwell walked into his office and told him about Great Lakes. Says Sanderson today, "You bring in partners for two reasons. One is you need their money, but two, you need their expertise, global connections. I mean, I don't think they came over to see me because I'm the nicest guy in the world; they came over to see me because money was Merrill Lynch."

Sanderson had based a building strategy on just this kind of connection, so he was pleased to be included by Jack Cockwell. So was the Canadian Imperial Bank of Commerce, which slowly had been rebuilding its relationship with Brascan since it had acted for Brascan, the losers in the 1979 takeover by the Edper group. Trevor Eyton, Jack Cockwell, and Brascan's Bob Dunford approached the bank with their plans to recapitalize the Great Lakes utility company. The idea fit in with the bank's recent internal restructuring, which included a special department to deal with corporate banking for investments and stock trading. The chance to invest in an unregulated part of the financial business looked attractive. A senior executive at the bank at the time says he was happy to have the ties to the other members of the board. "It was really a double-barrelled opportunity.'' The Canadian Imperial Bank of Commerce became the second largest investor in Great Lakes next to Brascan. The bank contributed nine per cent, or about $40.5 million, to Great Lakes' coffers.

Other financial institutions also made their way to chairs at the Great Lakes board table. The Brascan group held sixty-five per cent of the company's common stock; the CIBC and Merrill Lynch held eight per cent; Canada Permanent Trust held two per cent. Four other trust companies held preferred shares: Canada Trust, First City Trust, National Victoria and Grey Trust, and Standard Trust.

In classic fashion, Ken Clarke, a British-born corporate-finance expert, was plucked from Merrill Lynch to head Great Lakes Group. Before his stint at Merrill Lynch, Clarke had worked at Touche Ross with Jack Cockwell. While he was at Merrill Lynch, Trizec Corporation was one of Clarke's prime accounts. With Michael Sanderson, he was the main link between Merrill Lynch and the Edper group; Clarke's participation was on a work-a-day level. Like his old friend Cockwell, Ken Clarke thought dealers had taken advantage for too long of companies that issued stock. "When you're dealing with a dealer, you're dealing with somebody who has an inherent conflict of interest,'' Clarke says. He explains that the broker is considering the reaction of the client who is buying the stock as well as the interests of the seller. Sellers need someone who will ensure that they get the most money possible. "That is a different standard than what the dealer thinks he can sell easily and profitably with the least amount of trouble,'' Clarke explains.

Clarke also thought there was a need for a more constructive link — perhaps a central agency for group financing — between dealers and the Edper group. From the dealer's point of view, Clarke says, the group is a very difficult account. "One has to be cognizant of the central values,'' he says, while also realizing that individual managers make their own decisions. And with the amount of money the group was raising, he adds, "If anyone needs it this group does.'' But while Great Lakes could interpret the group to the investment world, that was not the main agenda. It was clout that Cockwell envisioned, a way to gain the best value for his dollar through concentrated buying power.

In the nether world of corporate-finance specialists, secrets are paramount. "They always sit in the back, in the corner, and they take notes and they don't talk to people," says one broker. "That's what corporate finance is all about." In the early days, the Great Lakes Group was part of the "exempt market," a catch-all phrase that included everyone: film syndicators, MURB dealers, tax-shelter artists, venture capitalists, and big-deal players. The exempt market was already a potent force; a 1984 industry study showed that, between 1979 and 1983, half the security issues were done in the exempt market. The exempt market also included debt issues and bought deals. Says Garfield Emerson, "They were at one end of the spectrum of a broadening group providing financial services [who] are not part of the normal investment dealer community."

The new role had new rewards. The Great Lakes Group offered the industry access to capital — at a nice fee. It offered to buy stock that brokers couldn't sell, through what it termed a "dealer-support system," and to warehouse the stock — at a nice discount. It offered to provide advice to issuers and dealers on how to set up stock offerings. For an issue of $100 million or less, Great Lakes' fee was one-tenth of one per cent; for larger issues the fee was one per cent. The company also offered to syndicate large issues, or to place them privately. The group committed capital to a venture-capital fund and brought in other partners; by 1985, there was a $50 million fund for investment in private business. Great Lakes bought a partnership position in a mutual-fund company, 20/20 Group Financial. In 1986, it bought a position in an investment-management company, Connor Clarke. To Great Lakes' chief executive Ken Clarke, the key word for Great Lakes' operations is hustle. It is a business philosophy he believes in. The group has the ability to spot a deal, do a job, move into a new area quickly and with finesse.

From the beginning, the business community has confused Hees and Great Lakes. In many ways, Great Lakes was the "son of Hees." Hees first developed the expertise to deal with "special situations," to take risks for a longer term. Ordinary dealers didn't or couldn't do this, because they didn't have the capital, and they weren't in that business. They were traders. In contrast, Hees, and later Great Lakes, acted as principal, not agent. Both are willing to step into the breach and buy an issue of stock and hold it until the market turns around. Both look at risk the same way. and both are geared to rewards. "We're not interested in lending money for half a percentage point over prime [rate]," says Clarke. "We're interested in good 'super profits' out of the transaction. By super profits, I mean something beyond a nice banking return." Both Hees and Great Lakes turn away a lot of deals. "We probably look at twenty deals before we do a deal," says Clarke.

But there is a distinct if subtle difference between the two companies. Hees is a longer-term investor; Great Lakes is, in Michael Sanderson's words, "more of a transaction company." In many stock deals, it acts as the buyer of last resort. Although there is nothing like Great Lakes Group in the more liquid U.S. stock-market scene, Sanderson says that "Great Lakes in a classical sense would equate to any of the large merchant banks in the world."

The Edper group, which comes to market at least a dozen times a year, was looking for ways to outwit the underwriters, who were cautious by nature. The bought deals of Gordon Capital's Jimmy Connacher had started to change the underwriters' attitudes, but there was still what one observer called the "station-wagon attitude." "Partnership capital is risk capital," the observer explains. "You've got your house and your station wagon in hock for your company. You are asked to underwrite a Brascan issue and the market is soft and you can't really do the issue at the size you promised except by lowering the price."

Great Lakes provided a formal backstop, or sub-underwriting agreement, first for group issues and later for other companies. For a hefty fee, it would guarantee to pick up the stock so the issue price could be kept up. The more money raised in the stock market, the better the company's balance sheet, the more it could borrow, and the better its credit rating. "If, by putting up a dollar, we can help a company raise $20 in the equity market, that company can then probably borrow another $15," explains Ken Clarke. "So by putting up a dollar, we've given that company $35 of funding." It was the classic risk issue again reworked by Jack Cockwell for his own benefit. Minority shareholders at times objected to the back-up or "greenshoe" idea. They wondered why they were paying a fee so that a group company in which they didn't hold shares — Great Lakes — could buy stock issued by their company, for example Trilon, in which there seemed to be good market interest. In fact, the back-up idea became a controversy, and would bring Brascan under government scrutiny; in reaction, the group changed its policy and brokers began to pay Great Lakes' fees.

Many brokers didn't approve of the idea of a sub-underwriter; large firms thought they didn't need this type of back-up. But they adjusted to circumstance. As Michael Sanderson explained, "You do create change because people react to it. I know when Great Lakes started, people pooh-poohed the idea. They were never invited to be a sub-underwriter in any deal. As time went by, more and more they improved their effectiveness by being a sub-underwriter, and now it is not unusual to see them at all. And also, I think they've increased the tempo of the deals on the street. Deals can now come faster, cleaner, quicker, bigger."

Ken Clarke explains Great Lakes' motives: "For our group, or any group, to get the best out of the market, you've got to have the goodwill of the distributors, the dealers. Here we have a bought-deal environment — show us your best, and slit your throat to do the business. In the end, enough people slit their throats, there are no bodies left. That's not in our interest. That's not in the interest of the marketplace." Instead, he says, Great Lakes helps to "foster relationships" with the dealers. "We haven't tried in any way to push the role of the traditional investment bankers aside. We have tried to complement and enhance it, to the benefit of the [stock] issuer." The Great Lakes Group shapes deals and hands out advice to group companies about the timing of deals, strategy, and tactics.

Great Lakes Group, like Hees before it, developed a pattern upon which others could fashion merchant banks. In the next three years, several family-dominated organizations set up similar merchant-banking businesses, for example the Belzbergs (First City Capital) and Reuben Cohen and Leonard Ellen (Central Capital Corporation). At the same time, brokers were adding to their capital and a few were taking principal positions when they cut deals. The success of Great Lakes showed that taking risks for a fee could make money.

In May 1986, one of the biggest warehousing deals showed that others could do what Great Lakes did. Merrill Lynch and Gordon Capital, the latter in partnership with Genstar Corporation, which had a ten-per-cent stake in Gordon Capital at the time, joined with Great Lakes to warehouse forty-two per cent of British Columbia Forest Products Limited stock, worth $250 million. They sold nine months later to New Zealand's Fletcher Challenge Limited at a profit of $225 million, doubling their money. Sanderson says the deal reflects his own willingness to act as principal. Great Lakes legitimated this kind of deal. But, Sanderson says, "I would have done it if Great Lakes Group didn't exist. It's a matter of philosophy and opportunity."

Changing opportunity makes for changing philosophy. In May 1987, Great Lakes issued its first common-stock offering, with Hees stepping in to provide a one-time backstop agreement. The renegade had joined the public markets. The deal was not entirely smooth. The issue did not sell well; it was a victim of the tag end of a bull market, which was softening for new issues partly because of uneasiness before Michael Wilson's reform-minded budget, which was expected to hurt the stock market. And people still did not understand Great Lakes. But after that, Hees took a large position in Great Lakes, and the two firms declared their separate roles: Great Lakes as a registered dealer in the new, more open securities markets of June 1987, and Hees as a merchant banker that would look to Great Lakes for public issues.

At the time of Great Lakes' inception, the brokerage business was examining itself to death while still attempting to stem the tide of change. Placing capital on the line — a necessity once the bought deal arrived — meant that brokers needed to have the capital to risk. Brokers had to grow larger, and in the next few years there were several mergers on the Street. As brokers struggled to maintain a position in a newly competitive world, other players tried to enter the market. In mid-1983, the Toronto-Dominion Bank's entry into discount brokerage sparked a public hearing into the role of banks in the brokerage business; in 1984 there was another hearing, this time into brokerage capital and who should be allowed to invest. In late 1986, Ottawa and Ontario were ready to throw the doors open. The banks, the foreigners, all would be allowed into the brokerage business. Those brokers who had fought against change — dubbed "the Flat Earth Committee" by their detractors — found they would have to cope. James Pitblado had argued against change: "Once you cry havoc and unloose the dogs of war, you can't control them, so you've got to go all the way."

There were many pressures, but three factors dictated change: internationalization of markets; the push by banks for a place in brokerage; and a difference in attitude in Canadian markets. The third factor is reminiscent of the Royal Bank bought deal, which changed the brokerage industry. The laurels went to those who dared, says Pitblado: "It was the ability to be, if you will, psychologically comfortable with taking risks, rewarding those who are good at judging." The brokers have scrambled to increase their capital, making deals with other financial institutions or private backers in order to compete in the new international market.

Some argue that the brokers didn't really need all this new capital; they just needed to take advantage of the system that was being developed for them. The capital base of the investment community was adequate for the type of business it was doing before Gordon Capital pioneered the bought deal, some observers argue. Great Lakes Group and others like it could have provided the capital needed for the bought deals. Many people say it was mind-set, not money, that was the problem. It was a time of international deregulation, and Canada opted to throw open the doors. Now, with foreign investors moving in and positioning themselves to gain market share, and banks controlling the top six Canadian brokers, there will be very "patient" money not at all worried about profits at first. Everyone sees increased competition. And competition will be good for the clients, the Brascans of this world.

The stock-market "crash" of October 19, 1987, meant the demolition of stock prices for companies that Jack Cockwell had laboured years to raise in public esteem. The price of Hees stock plummeted to less than half its pre-stock-market-crash level; other group companies fell with the market, or farther. But the crash came at a time when most of the companies were well financed; Cockwell had been proclaiming a few months earlier that the group was at last secure.

The stock-market crash did something for the Edper group that nothing else could have done: it proved that Edper was not a "paper mountain," whose managers would run when the market crashed. All the talk about one group company propping up another, about executives who were sure to cash in at the top of the market and decamp to sunny climes, all the posturing by the old-liners on Bay Street was proven to be totally false. Certainly, everyone in the group lost money on their stockholdings. Peter and Edward Bronfman lost about $600 million; the loss cut their worth to about $1.1 billion. Some stockbrokers speculated that Hees stock was a "house of cards," and would continue to tumble. Individual group managers who had been borrowing to buy stock now had a very long-term commitment to building their businesses. But, by the late autumn of 1987, the group had become so central to the lifeblood of the Canadian financial system that, rather than becoming a source of worry for brokers and financiers, through Great Lakes, they became the saviours of the most "establishment" brokerage firm of all.

In the weeks following the October stock-market crash, the company most threatened was Wood Gundy. Wood Gundy represented everything that was the old way of doing business.

Its domineering chieftain, Edward (Ted) Medland, had been the spokesman for the Flat Earth Committee. Wood Gundy had emerged as the top-of-the-line, pace-setting broker during the later seventies and early eighties as its major rival, the old-line A.E. Ames, floundered, and finally disappeared into the maws of Dominion Securities. But Wood Gundy had been showing signs that it couldn't adapt to the new investment climate of the mid-eighties. Indeed, Medland had written his own epitaph. During a 1986 press conference to announce a merger between Wood Gundy and Gordon Capital, Medland said that, without a partner, Wood Gundy would wither and die. The merger with Gordon Capital lasted only a week before it fell apart, and lengthy negotiations with the Royal Bank of Canada also failed. Staff began to leave. The eighty-year-old organization began to crumble. Then, in mid-1987, Medland announced a very lucrative deal with First National Bank of Chicago; he was, for a short time, again a *wunderkind*. But after the crash, the deal was up for renegotiation; finally it, too, foundered. It was rumoured that the deal fell apart because Medland would not agree to resign.

Amidst the chaos, Wood Gundy struggled to maintain its credibility. But while the industry was aghast at its merger attempts, no one really thought the company was in danger of going under — at least, not until Friday, October 23. That afternoon, at a meeting with its brokerage partners on a major international underwriting of the shares of British Petroleum, Medland suggested that Wood Gundy might back out of the bought-deal agreement the firm had signed with the British government. If it didn't back out, Wood Gundy could lose up to $60 million on a $385 million commitment because it had agreed to buy the shares the week before the stock-market crash at a price it couldn't hope to recoup a week later. And Wood Gundy didn't have that kind of money.

But if it backed out of the deal, Wood Gundy would lose its credibility. It would lose its ability to make deals on a hand-shake, the trust that is the essence of dealmaking. It could be sued. And the Canadian public would see that a blue-chip firm was in trouble. If Wood Gundy could be in trouble, people might start thinking that the entire investment community could be shaky. For Wood Gundy, and for the industry, there had to be an alternative.

The deal closed at the end of October. On Thursday, October 29, the day before the close, Wood Gundy was at the end of its rope. Its bankers were refusing a loan, saying that any loan of that size must be looked upon as an investment — and this was one investment the bank didn't want. Medland and his team of executives had only one place left to turn.

While Wood Gundy was facing a life-or-death situation, it was business as usual elsewhere. The folks at Great Lakes and Hees spent the day sorting through the deals that had started to come in after the crash. They also discussed the fact that some brokers were breaking bought-deal agreements by using a special "out" clause. The clause let brokers out of a deal if there were a substantial change in the market. The Edper people were upset about the clause. Ken Clarke and Jack Cockwell both received calls from Wood Gundy asking that they contact Ted Medland; they thought Medland must want to discuss the bought-deal controversy. They called him from Cockwell's office , and he asked if they could come right over. After they hung up, Cockwell and Clarke agreed that they would both be happy to stroll over to Wood Gundy and tell Medland exactly what they thought about people who welched on deals.

It was three-thirty when they arrived at Wood Gundy. All the other people at Wood Gundy knew that, at five o'clock Toronto time, the Chancellor of the Exchequer would rise in the House of Commons in London, England, and announce whether the government would go ahead with the British Petroleum privatization stock issue. Wood Gundy had to be ready for whatever the government decided. Clarke and Cockwell sat on one side of the board table; Medland sat on the other, flanked by Wood Gundy vice-chairman Ed King and partners John Abell and Gord Homer. Unbeknownst to Clarke and Cockwell, government regulators were sitting in a room down the hall. Medland tersely outlined the situation: the chancellor would announce that the deal was to proceed. It would close by ten o'clock the next morning, Toronto time. Wood Gundy needed money quickly. What terms would the Edper group ask for a $137 million loan?

As Cockwell and Clarke sat at the table, facing the representatives from Wood Gundy, images raced through their minds: Wood Gundy failing; the entire financial system being shaken; line-ups outside investment houses. The pair asked for a few minutes together. They didn't want to hold Wood Gundy to ransom, they decided. One percentage point above the prime rate (the rate the Bank of Canada charges its best customers) would be fine. This wasn't a time for Clarke's "super profits." But they would need the BP shares as security. The Wood Gundy officials also offered the firm's holding company as collateral for the loan; Clarke and Cockwell agreed. They would need an hour, to go back to Commerce Court West and discuss the plan with the rest of the guys. As long as the others agreed, Wood Gundy could have the money. Great Lakes made the loan, and spread the risk to Hees and Brascan by borrowing some of the money from those companies. The group never sat down and mapped out the details. Says one insider, "The accountants come by with a brush pan and a broom later." That night, the two groups signed a simple, two-page agreement, and the bank provided the money to the British government the next morning.

When the chancellor made his announcement, he included some protection. The British government set a floor price below which it would buy back shares. The loan was a bit better than the group originally thought: Wood Gundy ended up losing $20 million on the deal. Whenever it sold the stock, the money was turned over to Great Lakes. And the group became parties to bi-weekly briefings by Medland and his partners on negotiations with a number of potential buyers for Wood Gundy. By the end of January, Wood Gundy had repaid $100 million of the loan. During the last week of January, it announced a merger with the Canadian Imperial Bank of Commerce.

A few people say that Great Lakes pushed Wood Gundy into the arms of the Commerce, that they strong-armed the brokerage firm so they would be paid back. But general sentiment is very much on the side of the Edper group. Except for

Great Lakes and the group, no one was ready or willing to save Wood Gundy from immediate disaster. Wood Gundy's problems proved the need for and the value of a company like Great Lakes, which was full of cash, prepared to provide a backstop, and willing to take a risk. "It was a fundamental need of the system," says one insider. Great Lakes also showed the hustle it liked to brag about. They weren't the first ones Wood Gundy turned to, but when asked they made a decision within an hour. The group hoped the deal would engender goodwill, that this time, no one would accuse the group of under-the-table arrangements with old friends like George Mann and Jim Leech. The Wood Gundy loan was certainly a public-relations coup; the group was cast as the hero of the post-crash panic. After the bailout, one critic of the group said he had to congratulate Great Lakes. "I hate to say it, but it was a very responsible thing to do, and they deserve the credit." Added Clarke shortly after the sale of Wood Gundy to the bank: "I've been told by a lot of people that our writings, our views of the world have been vindicated in the last six months."

The corporate-finance market was gone with the crash, so Hees and Great Lakes looked at merchant banking deals in late 1987 and early 1988, deals like the Hees bailout of a company called National Business Systems. Ken Clarke estimates he saw ten deals a week, but they only chose one or two a month. They managed to patch together a few financings in the market, even a bought deal or two, but Clarke says it was a time "when merchant banking takes over from corporate finance." Of course, for the group, one is as good as the other.

In little more than five years, a financial system that Jack Cockwell had approached as a distrustful outsider had adapted to his rules and, finally, taken him to its heart. Playing by Cockwell's rules is now seen as the best way to negotiate a deal. Andy Sarlos says Cockwell's motivation in forcing change in the brokerage industry is easy to understand. "He became the largest user of equity funds needed in Canada," Sarlos explained. Ken Clarke says that the group raised $6 billion in equity between 1985 and mid-1987; it was important to Cockwell that he have a network of brokers who did things his way. "He needs players who are willing and able to do these deals with the minimum cost to him." Sarlos adds that the group turned to the stock market to raise money as inexpensively as possible. "We are talking billions of dollars a year, and if you have to pay five-per-cent commission on every one of these deals it kills," he says. "If you can do it for one per cent, you save four per cent for your shareholders. We are talking hundreds of millions of dollars."

In 1988, with the new entrants, the mergers, the crash, and its fall-out, the people making the decisions at brokerage firms are very different, in background and outlook, than the people who headed the old selling groups Cockwell disdained in the early eighties. "I think that the dealers were playing King Canute for a long time," muses Clarke. "It was absolutely in their interest to do so, and nobody should blame them, but now they are thinking differently, totally differently. The old syndicate managers who used to get together and have lunches and decide what an issue should be, without any real knowledge of the market or the issuer, that little fraternity — either the guys have changed as individuals or the individuals themselves have changed." He sees the group as the vanguard of that change. "I'm a representative of a new generation of people, who didn't feel happy feeding off that sinecure, that franchise."

Like the Edper group, Gordon Capital, once a renegade, is now the role model in a radically different business. But for some people, Jimmy Connacher's personal style will always be anathema. Even in 1988, when it is widely acknowledged that the shake-up was needed and good for the country, the private grudge against Connacher's bought-deal coup remains. "It was a brilliant stroke; they should build a statue for him on Bay Street," admits one financier. "I don't know whether they should get the pigeons to come and shit on it."

CHAPTER ELEVEN

The Invisible Hand

*They were different than we were. But it is not our
style to try to tell people what to do.*
— Trevor Eyton, testifying at an Ontario Energy
Board hearing into the takeover of Union Enterprises
Limited

The June Ontario sun warmed the plank dock on Lake Ros-
seau. Jim Leech was relaxing with some favourite cottage reading: the *Globe and Mail*'s Report on Business. He had just
spotted a small item on a proposal to reorganize Union Gas
Limited into a holding company, a move that would permit
diversification, restructuring, and all those other good things
of the 1980s. Union Gas was a plum — a utility that distributed
natural gas to half a million customers in the stretch of prosperous south-western Ontario from Windsor to just west of
Toronto. Union Gas had a guaranteed income for as long as
there was snow in winter.

But until the proposed reorganization, which in effect put
a holding company on top of the utility, the province restricted
anyone from owning more than twenty per cent of it. The
board of Union Gas was dominated by comfortable, rural
Tories who passed for aristocrats in London and Chatham.
They were demonstrating their *In-Search-of-Excellence* savvy

255

by proceeding with restructuring the share ownership of the company to allow it to take over other businesses. Other utilities had been restructured to escape government regulation. But Jim Leech's morning perusal of the newspaper triggered a series of events that would, in the following six months, signal one of the last hurrahs of the old guard of corporate Canada, and raise unresolved questions about the exercise of power and decision making within the Edper empire. With a little help from its friends at Brascan, Hees, and Gordon Capital, the company of which the thirty-seven-year-old Leech was president, Unicorp Canada Incorporated, would turn the country's business world on its head, making bad guys into good guys and good guys into jerks. Two public regulatory hearings, several court actions and large public advertising campaigns would give Canadians one of the most awesome public disclosures of corporate power in operation ever seen. It would also demonstrate the insidious nature of corporate concentration. During 1984, for the first time, Canadians would understand that Brascan's influence in the Canadian business community was persuasive. It was not just what it owned, the interlocking boards of directors, the interrelated corporate holdings and business dealings; it was the friends it made and informal IOUS it had collected. It was the contacts with politicians, investment dealers, accountants, bankers, and lawyers. That group, which values its anonymity, wanted to be close to the Brascan executives; they hustled after Brascan business and were careful not to cross Brascan unless there was no other way.

The invisible hand of Brascan and its friends had the power and the will to make events happen. In 1984 Brascan wanted something to happen at Union.

Leech went in to telephone his boss, George Mann, chairman and sixty-eight-per-cent owner of Unicorp. If Hollywood were casting the part of unsettling upstart on Bay Street, Mann would cinch the part. As far as many of the members of the establishment were concerned, Mann had three strikes against him: he was Jewish, slick, and had a chequered past in mortgage lending. His fortune was built on astute stock-market moves.

At the opposite end of the spectrum stood Darcy McKeough, the chairman and chief executive of Union Gas. McKeough was fifty-two, and he had all the proper credentials for the old guard. Born and bred in the prosperous farming town of Chatham, the scion of a prosperous family in the plumbing contracting business, he had the confident bearing of a WASP sure of his place in the ruling class. He had spent fifteen years of his adult life as a member and Cabinet minister in provincial Tory politics, building a legendary reputation for connections. At one time, as treasurer during the halcyon years of the Bill Davis regime, McKeough was Ontario's second most powerful politician. He resigned from Cabinet in 1978 over a point of principle, and later landed the chief executive post at Union Gas.

George Mann was a businessman who read annual financial statements for fun; he immediately grasped the significance of Leech's find. The restructuring, said the *Globe and Mail*, would formally take place on December 31. Leech and Mann set about acquiring a hundred shares of Union — something they routinely did with any company they were even mildly interested in. From June to November, they collected information about Union. By November, they were aware of an unsatisfied shareholder who wished to sell sixteen per cent of the company's shares: GLN Investments, a subsidiary of Great Lakes Group, which itself was a subsidiary of Brascan.

The Union Gas investment had been a thorn in Jack Cockwell's side for several years. When Leech and Mann started buying, Cockwell saw a chance to sell — at the price he wanted and in the way he wanted. The group's involvement with Union Gas had been difficult from the beginning. In 1980, two Calgary oilmen who ran a small company had approached Cockwell for some help. Their company had run into trouble financing the purchase of a sixteen-per-cent block of Union stock. Cockwell hit on the idea of approaching Union for two board seats for the Calgary company. As part of a workout deal, he had secured a promise from the company's bankers that, if the company could "equity account" the stockholding — that is, treat it financially as a subsidiary holding rather than as a stock-market investment — then the bankers would lend more money. But to "equity account," a company must have board representation. And that was a problem.

When he took the job at Union, McKeough brought in outside advisors to ensure his success as a newly minted businessman. John Evans, a senior partner at the venerable law firm of Blake, Cassels & Graydon, had been retained as chief legal advisor; Tom Kierans of McLeod Young Weir had won the job of investment advisor. Dealers Dominion Securities and A.E. Ames had held the Union account for some time, and when Kierans won the business, despite an open tender, there were mutterings of a political fix. Kierans was one of the fabled Big Blue Machine back-room boys, one of a handful of men whom Ontario Tory premier Bill Davis had relied on for advice at Tuesday and Thursday breakfast meetings at the Park Plaza.* Evans and Kierans quickly became involved in the affairs of the company, often eclipsing senior officers of the company.

It was clear that McKeough needed the help. He was a facilitator, a politician, a good guy. He found it hard to say no — and in business that is often necessary. One Union Gas insider says: "Everything is smoothing over, patting the edges." Even Tom Kierans acknowledges: "Darcy is a visionary and a leader. When it comes down to the nitty-gritty of saying no, however, this is something best left to others."

Cockwell began his campaign to get the two Calgary oilmen on the board of Union Gas. McKeough and the board members resisted; they thought the two businessmen weren't up to snuff. Cockwell persisted. One Friday evening,

---

*Tom Kierans advised William Davis and the Ontario government to buy the Canadian subsidiary, Suncor, from Sun Oil Company of Pittsburg, Pennsylvania. The government spent $600 million to acquire twenty-five per cent of Suncor; that shareholding, by the estimate of the auditor general of Ontario, is now worth $225 million.

McKeough was flying back to Chatham from a meeting in Montreal in McKeough's private plane with Kierans, Cockwell, and Trevor Eyton. McKeough chatted amiably and leisurely; he offered drinks. Cockwell declined; it was, after all, strictly business. Finally Cockwell asked what McKeough was going to do. McKeough let Kierans explain why the board objected to Cockwell's two nominees. "So I go through this whole thing about why this little company isn't worth a hill of beans," recalls Kierans. "And how their little paper shuffling looks like hell, and how I can't understand why Jack has got himself in bed with such guys, but in any event, there is no goddamn way they're going to go on the board." Cockwell lost his temper. The merchant-banking deal he had worked out was not going to fly. Cockwell explained the deal to Kierans again in a final attempt to make his argument for board seats. But Kierans's instructions from McKeough and the board were clear, and he remained adamant. The deal was dead, and Cockwell blamed Kierans.

By the time the aircraft landed in Toronto, Eyton, ever the diplomat, had calmed things down. Eyton went off in one car; McKeough stayed on the plane, destined for Chatham; and Cockwell and Kierans shared a car into town. Cockwell immediately began pitching another deal; he had recovered from the episode in the plane. He told Kierans that the group had decided to sell Great Lakes Power, the electric power utility in Sault Ste. Marie. He believed Union Gas should buy it, and he asked Kierans whether he would take a look at the company. Cockwell pulled a package of information out of his briefcase and handed it to Kierans, saying he would call Sunday to discuss it.

The power company had been set up brilliantly by Cockwell. It was a money machine. The key element in Cockwell's creation was that Great Lakes was a private utility that negotiated its rate of return behind closed doors with Ontario Hydro, rather than in public with Ontario Energy Board regulators. Because of Great Lakes' special situation, the company could use its cash flow to spin off lucrative side businesses.

For that reason, Cockwell wanted three and a half times the book value for Great Lakes.

On Sunday, Cockwell called Kierans for a response. Kierans began, "Jack, this arrangement is the second coming of Jesus Christ. But what the cash flow is worth to you and what it's worth to Union are two different things." Because Union Gas was regulated in a public arena, Kierans feared that the Ontario Energy Board would not approve the deal and that it would cause a public outcry. Cockwell exploded, launching into a tirade. Despite his reservations, Kierans offered to show the proposal to McKeough and Union's chief financial officer, Paul Little, a long-time political aide of McKeough's. "There's no goddamn point," responded Cockwell, and he slammed down the telephone.

In the meantime, Brascan had acquired the block of Union Gas stock from the Calgary oil company and Trevor Eyton and Bob Dunford, a Brascan treasurer, had joined Union's board. At various times during the next three years, Cockwell tried to convince Union Gas to buy Great Lakes — but without success. Those episodes and others contributed to Cockwell's growing irritation over how Union Gas was being run. He objected to the acquisition of an energy company, Numac Resources, "which," said Cockwell, "would not have been made if there had been senior management in the company." He was angry with the time it took the management at Union Gas to tackle problems. He chafed at the price of the utility's stock, which had failed to move from the $10 to $12 range since 1971, when it had hit a high of $18. But what really rankled Cockwell the most was a plan to issue more common stock in Union Gas in 1982. Cockwell resented the dilution. He believed it was "an easy way of life for the management and the company to issue common shares, because you don't have to service them if you are not performing." When Union Gas pushed ahead on the idea, Cockwell tried to talk company officials out of it. He offered alternatives. He suggested preferred shares as a way of raising capital for Union, or some sort of debenture financing. Anything but common shares, which he believed no one should issue in the high-interest-rate climate of 1982. Union Gas executives later claimed that, at one meeting, Cockwell urged them to "start milking this utility." Cockwell vehemently denied making the statement.

One of the "bad management practices" that drove Cockwell especially nuts was the fact that Union Gas paid income taxes. Cockwell approached Union Gas with yet another proposal: Union would buy $300 million of preferred shares issued by the group and, in the process, avoid paying current income taxes. The idea was enthusiastically received by some Union Gas officers, less so by others. McKeough called for his advisors. It was a brilliant scheme. The preferred-share structure was still new, and Kierans saw that there was nothing unethical or illegal in Cockwell's idea. But for a regulated public utility, he felt the scheme was too dangerous, and Kierans once again argued against a Cockwell proposal. McKeough sent Kierans and the treasurer of Union Gas, Doug Shields, to Cockwell's office to give him the bad news. After they delivered their message to him, the two men watched in amazement while Cockwell threw one of his legendary temper tantrums. He screamed, kicked filing cabinets, jammed chairs around the room. Finally, he calmed down enough for Shields and Kierans to leave.

For Cockwell, the frustration was twofold. He couldn't get his way, which was always a difficult thing for him to accept. Also, he was just getting his preferred-share scheme off the ground, and that $300 million formed a significant part of it. Cockwell was tiring of the game at Union Gas. He and Eyton were unhappy that little had changed in the way the company was managed, despite an avalanche of helpful suggestions. Many in the business community agreed with them that Union Gas was not well run, and that Darcy McKeough was inadequate as a hands-on manager.

Cockwell and Eyton had decided to put their block of Union Gas stock up for sale. They could effect no real change from their position, and they had failed to persuade the Davis government to change the rules that prohibited them from owning more than twenty per cent of the utility. They quietly let it be known that they were interested in selling. At one point,

Cockwell was approached by a prospective buyer who planned to go to McKeough with an offer. Cockwell advised bluntly: "It's a fucking waste of time to see McKeough; if you want a deal done, go see Kierans." Cockwell saw McKeough as a stubborn good old boy from south-western Ontario and Kierans as the obstreperous brains behind the throne.

In October 1984, Gordon Capital floated an idea that could help Cockwell. Neil Baker, who was on the board of GLN, the Brascan holding company that actually held the Union Gas shares, took a proposal to Union Gas's management. He wanted a group of executives to buy GLN's block of Union Gas stock at a price palatable to Jack Cockwell. Price had been a sticking point for Cockwell for some time. He had acquired the shares at an average price of $11.75. Then there was the accrued interest on the investment — the carrying costs. Cockwell would not take a loss on the books; indeed, any unloading of the shares must show a profit on paper. Baker outlined a plan to have the executive group effect a leveraged buyout through a sidecar company. Once again, some people at Union Gas greeted the idea with enthusiasm; others argued against it, claiming it was unethical and constituted, in effect, a raid on the widows-and-orphans stockholders of Union Gas. The latter side prevailed. Cockwell still could not sell his shares. An angry Baker warned Union Gas that he might "show the block to somebody Union won't like."

The management group at Union Gas, meanwhile, was busy with its proposed reorganization. It was steadfastly determined to reorganize, despite its awareness that the company would lose its protection from an outside acquisitor. One part of the utility stored gas in huge underground caverns and tanks located in south-western Ontario. To avoid that vulnerability to takeover, someone floated an idea to leave that part of the utility in the proposed holding company, which would be called Union Enterprises Limited. That section of the holding company would then still be regulated by the Ontario Energy Board, and the twenty-per-cent ownership restriction would continue. But McKeough and others, including John Evans and Paul Little, argued that a takeover precaution was ungentlemanly and not what the marketplace was about.

Also unhappy with the proposed reorganization were the Brascan boys. At the Union board table, Trevor Eyton and Bob Dunford worked hard at influencing the direction of the restructuring. Eyton offered to lend people to Union Gas, largely because he and Cockwell considered the Union Gas staff ill-prepared for the job. "I had the feeling," Eyton recalled, "that Union Enterprises with the reorganization was like a pretty gal all dressed up with nowhere to go."

On November 15, Jim Leech of Unicorp saw Ken Clarke, the newly appointed president of GLN, at the GLN offices. They discussed, among other things, GLN's block of Union Gas stock. A week later, Leech and Mann had Tim Price and Jack Cockwell to the Unicorp offices for lunch. It was part of a larger networking routine that the Unicorp guys tried to do with some frequency, and Unicorp and Hees had already done business together in the United States. The Edper people were happy to meet for lunch. After all, Eyton later said, "We follow them as a matter of course. Mann's record is one of making money. We try to identify those who are winners and those who are losers." Over lunch in the boardroom, Mann and Leech received the happy news that the Union Gas stock was not one of the Edper group's "strategic investments." Later that day, Leech contacted Unicorp's lawyer and fellow Unicorp board director Lorie Waisberg, of Eddie Goodman's firm Goodman and Goodman, to advise him they were seriously thinking about taking a run at Union Gas once the reorganization was in place. Two weeks later, in early December, Leech approached Jimmy Connacher to ask him to take charge of the acquisition of ten per cent of Union on Unicorp's behalf. Connacher checked with Cockwell, because Connacher had tried to sell the stock for Cockwell in October, then agreed. Cockwell had no objections to Connacher acting for Unicorp.

Meanwhile, Leech and his vice-president of finance, Michael Kordyback, began to arrange financing for the ambitious takeover. If they succeeded in winning the whole company, they would need $400 million. Instead of going to their corporate banker, National Bank, whose board counted Mann as a director, they arranged a $40 million line of credit at the Continental Bank during December. Later, they would get another $200 million from the bank to finance the takeover. Continental was nineteen per cent owned by the Bronfmans; Peter Bronfman and Jack Cockwell sat on its board, and Cockwell closely monitored its affairs. Leech and his people also arranged for the printing of a draft prospectus; they pushed their auditors to speed up the year-end audit of Unicorp. The plan to win Union Gas began to form. The code name for the takeover was "Strike."

Union Enterprises was a New Year's baby, a new holding company formed by Union Gas, unfettered and unprotected by government regulation. The company was in play. On January 8, Gordon Capital went into the market looking for three million shares at $12.50 each. There were few takers, and Gordon got permission from Unicorp to offer $13 and the promise that a higher price would not be offered during the following six months.

In the two weeks that followed, Gordon Capital scrambled to fill orders made by its client, Unicorp. In the process, Gordon Capital acquired a massive short position in Union Gas stock, something of which Unicorp officials were unaware. Unicorp also did not know that its agent, Gordon Capital, was selling Union Gas shares that it had purchased after December 11 — the date Gordon Capital was hired by Unicorp — into the Unicorp order. Gordon Capital was, in effect, actively bidding for stock to cover its short position and, in the process, upping the price that Unicorp would have to pay for Union Gas stock. By January 15, Unicorp had acquired ten per cent of Union Gas, and it looked very likely that Mann and Leech would go ahead with a takeover bid. A week later, on January 21, with an additional $20 million line of credit from the Continental Bank, Unicorp told Gordon Capital to buy 1.3 million more shares.

Gordon Capital's short position had diminished somewhat, but it quickly became apparent that it would be difficult to secure 1.3 million more shares on the market. Gordon Capital traders became desperate. They telephoned the large institutional holders of Union Gas stock, and pressured them into selling. The message to these shareholders was: this is the end of the buying at $13 a share. There is no more cash available, and Gordon Capital might approach a shareholder of Union Gas who held a fifteen-per-cent block, putting Gordon Capital's client at thirty per cent. In that case, Gordon Capital traders warned, any mopping-up purchases would not be as attractive as $13 cash. Even after employing that high-pressure sales pitch, Gordon Capital could not scare up enough Union Gas shares to fill the order by January 22 without taking a short position again. But two days later, Gordon Capital bought 314,000 shares from National Victoria and Grey Trust. However, Gordon Capital reported the purchase "as of" January 22 on its books, and chose not to do the deal through the Toronto Stock Exchange. Through Gordon's manoeuvres, Unicorp had acquired 4.5 million shares — 13.3 per cent — in Union Gas, at a cost of $60 million.

On January 23, the board of directors of Unicorp met to approve a formal takeover bid for Union Gas. Jim Leech arranged to meet with Jack Cockwell and Trevor Eyton the next day to discuss GLN's Union Gas stock. Leech says that several ideas were discussed at that meeting, including whether Brascan wished to buy Unicorp's shareholding. But, Leech recalls, "It was clear at that point that Cockwell wanted to unload his shares." Leech could not offer cash. To his surprise, the Brascan boys indicated that something else would be just as satisfactory. Their paramount concern, it seemed, was to get a price that would look good on the books. For the next three days, Leech and Michael Kordyback, Unicorp's vice-president of finance, worked feverishly. They structured an offer with representatives from Gordon Capital and Midland Doherty, their usual investment dealer. On January 29, at eleven-thirty in the morning, Leech rushed the proposal to Cockwell and Eyton.

The proposal was contained in a letter. Unicorp would proceed with a takeover bid on the same terms as its purchase of GLN's block of Union Gas. Unicorp offered one $1.17 Unicorp preferred share and one-half warrant for each common share of Union. As well, Unicorp wanted a lock-up on

GLN's block — that is, GLN could not withdraw from its commitment to tender its shares in a takeover bid if a more lucrative offer came along. For the tough negotiators at Edper, Leech's offer was unusually restrictive. But, they said later, they felt they had boxed themselves in. Unicorp had enough Union Gas stock that, if GLN wanted to preserve its position as a major shareholder, it would have to take Unicorp out. But if GLN wanted to sell, this was the best deal going.

Later, during the second of three government inquiries into the takeover, Jimmy Connacher explained why the offer was such a good deal for GLN. "These preferreds had rates of return on them of approximately twelve per cent after tax, compared to other preferreds in the market that traded in the neighbourhood of eight and a half to nine per cent. If you sold off your half a warrant, you were putting the preferred shares on your books at roughly $12 a share. These preferreds are retractable in seven years at $13 a share. So there is a dollar pickup there. Plus they had a dividend yield that paid $1.17, which, at $12, worked out to somewhere around eleven or twelve per cent. So if you added in the dollar you received in seven years on top of the dividends, the yield was in the neighbourhood of twelve per cent after tax."

Shortly after he received the proposal from Leech, Eyton telephoned Darcy McKeough and read him the offering letter. Eyton told McKeough that Brascan and GLN were evaluating the offer, and that the offer would go before the GLN board the next morning. Eyton and Dunford, as members of the board of Union Gas, absented themselves from the GLN board meeting — although they later helped to write memoranda about the meeting. The discussion at the board table was heated. Directors wanted to know why Cockwell and Eyton had agreed to waive any rights to get a better offer if another bidder came along. After lengthy debate, the majority of the directors approved the sale. Two directors who represented large minority shareholders disagreed: one was the representative from National Victoria and Grey Trust; the other was from the Canadian Imperial Bank of Commerce. Canada Permanent, a relatively new shareholder, abstained from the voting. Cockwell signed the offer on behalf of GLN. Eyton, mindful of his "good relationship" with McKeough, wrote a long and detailed letter of explanation.

In the letter, dated January 31, Eyton explained that the decision to sell GLN's Union Gas stock had not been inspired by any disappointment with Union Gas or the relationships that Eyton had enjoyed there. Rather, it was a combination of the hard, cold attraction of Unicorp's preferred stock netting out above the desired $12.50, and the formidable determination of Unicorp to win control. Eyton offered to attend the next Union Gas board meeting to proffer further explanation, and signed off wishing "best personal regards." Four days later he received a terse response from McKeough: Eyton need not attend the board meeting.

McKeough had known something was up before he received Eyton's letter. By mid-January, the heavy trading in Union Gas shares was obvious. Then, on January 26, at the provincial Conservative party leadership convention in Toronto, where Frank Miller was elected, Eddie Goodman spoke with McKeough. Goodman promised McKeough that he would find out who was buying up the Union Gas stock. Three days later, McKeough was in Calgary on business when he received a telephone call at eight o'clock in the morning from Goodman, who said that Unicorp was the mystery buyer of all the Union Gas shares, and that Unicorp would be offering to buy GLN's block of shares that day.

Goodman's news and Eyton's letter touched off an emotional reaction at Union Gas. On January 31, the board of directors of Union Gas convened in Toronto. Several directors were beside themselves. They already harboured a deep distrust for aggressive businesses such as Brascan and Unicorp, and for upstart businessmen such as George Mann and Jack Cockwell. The prospect of such people owning Union Gas was too much. William Somerville, president of National Victoria and Grey Trust (NVG), was most vocal. NVG, which was part of the financial empire controlled by Hal Jackman, held two million shares of Union Gas directly, and another one million in client accounts. Somerville vowed not to sell, and urged others to do the same. But Somerville was in a peculiar position: NVG owned a piece of Union and a piece of Great Lakes. While Eyton had absented himself from the GLN board meeting when it discussed the Union Gas sale because he was in a conflict of interest, the NVG representative did not. Strictly speaking, there was no conflict for Somerville, but the question remained: did one hand of NVG know what the other was doing? The Union Gas board was unanimous in its resolve to reject the offer by Unicorp. Other advisors to McKeough, such as Paul Little, Kierans, and John Evans — whose law firm, Blake, Cassels, had been on the losing end of the Edper-Brascan takeover battle in 1979 — urged him to fight.

Unicorp had sent out a takeover-bid circular to the "widows and orphans" shareholders of Union Gas on February 1. In fact, those shareholders were — aside from the institutional investors — more likely to be Union's customers and the solid citizens, the farmers and merchants and public servants of south-western Ontario. It would be a tough fight for Unicorp. The offer — the same one made to GLN — was complicated. And Union Gas shareholders identified more easily with McKeough and with board directors like William Somerville, who came from nearby St. Mary's, and Merv Lahn, chief executive of London-based Canada Trust. McKeough issued a public letter to Union Gas shareholders, recommending that they not tender. Unicorp and its investment dealers were expecting shares to come through Midland from small "retail" shareholders, but those shares did not materialize. The Unicorp package was supposed to be worth a little more than $13 a share, and Union Gas shares were trading as low as $12.25. But a major bond rating agency had rated the package at a low "P4." McKeough muddied the waters for his shareholders by warning them that Union Gas customers might face higher gas bills if Unicorp succeeded in its takeover bid and then had to finance it.

Meanwhile, rumours circulating on Bay Street had finally surfaced at the Ontario Securities Commission. On February 8, the OSC convened a hearing to decide on a request from Union Gas that Unicorp be prevented from proceeding with its bid. Union Gas lawyers, led by Howard Beck of Davies, Ward and Beck, argued that Unicorp was guilty of violating a securities regulation that provided for the equal treatment of all shareholders during a takeover bid. "The principle of equality goes to the root of public confidence in the securities market," Beck told the OSC. He contended that Unicorp's takeover had started as early as January 9, when Gordon Capital was buying shares for cash from large institutional shareholders in private agreements. Smaller shareholders had not been contacted by Gordon Capital and thus were treated unfairly because they were only offered paper as part of the official takeover bid announced on February 1. Leech, who had worn his Royal Military College blazer to the hearing in an attempt to combat the image problem Unicorp had in some circles, was surprised to see Beck acting for Union Gas. Beck was a friend, and he had been at a meeting on December 5, acting as counsel to Gordon Capital. The below-the-belt battle escalated when Jim Pitblado, president of Dominion Securities, which, with McLeod, was running the Union defence, accused Gordon Capital of market manipulation and called Unicorp's stock package "Monopoly money."

After a week of hearings, the OSC decided that Unicorp had not violated regulations: a takeover was considered underway when twenty per cent of a target company's shares had been purchased, and Unicorp had only thirteen per cent. The takeover was allowed to go ahead.*

But the commission chose to overlook some startling evidence that had emerged from the hearings. Two witnesses testified that Gordon Capital had leaked insider information about the impending takeover bid. First on the stand was William Rogan, president of an investment counselling firm that

---

*However, the commission found Gordon Capital guilty of misrepresenting its short position in Union Gas stock to Unicorp and of staying in the market to cover its shortfall after the takeover bid was official. Gordon Capital's buying could have had the effect of propping up the price of Union Gas shares, which would have misled investors who evaluated the Unicorp share-swap offer partly on the basis of the stock-market value of Union stock.

managed $100 million for wealthy investors. Rogan's firm owned 175,000 Union Gas shares. During a rare Saturday hearing, he testified that a Gordon Capital official had told him on January 18 that coming up was "the last day that I could sell my shares for $13 cash and that the follow-up was coming and would not be as attractive." Rogan had told the story to Paul Little soon after it happened. He called Little at the Union Gas downtown Toronto office and arranged to drive home with him that evening — both men lived on the same street in Toronto's Moore Park area. Rogan had agreed to testify at the OSC hearing on the condition that he be permitted to make a speech on the erosion of ethics in the securities industry. Unicorp's lawyers quickly tried to discredit him, describing him as a "naive zealot."

But several days later, a second institutional investor stepped forward. Duncan Baillie, a senior vice-president at National Victoria and Grey Trust, said that a Gordon Capital trader had telephoned him on January 22 or 23 and applied pressure to sell his Union Gas shares. Baillie said that the Gordon Capital employee told him that the "next offer would be in the form of paper and that we would not be particularly intrigued with the issuer." Baillie had to be subpoenaed to testify. "I don't particularly have an axe to grind," he told the commission, adding that his company wished to stay on good terms with Gordon Capital, Unicorp, and Brascan. Days before he testified at the OSC, Baillie was asked by his boss, Bill Somerville, to go to the offices of McLeod Young Weir to tell lawyers for Union Gas about the leak from Gordon Capital. He was questioned for three hours.

Although the OSC had found in its favour and had chosen to ignore the revelations of Rogan and Baillie, Unicorp was forced to extend its offer to March 11. More time for a search for a white knight by Union and more time for political fixes, said a bitter Leech. Later it was again extended, to March 15. But only a day after its victory at the OSC, Unicorp faced another hurdle thrown up by Union. Citing "hundreds" of letters of concern and complaint, the provincial energy minister announced that the Cabinet had ordered the Ontario Energy

Board to hold a hearing into the takeover bid, to investigate the impact of the bid on natural gas supplies and prices. If the takeover was deemed undesirable, the OEB had the power to retroactively disallow it.

The energy minister's announcement had come at the end of an agonizing Cabinet struggle. McKeough had counted on his political friends for help in fending off Unicorp. But times had changed. In December, with Bill Davis still at the helm, the Ontario Cabinet had waived a requirement that the OEB approve the reorganization in Union Gas as a subsidiary of Union Enterprises. Now, as Eddie Goodman and others in the Unicorp camp with political clout lobbied for their side, the Ontario Tory establishment was split. Premier Frank Miller's Cabinet did the smart thing: it sent the Union Gas requests for intervention to a regulatory body.

For the McKeough camp, the options were narrowing. At a board meeting in late February, Union Gas directors authorized a move that, in the takeover jargon of corporate America, is called a "scorch-the-earth tactic." McKeough was given permission to have Union Gas acquire another company. The move would make Union Gas less attractive. And if shares were issued to do the deal, Unicorp's holding in Union Gas would be diluted. McKeough first considered buying brewing company Carling O'Keefe, which he knew was for sale. That did not work out. He then re-examined a company Union Gas had once contemplated buying, Burns Foods Limited, a Calgary-based meat-packing concern owned by the Webster family of Montreal.

Howard Webster is a Canadian blue-blood, rich and influential in his own right. Webster preferred to sell for shares rather than cash, for tax reasons. McKeough and his advisor, Paul Little, met Webster in Montreal on February 28, and signed a deal that gave Union Gas control of Burns Foods in return for $125 million in preferred shares. Union Gas issued ten million preferred shares. Each carried a four-fifths vote, and the issue had the effect of diluting Unicorp's stake in the gas company.

But the acquisition of Burns Foods was the undoing of Darcy

McKeough. It was a flagrant abuse of the rights of the widows-and-orphans stockholders, whom McKeough had claimed he was protecting. It was an expedient tactic aimed at preserving the old guard's power. And it sickened Bay Street. When Trevor Eyton heard about it, he immediately sent a letter to every Union Gas shareholder denouncing the manoeuvre. Jim Leech says that, with the Burns Food deal, "the whole thing changed, the Street crossed the street." As Leech recalls, acquaintances literally crossed the street to tell him, "I don't necessarily like the takeover that you started, but what was just done to you was obscene."

That feeling was shared by people close to the takeover fight. Tom Kierans got on a flight for Bermuda, although he kept in telephone contact. "With the Burns purchase," recalls Kierans, an old friend of McKeough's, "Darcy took off the white hat and put on the black hat." Returning home from out of town on a Sunday, Hal Jackman immediately called David Weldon, a Tory friend, the president of Midland Doherty and a member in good standing of the Ontario establishment. Jackman asked if there would be a buyer for all of National Victoria and Grey's two million Union shares at $12.50 cash. Weldon said yes. On Monday morning, Jackman telephoned William Somerville to tell him that the shares were sold. Somerville recalled later, "I was amazed. I didn't think we would be able to find a buyer." Somerville had watched uneasily from his board seat while the Burns Foods deal had been negotiated. He had disagreed with the deal on business grounds, and he was disturbed by the growing wastefulness of the takeover fight. "I told them if they persisted, that we would reserve the right to sell. I hate that kind of move; nobody wins," Somerville said. When McKeough had brought the letter of intent to buy Burns Foods to the board for approval, Somerville had reluctantly given his vote after McKeough agreed to several conditions, including a face-to-face meeting with George Mann and Jim Leech.

The meeting was a disaster. The Unicorp people were irritated because they couldn't get McKeough alone to talk to them. McKeough's advisors stuck close by. That afternoon,

Union Gas publicly announced the Burns Foods deal. Several days later, on March 11, at the end of a two-hour meeting of Union Gas directors called to discuss defence strategy, Somerville announced that National Victoria and Grey was tendering its shares. Jackman's shares had sold through Midland Doherty to the Unicorp bid. Gordon Capital had then provided a buyer for the Unicorp units at $12.50 cash each.

On the eve of the bid's expiry, Unicorp needed two million more shares. Jimmy Connacher had a suggestion for George Mann: contact Paul Reichmann and ask him to consider an investment in Unicorp preferred shares. Early on Friday, March 15, Mann went to see Reichmann in his office in First Canadian Place. Mann went over the events of the takeover and explained that, as a result of the Burns Food deal, Unicorp had about forty-per-cent ownership in Union Gas. Mann thought he could win a proxy contest, however messy it might be. But he preferred to have clear control. He gave Reichmann Unicorp's latest financial results and asked him to consider buying Union Gas shares and tendering to the Unicorp offer. Reichmann said he would think about it, and the twenty-minute meeting was over. "The shares traded," says Jim Leech, "before the elevator hit the ground floor." After a few hours of study, Reichmann had telephoned Connacher and issued buy orders for two million shares of Union Gas at prices up to $12.50. The shares Reichmann bought came from Gordon Capital, acting as agent for some of its clients, and other brokers on the Toronto and Montreal stock exchanges. The Union Gas shareholders who were using Gordon Capital got $12.50 a share; shareholders using other firms on the two exchanges received between $11.25 and $12.375 for their shares. Reichmann tendered to the Unioncorp bid; George Mann had won Union Gas. But the fight was not over yet.

The day Unicorp announced that it had secured sixty per cent of Union's common stock and forty-eight per cent of the votes (because of the voting preferred shares), Darcy McKeough responded with a lawsuit. It was remarkable for its broad range of defendants: McKeough's old friend Hal Jackman was named along with Jimmy Connacher, George

Mann, Jim Leech, Midland Doherty president David Weldon, and chairman Phil Holtby, who sat on Unicorp's board.* McKeough claimed to be fighting for the "widow in Wallaceburg," and the Union Gas writ alleged that, in the case of the Jackman sale, the Unicorp forces had acted together to provide Jackman with access to cash and a good price for his Union shares, while smaller investors were given the choice of a share exchange or selling on the stock exchange for less than $12.50. Paul Little of Union Gas claimed that, of the 14,600 Union Gas shareholders with less than 5,000 shares before the takeover bid was announced, 14,100 were still Union Gas shareholders.

One "Wallaceburg widow" was Victor Beynes, who owned and operated an import-export business in Toronto. He held six hundred shares of Union Gas, and had found it difficult to evaluate the worth of Unicorp's offer because of conflicting assessments coming out of different brokerage houses. He knew about the grey market that operated outside the bounds of the stock exchange, and that some shareholders were getting $12.50 a share in cash. He had called Gordon Capital and offered his shares for that price. The Gordon Capital official told him his block of shares was too small; they weren't interested. Beynes then sold his shares on the Toronto Stock Exchange. He got $12.25 a share, doing much better than many small Union Gas stockholders, who got prices closer to $11 during the bid. The stock market, Beynes told the *Toronto Star*, "is a game in favour of the big boys."

When McKeough launched his lawsuit, Jim Leech immediately cloaked himself in righteousness. He said the lawsuit gave "corporate Canada a black eye," and he urged both sides "to stop their fighting and get back to business." People in McKeough's own camp were urging him to reconcile. Tom Kierans and Alex MacIntosh, a senior partner at Blake Cassels, began pressuring McKeough to negotiate a truce with Unicorp.

---

*Jackman and McKeough went back a long way and they saw each other socially with their wives. Since the takeover, McKeough has resigned from the board of Jackman's Algoma Central Railway and Jackman and McKeough have not spoken.

Finally McKeough relented, and the two sides met in a corner suite of the luxurious King Edward Hotel in downtown Toronto. Largely because of the goodwill of two lawyers present — Eddie Goodman, who represented Unicorp, and Jake Howard, a partner at Blake, Cassels, who represented Union Gas — an agreement was hammered out. Union Gas would drop the suit and co-operate with the new owners. In return, Unicorp agreed to hold eleven of the twenty board seats, leaving room for a strong "minority shareholder" faction. Most astonishingly, the two sides agreed to leave McKeough as chairman and chief executive officer. The deal concluded, Mann and McKeough shook hands and went down to the main-floor dining room, Chiaro's, to seal the pact with a meal. Also at the dinner table were Leech, Howard and Kierans. "It was," recalls Kierans, "one of the most uncomfortable meals I have ever sat through in my life."

Whispers of a conspiracy had been floating around the fight almost from the beginning. Was it a Brascan-orchestrated *coup d'état*, a Jewish conspiracy, or an unholy alliance of the new guard? How could little Unicorp *afford* to buy Union Enterprises without having made a pact with the devil somewhere along the way? Was there an owner behind the owner? Twenty-six days of dramatic hearings at the Ontario Energy Board did nothing to dispel the suspicions. By the time the OEB met for the first day of hearings into the takeover, on April 9, the two sides had ostensibly merged. But as the witnesses trooped into the hearing room, old wounds were reopened.

The energy board was charged with determining whether the acquisition would hurt the gas consumers of south-western Ontario; whether the costs of the expensive takeover would be passed on in the form of higher gas prices, supply cuts, or deteriorated service. When Ontario Energy Minister George Ashe had announced, only an hour after the OSC had cleared Unicorp's bid, that there would be a hearing, he had left open the possibility that the energy board could overturn Unicorp's ownership. But the hearing quickly focused on the stock-market games that had been played during the takeover. OEB chairman Robert Macaulay was an old hand at Ontario politics. His brother, Hugh, a long-time adviser to Bill Davis, had gone to his reward as chairman of Ontario Hydro. Bob Macaulay was known as the "Minister of Everything." He had held a number of portfolios in previous Ontario governments, including energy, and had emerged as the kingmaker during the leadership convention that had elected John Robarts as leader of the party. He was widely considered a bright, extremely ambitious, impatient, irascible man. He has, one admirer says, an ego the size of a house. Macaulay was disturbed by the extent of the energy board's power; he called it "one of the illusions of life," because the board had to seek the permission of the government to impose penalties such as injunctions, fines, or prison sentences. As the hearing began, the power structure in Ontario was changing dramatically. Frank Miller was waging a tough election battle, the Big Blue Machine was on the outs, and the Liberals, under David Peterson, were on their way to power for the first time in forty-two years. Macaulay saw an opportunity to make something of this hearing, to solidify the place of the OEB. The Union Gas hearing, Jim Leech likes to say, furnished two new hearing rooms and doubled the staff of the energy board.

Macaulay had chosen a lawyer, John Campion, from the Toronto firm of Fasken and Calvin, to act as board counsel, or, in effect, as chief prosecutor. Campion was an ambitious lawyer who wanted the energy board to extend its mandate to cover all aspects of the matter, even if it meant infringing upon the territory of the OSC. He had a sense that the shareholders of Union had not been fairly treated, but no solid information. Campion could not probe too far without facts of actual wrongdoing surfacing early. Otherwise, Macaulay would limit the inquiry to strictly energy matters. At the same time, Campion could not turn the thing into a three-ring circus. He had to be careful not to ruin careers and draw uninvolved people into the limelight.

But before a single witness could be called to testify, Unicorp, represented by Eddie Goodman, sought a court order to restrict the OEB's mandate. The OEB, as a part of its directions from the government, was supposed to determine whether the public interest was affected by the nature of existing or potential shareholders of Union. In other words, did the ability of Union's new owners to finance the takeover affect the long-term health of the utility. To determine that, the OEB had to find out exactly who would own Union — Mann, or some unknown purchaser waiting in the background. Unicorp clearly did not want the hearings to stray into the share-ownership question. Goodman wanted an order restraining the OEB from looking at both the way the shares were acquired and who had acquired them, and he wanted restrictions on the OEB looking into the effect of the takeover on Union shareholders. The court turned him down.

The hearings began on April 9, and the burning question was who had helped Unicorp. Unknown benefactors had purchased $135 million worth of Unicorp securities from large investors, who had accepted them as temporary payment for Union Gas stock only because they were assured that they would soon receive cash. The *Globe and Mail* wondered how a small company like Unicorp, with only $400 million in assets, could buy Union Gas, a corporation four times larger. The newspaper noted speculation in the investment community that Royal Trustco, Brascan, and other companies connected to the Bronfman family business empire held most of the shares. But the general expectation that the hearing would provide Bay Street fireworks was mitigated somewhat by the truce negotiated between Unicorp and Darcy McKeough.

Leech took the stand the first day and promised to provide a list of current Unicorp shareholders. Campion wanted to uncover the recent buyers of Unicorp's preferred shares. Ownership of the shares was largely in "street names" — the stockbrokerage houses or trust companies who held them for unknown clients. The Unicorp people had been less than helpful in helping Campion find out who they were. But the dividend list filed by Leech the next day revealed only that eighty-three per cent of the 15.3 million shares issued by Unicorp as part of the takeover bid were held by GLN, National Bank, Continental Bank, Midland Doherty, and Gordon, representing undisclosed clients. Campion could subpoena the brokers to find out who their clients were, but in the meantime he asked Leech if there had been discussions at Brascan or its affiliates about buying preferred shares. "Not to my knowledge," replied Leech, who also denied a rumour that there was a secret deal to sell Unicorp's 6.2 per cent holding in Canada Trust to Brascan in return for favours rendered during the takeover.

Truce or no truce, when Darcy McKeough took the stand a few days later, it was clear the gloves were still off. McKeough was hoping for a miracle, a roll-back order from the OEB. During most of McKeough's testimony, his new boss, Jim Leech, sat in the audience listening. McKeough urged the energy board to acquire the power to examine, in any takeover of a utility with monopoly status, not just the immediate owners but the ultimate owners as well, such as Unicorp. "When somebody acquires a natural-gas utility, they take on a different obligation than when somebody buys a Coca-Cola plant. There is a trust," he said. He also offered the energy board the opinion that undoing the takeover would not be a great problem. Finally, McKeough trained his bitterness on the Brascan group. He told the hearing that Brascan had tried to acquire more than the allowed twenty per cent of Union Gas in 1982, but that they "ran into a stone wall" at Queen's Park. He related the disagreements about Union Gas's financing plans, saying the company had strong views on "who we should finance with." Under questioning, McKeough changed his mind: "I withdraw that suggestion, it was not very strong," he said.

The board's attention gradually moved from Unicorp to Brascan. Testimony from Tom Kierans had shifted the focus. He was the key in helping Campion understand the significance of the huge share crossings that had occurred during the Unicorp bid. Kierans had taken a few swipes at the Unicorp side during testimony at the OSC hearing in February. At the

OEB, he called Unicorp's stock offer "the Canadian equivalent of American junk bonds." He mentioned the possibility
that the Brascan group — "a huge conglomerate with a reputation for turning a utility into a cash machine," according
to the *Globe and Mail* — would be exerting influence over the
business affairs of Union Gas. The hearings had yet to determine the mystery buyers of Unicorp's shares; there were still
rumours that the buyers were affiliates of Brascan. Kierans
took the energy board through the financial restructuring of
GLN. He pointed out that, unlike public utilities, GLN
negotiated its rates in private with Ontario Hydro. That, said
Kierans, put the private utility in the position to capitalize
"aggressively." In other words, GLN could take on a larger
debt-to-equity ratio. GLN used "double leveraging" as a way
of reducing payable taxes, Kierans said. The utility would
increase cash flow by borrowing, write off the costs, and re-
invest the money to increase cash flow. Brascan, testified Kierans, saw GLN as a "cash cow." The implication was clear for
Union Gas.

The OEB inquiry was proving too much for the officials at
the OSC. In an unusual step, they revealed that their investigation into the Union Gas takeover was continuing. Current
investigations were rarely, if ever, publicly disclosed in mid-
stream. Clearly, civil servant noses were out of joint.

On May 3, after the provocative statements of McKeough
and Kierans, GLN issued an unsigned manifesto explaining
itself and its actions. The eleven-page document, prepared prin-
cipally by Jack Cockwell, was intended to address "reported
comments by Union management and its professional advisers
which have created an unwarranted diversion from the basic
issue before the board." The war between Kierans and Cockwell began to rage. The GLN statement denied that long-
simmering disputes with Union Gas over how the company
should be run and financed had anything to do with GLN's
decision to sell its Union Gas shares to Unicorp. Cockwell cited
"a special relationship" with McKeough, although GLN
admitted to a number of discussions with him about the need
to attract more high-quality executives to replace outside

professional advisers. The Statement of Facts patiently explained for the board how the Brascan group worked and, in a defence of Kierans's comments about the operation of GLN, noted that Brascan had a wealth of knowledge in the utilities area because of its Brazilian past. The statement did not mention that it was an entirely different company now, with virtually none of the old Brascan executives.

Finally, the GLN statement got to the point. "At the specific request of the board, Great Lakes Group has made enquiries of companies in which Edper Investments Ltd. and Brascan (the Edper/Brascan group) have an interest relating to their possible dealings in Unicorp preferred shares." The statement revealed that, "in the normal course of business" and based on "the investment merits afforded by the Unicorp securities," several associated companies had indeed invested. Royal Trust had roughly $5 million; Continental Bank owned $13 million; and Jimmy Kay's holding company, Hatleigh Investments Incorporated, held about $24 million.

The news exploded over Bay Street; the rumours had been true. It appeared that four companies controlled by Edper and one individual with heavy financial obligations to the Edper group had, in effect, bankrolled the takeover. Edper had ended up with $135 million of the $190 million that Unicorp had issued to finance the takeover. Edper had allowed the bid by Unicorp to succeed.

Ninety per cent of the preferred shares were now in the hands of Continental Bank, GLN Investments, Hatleigh Investments, National Bank, North Canadian Oils, Royal Trust, and Olympia and York. More than twenty-six per cent of the shares issued by Unicorp for the takeover were owned by North Canadian Oils and Hatleigh Investments. During the bid, slightly more than twelve million Union Gas shares had traded on the Toronto Stock Exchange. Of those twelve million, more than half had changed hands at less than $12.50. Just as important was the timing of some of those purchases. On the eve of the first expiry of Unicorp's offer, Continental Bank had stepped in to buy large blocks. And, at the last moment, as the second deadline was about to expire, the Reichmanns, National Bank and North Canadian Oils had saved the day with large purchases. It was a masterful orchestration. How had it happened?

In late February, arbitrage traders Andy Sarlos and Barry Zukerman had held a large block of Union Gas shares. Frank Constantini, the head trader at Gordon Capital, knew this; he wanted those 769,700 shares. But Sarlos had instructed his stock trader not to tender to the Unicorp offer; Sarlos did not want Unicorp preferred shares. Constantini persisted, finally proposing that Sarlos tender to the Unicorp bid on the understanding that Gordon Capital would guarantee that the Unicorp shares could immediately be sold at a net profit of twenty-five cents a share. Sarlos tendered; Gordon Capital bought the Unicorp shares and paid Sarlos cash. Meanwhile, early in the takeover, Unicorp's Michael Kordyback had approached the National Bank about investing in Unicorp preferred shares. On March 5, the bank bought 800,000 Unicorp shares from Gordon Capital on an "if, when and as needed" basis, at $12.25 each, providing Gordon Capital with the cash to buy the Sarlos and Zukerman shares.

A few days later, on March 8, Constantini contacted Jimmy Kay, a close associate of Hees, to ask whether his holding company, Hatleigh Investments, would buy 400,000 Union Gas shares at $11.50 and tender them for Unicorp shares. Kay said yes. Three days later, Constantini called again and suggested further purchases. Kay decided to buy another 1.9 million Union Gas shares. But soon after the trades had been done, Kay changed his mind; three days later, he sold 400,000 Unicorp shares back to Gordon Capital. That left Hatleigh Investments with a whopping $27 million in Unicorp shares — ten per cent of the company's entire investment portfolio. The entire amount had been financed by a $60 million line of credit Hatleigh maintained at Hees.

The same day Constantini phoned Kay about Hatleigh's participation, he also contacted an executive at North Canadian Oil, where Kay was chief executive officer. Hees held a stake in North Canadian Oil. Constantini offered the North Canadian official a choice of buying either Union shares or Unicorp units; both were available for purchase. On March 11, the

North Canadian official called back and said he would be willing to buy one million or two million Unicorp units at $12.25 to $12.50 a unit on an "if, as and when" basis. The purchase was financed by a line of credit maintained at Hees. The shares were the ones Hal Jackman had sold. North Canadian bought them for $12.50 and tendered them to the Unicorp bid.*

Trevor Eyton took the stand at the energy board on the twenty-fifth day of hearings. Here was the main event. But as the *Globe and Mail* reported later, Eyton's testimony "sometimes stood in sharp contrast to other evidence that has been given at the inquiry." John Campion broached the idea of a concerted effort by Brascan affiliates to ensure that Unicorp's bid was successful. Eyton replied: "I have been intrigued by the proceedings of the board because there seems to be an emphasis on Brascan, and what would Brascan do if it were to run Union Enterprises, and how it would be for Union Enterprises. To us, you know, the question is preposterous and irrelevant." There was no conspiracy, he said; the fact that so many of the preferred shares ended up in the portfolios of affiliated companies simply reflected the unparalleled reputation of Brascan and Hees as preferred-share players.

Eyton also quarrelled with McKeough's recollection of a telephone conversation that took place the morning the GLN board met to consider the Unicorp offer. McKeough's notes of the conversation showed him asking Eyton how attractive the Unicorp preferred shares could possibly be, with Eyton replying that the offer could be treated like cash because "the Brascan group really makes the preferred-share market in Canada." Eyton disagreed. "I may have said that we are

---

*The operation held a powerful resemblance to an earlier takeover. In 1981, a group of blue-chip establishment businessmen, the kind Darcy McKeough felt comfortable with, had rallied around Ken White, chairman of Royal Trust. The Old Boys in the banks and brokerage houses and other friendly allies had mounted a successful defence against would-be acquisitor Robert Campeau, an outsider, by buying up Royal Trust stock. Now, the old guard was on the opposite side and the new breed seemed to be using the same tactic.

familiar with preferred shares; I wouldn't have said that we made the preferred-share market."

On it went. Eyton criticized Tom Kierans for "speculating entirely" on the affairs of GLN. "The comments he was making were sheer nonsense." And he vigorously denied McKeough's suggestion that Brascan had wanted to control Union Gas, and had gone so far as to lobby the provincial government. "There was certainly no discussion whatever of increasing the stake beyond the twenty-per-cent level that I have seen referred to in the newspaper," Eyton told Campion. "It has never been discussed by our group, either within or indeed without. I was intrigued by suggestions, at least in the newspaper, that we had been rebuffed by the Ontario government. It simply wasn't in the cards. There was never, so far as I know, any approach to the Ontario government. I go further and say that, had we thought about it in those terms, I am confident that we would be received at least as well as any of the other holders of major gas utilities in the province. It just never occurred to us that we wouldn't be accepted, should we want to go beyond twenty per cent."

Why had his group decided to sell its stake in Union Gas? Eyton said he was sorry that things hadn't worked out better with Union Gas, and sorry they hadn't listened to the helpful suggestions emanating from the Brascan contingent. "They were different than we were," he said. "But it is not our style to try to tell people what to do."

Jimmy Connacher stepped off the elevator, head down, flanked by his two lawyers, John Petch and Bruce Bailey of Osler, Hoskin and Harcourt, into a waiting horde of news photographers. Until the day he was called to testify at the energy board, there were only two known photographs of Connacher, which newspapers and magazines had used again and again. One showed a shadowy figure, half hidden, darting to his garage; the other was not much better. Now the papers had a third shot — of Connacher hiding his face in his hands, like a reluctant witness at a trial.

When Connacher arrived at the OEB hearings, he hid from the news hounds by diving into an office near the hearing room. It did not matter that it was occupied. When his turn came to testify, he sat flanked by his lawyers — the only person to do so. Campion asked Connacher to name buyers of Unicorp's preferred shares that were not related to the Brascan group. Connacher could only name National Bank and a numbered company, 499977 Ontario Inc., a Gordon Capital client with two million Unicorp shares. Why hadn't other buyers participated? Connacher's firm had attempted to interest clients outside of the Edper group. "Most of them were not prepared to act because they wanted to wait to see what the result would be," said Connacher. "Most of these companies that did buy it are very sophisticated in the preferred-share market. We probably trade $400 million to $500 million worth of preferred shares with this group of companies in a given year." If it was such a great deal, why had only 500,000 of 7.5 million warrants been traded? "It takes time for people to understand it," said Connacher. Who was the mystery buyer? Confidential, but he assured the board the buyer had no connection with Brascan. Connacher seemed to have forgotten that the Reichmanns had a link to the Bronfmans through Trilon and Trizec. Campion knew that 499977 Ontario Inc. was owned by Paul Reichmann. But it was only after the hearings had closed that he finally made the connection between the Reichmanns and the Bronfmans — after Robert Macaulay read an article about them in *Maclean's* magazine.

Campion had arranged to take an affidavit from Reichmann explaining his role. The energy board lawyer went to Reichmann's office to take the evidence. He found the reclusive billionaire to be open and helpful. Reichmann told the story of his meeting with Mann on the eve of the bid's expiry. With the final piece of the puzzle in place, Campion took the unusual step of reopening the hearing to file Reichmann's affidavit for the public record. Reichmann had testified that early in the takeover battle he had been approached by Union Gas as a possible "White Knight" bidder for the company. Reichmann had referred the request to his ninety-three-per-cent-owned forestry giant, Abitibi-Price, which had declined. Reichmann claimed to have known George Mann for many years. But he said, "I do not believe Olympia and York has had prior business transactions with him." It was careful wording, because a year or two before, Olympia and York had seriously looked at becoming a significant shareholder in Unicorp. Olympia and York people had spent some time analyzing Unicorp and, until the deal was called off, had come close to becoming almost as large an investor as George Mann. In his affidavit, Reichmann insisted that he had decided to buy the shares in Union Gas and tender them to the Unicorp offer because it was "a good investment." But, he added, "One fact that may have made me more sympathetic to Mr. Mann was that I did not think that the purchase of Burns Food by Union Enterprises was an appropriate transaction to have taken place during the course of a takeover bid." There may also have been another motive for Reichmann. Says Leech, "As a non-Jew, I think there was a feeling in their minds that to have a bloodbath on the street [a proxy fight to get control of the company] would not help their [Jewish] community. I think there was a sense of that and so maybe they were investing in that. That is an absolute guess and no one has ever said that."

The energy board hearing was finally over. Jack Cockwell had testified last and, save for an peevish altercation with chairman Macaulay over why he had to come back a second day, his testimony had not added a great deal. He had disputed Kierans's "junk bonds" comment and accused Kierans of misusing confidential information on GLN. Cockwell confirmed the series of irritations over the way Union Gas was being managed and financed, and the "substantial cost" of retaining outside advisers, contradicting Eyton's assessment.

With the closing of the hearing in early June, Campion, as the board's counsel, recommended that the OEB approve Unicorp's takeover of Union Gas. But in his 202-page submission, Campion argued that Union Gas shareholders had been unfairly treated as a result of the way the takeover bid had been played out. Campion stated: "The objective fact of the Unicorp $1.17 preferred share ownership would have led one to conclude that the Edper-Brascan purchases were a concerted effort by that group to make the bid successful for some undisclosed reason, except for the evidence.''

By figuring out the complicated trades and share crosses, Campion had brought together those who had helped move the deal. The hearing had peeled back the layers that usually hide the way business is done. And that made some people uncomfortable. In his final report, Campion recommended greater regulation of gas utilities and their holding companies. As for Unicorp's fitness as an owner, ''The public review has more than satisfied any concern,'' Campion said. Two months later, in a report to Cabinet, Macaulay's board generally agreed with Campion and recommended some tinkering with the board's regulation of gas utilities.

For Jim Leech and George Mann, the way finally appeared clear. Leech told the *Financial Post*, ''Union is for us what Brascan was to Edper'' — that is, a corporate turning point. In mid-April, Mann called Trevor Eyton to ask him and Bob Dunford to remain on the board of Union Enterprises. Eyton said he wanted to think about it, and called back the next day to accept. ''I thought we would want to carry on,'' he said in his characteristic conditional tense, which makes his thoughts seem weightier than they actually are. ''I thought it would be useful to try to help patch up the difficulties that had developed during the takeover, to try to dampen down the criticisms and the rumours and innuendoes.'' Eyton also saw it as an effective way to oversee the most important holding of Brascan's own new investment, Unicorp, although Cockwell admitted that ''it would be somewhat unusual for us to sit on boards where we don't have a direct common equity interest.'' The Brascan influence continued.

Darcy McKeough also remained on the board. As part of the peace settlement, he retained the post of chairman and chief executive of the utility, Union Gas. His relations with Unicorp remained strained, however. ''He stayed,'' said one supporter, ''because he didn't want to be a quitter; he stayed to try to do something for the minority shareholder.'' But in truth, with his image blackened as a result of his purchase of Burns Foods, there was little else for him to do.

There was still the matter of the OSC investigation. The OSC had been criticized for ignoring revelations made at its hearings in February. In late March, OSC officials had launched another inquiry. With the usual OSC staff investigators and accountants, the commission had hired Thomas Lockwood, a leading securities lawyer with the firm of Lockwood, Bellmore and Moore. Lockwood was to head the investigation. For the next seven months, securities detectives dug through documents and interviewed almost a hundred witnesses. Recalled Lockwood, "We had a very broadly framed mandate, with wide powers to subpoena both individuals and documents." As part of the investigation, witnesses swore that they would not even reveal that they had testified. It was, as one participant described it, "a star-chamber inquiry." By late August, the commission staff felt there was enough evidence of securities violations to recommend laying charges against Unicorp and Gordon Capital. The OSC commissioners could accept or reject the recommendation. They chose to hold a hearing and scheduled it for November. Unicorp and Gordon Capital stood accused of treating shareholders of Union Gas in an unequal manner, of misusing insider information, and of violating securities legislation. If the OSC decided they were guilty, it could force Unicorp to offer other Union Gas shareholders the terms it had made available to its friends. Gordon Capital could find its licence to do business revoked. The largest OSC investigation ever could, potentially, yield the most severe punishment ever meted out to stock-market players.

The announcement of the hearing in mid-September effectively scuttled discussions between Unicorp and Union Gas minority shareholders about a settlement. At one point, they had come close to signing a cash settlement. Instead, it seemed there would be yet another public hearing. Unicorp and Gordon Capital resolved to stall the matter in court; the OSC hearing could take years to commence. On December 20, a little more than a year after Jim Leech and Jack Cockwell had first talked about Union Gas, the OSC announced a settlement. It was a complex arrangement. Gordon Capital and Unicorp would pay $7.1 million into a fund that would be used "to top up" minority shareholders who had been squeezed by the big players during the takeover. The agreement between the OSC and the two companies left unresolved the question of larger wrongdoing. Unicorp and Gordon Capital did not have to admit to any transgressions, aside from Gordon's conviction on illegal short selling. They just had to pay out millions of extra dollars — and Gordon was barred from takeover bid work for sixty days. The OSC hailed its decision as a landmark victory, a show of strength. "It was a lot of nickels," commented Gordon Capital's Gordon Eberts to one insider. But others thought that getting Gordon Capital for short-selling was an inadequate compromise.

Two years after the rancorous takeover, the healing job that so appealed to Trevor Eyton appeared to have gone as far as it would ever go. Eyton had left the board; he was replaced by Tim Price from Hees. Darcy McKeough has continued to run Union Gas; Unicorp cannot remove him, and Jim Leech says he now values McKeough's understanding of the regulatory side of the energy business. But even McKeough's staunchest establishment supporters privately admit that under Mann, Union Gas is managed "ten times better than it was under McKeough." Undertakings pledged by Unicorp when the OEB was flexing its muscles in 1985 have yet to be signed by either side. Unicorp struggled to sell off parts of Burns Foods. Unicorp executives remain sensitive about appearing to be too close to the Edper-Brascan group. When Unicorp was selling off Burns Foods' attractive Alberta-based Palm Dairies division, Mann and Leech distanced themselves from interest expressed by Labatt's dairy division. "We started getting paranoid," recalled Leech. "Should Tim Price go to the Unicorp annual meeting? Or will there be a goddamned article written in the newspaper the next day?"

But the self-consciousness was a positive sign. The cutthroat tactics and layers of deception that enveloped the Unicorp takeover bid forced not only self-satisfied Bay Street but also the general public to a new level of awareness. For the first time, ordinary Canadians detected the hidden hand of Brascan. People were suddenly aware of the tremendous power and influence of the Bronfmans' Edper group, a corporate empire that could single-handedly make a takeover happen. People learned how friends did business with friends, sometimes to the detriment of an ignorant outsider.

"It was a large takeover bid that raised fundamental issues about the process of acquiring companies," says Joe Groia, counsel for the Ontario Securities Commission. Ermanno Pascutto, director of the OSC, says, "One of the most difficult problems in regulation of takeover transactions is the concept of 'acting in concert.' That is, when friends or associates of the participants in the transaction do things to assist the participant that the participants are not able to do directly — or would have to be required to disclose." The arrangements can range from a written contract to a "wink and a nod" he adds; in any case, the most basic objectives of takeover bid regulation — the protection of public investors — can be completely undermined. "The shareholders may be misled, they may not have access to a fair price, and markets can be improperly influenced." But, says Pascutto, "like any private and secret arrangement, it's very difficult to prove."

Through the summer of 1987, Unicorp tried to hammer out yet another settlement for minority shareholders. They were negotiating with a group of old-guard Union Gas directors who had been designated guardians of the minority. They came up with a complicated proposal to restructure Union Enterprises and Union Gas so they would be much the way they were before; the proposal also included an offer of paper. But when it came to a vote at a special shareholders' meeting in September, Mann and Leech were humiliated by strong opposition, and they withdrew the proposal. Afterwards, Leech attributed the minority shareholders' negative reaction to a general mistrust about "paper shuffling." But Mann had thought he was offering a very attractive deal. When it was pointed out to him that it cost less than he had paid to Brascan two years before, Mann brushed that idea aside. "Yeah," Mann replied, "but that was different."

CHAPTER TWELVE

The Public Service

*Within the group there is a strong value . . . a com-
mitment to, as I generally describe it, public service.*
— Trevor Eyton, on October 10, 1986, at the Parker Commission inquiry into conflict of interest by
Sinclair Stevens

Like so many other business deals, it began with a telephone
call. In late September 1984, Sinclair Stevens, Brian Mulroney's
Minister of Regional and Industrial Expansion, called to ask
Trevor Eyton to drop over to his King City Hereford breed-
ing farm. The minister had some ideas he wanted to run by
the industrialist. At that point in Eyton's rigidly scheduled
career, very few people had the clout to make such a casual
request; Stevens, a key economic minister in Mulroney's Cabinet, was one of those few.

When Eyton approached the Stevens's front door that Sunday, the 29th, he was prepared to visit a man he had known
casually for years, but always met in a crowd, whether at political or business gatherings, and never as more than a nodding
acquaintance. "I trod the downtown streets of Toronto for
many years," Eyton later recalled. "I am sure I ran into him

there. I do not recall ever doing any business . . . with Mr. Stevens or Mrs. Stevens, but I knew about them and I certainly would have recognized Mr. Stevens."

It was Sinclair Stevens's wife, Noreen, who answered Eyton's knock. The meeting began as a brainstorming session on the potential for the government's plans to sell its interests in a host of companies, including a group held by the Canada Development and Investment Corp (CDIC). Stevens also had a more direct question: would Eyton and his group of executives be prepared to help out in the government's privatization push? Would Eyton head the government's aggressive retreat from the corporate state? Eyton, flattered by the question, allowed that he had prepared for the meeting by refreshing his memory on CDIC's holdings. They certainly weren't the kind of companies the Brascan group would be interested in. In fact, the CDIC companies desperately needed new management and financial overhauls. Their financial shape was a perfect example, in Eyton's view, of the reason the government should bail out of the business of running companies. Aircraft manufacturer Canadair was an example. Eyton said that, in 1984, "For every dollar in sales, they lost approximately one dollar. Every time you sold something for a buck, you lost a buck." Canadair wasn't the worst case. "For de Havilland [another aircraft manufacturer] I think the ratio was probably one dollar of sales to something like two dollars in losses," Eyton reported. Eldorado Nuclear, a uranium mining company, was making money but had a mountain of debt; telecommunications company Teleglobe Eyton saw as "a creature of the government"; it made money only because it had a monopoly. "On Massey Ferguson, I hardly need say more than mention the name," said Eyton. Even Canada Development Corporation, in which CDIC had a twenty-per-cent interest, had piled up debt to expand its holdings in other companies. "I think it was a perfect demonstration, at least in my own mind, of the need for privatization," Eyton concluded.

But asking Eyton to set aside his own business affairs and head the CDIC for at least a year was reaching too far, even for an original thinker such as Stevens. Eyton gently steered

Stevens away from that idea before it was even fully broached. Still, Eyton was prepared to listen to Stevens's other tack: that the group help shape the country's privatization efforts. Trevor Eyton believed Stevens was referring to not just the people at Brascan, but to the executives at all the Brascan corporate affiliates and even associates in the Brascan orbit. He was proud that Stevens recognized the calibre of his circle: "People that I had worked with, people that we were comfortable with, people that had special qualities who could contribute particularly to something like privatization."

Back at his Commerce Court headquarters, Eyton and his confrères agreed: it would be tough to make the time, but they felt something should be done. They obviously couldn't do everything the minister had originally envisioned. "He was really talking around the possibility that I and some of my colleagues would become, in effect, the merchant banker for the federal government." In fact, that was exactly what Stevens was touting to the prime minister, in a letter reporting on his chat with Eyton. The grandiose merchant-banking scheme was not to be, but Stevens did get some help. Eyton cast around for a point man for the project. Paul Marshall, chief executive officer of Brascan subsidiary Westmin Resources in Calgary, was the answer. Marshall, at sixty-three, was an experienced oil man who had joined Westmin Resources in 1978. Westmin was healthy, but the oil industry was in trouble, so the company wasn't doing any new business; Marshall could be spared. Besides, he had experience in Ottawa; three decades earlier he had been an executive assistant to the minister of defence. Marshall was surprised at Eyton's request, but he didn't refuse. "Mr. Eyton is no different than anybody else," Marshall ruminated later. "He tends to be a little flattering on those occasions when he is seducing you into something." Stevens and Eyton talked again at the minister's farm the next weekend, and by mid-October it was agreed: Marshall would quarterback operations in Ottawa. The two Brascan men and the minister had lunch on October 16 in Ottawa, and Marshall officially accepted the assignment.

Marshall pushed Eyton to take a place on the CDIC board.

Eyton felt that giving up an executive for a year should be enough of a contribution. But Marshall didn't want to be a token offering. He knew that as soon as he stepped into the CDIC role, he would be somewhat distanced from his corporate home. Eyton's personal interest as a board member would ensure co-operation from others in the group when he wanted to call on them, and would keep him plugged into the group. "Large corporations have a tendency to close ranks when somebody goes off on a do-good operation. I did not want Mr. Eyton to forget my name at all, or where I was."

Stevens appealed to both Eyton and Marshall for other potential CDIC board members. Eyton easily named fifteen, but only "clicked" on one, Patrick Keenan of Keywhit Investments, a name Marshall had also pushed. Still, when the CDIC board appointments were made by an Order in Council in late October, eyebrows rose on Bay Street about the number of Brascan people who were involved. The list included Eyton and Marshall; Keenan, a Brascan director; and Antoine Turmel, a director of Brascan-controlled Noranda. Three other new directors joined the sixteen-member board: Frank Stronach, of Magna International; John Grant, a Halifax lawyer; and Lucien Bouchard, a Chicoutimi lawyer. The Brascan view was that neither Keenan nor Turmel could be considered "Brascan people." Keenan was an independent director of Brascan and a long-time personal friend of Eyton's. He had been a joint-venture partner in Edper's 1979 takeover of Brascan, along with the Patino family. In 1981, he sold his stake but stayed on the Brascan board. Antoine Turmel had not always been so friendly to the group. The head of the Montreal-based Provigo food-store chain until his 1987 retirement, and one of few living members of the Canadian Business Hall of Fame, he had been a director of Noranda Mining and had tried to fight off the Brascan invasion in 1980. "He was very much a part of and approved a series of steps by Noranda and Noranda senior management to frustrate our attempts to gain a significant stake in that company," said Eyton. "He was really not a Brascan man but quite the reverse. Since then, of course, he has come to know us and, I hope, he has come to love us. At the same time, he surely is independent.'' All of which is fine, but it didn't stop the talk on Bay Street. It was the first whiff of a potential scandal; the gossip-mongers began to try to figure out Brascan's angle on the government deal.

Indeed, alert journalists immediately asked what rules Brascan companies would follow in overseeing the sale of government-controlled companies. Stevens said that there was nothing to worry about: no company associated with a board member would be able to bid on CDIC assets. Eyton, ever-alert for news reports, noted the statement, and said, ''It did not really bother me as a Brascan man. In terms of a policy that none of the companies in which we had investments could be a bidder, I found it surprising, particularly when I did not recall any discussion along that line.'' But he didn't take the idea seriously. After all, business people deal with conflicts among directors all the time; any director with a conflict simply declares it and leaves the room. This classic strategem is most often noted in bank boards, where most directors are in fact major borrowers of the bank. The strategem relies on the honour system, and it is prized in business. As well, Eyton thought it would be unfair to exclude some companies only because a Brascan company had an investment in them. In Noranda, for example, Brascan had about a thirty-one per cent interest. The government was looking for as many bidders as possible, Eyton said, and, ''It struck me as wrong and difficult for other shareholders, the public shareholders in those autonomously managed companies, that because I was doing something that I considered was for the public good that they would be precluded from ever considering any of the assets that were involved.'' Eyton discussed the exclusion policy with Marshall as a point of principle, but he never expected it to have a practical application; he couldn't see why any companies in Brascan's orbit would be interested in the CDIC assets. But that was only one score on which Eyton would later be proven wrong.

In fact, Noranda chairman Alf Powis was very interested in some of those assets Eyton scoffed at. He also thought the exclusion policy was unfair. Just because Trevor Eyton chose to get himself and Paul Marshall involved in the government's privatization drive, Noranda was precluded from bidding on resource assets. Powis had his eye on some sort of joint venture with Kidd Creek Mining, or a possible acquisition of Eldorado Nuclear. Both companies were controlled by Canada Development Corporation (CDC). Powis told Eyton he found it disturbing that Noranda wouldn't be able to consider either company as an investment. Eyton told him not to worry; after all, in a government deal, there would be an open auction and plenty of scrutiny by parliamentary committees afterward. Everyone would see that the process was above-board, and Eyton was certain there would be no problems.

Paul Marshall rolled up his sleeves as soon as his chief executive officer appointment was official. He insisted on operating from the CDIC's Toronto office, just a few floors below Brascan. He had a special aide appointed to interpret "bureaucratese" and to act as his "Ottawa spy" on the political world. He used a no-nonsense style with the board. At times, he would need quick decisions. At the first board meeting, a special Divestiture Committee was selected. It was chaired by investment whiz Richard (Dick) Bonnycastle, chairman of Electra Investments, and included Trevor Eyton, Pat Keenan, and Antoine Turmel. It also included Bernard Lamarre, chairman of the CDIC board and chairman of Lavalin Incorporated, an international engineering firm; and William Teschke, Stevens's deputy minister at the Department of Regional and Industrial Expansion (DRIE). The appointments helped fuel the murmurs on Bay Street about Brascan people shaping government policy on privatization.

The committee turned out to be very active. Marshall turned to the small group for a consensus and let the board approve matters later. One of the key decisions the committee would ruminate over before turning to the board for a final decision was what type of professional help to bring in to bolster CDIC's own resources. The staff wanted to shop the companies around all by themselves. But the new brooms didn't buy that. As Eyton saw it, "It was a hard-working bunch, but they did not have a lot of support staff, and in some areas they did not have a great depth of experience.'' This was a selling job on companies that were "not the prettiest in town," and they wanted to sell the money-losing companies as quickly as possible.

On Monday, January 21, Marshall's hand-picked committee met with Minister Stevens for dinner in his Ottawa DRIE boardroom. The politician and his business advisers discussed the question of bringing in professional help from the investment community. In a morning meeting, before they flew out of town, the committee members chose the firms that would have the pleasure of serving the government. Details of the lucrative contracts would be negotiated and discussed with Stevens, since they were bound to be politically sensitive.

Mike Carter, the vice-president of finance at CDIC, had written Marshall a memo with some suggestions for places to look for professional help. McLeod Young Weir would be a good choice for Teleglobe, Carter said. Wood Gundy had long been associated with Massey Ferguson, and Burns Fry and Richardson Greenshields were possibilities. The investment bankers had all been making their pitches. But the final choices differed substantially from Carter's memo.

Burns Fry Limited — as it happened, a favourite of the minister — was chosen to sell the two aircraft companies, de Havilland and Canadair. Merrill Lynch would help from New York, and Warburg would help internationally. Burns Fry was also chosen to handle the sale of Eldorado Nuclear. The senior staff at CDIC had originally envisaged de Havilland, Canadair, and Eldorado as a package, reasoning that Eldorado would be easy to sell and would therefore offset the hard-to-sell aircraft firms. Dominion Securities Pitfield, the country's largest broker, was chosen to sell the profitable Teleglobe, the easiest sell. Geoffrion Leclerc of Montreal was the back-up firm, a bow to "regional considerations."

All the firms had been lobbying for the business, ever since the government took office. Stevens had heard from firms, and Marshall and CDIC officials had received presentations as well. Some firms were being ignored, and others, particularly Burns Fry, were being handsomely rewarded. The actions of the divestiture committee would be minutely scrutinized by the financial world. Trevor Eyton, as much as Sinclair Stevens, would face the fallout from these appointments in the months to come.

Eyton was a corporate mogul, so he was used to juggling different balls in the air. But in the third week of January, 1985, he made the mistake of handling two separate matters at the same time: a personal commitment to aid Sinclair Stevens's private company, and a commitment as a CDIC board member to choose securities-industry advisors. The timing was too pat for too many people. Eyton would find his own reputation in jeopardy as it had never been before because of the way he used his Bay Street connections.

When he had agreed to help the Cabinet minister privatize Crown companies, Trevor Eyton's knowledge of Sinclair Stevens's business affairs was vague at best. He knew that the Stevens family controlled a company called York Centre, which traded inactively on the Vancouver Stock Exchange. Eyton called it, "one of those bits of business knowledge or business trivia that I might be expected to have tucked away somewhere." According to Eyton, he and Stevens never discussed the minister's personal financial affairs.

But when he was appointed as a board member of CDIC, Eyton began to be pulled inexorably into the Stevenses' business affairs. He allowed himself to become involved out of a sense of personal obligation towards a man who was spending all his time on the public weal, to the obvious detriment of his personal fortunes. But here Eyton was dealing with a very different set of circumstances. He was not a corporate executive helping the government; he was a corporate executive wielding personal influence to try to help another individual, one who happened to be a Cabinet minister. As far as Eyton knew, Stevens never knew of his fairy godmother role. Still, Eyton was taking a big risk.

Part of the risk emanated from the reputation of the man he was helping. Stevens never clearly separated his public and private personae. He has always been a businessman, an entrepreneur; and he has always been a politician. A farm kid raised near Toronto, he received a degree in journalism from the University of Western Ontario; then he became a night-beat police reporter at the *Toronto Star* in order to pay his way through law school. He put himself through law school in the mid-1950s, and that was where he met his wife, Noreen. Even then, Stevens was making deals. In fact, his piece of a $290,000 profit on a $10,000 land investment laid the base for an empire of real-estate and financial-services companies. By 1964, his empire had an asset value of $78 million; two years later he was granted a charter to found the Winnipeg-based Bank of Western Canada. He chose as president James Coyne, who had been the governor of the Bank of Canada. But Coyne soon quit after complaining publicly that Stevens wanted the bank to lend money to one of his own companies. Stevens denied the charge, and a House of Commons committee investigation backed him up. But the bank couldn't withstand the controversy. Stevens's other investments, including Ontario-based York Trust, had overexpanded, and were in trouble as well. Investors demanded more information as York's stock price fell, and it was on the brink of collapse when Stevens sold it to another firm. Stevens managed to restructure his holdings, but his business empire never soared to the big time again, and suspicions about his business methods lingered.

Bay Street never really accepted Sinclair Stevens. When Joe Clark was forming his Cabinet in 1979, a delegation of senior financial figures urged the prime minister not to appoint Stevens as finance minister. Some of Stevens's problems emanated from the essential conflict of political and business life. For instance, as minister in charge of the Anti-Dumping Tribunal, he had to make a decision in 1984 on shoe quotas. He decided to let more foreign-made shoes into the country. Meanwhile, a shoe company his family group controlled went into receivership. At the same time, his oil and gas company was in deep trouble because of his own government's decision to cancel special grants to the industry — a decision Stevens applauded.

After the Conservative party was elected in September 1984, the business community began to whisper about instances where it believed Sinc Stevens was crossing the line between his public role as a politician and his private one as a business-man whose companies were in trouble. Stevens seemed to think it was acceptable to involve in his private affairs people who were aiding him in his public role. Edward (Ted) Rowe, Stevens's political campaign aide and his substitute at the family's York Centre Corporation (named after Stevens's rid-ing, York Simcoe), was appointed as a director of CDC. In the fall of 1984, Rowe was working hard to save York Centre, the centrepiece of the shaky family finances. Stevens suggested to his wife, Noreen, and to Jim Davies, a financial advisor and a vice-president at Richardson Greenshields of Canada Limited, that they ask Trevor Eyton for advice. Then Stevens had to give over his affairs to a "blind trust," a rule for all Cabinet ministers.

Rowe called Eyton at about the time Eyton was appointed to the CDIC board, to ask for advice on how to raise money for York Centre. As well, Eyton received a letter from Jim Davies. Although Eyton and Davies had known each other for years, Davies let Eyton know that the contact was "at the sug-gestion of the Honorable Sinclair Stevens, PC MP." Eyton didn't feel alarmed at the requests for aid, or at the timing. After all, he and his colleagues had an open-door policy to all refinancing requests; this was only one of myriad approaches. He looked on it as a request from Ted Rowe, a man he had never met, and Jim Davies, not a request from Sinc Stevens. He didn't even think about a potential conflict between the request and his work with CDIC. "At this stage, it was just simply somebody asking for advice." His mind didn't stretch to encompass Stevens's own position. Nor did he think of telling his man at CDIC, Paul Marshall, about the request. As Eyton explained it, "I considered my commitment to the CDIC to be one where I was giving, not receiving. This would also be a situation where I was giving and not receiv-ing. I did not see any conflict whatever."

Instead, Trevor's mind kicked into deal-maker mode: who in the group should look at the request, and what could they do with it? Eyton met with Ted Rowe in November; then he contacted Manfred Walt and Tim Casgrain at Hees International and asked them to do a preliminary assessment of the York Centre proposal. Rowe's proposal had already passed first base; many proposals are turned down by the group without even an assessment. This one fell into the second group, where courtesy seemed to demand at least a glance. Third base was the key: getting a positive response after a preliminary appraisal, at which stage the group moves into high gear for as much as a month to analyze every aspect of the opportunity. Although Walt and Casgrain met with Rowe in December, York Centre didn't make it to third. On December 11, the Hees vice-presidents delivered a short report to Eyton stating that Hees wasn't interested. They also let Rowe know their decision. Eyton went out of his way to telephone Rowe and let him know personally as well.

Eyton was not the only one to whom Rowe and Davies were turning for advice. By late November, they had contacted Keywhit's Pat Keenan, the director who was being talked of in some circles as one of the four Brascan appointees to the CDIC board. And they weren't shy about using Eyton's name. Keenan was told of Eyton's interest in the transaction, and he contacted Eyton to see what the Brascan chief thought. Eyton replied that York Centre had cash-flow problems and probably wouldn't interest Keenan.

There was one more avenue Eyton could follow to try to aide York Centre. With Jim Davies's ideas falling through, Eyton told Rowe he'd help him check out the possibilities for a public stock issue. He couldn't help right away, because it was time for his annual Florida Christmas break, and he was loaded down with travelling engagements for the next month. But he didn't forget his promise. In late January 1985, Eyton decided to use what influence he had within the investment community to introduce Rowe and his problems to a few dealers. With Eyton, that meant starting at the top. It was time for what would come to be known as "The Bay Street Walk."

Eyton contacted two of the industry's most powerful men,

Jack Lawrence, chairman and chief executive officer at Burns Fry, and Anthony (Tony) Fell, chief executive officer at Dominion Securities Pitfield. Both were close personal friends; both would look at any proposal introduced by Trevor Eyton. Coincidentally, both firms were involved in the privatization efforts of CDIC. In fact, they heard from Eyton about Stevens's private affairs the same week they received news of their CDIC appointments, the week of January twenty-first, after the Divestiture Committee's Monday night dinner with the minister.

Eyton chose Lawrence and Fell because they were friends; he was looking for personal advice, "a quick feel" as to whether anything could be done. "I recognized that this was not the opportunity of a lifetime, but at the same time I was trying to help," Eyton said. He was following through on a commitment. In retrospect, he thought he might have done better to let Rowe do his own checking.

Still, Eyton saw his role as a noble one, stretching himself to help this pipsqueak company with money troubles. Eyton believed York Centre's problems were caused in good part because Stevens had taken on a role in the public sector at his own personal expense. Eyton thought people who believed in the involvement of businessmen in public policy-making should help out when a public commitment hurt a businessman's livelihood. Eyton's gut instinct was to help the family company as much as he could. "It had as much to do with my involvement with CDIC as it has my effort to try and provide advice, and that is a concern as a Canadian that the private and public sectors are much too remote from each other, that there is not enough exchange or interchange between them. I think we are the worse for it."

Stevens had made that public commitment, and Eyton felt it should be appreciated. "The same kind of thinking applied to Mr. Stevens who had gone into public life, who was a Cabinet minister and was trying to serve in the Canadian government, and really it was at a time when his own personal affairs and York Centre were in some difficulty. They had a cash problem. I felt some sympathy for Mr. Stevens, because he

had made that public commitment and left behind in effect
a family enterprise that was in some trouble. Feeling as I did,
that that exchange from the private sector to the public sector
and for that matter back again is a good thing and a healthy
thing for Canadians, and wanting to encourage that process,
I had a certain sympathy to see if in the right kind of way I
could provide advice and help in a circumstance where it was
clear to me that the minister himself could not help."

Eyton didn't believe it mattered that the people he was asking
to help the minister would directly benefit from the minister's
policies and decisions. These were captains of industry he was
dealing with, after all. "I would have distinguished entirely
between that phone call on the question of advice for York
Centre and a meeting of the Divestiture Committee. I think
it is fair to say that all of them have enough standing and
enough reputation that you would expect them to be assigned
to the tasks at hand." That Eyton's request for aid came at
the same time as the government appointment was not rele-
vant. After all, Lawrence and Fell were only being asked for
advice.

It also never occurred to Eyton to ask himself whether
Stevens would have any knowledge of the affairs in his family
company. If Eyton had ever thought that the minister was
aware of his attempts to aid York Centre, he would have been
personally offended. "If I thought that the minister was tying
together the assignment of work to the investment bankers with
some kind of favourable response or some kind of help, even
at this stage for his family company, I would have nothing
to do with him."

The very idea that Stevens might know about his help, even
if the minister wasn't using his knowledge, would have made
Eyton draw back. "Had I assumed that Mr. Stevens was aware
of my discussions with Ted Rowe and Jim Davies . . . I might
simply have, let us say, been less helpful in trying to provide
advice."

Jack Lawrence and Tony Fell would be as helpful as they
knew how. Lawrence had known Sinc Stevens casually for a
decade, but Burns Fry had never done any substantial busi-

ness with him. Lawrence had helped Stevens a few times on business matters, but he usually talked with him about politics, not business. After Stevens was appointed to the Cabinet, Lawrence was pleased to see his commitment to privatization. "I had preached that philosophy really across the country and to both governments." And privatization was good for business. In late 1984, Burns Fry wrote to CDIC and to Stevens offering to act as broker. Many brokerage firms were aggressively trying to become part of the privatization scheme.

As part of the Burns Fry strategy, different executives were assigned targets to talk to about their potential participation. Lawrence was given Canadair president Gil Bennett and Paul Marshall at CDIC. Trevor Eyton was a target for another Burns Fry executive. Lawrence and another Burns Fry executive, Bob Bellamy, were to tackle Stevens together, but Lawrence says they never actually talked to him. Instead, Lawrence wrote to Stevens in November 1984, and in the letter referred in passing to a recent meeting. The firm's lobbying efforts went on through the winter. They mainly concentrated on Marshall and the CDIC; the mergers-and-acquisition people led the charge. Lawrence's role had been to write the initial contact letters; it was a standard tactic.

To Lawrence, the fact that a CDIC director was calling upon him for advice on the minister's personal affairs was not a big deal. As he explained, "The call came in and it was one of many phone calls in a day." The fact that it was a Stevens company "raised a few questions, that was all . . . I was curious as to what the real ownership was." But Lawrence didn't bother Eyton for details. He assumed he would get them from Hees. He handed the matter over to Willmott (Wil) Matthews, a vice-chairman at Burns Fry. As it happened, the next Monday, January 28, Matthews was plunged into the very public life of Stevens during a discussion at Canadair. At that meeting, the Burns crew finally learned that their lobbying had been successful; they would be handling the de Havilland, Canadair, and Eldorado privatization contracts.

Three days after his meeting at Canadair, Matthews, who has a habit of taking copious notes of all telephone calls, heard from Ted Rowe. Rowe told Matthews that he needed to do a deal quickly. He had wasted time with Hees only to find out that Hees wasn't interested. He said one reason Hees turned him down was a potential conflict with Eyton's Ottawa involvement. Matthews later said that his own company had adopted a wait-and-see attitude about conflict: "If it had turned out, on investigation, that it was financeable, at that time we would have taken a more serious and rigorous look at whether there was a potential conflict of interest or not."

Matthews looked at York Centre until March; he met with other Burns Fry analysts and with York Centre people, but the company didn't warrant the detailed evaluation. Dominion Securities was going through the same motions at the same time, and on occasion they worked in tandem. The zeal on Burns Fry's part, Matthews said, was not because of Sinc Stevens — it was because of Trevor Eyton. "I think if any man of Mr. Eyton's stature in the business community were to ask us to look at a company we would make the effort," Matthews said. But York Centre was a bad investment. On March 25, after being told that Burns Fry did not want to deal, Ted Rowe requested the company's private corporate documents back from the brokers. Fell and Lawrence let Eyton know the results.

Rowe didn't give up; he just shopped around. Before he was through, he would visit twenty-two brokerage houses. Still, he couldn't distill the kind of magic that would save York Centre. Finally, in May, he turned again to Trevor Eyton for advice. This time, he had a broker from Gordon Capital, Jocelyn (Jo) Bennett, at his elbow. Bennett knew Sinclair and Noreen Stevens. In fact, she had been trying to help York Centre restructure its affairs for five years, on and off. Coincidentally, Stevens contacted her at Gordon Capital at about the same time she arrived at Eyton's door with Rowe. Stevens was calling her to discuss the idea of Gordon Capital representing the government to negotiate the fees of other brokers' privatization contracts.

Eyton was surprised that Rowe had managed to interest Gordon Capital. He met with Bennett and Rowe on May 17 to discuss possibilities. Ken Clarke from Great Lakes Group flanked Eyton at the meeting, and Rowe brought Noreen

Stevens, the Cabinet minister's wife, a family member in a family company. "The discussion was in effect led by Jo Bennett and supported by Ted Rowe. Mrs. Stevens was there, but my memory is that she played a small part in the proceedings," Eyton recalls. Clarke took away Gordon Capital's financing proposal. In June, he told Bennett she should shelve her somewhat circuitous suggestions and try to keep the deal simple. His advice was to look for the smallest amount of money possible and to get the bank to back the share issue.

Bennett wrote to Eyton on June 13, and the notes he scribbled on her letter revealed his uneasiness about the deal. He was worried about the size; an investment in frontier exploration in the Beaufort Sea was not "up their alley." Management would have to put their own money on the table before anyone else would; so would the bankers. The company needed to play hardball with the bank — they needed to "negotiate tough." They needed a sensible business plan, and that could include a partial liquidation. The way the present deal was being suggested, any upside would go to the Stevens family. On July 5, Rowe and Bennett again met with Eyton, and urged him to respond to Bennett's idea. Eyton, spurred on by this "reminder and a tickler and a bit of urging," again "contacted different friends of mine on Bay Street." Those "friends" included Fell and Lawrence, and Gordon Capital's Jimmy Connacher as well. Eyton pointed out the difference in size and form of the financing. He knew Burns Fry and Dominion Securities hadn't been interested before, but at least they knew the company. "I was trying to get a quick response. I have to say that I was pessimistic that we were going to be able to help. At the same time, I wanted to give it my best shot." Eyton didn't worry about their CDIC connections: "Anybody I might have chosen to talk to would already be doing substantial business with the federal government in any event."

At a meeting with Jack Lawrence and Tony Fell on July 7, the fact that York Centre was a Stevens family company and that Stevens was minister of CDIC did come up. Eyton says they all agreed that, because of Stevens's political power, any help for his private company would have to make very good business sense — and it had to be perceived to make sense. Edper group executives had already reached the same conclusion. Says Eyton, "There was a double test. It was a tougher test than you would have with anyone walking in the door."

Eyton scheduled another meeting, his final attempt to help Rowe. As he recalls, "The August 7 meeting was one where all of the people who had been asked for advice were going to get in one room and were going to discuss the possible public or quasi-public financing and then come to some kind of a conclusion." Eyton and Clarke met with Fell, Lawrence, and Neil Baker from Gordon Capital. Eyton looked upon them as individuals at a brainstorming session, not company heads. Of course, back in February, after he asked for their advice, they did bring in their corporate power to analyze the situation. But that was only natural, from Eyton's perspective: "As in all of these things, Tony Fell is a busy fellow and so I am sure he has someone to help him, but I really wanted his judgement as to whether or not it could be done." Eyton wasn't optimistic, and he was proven right.

The meeting lasted about twenty minutes, and his conclusions were echoed by the others. They couldn't see the issue working. The deal Rowe and Bennett proposed was too small for these top-drawer firms, and too risky. The investors were being asked to take too much risk, the family too little, and the company might need more money within a year. No one was comfortable with the package, and no one thought it would sell. Then the perception question came up again, because of the Stevens family and its public position. As Fell later said, "I think there was a comment and a recognition by everyone at the meeting that there was the potential here for a serious conflict of interest." From Fell's viewpoint, even if the Rowe-Gordon plan had worked, any brokers involved with the government couldn't have been involved with York Centre. Eyton thought if the deal had made commercial sense, any broker who accepted it would have to openly declare that it wasn't a special favour. He later admitted, "I think it could have been difficult for us, had we got over the first hurdle, to satisfy ourselves that the second hurdle was one that we could deal with properly."

On August 8, Eyton delivered the bad news to Ted Rowe and Noreen Stevens. Then, and in a few later meetings with Rowe during the autumn, he tried to give general advice about how York Centre could dig itself out of its hole. Liquidation seemed one of the few alternatives. Hees, Eyton suggested, might be able to help with that. But Rowe wasn't interested in liquidation — he didn't want Hees or any other company moving in and taking control and getting first claim on assets. Eyton didn't tell Rowe that he and his colleagues felt that they had a conflict problem — it wasn't germane. He met with Rowe again in September and November, but these were hand-holding sessions. For Eyton, the discussion was closed, but his door was still open to Rowe. He thought Rowe was "still on the prowl looking for financing and, I think, was going around in ever-decreasing circles and was not having a great deal of success."

In the spring of 1986, York Centre began to liquidate its oil and gas holdings. By that time, the story that Trevor Eyton had helped Ted Rowe and Noreen Stevens look for financing was all over Bay Street. Reports of the meetings with the brokers had begun to appear in the newspapers. When stated in black and white, the news didn't look promising for Eyton. No matter how he explained it, it couldn't be denied: his group had, after all, bid on CDIC assets while he was playing match-maker between Stevens's family company and the brokers given contracts by Stevens's ministry. In 1985, some people believed that Eyton and the Edper group were planning to pick out CDIC's best assets, and that, with the aid of their friends, they planned a creeping takeover of CDC. Neither event took place. But coupled with Eyton's interest in Stevens's personal fortunes, the stories made a good conspiracy theory. Eyton would not be able to escape the consequences of all that gossip.

At its most basic level, business is a handshake and a signature. Two people make an agreement, which they acknowledge

with the handshake, the symbol of trust, and with the signature, the symbol of law. And, although the business world sur-
vives on mutually advantageous decisions, wily deal-makers
know there can be a hidden agenda behind seemingly disarming decisions made by their counterparts on the other side of
the table. Indeed, in a business deal, there must often be a winner and a loser. The boys at Brascan are deal-makers, and they
are respected and feared for their profitable and sometimes
circuitous approach to agreements. Many financiers automa-
tically look for a hidden agenda when the Brascan group
appears on the scene.

That's how it was with the bid to aid CDIC in privatizing
companies in 1984 and 1985. Eyton might have said he was
performing a public service, but others thought he was doing
business, and were suspicious from the start about Brascan's
motives. When reporters asked Sinclair Stevens whether the
Edper group would be able to bid on CDIC companies, they
were looking for hints of insider information and secret deals.
Then the stories began circulating that Trevor Eyton was helping the Stevens family companies try to sort out their financial collapse, and was involving brokers who were also working
for CDIC. Cynics thought that their worst fears were confirmed. Brascan was in this for something big — but what could
it be? What particular CDIC assets did Brascan want? Michael
Cassidy, an Ontario NDP MP, suggested on CBC radio after
Stevens had appointed his board that Brascan was only interested in "cherrypicking" CDIC's best assets, and that there was
an informal coup going on; the Brascan boys were making the
day-to-day decisions and slowly taking over CDIC's operations.

Some accusations were more specific. It was known even
before the Conservatives began the privatization push that
Noranda wanted to consolidate its operations by merging some
functions with Kidd Creek Mines, which was controlled by the
Canada Development Corporation (CDC). And CDIC was
CDC's largest shareholder.

As a matter of fact, Noranda was very interested in such
a merger; it would save the company a badly needed $20 mil-
lion, by some estimates. Noranda also thought some other

CDIC assets were interesting — the mining assets of Eldorado Nuclear, for instance. Noranda chairman Adam Zimmerman sent a memo to group executives at the end of October 1984, at about the same time Alf Powis questioned Trevor Eyton about the news reports on Edper companies being barred from bidding on CDIC companies. Zimmerman asked for a general review of Ottawa's portfolio. "With the government's plan . . . to dispose of its holdings in CDIC (and thereby CDC) now in place, we should concentrate our minds and talents on deciding whether any of them are attractive to us," Zimmerman said in his letter. "The obvious candidate that fits with Noranda is the CDC, or large parts of it." He added that Canadair, Teleglobe, and Petrosar all held interesting possibilities, and Noranda received an information booklet on Eldorado in late November. But Kidd Creek was the most tantalizing.

That may have been what Jack Cockwell had in mind when he answered the telephone at Brascan and chatted with Rod Foster from Imasco on March 21, 1985. Foster had a message for Paul Marshall, chairman of the CDIC, who was out of town. It wasn't Cockwell's usual style to write a memo; he preferred direct, verbal communication. But Cockwell was about to leave town and Paul Marshall wasn't in his office, so Cockwell drafted a note for Marshall. Imasco, which was a partner in the domed stadium, had talked of an interest in CDC shares, which never finally amounted to anything. But Cockwell thought of another possibility: group involvement in the sale of CDC shares.

Cockwell was in the midst of sorting out problems at Noranda. He was involved with the company's long-term restructuring for much of 1985/86, and he was interested in any possible contribution to the final leg in his long-term investment strategy for the group. In CDC, Cockwell saw the potential for a classic group offensive. Great Lakes could line up two or three major buyers for a special government bond issue with CDC share warrants attached; Brascade or Noranda could make the deal. Ted Medland at Wood Gundy had first thought up the link to a government bond issue. Ottawa might extract a better price for CDC by issuing government-guaranteed bonds. They would carry a warrant that could be converted into stock in CDC. But large companies would have to be interested in buying the bonds, and they might be hard to find because of the size of the issue and CDC's debt problems. Cockwell thought Edper group companies should be looked at as investors. It was a long shot. Eyton, who received a copy of Cockwell's memo, said: "The effort there and the thinking there was to make the offer a success from the point of view of the government and CDIC, not from any personal or selfish point of view." Still, the result would be a position in CDC that could be used to negotiate the Kidd Creek deal. A CDC investment fitted Powis's thinking on Kidd Creek, as well, and at about this time it become common currency among investment dealers that Noranda might buy a piece of the CDC share issue. It wasn't discussed by Noranda's board of directors for some time, however, and Eyton says he didn't know it was part of Noranda's game plan.

No matter who bought the shares, the idea of a few large shareholders for CDC appealed to the CDIC board members. Dick Bonnycastle and Trevor Eyton were particularly enthusiastic about finding large, vocal shareholders who would pressure the company to clean up its books. Active shareholders would also reassure the investment community about CDC's future prospects. The CDIC forced CDC to appoint four CDIC directors to its board, with Pat Keenan as chairman. Tony Hampson, the chief executive officer at CDC, didn't like the prospect of outsiders clamping down on the way he ran his company. Block shareholder control is certainly a Brascan tactic, but Hampson believed the Brascan boys and their friends were about to make a power play for his company. Past negotiations with Noranda over Kidd Creek fuelled his fears about a potential Brascan takeover. He discussed those fears with politicians, bureaucrats, and people on Bay Street.

Eyton wasn't worried about any potential conflicts of interest, however, until May 13. At a CDIC board meeting that day, he learned that others were very worried about a conflict. The issue of who could and couldn't bid for CDIC assets had been ignored, but it hadn't disappeared. Meanwhile, the government had appointed a ministerial task force on privatization. The task force included Sinclair Stevens, Robert De Cotret of Treasury Board, Minister of State for Finance Barbara McDougall, and Energy Minister Pat Carney. The task force suggested that any companies related to people closely involved with CDIC not be allowed to bid on any CDIC assets. Brascan was the group the Cabinet ministers had in mind when they drafted the informal directive. Eyton was enraged.

"I was offended because, in particular, we had been identified as someone who needed to be prohibited," recalled Eyton. "I do not think I need prohibition in order to behave properly. In the context of the ways in which we deal with conflict, which I think set a good standard, and in the context of the kind of selling process we were talking about, the full and the fair and the open process, it was, I thought, an insult to me and the people at Brascan."

But it had taken Eyton more than eight months to say formally anything about the ministers' position. Initially, the suggestion of a bidding prohibition had been offensive but not damaging; eight months later, when Noranda was interested in bidding for a CDIC asset, the new rule threatened to hurt an affiliate. In any case, Eyton was incredulous that when the government was trying to sell companies and everyone in the country knew about it, anyone should be excluded from buying. "It just seems inane to suggest that because one of the directors on CDIC happens to be associated in one way or another with a prospective purchaser, that that prospective purchaser cannot buy. I do not think that it serves any public purpose whatever," Eyton said. Those on the outside were not worried that directors had an opportunity to buy, but that they had an opportunity to get knowledge or to get a favoured place as a bargainer. Eyton did not recognize that fear.

Eyton would have lived with the government's restriction if Brascan Limited, the holding company, were the only group organization affected. "Sometimes you say to yourself, 'Well, on principle it is a little offensive, but if the government feels I can serve, I will accept that prohibition.' " But he couldn't accept the prohibition when the business of affiliated companies was being interfered with.

It turned out that he didn't have to worry: the board of CDIC met and sided with Eyton, and agreed to draft a code of ethics that would suggest the same rules used in the private sector — an individual declaration of conflicts — be used by CDIC. After the meeting, Eyton contacted Sinclair Stevens's executive assistant, Paul Brown, and filled him in on the problems. Two days later, Stevens received a memo from Brown describing the reaction to the task force suggestion: "Trevor Eyton was concerned (and offended) about a specific exclusion of Brascan-related companies in the purchase of public CDC shares. A code of ethics was drafted and is attached." Marshall also sent Stevens a memo — which had been vetted by Eyton — about the meeting the same day. Marshall stressed that the ban could force business executives to choose between government service and private interests. "The thought that any company would be precluded from bidding on one of our companies, even though its bid were patently the best bid or conversely, that the director concerned would be obliged to resign and deprive CDIC of his or her services, would to my mind be a retrograde step," Marshall's letter concluded. After the double-pronged indirect message from Eyton, the task force caved in. CDIC board members would use the time-honoured business community rules of behaviour; when a board member had a conflict, he would disclose it and withdraw from discussion and voting. By summer's end, Eyton would be in exactly that position.

Meanwhile, Sinclair Stevens was covering all his bases. In April, he had called his old friend, Gordon Capital director Jocelyn Bennett, and suggested that perhaps Gordon Capital could act as policeman on a number of the privatization contracts with other brokers. Gordon Capital would suggest and negotiate the other brokers' fees and analyze the brokers' alternate proposals about privatizations. Bennett and her boss, Jimmy Connacher, made the trek out to Stevens's farm to discuss the job, which was essentially insurance that the government was getting the best possible deal. The idea was adopted from the British, who had used a "shareholder's broker" in their privatization schemes; besides saving money on fees, the scheme would look good at House of Commons hearings into the sale. After Stevens suggested Gordon, Paul Marshall, with board approval, started involving Jimmy Connacher and other Gordon Capital brokers in negotiations in early May.

The firm Connacher and his confrères were negotiating with was again the lucky Burns Fry. Jack Lawrence had again written to Stevens and Marshall, and he met with both in April to explain that he had been lobbying for the sale of the government's interest in CDC for years. He had spoken with Tony Hampson at CDC, who also wanted the government out of the company. A group of Burns Fry executives were told by the minister at a meeting May 9 that they had the job. "It was pretty strongly indicated, if not actually confirmed," recalls Lawrence. But it was only at the May 13 board meeting, immediately before the lengthy discussion on conflict of interest, that Marshall's recommendation of Burns Fry was confirmed. Eventually, Burns Fry would lead a team of seven brokers distributing the issue.

Marshall later described Stevens's methods: he never issued orders, he only made suggestions. "He said he was impressed with their brochure, and of course that is the nature of the man; he does not issue edicts or instructions, he tends more to bounce things off you." But Paul Marshall was very attuned to what the minister "would tend to prefer," so Stevens's suggestion became the course of action.

When Lawrence and the Burns Fry team walked into Marshall's office on May 16 to settle the company's fee and to begin strategizing, Lawrence saw Jimmy Connacher sitting at the table. Marshall felt good about the decision to use Gordon Capital as a shareholder's broker. "Lawrence said, 'What is Jimmy doing here?' " Marshall jokingly replied, "He is just here to keep you honest, Jack."

They didn't settle on a fee that day, but they eventually decided that Burns Fry would receive four per cent of the money raised from a stock issue. At least, Burns Fry thought the matter was settled when the contract was signed later that month. But with Gordon Capital, a deal isn't over until the final deal is cut, a fact Lawrence would have brought home to him when the stock issue was ready to be completed later in the summer.

Before it could think about selling stock, however, Burns Fry had to find some potential buyers. It made up a "wish list," and employees began working the telephones and knocking on doors, looking for large private companies, pension funds, or other institutions that were interested. By summer, despite talk by Imasco and others, it was clear that the most interested candidate was Noranda. In fact, at a board meeting in Noranda's offices on the forty-fifth floor of Commerce Court West on July 10, Alf Powis mentioned to directors that when a public offering of CDC was done, Noranda was planning to expand its investment in CDC by picking up a block of shares. He was hoping the expanded investment would strengthen his position in discussions with Kidd Creek's senior management. Although Powis didn't go into details for the board, one Noranda executive had already talked with Neil Baker at Gordon Capital. The Noranda executive had linked the share purchase to a potential acquisition of Kidd Creek, with Gordon Capital in the driver's seat.

Just to be safe, Lawrence suggested to Marshall that he mention Noranda's intentions to Sinclair Stevens. The minister had no problems with the concept, but he, in turn, took the information to Cabinet. Marshall saw no problem as the head of the CDIC; it was as a Noranda board member, albeit inactive, that he was disturbed. "I do not know what the hell they are doing," he said to Lawrence in frustration.

The stock issue was set for September, when the summer doldrums would be over and the market would be looking for new investments. But in mid-August Connacher and Marshall realized that the market was quite active, and the company was ready. They decided to move more quickly. So when Trevor Eyton arrived back in Toronto late in the afternoon on Tuesday, August 20, from a business meeting, he was startled to hear that an important meeting of the divestiture committee had been called to decide the pricing of the CDC share issue.*

Eyton walked into Marshall's CDIC office shortly after seven o'clock, right in the middle of an intense bargaining session between Burns Fry and Gordon Capital. This was a "special" meeting before the full committee meeting; Marshall, CDIC's Mike Carter, and Dick Bonnycastle, as well as the hired securities-industry guns, were knocking out the details of the financing. Although an executive committee member of the Noranda board, Eyton says this was the first time he heard of the size of the potential Noranda share purchase — $75 million.

Eyton said, "As soon as I learned that, first, they were involved in actually setting the terms of the financing, including the pricing, and that Noranda were prospectively a fairly substantial buyer in the issue, I went into the boardroom where all the people who were not in the meeting had congregated and paid my respects and declared, in effect, my interest because of the Noranda involvement and left." It was the appearance of a conflict that motivated him, more than a real conflict, he later said. After all, this was a Crown corporation and the public had a special right of accountability. "Given all that, I decided that the best thing for me to do was to get out."

By leaving, Eyton missed a knock-em-down shouting match between Connacher and Lawrence. It was a battle that it would have been worthwhile for him to hear. Histrionics aside, the clash of tempers was about a specific issue: some of Gordon Capital's trading tactics. Some people in the investment community, still on the look-out for a conspiracy by Brascan to pick off government companies, were adding Gordon Capi-

---

*Marshall was criticized for using the divestiture committee rather than the full board to make such an important decision. He explained that he had told any members who were going to be in town to come if they liked, because it was such an important meeting. But he wasn't going to wait for people to arrive from points east and west. "We did not want to bring people in from all over the country. The whole issue had been approved in principle. It was a question of getting down to the nitty gritty of pricing."

tal's trades and Noranda's share purchase to the list of Brascan-related deals tied somehow to Sinclair Stevens.

Lawrence had two bones to pick with Connacher, and both were rooted in the way Connacher and Gordon Capital do business; Lawrence thought Connacher was changing all the rules. For starters, Connacher wanted to reduce Burns Fry's fee, which had been agreed upon at four per cent of the money raised. Connacher's view was that, since one company was buying a large chunk of the shares, it was an easier job for Burns Fry to sell them, so the fee should be two per cent for that large sale. Although they had already signed an agreement with Burns Fry four months earlier stating the fee, Marshall thought Gordon Capital was right. "I would not have been satisfied unless we had pushed."

But the matter the Burns Fry executives were really up in arms about was Gordon Capital's trading activity on the stock market that day. Gordon Capital had bought $1.4 million in CDC shares that afternoon; Burns Fry thought Gordon Capital was deliberately driving up the share price before the issue, so the government could raise more money. Burns Fry thought that was bad strategy; they knew how much their clients were willing to pay. As well, for the issue to be a success and to make people happy about the government's privatization plans, the stock should rise in value after the issue. By overpricing it, the government would cause it to fall in price, creating unhappy customers who wouldn't be as interested in future privatization stock issues.

Connacher did most of the talking. Lawrence thought the Gordon Capital chief was not "too interested in what our rationale really was." Lawrence demanded that Gordon Capital's trading that day be ignored in setting the price of the stock. Connacher bluntly disagreed. They fought for almost three hours, Lawrence said, "with neither side giving any ground." Lawrence tried to appeal to his client, Marshall, but Marshall was satisfied with Connacher's explanation of why Gordon Capital bought the CDC stock. "My only question for Mr. Connacher was: 'Were you buying these for a client? Did you have an order for these shares?' He said, 'Yes, we did.' "

Connacher's reply might have satisfied Marshall, but it didn't answer Lawrence's questions. "We felt that it was a remarkable coincidence that Gordon [Capital] was active in the trading of CDC shares during that day." Lawrence believed Gordon Capital was manipulating the market, and he said so. "Of course, to this day, I do not really know whether or not it was just a complete coincidence that there was all this activity in those shares at Gordon or whether there was any other explanation for the heavy volume," Lawrence said.*

Finally, the group agreed to try to resolve its differences by contacting Minister Stevens, who was in Vancouver and expecting a call to hear the upshot of the pricing meeting. Members of the divestiture committee had been dropping in and out of the pricing meeting from the next room; they finally sat down with Marshall at about eleven that night, while the call to Stevens was being arranged. Lawrence clearly objected to Gordon Capital's strategy and trading activities; Marshall said the divestiture committee had unanimously plumped for Connacher's price of $11.50 a share for CDC stock — twenty-five cents higher than Burns Fry's price. Stevens decided to follow the divestiture committee's advice, even though Lawrence made it clear that at the higher price — and a compromise fee of three per cent — he would have to check with his selling partners before agreeing to go ahead. After all, if they couldn't sell the shares, they would have to sit on them and pay the government the money.

They did sell the issue, with Noranda taking 6.5 million shares instead of the hoped-for eight million, and Canada Trust

---

*When he wrote Lawrence to compliment him on his work on the issue, Marshall had to address the acrimony. He later added he was at his most diplomatic when he stated simply that "there were things said that would have been better left unsaid." Marshall added that, in his years as a businessman, "I have never before experienced one [a meeting] in which emotions surfaced to the extent they did that night." Since Lawrence told his six partner firms, who were helping to sell the issue, about the argument, and other directors in the next room witnessed the acrimony, word was bound to get out that there had been a major disagreement between Gordon Capital and Burns Fry. The meeting gained notoriety when it trickled out to the press just what a fight there had been.

picking up the 1.5 million slack. Gordon Capital's actions saved CDIC $920,000 in fees, and the higher price earned CDC $5 million. Still, a number of buyers did back out. In fact, a few institutions threatened to complain to the Ontario Securities Commission about Gordon Capital's action. They were more upset when they discovered who Gordon Capital's client was.

The buyer had been Jimmy Kay, a clothing merchant widely considered to be in the Brascan orbit. The label had been confirmed when his North Canadian Oils had purchased shares of Union Enterprises and sold them to Unicorp during a bloody takeover fight. A number of other Brascan-related companies had also done this. And now here was Kay, only months after the Unicorp deal, buying shares of CDC just before a stock issue in which the major purchaser would be Noranda. Where did he find the cash? As with the Unicorp purchases, he used his line of credit to borrow money from Hees. Rumours floated around that Kay was being used as an "accommodation account" — that he was acting as a shill for someone else. But who? Gordon Capital wanted to ensure that the issue sold for a higher price. But why would that benefit them, when their fee was already set? Noranda or another Brascan group must be behind Kay. Still, Kay's actions only drove up the price of the shares, costing Noranda or another buyer more money. It didn't make sense. Was he acting as an advance party for the group? Was he driving others away from the CDC share issues so the group could scoop them all up? The coupling of the same familiar names was just too much coincidence for some people.

It fit in with a theory propounded by Tony Hampson at CDC that the entire Brascan group was going to take control of CDC, one way or another, and pick out the assets they wanted, especially Kidd Creek. The events surrounding the CDC share issue tied into the CDIC board's decision that there should be larger shareholders at CDC, using this scenario. Before there could be large shareholder blocks at the Crown corporation, however, there would have to be a change of legislation. Funnily enough, a number of Brascan-related companies wrote letters to the legislative committee that was reviewing the idea, in support of the theory of control stakes by large shareholders. NDP committee members were openly derisive of the group's motives. But Marshall points out that Hampson had his own agenda. "Certain members of our board felt that his [Hampson's] concern was that he did not want a large shareholder; he wanted to perpetuate management control. That may be unfair to Tony, but I am sure that thought was in the minds of a number of our board." Marshall wouldn't even consider the potential for a Brascan takeover of CDC; his job was to sell assets, not to deal with conspiracy theories.

But, like all conspiracy theories, the idea of the Brascan group manipulating CDIC took on a life of its own, even after it was clear that Noranda didn't plan to take over CDC. Instead, as the news about Stevens's personal business problems emerged in the spring of 1986, the Brascan angle became part of the mythology of what was wrong with Stevens's performance as a Cabinet minister.

The story of Trevor Eyton and his group's involvement with Sinclair Stevens was only one item in a series of personal, business, and ministerial actions that created a pattern of crisscrossed objectives and obligations during Stevens's tenure in office. Because the business community in Canada is small, some of the coincidences were inevitable. For instance, the fact that Jack Lawrence of Burns Fry should be on Frank Stronach's Magna International board and that Stronach was on the CDIC board made it more delicious when Stronach's company bid for Canadair. For the sale, CDIC had appointed Burns Fry as advisor.

Then the press revealed that Stronach's partner had given Noreen Stevens a large personal loan for York Centre, and that Lawrence had attended meetings organized by Eyton to talk about refinancing York Centre.

It turned out that Lawrence did worry about the appearance of conflict because of the ties between his firm — Burns Fry — Stronach, Magna, and CDIC. He consulted legal counsel, and a few of his partners withdrew from Magna meetings when Canadair was discussed and steered clear of Burns Fry's advisory activities on Canadair. "I decided I would keep out of both sides of it," said Lawrence. "I did not know anything about anything. That is the way it was kept right up until I started reading about it in the papers." One Burns Fry executive Lawrence consulted later explained, "Our concern was always more with the appearance rather than the substance, as the substance was easy to deal with."

Still, for all his sensibility Lawrence couldn't escape being woven into the web of overlapping interests, along with others who weren't so sensitive to potential criticism. The best example is Frank Stronach. He openly approached Stevens about his ideas for Canadair, because he didn't think they were properly appreciated by the CDIC board or the bureaucrats. Paul Marshall was happy when Stronach eventually resigned his board seat after attending only one meeting.

The problem for anyone whose path crossed Stevens's was that there were just so many stories. Stevens asked Tom Kierans, the president of McLeod Young Weir, to give his wife, Noreen, advice on York Centre's bond portfolio while offering Kierans both a deputy ministership and a special financing project for Atlantic Canada. The former was refused; the latter never panned out. Another story reported dealings with banks with which Stevens had had personal relationships. There was gossip about the appointment of Ted Rowe to the CDC board. Some stories the media did not discover, but the *Globe and Mail*, the *Toronto Star*, and other papers uncovered enough about potential conflicts of interest because of the minister's financial problems — including the Stronach-related loan and the August meeting Eyton organized with the brokers to try to help York Centre — that Stevens was forced to resign his Cabinet position in May 1986. There was a federal inquiry into potential conflict of interest headed by Ontario High Court Justice William Parker, seventy-four, whose report was delivered nineteen months later. The inquiry was aggressive in its search for facts and kept the issue alive. Eyton and others were exposed to public scrutiny via a very popular cable-television relay of the testimony highlights.

Government inquiries take on their own flavour; their very existence alters people's perceptions of an issue. Eyton cannily pointed this out when asked why Brascan's name was on a Dominion Securities "wish list" of possible buyers of Teleglobe. Brascan wasn't interested, he said, and he would have told Paul Marshall so, but Marshall wouldn't have bothered to contact Dominion Securities to have the name removed from the list. "He would have seen it as an exercise meaning nothing. We were not aware at the time that we were going to have this inquiry and that we would be talking about it today," Eyton said. To the government researchers and to casual observers, seeing Brascan's name on a list would add fuel to a conspiracy theory.

It was easy to forget that the Parker inquiry was not a trial. There were ninety-three witnesses in seventy-eight days of hearings, which stretched from the fall of 1986 to the spring of 1987. David Scott, fifty, the aggressive Ottawa-based lawyer who headed the team representing the Parker Commission, is the brother of Ontario Attorney General Ian Scott, and had expressed a wish to enter politics. He had obviously singled out Eyton as the chief representative of Bay Street. Scott eventually recommended that Eyton be cited for his behaviour as the leader who involved other businessmen in Stevens's private affairs. Scott thought Eyton should have known better. During the hearing, he grilled Eyton on how conflict of interest should be defined. "He has defined in his own way the approach that corporate directors take to situations of conflict," Scott told Commissioner Parker. "There are no experts on conflicts of interest, otherwise presumably you would not have to preside here. It is a question of perception and what is appropriate." Eyton was thought to exemplify the public service; so the inquiry was questioning more than the ties between one politician and one businessman. Said Tom Kierans: "The interrelationship between politicians and the business community is very much on trial."

Those attacking and those defending Eyton and Stevens had

to try to discover how much Stevens knew about Eyton's activities on his behalf. Certainly, the wandering scrawls of Shirley Walker, Stevens's fifty-three-year-old secretary, showed that she had some knowledge. On July 11, for example, she scribbled, "Jo Bennett/Eyton — DSP — O&Y-Brascan $500,000 each, plus Gordon say .5." Her notes add up to $2.5 million in hoped-for financing for the Stevens family companies. It was a very hopeful scenario, and Eyton denied it. In another note, Walker wrote Eyton's name, as well as Andy Sarlos and "Mr. Reichmann," at the bottom of some notes about a discussion of a scheme for York Centre to issue special Christ coins with the Vatican's approval. Eyton dismissed knowledge of the discussion offhand. "I have never heard about it and I stopped collecting coins when I was about eighteen or nineteen years old." It was far from clear for whom these muddled musings were intended. It seems likely that Walker's actions were the result of Stevens mingling his public and private business over the years; she could have been telling the minister, or someone else, and she could have heard this from Rowe, Noreen Stevens, or someone else.

The allegation that most offended Eyton was the theory that the Brascan group became involved in order to control CDIC so it could cherrypick CDIC's best assets. There was absolutely no advantage, Eyton maintained. Noranda bought the CDC shares "at a price that was inflated to the benefit of the Canadian public. The benefit that they have achieved as a result of that investment is a pretty substantial financial loss," he added.*

It was also suggested that the brokerage firms were being pressured into helping York Centre. Eyton was adamant that that wasn't his intention. "There was never any suggestion of fear or favour," he said. He thinks the fact that the Brascan group tried to help York Centre shows that there is honour in government appointments. Eyton testified, "They did look

---

*Jack Cockwell never agreed with Noranda's purchase at that price. In April 1988, Noranda sold its stake in CDC (by then known as Polysar Energy & Chemical Corporation), during a bitter takeover — for a handsome profit — to Gordon Capital and others sympathetic to acquisitor S. Robert Blair of Nova Corporation of Alberta.

at York Centre, they did give their advice, they did say we cannot help, and the good news — and, I think, a demonstration that the system is working — is that they are still doing business with the federal government.''

Still, some people think the intermingling of the same firms in a Cabinet minister's personal and government affairs is reason to question the well-greased system of mutual benefit that supplies funds for political campaigns and contracts for financial panjandrums. People who understand how things operate in the business world — for example Sam Hughes, then president of the Canadian Chamber of Commerce — assumed the Brascan group would not be bidding for assets. Hughes said so to the newspapers, as part of his praise for the appointments. Tom Kierans, of McLeod Young Weir, was an intimate of former Ontario Premier Bill Davis during his years in office. But Kierans realized, when the furor broke over Stevens's financial troubles, that the minister's dealings with McLeod Young Weir were in question because Stevens had asked Kierans to advise his wife. "I clearly recognized that a delicate incident had occurred," Kierans said.* While the press has no special antennae up for the McLeod Young Weir chief, the way they do for the Brascan group, all such links will be looked at very carefully by the business community after the Stevens inquiry.

In December 1987, Judge Parker's four-hundred-sixty-one-page report was released. It condemned Stevens on a number of counts, including his appointment of Eyton to the CDIC board, his approval of contracts to Burns Fry and Dominion Securities, and the appointment of Gordon Capital as government advisor for the CDC sale. But with the same stroke of his pen, Parker dismissed the "creeping takeover" theory as "an intriguing but ultimately fruitless review." He said he believed that Stevens knew about Eyton's efforts to help York Centre, and was in a conflict of interest. But he underlined

---

*In early 1987, Kierans would take his own place in the public eye as he headed a long-range task force for energy minister Marcel Masse, to look into the future of alternate energy in Canada.

Eyton's suitability for the CDIC job: "It is important to emphasize that the conflict was Mr. Stevens's, not Mr. Eyton's." The same thinking was applied to Burns Fry, Dominion, and Gordon Captial. And there was a note of apology in Parker's summary: "The allegations of a conspiracy to aid Brascan were made on the basis of incomplete information, and have resulted in what I imagine to be significant damage to the reputations of those involved."

Parker was right about the damage done. In the end, it doesn't matter how much was known, or who knew what. People knew Eyton was acting in concert with the minister publicly and on his behalf privately. Eyton's public character, which he had been at such pains to build up over the years, was damaged in a very public forum. His high-school buddy and law partner at Tory, Tory, Deslauriers and Binnington, Lorne Morphy, pointed out just how serious the questioning at the inquiry was for Eyton. "There is hardly a more severe allegation to be made" in the business world, Morphy said. "His integrity as a leading businessman in this country has been severely criticized."

Because Eyton didn't question his own actions, others had a chance to second-guess him, and the results were not pleasant. *Toronto Life* magazine, which had featured Eyton on its cover as Toronto's most influential person in mid-1986, felt the Stevens inquiry damaged his public persona. The magazine ran a terse assessment of Eyton when they listed the powerful Torontonians of 1987: "Was embarrassed by the revelation that he extended help to companies owned by Sinclair Stevens. Our last year's number one, his influence has probably increased in the city and decreased within Edper." That's just one magazine's assessment, but it is such perceptions of the ebb and flow of power that give Eyton clout with the business community.

Indeed, before the inquiry was over, his motives questioned and his actions assailed, Eyton acknowledged that the perceptions of others could have an impact on his position. As he said about his decision to step back from the decisions about the CDC share issue: "You have to take the world as it is."

CHAPTER THIRTEEN

A Glass House

We are in a glass house.
— Jack Cockwell, addressing the House of
Commons Finance Committee, July 1987

Ridges of clean white snow still padded the shoulders of Highway 7, reflecting the lights of the mid-sized 1982 Pontiac sedan as it wound its way through the back reaches of the Ottawa Valley on Sunday, April 13, 1986. It was a solitary drive for Paul McCrossan, forty-six, a gnomish figure who had been larding on pounds since his September 1984 election as the member of parliament for Scarborough Centre. The backbench Tory MP had slept little in recent weeks; instead, he had spent the nights worrying about the consequences of a decision to fight the powers in his own party and the giants of the financial world. He was about to take a very public stand against large conglomerates owning financial institutions.

Events were pushing McCrossan and his confrères on the House of Commons Committee on Finance, Trade and Economic Affairs toward a confrontation with Trevor Eyton and his corporate counterparts at other family-controlled financial empires. McCrossan spent the entire drive to Ottawa mulling over a very unsettling weekend at home. Late Saturday morning, when he had finally drifted into an uneasy slumber, his wife, Sheila, shook him awake. She had been listening to CBC radio's weekly parliamentary program, "The House," and had heard Mervyn (Merv) Lahn, the plain-spoken head of Canada Trustco, speaking about the almost-settled sale of Canada Trust's parent, Genstar Corporation, to the giant retail drugstore-tobacco giant, Imasco Limited. In 1985, Lahn had fought against his company's takeover by Genstar, the construction and resource conglomerate that had merged Canada Trust with Canada Permanent Mortgage Company. During the radio interview, Lahn stated baldly that he knew of instances of self-dealing between Genstar and Canada Permanent.

McCrossan immediately telephoned CBC's Toronto radio studios, had them replay the interview, then drove downtown to pick up a copy of the tape. Lahn's statement confirmed his worst fears. The finance committee had been powerless to stop the Canada Trust takeover by Genstar in 1985. The Imasco sale was imminent, and still there were no restrictions on ownership in the legislation. McCrossan telephoned Elizabeth Roscoe, chief of staff for Minister of State for Finance Barbara McDougall, and insisted that she listen to the interview. What was McDougall going to do about these abuses? He got his answer that night, when McDougall gave Imasco an ultimatum: she would only approve the sale if Imasco agreed that there would be no deals between the trust company and Imasco's other holdings. As well, Imasco would have to reduce its holding in the trust company if Ottawa so decreed it at a later date.

That same morning, the Toronto *Globe and Mail* published a startling report in its business stock column, written by reporter Martin Middlestaedt.* The article outlined a couple

*Middlestaedt was the chief union negotiator for the *Globe* staff. He was loathed by the banking and stock-brokerage community for his irreverent attitude. An openly avowed socialist, in mid-1985 he wore a T-shirt urging support for striking T. Eaton Company workers to an interview with entrepreneur George Mann about Mann's takeover of Union Enterprises. The business community complained of biased coverage, but the *Globe* valued Middlestaedt and sent him, in mid-1986 to open its first Wall Street bureau.

of stock deals within the Brascan group, including one that involved Trilon Financial Corporation, the parent of Royal Trustco and other financial-services operations, and the Brascan-controlled merchant bank, Great Lakes Group. Great Lakes was receiving a large fee for what appeared to be no work at all: guaranteeing that it would buy any unsold portion of, say, the Trilon stock issue. In fact, it received a fee even if it didn't buy the stock.

As well, there had been disturbing comments in a recent speech by Bernard (Bernie) Ghert, chief executive officer of Toronto-based real-estate-development firm Cadillac Fairview Corporation. Ghert had said he knew people who could tell of instances of self-dealing by conglomerates that had hurt other companies and the financial system. Ghert was a "captain of industry" who, in fact, worked for a public company whose major shareholders were two of the largest private family fortunes in the country. Cadillac Fairview was started as the real-estate tentacle of the Montreal Bronfman family, the cousins of Peter and Edward Bronfman and the heirs of Seagram's founder, Sam Bronfman. A few years earlier, the Reichmanns had taken a significant stake in Cadillac. Ghert was a director of Wellington Insurance, a Trilon subsidiary, and was on the executive committee at Canada Trust. Lahn was on the Cadillac board. Ghert knew what he was talking about when he discussed corporate concentration.

He wasn't really biting the hand that fed him, but he felt he should point out the dangers of closely held empires owning financial institutions. He argued that, while concentration of ownership within the industrial sector is not necessarily harmful, a cross-ownership between large industrial conglomerates and financial institutions creates powerful conglomerates that could restrict access in the capital markets. Such monopolies create the potential for abuse of a public trust. He told Barbara McDougall of his concerns in the spring of 1985, after she proposed in a "Green Paper" that closely held companies be allowed to increase cross-ownership of trust companies, insurance companies, and banks. He also prepared, at her suggestion, a brief for the finance committee. Before he sent it, Ghert bounced the paper off two Cadillac directors: Toronto Dominion Bank chief executive Richard (Dick) Thomson and former Privy Council clerk Michael Pitfield, who is aligned with Paul Desmarais' Power Corporation. The committee rejected McDougall's idea and proposed instead a twenty-per-cent limit on ownership of financial institutions by large conglomerates. "Our feeling," says McCrossan, "was that someone who had the ability to influence decisions could be creative enough to get around any regulations we could come out with." But for all the proposals, no changes had been made in the system. Now they faced the threat of potential abuses of power by several big holding companies. It was time to go back and ask Bernie Ghert exactly what he meant by his allegations of self-dealing in the corporate-financial world.

McCrossan kept his eyes on the road and his actuarial mind on the problem of exactly how to pull all these threads together into a tapestry that would illustrate his argument in bold colours. The time was right for a back-bencher to take a strong stand on an issue. Only weeks earlier, new rules reforming committee powers had been passed in the House, and committees now had more clout than they had ever possessed in the history of Canadian parliaments. No one had yet used the new powers. The finance committee would need to summon some people, to get at the facts of particularly worrisome deals within conglomerates. When he arrived at the Ottawa Centre apartment he shared with York Centre back-bencher Bill Attewell, McCrossan eagerly rifled through the revised House rules and discovered he would have the power to get the information he needed. As of April, the committee could subpoena witnesses and demand documents. A House committee could hold a U.S.-style hearing into an issue such as concentration of ownership.

McCrossan huddled with Attewell and Don Blenkarn, the shoot-from-the-hip MP from Mississauga South who headed the finance committee. Before he ran for office, Attewell had been director of corporate planning at Guaranty Trust; he had worked for the McCutcheon family, one of Bay Street's most established examples of family power.* He had become a convert to the fight against corporate concentration only the previous autumn. Blenkarn, who is partial to aphorisms, believes that people should either "fish or cut bait," and that the financial world should be closely watched because "things move around in a twinkling of an eye." One observer compares Blenkarn to a hockey player who mucks it up in the corner while his deft teammate moves in to score. In this case, his paunchy teammates were hardly in better physical shape than the bulky Blenkarn. Still, he was fully prepared to have his committee push harder and go further than a Canadian House committee had ever ventured. He thought "the Ghert thing" and the Imasco takeover were symptoms of a larger problem, "the general feeling by the public that the four partners, the dozen families owned the country."

On Monday morning, key members of the finance committee met in a small anteroom, which shoots off the Parliamentary cafeteria. The eleven members crossed party lines: Blenkarn, McCrossan, and Attewell headed the seven-member Tory contingent; Aideen Nicholson was the more active of two Liberals; Nelson Riis and Simon de Jong were from the NDP. McCrossan had lists of potential witnesses, and had divided up the areas to be covered. "It wasn't just one or two members going wild; it had the force of the whole committee behind it," McCrossan underlines. "We got together and we choreographed the meeting." In the weeks to come, he also drafted questions for Nicholson and Riis.

The committee scheduled hearings for the next few weeks. Among the witnesses were Canada Trust's Merv Lahn; Genstar's Angus MacNaughton and Ross Turner; Brascan's Trevor Eyton and Robert Dunford, and Brascan-controlled Trilon

---

* The late Senator Wallace McCutcheon was one of the powers at Argus Corporation when Bud McDougald controlled Crown Trust. The senator's son, Fred, co-founded the stockbrokerage firm Loewen, Ondaatje, McCutcheon in the 1970s; he and his brother, James, controlled Guaranty Trust until mid-1987, when it was sold to Central Capital Corporation.

Financial Corporation's Melvin Hawkrigg. Later, the committee recalled executives from Genstar and from the Bank of
Montreal Leasing Corporation to discuss a particular Genstar
transaction. McCrossan and Attewell began poring through
reams of background documents, looking for instances of self-
dealing. Like investigators on the trail of a paper tiger, they
delved through reports filed with securities regulators in
Washington; the footnotes in annual reports; analysts' reports;
and stock and bond prospectuses. They had some help from
the outside: one Toronto stock-market analyst, a personal
friend of McCrossan's, travelled to Ottawa on the strict understanding that his name would never be revealed. Many callers
who dropped hints or told stories about self-dealing by large
conglomerates were equally circumspect about the use of their
names in public. Some said frankly they couldn't afford to
risk the loss of job opportunities. At moments, McCrossan
felt the same way. After creating this much fuss, would he ever
be able to find a job in business again?

But at other moments during the following weeks, there were
times of excited chatter between McCrossan and Attewell about
what had become an obsession for both. They made lists of
incidents any witness mentioned and tried to track each one
down, "So we wouldn't be seen as fishing in the dark,"
McCrossan said. McCrossan and Attewell would arrive at the
low-rise Centretown apartment that they shared to cut the costs
of homes away from home, spread their piles of documents
over the floor, the couch, every available space, and talk almost
through the night about their search. They began to perceive
a polarization among businessmen. For the first time in their
political careers, they saw an issue, as McCrossan says, that
caught "the imagination of the business community. We had
calls from people that you wouldn't believe, and I'm taking
about presidents of the Big Five banks and senior heads of
business associations and senior people, presidents of some
of the big corporations. [They were] all saying keep it up or
here's something you want to look at or here's something that
happened to us, and so we had all kinds of leads. These people just don't get up and call members of a parliamentary com-

mittee and start volunteering things.'' Blenkarn, Nicholson, and Riis also received calls; a few strictly off-the-record conversations were initiated by senior civil servants. Some leads didn't pan out; those that did were referred to the Superintendent of Insurance. ''The thing with what essentially is hearsay is that a lot of it is second, third-hand, and it gets changed,'' says McCrossan. ''By and large, I was impressed with the quality of information that came, the high percentage of the leads that were verifiable was very, very gratifying.''

The MPs-turned-investigators grew used to flying to Toronto on the supper run and back to Ottawa on the midnight flight to check out the leads they had received. During one of these trips, McCrossan and Attewell went to the Cadillac Fairview Building, a shiny white tower that juts out of the southern end of the company's flagship Eaton Centre in downtown Toronto. They met with Cadillac chief Bernie Ghert in his fourth-floor office, a pleasant room featuring Ghert's own photography. One of the most prominent photographs is of the wailing wall in Jerusalem; one small black-robed figure stands bowed in front of the sand-hued wall. The eerie image bears a strange resemblance to a Rorschach-test ink blot.

A man with a piercing, measuring look, a wide, ironic smile, and a personality that keeps many associates at arm's length, Ghert has been gaining attention in recent years as a personality in Canadian business. He believes in competition. His professional profile was heightened in 1986 by a story on the front page of the *Globe and Mail*'s Report on Business about his bicycle racing. Ghert rides his Vitus bicycle several kilometres most mornings, and races with a team of enthusiasts at home and in the U.S. The story was picked up by the wire services and appeared in papers as far away as San Francisco.

''One of the things that interested us, obviously, was what was motivating him,'' McCrossan recalls. When Ghert had first talked to McDougall, the issue had been academic: ''I want to make sure that capitalism doesn't destroy itself, that it is an unfettered free market,'' he said. A year and a half later McCrossan believed that Ghert wanted to discuss instances of conflict of interest. ''He wouldn't make public statements challenging the committee to summon people unless he did some corroborative work himself," McCrossan said. They were reassured by Ghert's certainty that there were actual instances of self-dealing. Ghert had been receiving calls of his own, but most he dismissed because he didn't know the sources well enough.

But two stories he did believe. Both stories had been told to him in the vaguest terms by chief executives — men who had, to Ghert's mind, "both credibility in their judgement to judge the circumstances and the fact, and the high credibility I have in them telling me something they honestly believe." Ghert told McCrossan and Attewell whom he had in mind when he made his public statements about businessmen who knew about self-dealing: Toronto-Dominion Bank chairman Richard (Dick) Thomson and Austin Taylor, chairman of stockbrokerage McLeod Young Weir.

Ghert didn't make the leap from theory to example without warning Thomson and Taylor of his plans. They were old friends, Thomson a director and Taylor the company's main fiscal agent. After he met with McCrossan and Attewell, Ghert told Thomson and Taylor of his conversation with the finance committee. He had always thought there was "a possibility" that his speechmaking would lead to this, but he wasn't pressing anyone else to step forward the way he had. Neither was pleased. But while Taylor was annoyed, he nevertheless would stand behind his story. Thomson, in contrast, was ready to kick up dust. Ghert puts it more circumspectly: "I just left it to them and, of course, they gave me two different reactions. One was, 'I'd rather not, but so what.' The other one was, 'Gee, I really don't want to.' "

For the finance committee, however, the two examples could make the difference between a set of hearings laden with technically correct examples of inter-corporate arrangements that might excite the business community but would not gain the public exposure their cause needed, and a real-live case of self-dealing that would make the country aware of the issue of who should own a financial institution. The hearings were being reported, but there was no spark to the news items.

When the hearings began, Genstar, the former owner of Canada Permanent Trust, was under scrutiny. One of the deals alluded to by Canada Trust chief Merv Lahn raised some very serious questions about whether the trust company had been abused by its conglomerate parent. Equipment had been leased by Genstar with a guarantee from Canada Permanent. It was very technical stuff, and besides, those folks had merged the trust company with Lahn's and then been taken over themselves. The deal was three years old, and there was no proof that it was still happening; indeed, Lahn swore it wasn't. It was an example of self-dealing; but it wasn't an example that would change the course of legislative events. Even after the Brascan subsidiary, Trilon Financial Corporation, sent executives to explain why their stock issues were guaranteed by Bronfman-controlled Great Lakes group — with a hefty fee to Great Lakes — there was no real excitement about wrongdoing uncovered. But the examples of self-dealing alluded to by Ghert were widely assumed to involve financial and nonfinancial arms of the Edper-Hees-Brascan empire. McCrossan began to speculate about media coverage. The committee had taken on its task because of belief, not because the issue was a vote-getter. Still, to influence the course of events, the issue would have to capture the country's imagination. The Brascan stories might do just that.

McCrossan saw his chance one night in mid-May, when Finance Minister Michael Wilson appeared before the committee. Marc Clark, a reporter for *Maclean's* magazine's Ottawa bureau, lingered after the session to talk to McCrossan. As they walked out of the Railway Committee Room and down Parliament's marble-floored Hall of Honour, McCrossan piqued Clark's interest by explaining that the first-ever use of the House's new rules for committees was focusing on the heavyweights of Canadian finance. They talked for an hour and a half; the next day, when Clark began digging, he found more than enough to pitch a story. There were rumours of self-dealing, hints of corporate intrigue in the air. Clark learned that Bernie Ghert said he could name two senior businessmen who had stories to tell about self-dealing. Clark wrote a three-page story, which ran complete with a large centre photo of McCrossan, Attewell, and Blenkarn with the headline, "A back-bencher crusade." McCrossan framed the spread and mounted it in his Parliament Hill office; Attewell used it to spark a survey of his constituents. But the question remained: would there be a John Dean to startle the House with details of deception?

McCrossan now had his media coverage, but he began to realize he wouldn't be able to control it, or its affect on people's perceptions of his goals. He insists that he was not looking for anything illegal; the committee had decided from the start that if it found anything illegal, it would have to stop its investigations. "Our purpose was to show that things which could be undesirable could be done under the current law." However, that was not the way the media interpreted the members' actions and statements. And the committee had gone out of its way to court coverage, as it believed it was right about the issues. "I think part of it was the fact that the committee used the power of summons at all," rationalized McCrossan. "Some people took this, because it was the first time it had happened, as a sort of 'we think you're guilty of a crime and if the police can't get the evidence, we'll get it.' " But the sleuthing, the whispers of high-level sources with tales to tell, played into this interpretation of events by the media, who were already hostile to the Brascan group. Blenkarn admits that the committee knew they were handling hot stuff: "No question about it, going after them was a popular thing to do. They haven't got all the friends in the world." Even after the *Maclean's* story, the committee tried to keep Thomson's and Taylor's names under wraps. But a follow-up piece in *Maclean's* two weeks later focused on Brascan, and printed both businessmen's names. The *Globe* picked up the story, but without printing the names. Still, the idea that the House of Commons was "after" Brascan became firmly entrenched in the public consciousness.

Ironically, the two weeks between the *Maclean's* magazine pieces were the most delicate moments of the committee's quest. After puffing up its role before the public, the committee had to decide just how far to push its power, and whether it could accomplish more by moral suasion, that classic Ottawa-Bay Street rite of negotiation and deference, than by muscle.

And first, the committee had to pin down the Thomson and Taylor stories. Ghert had supplied only the names; he didn't know the details. Unfortunately for the committee — since the existence of the stories had been exposed to the media — as soon as they were held to the light, the stories were disappointingly insubstantial, as any gripe can be when reviewed by strangers. Taylor told a tale of a financing deal with a Brascan company that was cancelled at the last moment, then revived with one of the Brascan group acting as broker. A brokerage firm had negotiated a stock issue with Royal Trust; at the last moment, Jack Cockwell stepped in and said, "Don't go ahead with it, we can do this ourselves." So the deal was shelved. Weeks later, one of the merchant-banking arms of the Edper-Brascan monolith did the deal. But in any financing, there is always room for cancellation. And in weeks, the market can change, and the factors behind a company's plans can alter. There is always complaining when a company decides against one source of financing, then raises the money later with other partners. Besides, there was no absolute proof that it was Cockwell pulling the strings. It was an assumption that almost had the quality of myth in its assurance. It was dynamite if it was provable; but therein lay the rub.

The story attributed to Thomson had more substance. Apparently Royal Trust was providing financing for a company, with Toronto-Dominion and others. At the last moment, word came down from the Edper-Brascan boys to back out. The reason: the company receiving the money, a paper company, was a competitor of another company in the Edper-Brascan group. If the story was true, it substantiated Ghert's theoretical worries about a potential lack of funding sources. Even more important, it demonstrated an abuse of power, an evil side to the ownership of a financial institution by an industrial conglomerate. And the story had been told by the head of one of the country's largest banks.

Dick Thomson is not just a banker who believes in limi-
tations of ownership for financial institutions; he is also a
partner with Brascan and the Reichmann family in Trilon
Financial, which counts Royal Trust as the most major of its
holdings. Thomson had placed the reins of power at Royal
Trust in Brascan's hands: in 1982 he had allied Toronto-
Dominion's ten per cent of Royal Trust with Brascan to help
Trevor Eyton kick out Royal's chairman, Ken White. Brascan was a major client of the Toronto-Dominion Bank. Thomson and Jack Cockwell may not have liked each other, but
Thomson was not willing to talk about Cockwell — as McCrossan discovered when he arrived at Toronto-Dominion's headquarters, the most eastern of a three-pronged imposing black
centrepiece of Bay Street called the Toronto-Dominion Centre.
In fact, the bank's lawyers, who did not fully understand the
House of Commons' new powers, initially refused McCrossan's request for documents relating to the transaction. They
were flummoxed when McCrossan, resembling a bantam
rooster in an alien farmyard — uncomfortable yet still cocky
— rhymed off the story of the last time a parliamentary request
for assistance had been refused. It was in Britain, in the seven-
teenth century, and the recalcitrant noble's head had been
chopped off. The documents were sent to Ottawa the next day.

But when the committee read the documents, notes McCrossan ruefully, "It became evident pretty quickly that what we
had was strongly held beliefs as opposed to facts." The committee had hoped that Ghert could provide the proof, and
Ghert had trusted his sources. Now the committee was faced
with a less than satisfactory result. "We had to question what
the public purpose would be in calling a series of people who
say, 'I was told,' 'I believe,' and all this sort of stuff," says
McCrossan, "stringing it out and, in some cases, besmirch-
ing people's names under parliamentary immunity, when, in
the end, we became convinced that nothing illegal or improper
was provable." Ghert believes the parliamentarians may have
decided it wasn't worth putting Thomson through the wringer:
"It may have been harmful to the TD Bank if Dick Thomson
had to testify, and they may have looked at that and said,

'Well, maybe we'd better not.' ''McCrossan points out that the committee was galvanized by Ghert's public pronouncements: "All the way along he [Ghert] said he believed there were people who if they were called under oath would say certain things. And he had reason to believe that they would, from conversations he had with them or with people who had talked to them. And he was probably right, that those people believed those things. But that wasn't the challenge he threw before the committee.''

The calls kept coming, and McCrossan and Attewell kept poring over documents. But the months of strain had begun to tell; McCrossan, particularly, was exhausted. They had been doing the work of researchers as well as parliamentarians. Sighs Blenkarn, ''I thought we went as far as we could go without the tools.'' But there was a general feeling that the inquiry was slipping away from them, that they were losing sight of their pure purpose amid the mountain of documents and the chance for media exposure. This was brought home to the close-knit group by a front-page column by *Financial Times of Canada* editor Terry Corcoran, who accused the committee of being witch-hunters. McCrossan attempted to arrange a meeting to discuss the charge, but their schedules never meshed.

The committee has never been able to explain why it didn't follow up the only stories that would have justified its aggressive activities to people like Corcoran. To Blenkarn, the story was there but it could not be pulled out of a miasma of uncertainty and prevarication. A decision was made: call Ghert, get him to name Taylor and Thomson, and have Trevor Eyton and Jack Cockwell up for questioning about their methods and their beliefs. Then go behind closed doors and write the report, before Parliament shuts down for the summer and the mandate is lost. A wide-ranging inquiry suddenly stopped short of its mark.

On June 11, 1986, the committee held its last day of hearings.

There were three witnesses: Bernie Ghert, Trevor Eyton, and Jack Cockwell. This was the second time Eyton had been scheduled to appear before the committee. He was originally summonsed to speak in April, the same evening Trilon Financial executives appeared. But Eyton's office called McCrossan that morning to "confirm" that Eyton would not be arriving. The secretary explained that Eyton had already cleared this with Blenkarn. But Blenkarn was out of the country with another House committee, and he hadn't left any message cancelling Eyton's appearance. McCrossan said as much, and added that Eyton had better send up a representative to explain his absence. John Tory, of the law firm Tory, Tory, Deslauriers and Binnington, grabbed a plane to Ottawa and explained that Eyton was in the middle of an important business deal. (It was the day Royal Trust bought a European company.)

Disgruntled committee members discussed issuing a subpoena, but decided that would be going too far, since they didn't know whether Blenkarn had simply forgotten to let them know about an agreement with Eyton. Later, they heard rumours that Eyton was laughing at them and telling cronies he had thumbed his nose at the summons. Whether or not that story is true, Eyton was definitely not impressed with the process. "If you listen to the level of debate in any House in the land," he said at the time, "you will understand that the kinds of issues and the way they deal with them don't make for . . . let me describe it as a meaningful debate." Indeed, Eyton didn't appreciate the second call to testify, which was scheduled for a night on which he was to host a party for hundreds of guests in Calgary. Privately he complained, "They don't give you a lot of notice." But he showed up — with Jack Cockwell at his side. For the final showdown, the Edper group realized it was time to parade the heavy artillery.

Ghert was greeted by the committee as a long-lost favourite son who had returned to his home. McCrossan had by this point lost perspective; the MP was almost sycophantic in his treatment of the Cadillac Fairview head. Ghert's role was key, in McCrossan's opinion. "There are very few people who are captains of industry who would, no matter how they feel, speak out publicly." Ghert did not enjoy his role; although he had chosen to become a public-policy maven, Ghert was a very private man. "I don't like being public property," Ghert says with his ironic smile. And his public airing of his views had caused reaction in some very powerful places. Senator Leo Kolber, the Montreal Bronfmans' chief advisor and Ghert's mentor, was approached by Bay Street heavyweights and asked to speak to Ghert about the wisdom of his actions. When Kolber didn't react, Senator Ian Sinclair was asked to push him into talking to Ghert. But Ghert, who is a sensitive man, had not been interested in public mud-slinging, and he resented any implication that that had been his intent. When he was pressured to back away, Ghert stuck to his guns. At the time, he was facing one of the most important periods of his professional life, the sell-off of Cadillac Fairview Corporation at the behest of the controlling shareholders, the Montreal Bronfmans. "You should do it right. It's something like bicycle racing. You can't finish the race if you give up. It's all mental attitude," he said later.

Much of his thunder came from the fact that he appeared at all, rather than from what he said to the committee that day. After all, he had already said his piece to the committee in the autumn of 1985, as well as speaking out elsewhere. But the committee chose to use him as a sounding board for its own evolving determination to change the rules. Ignoring Ghert's strongly stated antipathy to a retroactive rule change, members pushed him to state his own favoured upper limit for ownership. Ghert's most important words went almost unnoted by the MPs: at the end of his appearance, he named Thomson and Taylor. Then, at the end of the day, MP Nelson Riis moved that the banker and the broker be called to appear. Blenkarn refused to deal with the motion because, technically, this was not a full committee meeting.

Ghert was being watched by the media, and also by the next two witnesses. Jack Cockwell was not pleased with his performance. He fidgeted, openly impatient and belligerent. The committee had specifically called Trevor Eyton, but it was pleased to see Cockwell arrive. Now it would be able to get the details, the numbers, the facts of the cases it wanted to examine. As it turned out, Eyton and Cockwell couldn't answer every query; in some cases, they said they had been asked for the information too late, and promised to send it later. But they did a creditable job of explaining the importance of the financing links between Trilon and Great Lakes Group, Brascan and Hees, Lonvest and Noranda-controlled Canadian Hunter.

Eyton and Cockwell used the platform to argue their case. The group is honourable, they said; the executives do not try to influence management or outside directors, they do not break the laws, and they resent the inference that they are doing something wrong. Earlier, Eyton had said in an interview: "I think the media are having fun. I think some politicians are having some fun. I think that it's an issue that most responsible people have resolved in their own minds." They tried to adopt a high-minded tone, ignoring their more cutting earlier remarks, such as Eyton's tirade at the Brascade annual meeting the week before, when he referred to "pipsqueaks and adversarial media."

At times the two, but particularly Cockwell, were carried away by their vision of how the world should run. Blenkarn resented Cockwell's assertion that, for the Edper-Brascan group, Great Lakes performs the same function that the Bank of Canada performs for the country's banks. Blenkarn couldn't believe the arrogance of that statement. At another point in the proceedings, Riis couldn't resist pointing out that, by Cockwell's definition, Eyton sounded like a feudal lord.

Still, the well-briefed and sharp-witted pair was more than a match for the exhausted finance committee. Attewell attempted to ask a key question about the group's method of financing by preferred shares and how the financing affects the actual business of Royal Trust. But his question — how Royal Trustco spent the $200 million in preferred-share financing it raised in 1985 — was lost in the confusion of a long-winded discourse by Eyton on the definitions of the trust company's *actual* title and Cockwell's assertions that he didn't know *exactly* what investments the group made. The basic issue

— why Royal Trust raised the money and what it did with the cash — remained unaddressed.

Except for the allegations made by Taylor and Thomson, there were no cases of Brascan closing off markets or Cockwell or Eyton stepping in to dictate that the trust company be run to the best interests of the entire industrial-financial conglomerate. The 1985 purchase by Lonvest of gas wells from a Noranda Mining-controlled subsidiary, Canadian Hunter, while small potatoes, was the only case the committee had of a deal that had been done without being referred to any vaunted Brascan-style "independent review committee" for self-dealing, and without telling the Superintendent of Insurance. In this one instance, Eyton admitted, the company had been wrong; it wouldn't happen again.

Eyton and Cockwell ultimately carried the honours of the day. And the committee seemed to recognize it; the bogeyman had been flushed out and had turned out to be a solid citizen. In closing the hearings, Blenkarn repeated the title of the second *Maclean's* magazine piece: "The empire has struck back."

They may have carried the day with the committee, but Eyton and Cockwell still had to deal with the media. They would be punished for a remark Cockwell made, while still feeling the bile of having to sit through Ghert's presentation. His appalling breach of conduct was at the beginning of his presentation, and it coloured the paparazzi's reactions to his more collected later remarks. Ghert had remained in the committee room to listen to Eyton and Cockwell. Eyton began by saying that he wanted to clearly state the group's beliefs, since Ghert had summarized *his* position. Ghert began to fidget; he had not expected a personal reference. He did not view his public statements as a personal attack on any member of the group. Explains Ghert, "You can have people with whom you do not have a warm personal relationship and still agree on policy issues. You can have other people with whom you have close personal relationships and not agree on policy issues. That happens in business all the time."

Ghert's discomfort became pained embarrassment when Cockwell interrupted Eyton to give examples of what he felt a group with integrity should do. What it would *not* do, he emphasized, would be to allow executives to profit from only a certain portion of the group's performance, creating a bias towards certain projects. What it would *not* do was to allow executives to benefit from a rise in stock prices by granting options that could be exercised, but didn't have to be, meaning the executive didn't have to take any risk. "I contrast that with the practice of other companies such as Mr. Ghert's, where they promote phantom stock, cherrypicking of assets to participate in, and things like that. You will not find that within our group, and Mr. Ghert would not be employable, given the standards that we apply in hiring people." Ghert blanched. When the day's session ended, Ghert, normally circumspect, began to talk in front of a couple of reporters. He had heard Cockwell could act like that, but it was a shock to see it, he said; as a man who took pride in his public image as a business leader, Ghert would not be forgiving.

Yet forgiveness from Ghert was part of the Brascan game plan. Eyton regarded Ghert as "a good friend, in the social sense." He had already told Ghert, during a visit to the developer's office to raise money for the University of Waterloo, that he and Cockwell didn't agree with Ghert's philosophy and would like to discuss it sometime. After Ghert's public drubbing by Cockwell, Ghert wrote Eyton to let him know he disagreed with Cockwell's approach but was still willing to meet and talk about the underlying issues. Eyton telephoned Ghert and set a date and time; they would meet in Ghert's office. The day of the meeting, Ghert set aside a chunk of time. That was not to be. Eyton and Cockwell arrived about half an hour late, as Ghert recalls, and sat together on one of two couches arranged at ninety-degree angles in Ghert's office. "They just wanted me to come out and make a public statement that I knew nothing wrong about their operation," explains Ghert. "To say I don't know anything bad that Brascan has done. Write it out on the blackboard a hundred times, you've been a bad boy." He maintained he hadn't been pointing his finger at anyone in particular, so he didn't see the point of their request. "Cockwell was very difficult. He was like: 'You won't? You owe it to me! You must! You've got to! How dare you not?' And none of that had any positive impact on me."

Some weeks after he had refused their request for a public repentance scene, a letter arrived from Eyton. The Brascan board, it said, was upset by the allegations flying around, and wanted a written explanation from Ghert that he was not impugning any of the Brascan-related companies. Some insiders read "Bronfman" instead of "board" into that request. That explanation certainly fits with Peter Bronfman's obsessive character. Again Ghert refused, this time in a letter with blistering references to Cockwell's use of "veiled and empty threats" as an approach to mending fences. The Brascan board also asked for letters from Taylor and Thompson; both refused.

After the contretemps in Ghert's office, it was some months before Eyton and Ghert saw each other. The meeting took place in Chiaro's, at Toronto's King Edward Hotel, a favourite spot of Eyton's. Eyton was lunching with Eddy Cogan, a long-time Cadillac Fairview real-estate broker and a recent Eyton ally; Ghert was in the same restaurant, lunching with Cadillac Fairview's lawyer and a Brascan director, Eddie Goodman. Eyton was very friendly to Ghert.

While they failed to win over Ghert, Eyton and Cockwell succeeded on almost every other front. After routing the House of Commons committee, Brascan went on the offensive and launched a major public-relations campaign by initiating a series of meetings with selected members of the press, hand-picked for their interest in the group. That resulted in a front-page piece that revealed that the group was launching a press relations drive in the *Financial Post* in August. Then there was a series of public speeches at conferences, and before analysts and business agenda-setters. Eyton headlined, and there were also speeches by company heads such as Great Lakes Group chief Ken Clarke and Royal Trust president Michael Cornelissen. These speeches, and other prepared diatribes, were reprinted in the Toronto *Star*'s Monday viewpoint column whenever possible. Often, the topic was industrial concentration or the role of public companies in Canadian business, rather than a topic such as use and abuse of corporate power, particularly in financial institutions. During this time, Eyton was also in the news for his involvement in the domed stadium and the business affairs of Sinclair Stevens. But somehow he successfully managed to keep separate all these threads; his arguments about the good being done for Canada by his conglomerate and those like it were a separate issue.

Eyton and Cockwell were trying to dissipate what had been tagged "the Edper factor" by bureaucrats in the Department of Finance. There was an indefinable fear that the group couldn't be trusted, that it was taking advantage of the tax system and of the rules for ownership of financial institutions. They realized that, although they had succeeded in stalling the finance committee, Cockwell had not shone before the legislators. His surly personality had fulfilled their worst expectations. Even Eyton, who can shine in small gatherings with his witty turns of phrasing, can come across as pompous and repetitive in a larger public forum. So the pair retreated to a position of strength.

Before their House of Commons appearance, they had decided on a basic strategy. After the Commons appearance, Eyton and Cockwell began inviting Ottawa to lunch, one by one. McCrossan recalls meeting with Trevor Eyton, Jack Cockwell, and Gord Cunningham at the Brascan office in Toronto in July. "I spent about an hour and a half going over all the questions I had and their responses, sort of on a non-adversarial basis. Obviously, nobody's sworn, but you get a chance to ask, and they get a chance to ask you where you're coming from," McCrossan reported. In this much more Brascan-friendly environment, Cockwell was charming. Even Blenkarn unbent, and Attewell was frankly pleased to find out that Cockwell was a jogger. (Attewell, an avid runner, believes joggers to be a superior breed of people.) The Brascan group was, after all, an honourable operation with a first-rate team of managers. And although their point of view differed from the committee's, they came by their opinions honestly and held them sincerely. Such were the MPs' thoughts about a group that a few months ago had seemed their opportunity for a study of self-dealing and abuse of corporate power.

There were also more mundane factors at play in the change in outlook in Ottawa. The back-benchers on the finance committee had been beating the Brascan issue to the exclusion of all else. Then summer, their private lives and the realities of politics landed them in different circumstances. McCrossan, with lines of weariness etching his face, was presented with a double tragedy that summer. On the long weekend in July, less than a week after the committee finished its work, his sister died suddenly; his father never recovered and died in the airport scant weeks later after McCrossan saw him off with his mother on a trip to Disneyland. Then Attewell was offered and accepted the opportunity to sit on a United Nations committee from September 1986 to January 1987. It was a lifetime chance, but it effectively removed him from the debate.

The hard-working MPs of the finance committee, who had hoped that they would someday be promoted to the Cabinet, saw that their media recognition and their back-breaking labour weren't about to earn them that reward. Instead, those in power chose a very different type of MP to influence the ownership issue.

The stage was set for a new Cabinet appointment for minister of state for finance and a new approach to the issue by the time the committee's work was done. On June 25, after Don Blenkarn, Paul McCrossan, and Bill Attewell had presented their committee report at a press conference, they ran across another back-bench Tory MP, Tom Hockin. Hockin was also flushed with the feeling of a job well done: the international-relations committee he chaired had just held a press conference to present its study of free trade. Hockin was by nature a conciliator; he saw it as his task to lift himself above the parochial or national issues and take a broad approach. As he recalls it, "Instead of fighting partisan wars, we tried to find a number of practical things we could agree on." Hockin congratulated Blenkarn, McCrossan, and Attewell, although he didn't have much of an idea about what their report had been aiming at; he hadn't had time to keep track of the finance committee's agenda. Three days later, he was told by Prime Minister Brian Mulroney that Barbara McDougall was being moved on, and that Hockin would be the next Minister of State for Finance.

Hockin was no McDougall; he was never expected to have as high a profile. Indeed, there were some wags who said that was exactly what Wilson wanted in his department, a lieutenant who could act as second and would not upstage him. But the forty-four-year-old newly minted Cabinet minister happily adapted to his duties. Financial institutions were not the first of his priorities, although the industry let him know it was extremely tired of waiting. When he began to consider McDougall's approach to financial institutions — and the finance committee's rejoinders — Hockin brought a conciliatory framework and an international perspective to the agenda. He was definitely not averse to hearing the industry's viewpoints; indeed, he didn't feel he was lobbied hard enough, particularly by the trust industry. He had his staff arrange a series of lunches in Toronto, off-the-record sessions with antagonists seated together, so he could monitor the debate. The message he came away with was that the system certainly needed updating. What about the ownership question? In Hockin's opinion, the finance committee's report had been forged in "the heat of the moment" of the Imasco takeover. Certainly no self-respecting Conservative would consider roll-backs on ownership. One aspect Hockin didn't understand was Ontario's pronouncement, that autumn, that banks and other financial institutions could only own up to thirty per cent of a stockbrokerage firm. Hockin thought that wasn't workable; the banks would have to be let all the way into the business. After all, Ontario lived in an international marketplace, and could not shut out other countries who wanted to operate in the Canadian financial pool. After a scuffle with Ontario, Hockin won his point, and retired to polish off his report.

The finance committee was not so happy. Initially, Blenkarn, McCrossan, and the rest of the committee were sure that Hockin and Stanley Hartt, Mulroney's close friend and the recently appointed deputy minister of finance, were listening to them, and that the other bureaucrats in the finance department had been squelched. But while Hartt and his assistant deputy minister, Fred Gorbett, were telling Hockin about policy, the details were left to the same bureaucrats who had designed Barbara McDougall's strategy a year and a half earlier. In October 1986, Hockin promised to hold meetings to let the committee members have input on policy; Blenkarn said, "I think we've just about won the debate." But the meetings never materialized.

It was in early December, only a week before the release of his blueprint for the financial sector, that Bernie Ghert went to Ottawa to see Tom Hockin. Ghert had written to the minister a while back, but, good-natured as Hockin was, he just couldn't get around to seeing everyone. This time Ghert was there as a part of a high-level real-estate lobby group; Hockin asked him to stay behind for a chat. He knew Ghert's position, however, just as he knew Brascan's; after all, he had read the hearing's transcripts. Hockin summed up his understanding of Brascan's reaction to the finance committee hearings: "They felt that they were being put into the penalty box even though they hadn't committed an infraction on the ice." Ghert wasn't going to change Hockin's mind, but Hockin didn't mind picking Ghert's brain for ways to institute the regulations that would be needed to stop self-dealing. "I'm sure Bernie would have liked us to just go widely held [adopt ownership restrictions], and not to give advice on my terms, but he gave me good advice," says Hockin.

Hockin was surprised that he hadn't personally heard more from Brascan. Even though he understood their position, he had expected them to present it to him again. But though they seemed to have lunch with everyone else in the nation's capital, the Brascan boys contented themselves with appearing at Hockin's invitational noon-time events. And Hockin thought Eyton was strangely circumspect on the many occasions they met socially. They travelled in the same circles. After all, Peter Widdrington, president of John Labatt, is one of Brascan's much-vaunted independent managers; he is also Hockin's next-door neighbour in London. But at a Stratford opening during the 1986 season Eyton never once mentioned to Hockin anything about the upcoming financial industry legislation. Hockin was puzzled by his reticence. "Maybe it's just not polite to mention at social occasions."

Through the fall of 1986, Eyton's busy social calendar continued to place him near the reins of political power. For example, in November, he was one of four co-hosts of a first-rate Toronto fund-raiser for Brian Mulroney, prime minister of Canada.

That fall, there were rumours of a Cabinet split: Wilson was apparently opposed to Hockin's financial-industry legislation; McDougall and Mulroney favoured it. Hockin says that any Cabinet-level questioning was about details, requests for more information, not disagreement on substantive issues. When his policy was announced, it essentially presented a status quo for present industrial conglomerates with financial holdings — a sixty-five-per-cent ownership limit for large companies that already were in both businesses. The exception was Imasco, which had to reduce its holding of Canada Trust from ninety-eight to sixty-five per cent, on the basis of its old deal with McDougall, in order to conform to new legislation. The policy proposed a ten-per-cent ownership limit for new entrants, and an open door for every type of financial institution to move into the business of the others.

The stories of direct pressure on Mulroney by Eyton, as well as the prime minister's old friend Paul Desmarais, took on the status of common knowledge. Whether or not they were true hardly seemed the point, however. The Brascan group had thought its public image was at stake because of the beliefs and actions of "pipsqueaks and adversarial media." Now the group could rest assured that its view of the world was shared by those in power, legitimatized to the world at large. Eyton and Cockwell still had a lobbying job to do, and a big one, from their perspective: the "status quo" seemed to mean that they may not be able to expand their holdings to new commercial areas. But the draft legislation, released in December 1987, allowed for some ministerial discretion. The Edper group's Business Conduct Review Committees were enshrined as a tenet of good corporate governance. There were sensitive men in power after all.

In the final analysis, what had wounded Eyton and Cockwell was the idea that their vision of the way Canadian business should run was found lacking — so much so that it was held up to public scrutiny. Eyton emphasized to the NDP's Nelson Riis during his day before the committee that he and Cockwell wouldn't think of imposing decisions on directors and management; that wasn't the way things worked. Instead, managers and directors must operate within their own beliefs, their own value systems. As Eyton stated: "Can I get to the question of power? Any power we have is really, if we used it or would think of it, the power of persuasion, but it is persuasion that has to be based in logic, and we see that as compelling power."

Certainly, it helped that the Brascan push for acceptance of their right to do business as an industrial-financial conglomerate dove-tailed with international forces that wanted to open the Canadian financial system to outside competition. Brascan would use the international argument when browbeating Ottawa to remove any restrictions on their expanding operations. But despite the curbs on their growth, there was a crucial personal victory for Eyton and Cockwell. Their viewpoint was acknowledged by Ottawa as the right one, and the finance committee's viewpoint was seen as heated rather than reasoned. Or, as Lloyd's Bank of Canada president David Lewis said with a chuckle, "They sure came out of that one smelling like a rose."

Invidious Canadians

*In Canada, when they hold a beauty contest, they
don't give the first prize to the prettiest girl, because
she already has something.*
— Canadian-born actor and comedian Rick
Moranis*

A lingering question hangs over the Edper-Brascan-Hees
empire like industrial pollution. People suspect something. On
Bay Street there are still whispers of a pyramid built on paper
that will someday collapse. Whispers of confidential information received by one Edper company being sent over to another
group company. Whispers of unethical behaviour, of a
malevolent presence among the pristine inhabitants of corporate Canada. People submit the empire to rigorous examination. The Brascan annual meeting was for years a

---

* Moranis starred in the popular comedy show *SCTV,* which was
initially rejected by Canadian networks but became a hit on American
television. It was then picked up by Canadian stations. When the
purse-lipped CBC demanded more Canadian content on the Canadian
produced, financed, directed, written, and acted show, the writers
responded with a regular segment featuring the beer-swilling, toque-
attired, hopelessly stupid McKenzie brothers. Moranis was Doug
McKenzie.

cross-examination by shareholders and investment analysts. The tone was adversarial. The message was: What are you doing wrong?

To Trevor Eyton's mind, the question is prompted by jealousy, pure and simple. "You know," he explained in pained tones in mid-1986, during the worst of the mud-slinging, "Canadians tend to be and have been encouraged to be invidious people. You look at somebody and say, 'He's too rich or he's too powerful or he's too good or too talented,' and you've got to knock him down. It's not a question of saying, 'I can be better, I can strive, I can achieve,' but rather of saying, 'He's gotten too big, or too powerful, or too talented.' " Eighteen months later, when asked about this categorization of Canadians, Eyton replied, "I would have thought that the observation would fall within the realm of public knowledge." He points, with no hint of irony, to the proceedings of the House of Commons and the press as examples of daily attacks on successful Canadians of all stripes. "Obviously, we are sensitive to the charges and invidious comments that are levelled against our group," Eyton pontificates, "and our peers in Canadian business, including the Reichmanns, Conrad Black, Ken Thomson, and others."

Trevor Eyton is right. Canadians often do resent the rich and famous. They do not worship entrepreneurship as Americans do; in fact, Canadians prefer big government to big business. But while he is correct in his comment, Eyton is attempting to portray the Edper group as the passive victim of muddle-headed thinking. The group has stood out as the representative of big bad business because of its ever-increasing clout in corporate Canada. The Brascan-Edper group has changed the way business is done in Canada's inner corporate circle. Jack Cockwell and his boys set an agenda for change years before anyone outside the group realized it, and the group has assiduously followed it. The result is that the group has become representative of the way business is done in this country in the 1980s. The group has also upset a lot of people. That is one reason for all the back-biting and bad-mouthing. The more reasoned criticism is pointed at the rigidity of the group's ideas and approaches.

Some of their ideas are good. But their blind spot is that they believe everything they do is good and right and proper — the only way, in fact, to act. It is a very big blind spot.

The group's creed assumes that their devotion to the bottom line is good not only for their shareholders, but for the capitalist system. This assumption imposes a morality, the group's morality, on capitalism. But a more realistic assumption would be that their way of operating, like the capitalist system and like most things in life, has some warts. They operate with a very competitive approach, a style that urges aggressiveness. But no institution can inculcate morality. That is, in the end, in the hands of individuals. To counterbalance individual weakness, society has created a set of rules for proper behaviour. Company executives need regulations to curb their excesses. But there has always been a weakness in the contract. Regulations governing the way business operates in Canada have been weakly articulated and are ineffectually enforced. Edper's executives see this, and are scornful of the slower moving, slower thinking regulators. But laws should not be discounted because they have not been enforced in the past. Laws help to define what is right and wrong. No individual group should assume it can make decisions for society.

Jack Cockwell's text on life is a hard-driving essay on making money. He identifies many aspects of human endeavour in terms of money. This is a dangerous practice. In a lucid, thought-provoking round-table forum on the morality of capitalism, published in *Harper's* magazine in December 1986, *Harper's* editor Lewis Lapham declared, "If you substitute the profit motive for all human values, if you identify wealth with freedom and judgement with the worship of the bottom line, then you are able to justify any means of obtaining money. After all, wealth, being the greatest good, buys all the other goods." If the word *profit* is substituted for the word *wealth,* countered Walter Wriston, former chief executive at Citicorp, then it is an old, old story. "We're talking about the profit motive," which operates in all institutions, Wriston says. "Sometimes it's prestige, sometimes it's a parking space. But some form of reward system operates in every society."*

In the 1980s, the belief that what's good for General Motors is good for the country came back into vogue after it had fallen out of favour in the late 1960s and 1970s. The old business chieftains were then the only ones who believed in it fervently.

But now the group has the power to impose its standards on others. And its members sell their vision very aggressively. As in any religion, there is a strong sense of dogma. Trevor Eyton seems to display an alarming lack of self-knowledge when he says, "The only power we have is the opportunity of dealing with people who respect us and the Edper group, and who are prepared to listen to our ideas and suggestions." The record shows a very strong force of suggestion. Peter Bronfman says flatly, "I don't see myself as being in a position of power." He adds that he doesn't think a lot about power, since he isn't interested in fashioning his life around it. But Peter Bronfman must get his kicks somewhere. And Jack Cockwell and Trevor Eyton, while they have different styles and aims, are certainly both keenly interested in power.

Cockwell attributes his development of the group's operating principles as the reaction of an immigrant to "North American companies where management effectively appoint themselves, assess their own performance, determine their own rewards . . . and seek status symbols, while paying scant attention to shareholder interests, since they rarely hold more than the minimal number of shares." When Ken White kept Robert Campeau out of Royal Trust, he believed what he was doing was right. The Edper creed was designed to replace an admittedly corrupt and outmoded approach to doing business. The group was an outsider fighting to open doors, and it welcomed newcomers. Jack Cockwell listened to the Calgary

---

* The forum was adapted from a discussion held at the Cooper Union for the Advancement of Science and Art in New York City. The other participants were Robert Lekachman, a left-wing economist who teaches at City University of New York; Michael Novak, a right-wing advocate of the capitalist system; and Peter Steinfels, a neo-conservative Catholic theologian and editor.

entrepreneurs when others did not want to give them a seat on the board of Union Enterprises.

Cockwell prides himself on the changed Canadian corporate scene. "As a group, we have made some progress in restoring the owner's voice and focusing management's attention on building long-term values for shareholders, partly by requiring senior management to become important shareholders. Others are picking up on this theme," he declares.

The group's philosophy and its ability to wield influence are even more important in the context of the place of business in our society. There are undeniable links between economic power, political power, and cultural and societal influence. During the 1980s, economic heavyweights set the agenda for the political and cultural system more openly than in previous decades, led by Ronald Reagan and backed by an increasing need for corporate support of the voluntary sector. In Canada in 1988, a new business daily paper was started, backed in part by Conrad Black. Jack Cockwell helped to inspire Black's plan to create a paper with a more positive attitude towards business. The paper is a voice for business; its aim is public influence.

The group likes to talk about "real" and "spurious" issues. Concentration of ownership they class as nonsense. During the mid-1980s, when politicians were pointing fingers and the media were against big bad business bogeymen, Trevor Eyton was asked whether concentration of ownership is an issue for Canada. He replied, "Well, it's an issue. Whether it's a real issue is another question. . . . Concentration in Canada — that doesn't mean anything. That just means that some people see you as powerful and big. By itself, there's nothing wrong with that. What you've got to do is demonstrate harm." He demanded an accounting of how the group's position in the beer business makes Canadians suffer, or how its aggressive growth in financial services hurts the average customer. He pointed to the competitive real-estate business and asked how Edper's control of Trizec and three other major developers had closed off any markets. In every instance, he emphasized, the average Canadian is well served by the marketplace. His argument assumes that politicians and the public are paying attention, and that the powerful families follow the rules.

In any case, the Edper-Hees empire is moving beyond the invidious confines of Canada, out into the international marketplace. That is where future acquisitions are likely to be, says Eyton, in part because of a "recognition that there are a number of critics in Canada who consider the Edper group sufficiently large now." Indeed, a favourite argument of business — and Eyton has used this one often himself — is that corporate concentration is necessary if Canadian companies are to gain enough clout to compete in world markets and to compete with giant foreign interests in the Canadian marketplace. William Stanbury, professor of competition and regulatory policy at the University of British Columbia, has trouble with this argument. In an interview in the *Globe and Mail* in January 1987, he said, "The ones I love are the big-name Toronto lawyers who use the [international competiveness] argument when what they're defending is . . . Thomson's takeover of the Bay. Now what that had to do with international competitiveness other than that the Bay imports some British china and exports a few boxes of it to Americans in Texas, I don't know. That argument should have no force in cases like that, yet people are mesmerized."

At times, such as when Peter Bronfman claims not to have any power, an observer might be struck by the naïveté of some of the group's comments. Eyton, for example, rejects the notion that the group has political clout. He says, "The last thing we are is a powerful and significant voice in political issues. Collectively, we may have a voice, but it is only a voice that is compelling and is listened to when it makes sense. It ain't bad to have a voice, as long as you're expressing a right view, a sensible, rational view." Once more there is the group's blind spot, its unfailing belief in its own rightness. Says Stanbury, "Real power is having the option of *not* maximizing profits. If you have $8 billion in net wealth, your mind begins to think of things other than the next $100,000. You begin thinking of monuments, of extensions of ego . . . of things like imposing your political views on the nation, because, after all, they worked for you, and think how well off Canada would be if it followed your nostrums."

The group, because of its ardent self-righteousness, has been particularly threatened by media scrutiny. Ontario Premier

David Peterson, no foe of business, points out that this, too, is a classic case of the business mentality taken to an extreme. "Nothing these guys do is open for public examination. They see their name in the paper once — somebody saying something nasty about them — their whole life falls apart." Peterson claims to be a fan of criticism. "You can't accomplish much without accountability. But these guys, they don't have anybody to account to. They are used to dealing in secret; they are used to making their deals over the phone or sitting at the York Club working it all out."

Questioning the group's motivations is now old news. Politicians and the media might have been "having some fun," as Eyton said, at the group's expense. But he adds, "It is an issue that most responsible people have resolved in their own minds." After all, the businessman's ultimate responsibility is to the shareholders. The group believes that every public company has just as much responsibility to its shareholders as a financial institution has to the public. And people are placing trust in the company by investing in shares. The flip side of the coin is that the group has, in the past, said "trust us" without giving the shareholders or the public enough information upon which to base an informed decision. Still, the group has sometimes changed its habits because of public criticism. One example involved Great Lakes Group, which was paid a fee by various group companies for its financial backstop services on share issues. Minority shareholders complained that was costing their company money, money that was paid to Brascan and which benefited the Bronfmans. In response, Great Lakes began charging the fee to the stockbroker backing the issue rather than the company issuing the shares.

The group survived the 1987 stock market crash and helped to rescue Wood Gundy and National Business Systems; the group's public image in early 1988 was that of saviour of the system. It was an ironic turn for the group that, a year or two earlier, was seen as an octopus that was spreading its tentacles far and wide. Its practices hadn't changed; its behind-the-scenes role in the battle for control of Polysar Energy & Chemical in mid-1988 demonstrated that. But the perception of them had. As Trevor Eyton said, "We think that the public are now persuaded that the Edper group, with the quality and integrity of its senior managers, with their demonstrated competence, with their stated values, and with their evident track record, is entitled to say 'trust us' and have that entirely accepted.'' Eyton had the proof to back up the puffery: the 1987 Brascan annual meeting, held in the spring of 1988, displayed none of the old acrimony. Instead, it was in effect a tribute to the vision of Jack Cockwell, and an anointment of the executives who make the group run.

Certainly, Cockwell had proven that he and his group were smarter than the traditional corporate crew. He had capitalized on an obvious weakness. As well, according to Labatt's chief Peter Widdrington, simple economics assured that the group's approach to doing business would become the norm. ''Things are far tighter now than they were before. We don't have inflation any more. There was a sort of a pell-mell type of atmosphere, and inflation covered an awful lot of sins.'' Without that camouflage, Widdrington says, there was ''a toughening up all the way down the system.'' Whatever people want to call it, the tougher, leaner approach to business operations is now assured in Canada. As for the group, it has now secured its position through its dominance of the capital markets during the boom years of the stock market. And it has secured its place in the brokerage industry's heart by its never-ending deals and its bail-out of Wood Gundy.

The group's success and growth lead inevitably to questions about when and where the growth will end. Is there a point at which Cockwell's corporate asceticism must be replaced by the bureaucratization of a burgeoning empire? Leonard Spilfogel, who believes that day is approaching, asks, ''How many companies can you buy before you move from what was a highly efficient organization into a giant bureaucracy? At what point does power take over and begin to corrupt what is going on there — not from a corruption point of view, but from a mental point of view, philosophically, mentally. Jack can only work fourteen hours a day, and it may start to be at a point where it's just too much.''

Cockwell has attempted to secure his vision of the group by instilling his creed in the two dozen acolytes chosen as key group executives. In a way, Cockwell, the ultimate manager, is mirroring, with his protégés, the impulse at work in the Bronfman brothers. Professor Stanbury describes the ensuring of dynastic survival among Canada's richest families as "the ultimate expression of ego; you live beyond the grave by having your children fixed for life, and their children and their children and their children."

But it is family — the strong emotions, rivalries, indeed the very *closeness* — that threatens Jack Cockwell's buttoned-down planning. During 1986 and 1987, when Peter and Edward's Seagram's cousins, Edgar and Charles, squabbled publicly, in *Fortune* magazine and the *Montreal Gazette,* about which one of their sons would succeed them at the helm of the liquor empire, they demonstrated the friction that is inevitable when one generation supplants another. With their sister Minda dead and her children clamouring for their share of the family fortune, and with their own aims diverging, Edgar, Charles, and sister Phyllis Lambert eventually decided to split their CEMP trust and go their separate ways. To pay for the business divorce, they sold key holdings such as Bow Valley Resources and their Cadillac Fairview Corporation. As an investment, control of that real-estate giant was an excellent idea. But in the end, that was not the issue. "There are lots of reasons you might do that [sale] that are not necessarily driven by pure economics," says Arnie Cader, Edward Bronfman's chief advisor on succession. "There are the issues of working together, of independence, of future generations. Those kinds of things are as important as economics, sometimes more so."

In the end, the Edper empire, built by one man in the short space of twenty years, may be rent asunder by the most predictable of fates. Peter Bronfman believes the third generation's itch to take its money and make separate lives can be satisfied without "the sale of any major strategic holding," perhaps by taking Edper public. But there will be inevitable changes. Now, the Edward Bronfman trust holds half of Edper's shares; the Peter Bronfman trust holds the other half. Herb Solway, another of Edward Bronfman's personal advisors, explains why it was easier to split up the CEMP trust: "The difference was that everything wasn't tied up in Seagram's in that family. Everything here is tied up in Edper. There isn't anything else

. . . Edper has got everything. It all stems from Edper.''

However, H.N.R. (Hal) Jackman, a second-generation tycoon himself, sees a pattern that is hard to break: "There's no question in my mind the Brascan empire is going to fall apart. It will fall apart simply because the continued existence doesn't suit the owners, it doesn't suit the people involved in it. They need the money and they've got different priorities. I mean, every big family empire in this country has collapsed, and every one now will and that one will, too. And, in fact, that one is more vulnerable than most because it's got far more debt." Jackman, never one to avoid an issue, uses himself as an example. "I've got five children. They are all young and I have no idea what their ambitions are. There is no obvious acquisitive instinct in any of them. I've got to pay death duties, capital-gains tax split five ways. A family is as strong as its weakest link. If one wants to sell, where is the other going to get the money? And so it goes."

The Bronfmans and their Edper-Brascan-Hees group may become a historical footnote, like the Killams and the Gooderhams. They may be forced to dilute their hold on the empire, like the Molsons and the Southams. Certainly, the large, effective family empires in this country stretch, at most, for four generations. But in this, as in so much else, the Edper group may set a new standard for business operation in this country. No matter which direction the Bronfmans take, they are bound to be controversial. "What the ultimate judgement will be, who knows," says James Pitblado, president of Dominion Securities Limited. "But it is an important development." Three years ago, the fashion was to believe that Edper was a malevolent force; Edper survived the slander. Now the fashion is to lionize the group as a model of corporate perfection. This is also wrong-headed. But no matter what happens in the next decade and with the next generation, the family empire of Peter and Edward Bronfman has made an indelible mark on the way Canada does business. "It is," says Jack Cockwell's old Touche Ross boss, Don Wells, with the native pride of a satisfied mentor, "a story of remarkable accomplishment."

APPENDIX

WHAT BRASCAN COMPANIES PRODUCED IN 1987

Products		Units	Canadian Market Share (%)
Softwood Lumber	1,800	MMFBM	7
Market Pulp	1,191	'000 TONNES	14
Newsprint	712	'000 TONNES	7
Oil and gas (translated into barrels of oil)	33	MILLION BARRELS	4
Copper	113	'000 TONNES	14
Zinc	504	'000 TONNES	30
Gold	467	'000 OZS	12
Milk	2.3	BILLION POUNDS	14
Beer	8,401	'000 HECTOLITRES	41
Frozen Confectionery			24
Residential Mortgages Disbursed	4.3	BILLIONS $	11
Individual Life Insurance Premiums	540	MILLIONS $	15

BRASCAN'S ACQUISITION BINGE

Noranda	- First of 3 stages	1979
London Life	- Additional 20%	1980
Labatt	- Additional 10%	1981
Westmin	- Formation	1981
Scott Paper	- Acquisition of 25%	1981
Trilon	- Formation	1983
Royal Trust	- Acquisition of 50%	1983
Great Lakes Group	- Restructured	1984
Royal LePage	- Acquisition of 50%	1984
Wellington Insurance	- Acquisition of 100%	1985
Norcen Energy	- Option Interest	1986
North Canadian Oils	- Acquisition by Noranda	1987

The Edper Empire

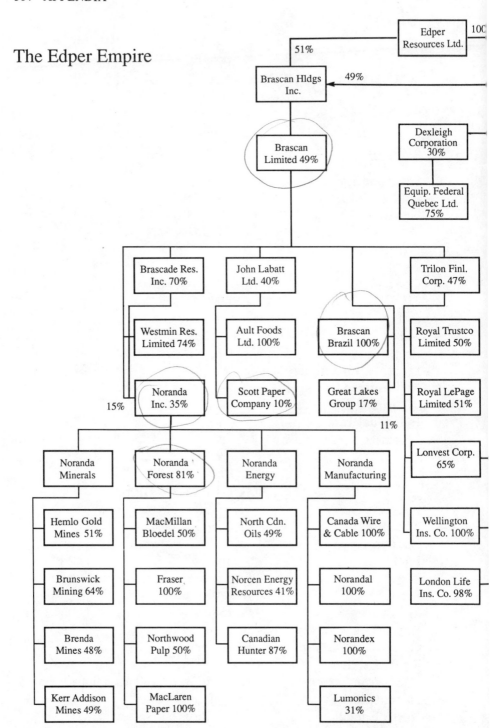

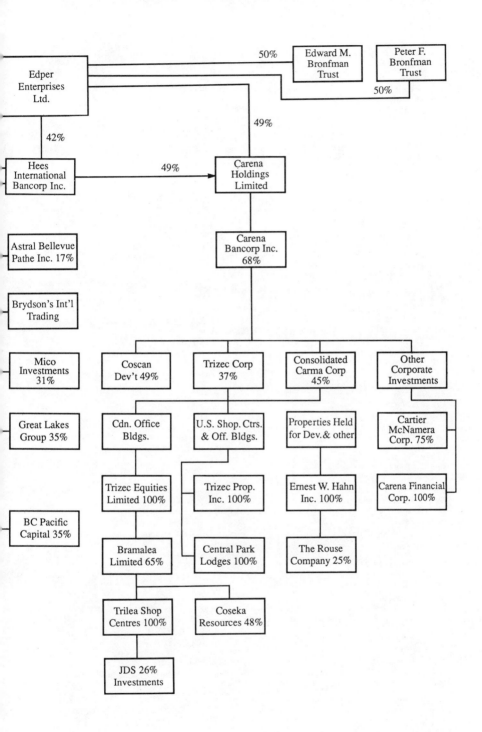

Index